NIMRUD

An Assyrian Imperial City Revealed

NIMRUD

An Assyrian Imperial City Revealed

Joan and David Oates

BRITISH SCHOOL OF ARCHAEOLOGY IN IRAQ

First published in 2001 by
The British School of Archaeology in Iraq
The British Academy
10 Carlton House Terrace
London SW1

ISBN 0903472252

Cover illustration: Lapis lazuli and gold jewellery from North-West Palace, Tomb II (published by courtesy of the State Organisation of Antiquities and Heritage, Baghdad).

Back cover illustrations: Open-work ivory panel depicting a winged sphinx, shown as it was found and as cleaned on the excavations; traces of gold leaf survive overlying the guilloche frame. From Fort Shalmaneser, room S 30 in the queen's apartments (ND 7550, 19 x 15 cm; now in the Iraq Museum).

Frontispiece: Reconstruction drawing based on the ground plan of Fort Shalmaneser, drawn in 1962 by Alan Sorrell with the assistance of David Oates. A major addition, made in 1963, is a door leading northwards from the south-west corner of the building into the outer bailey (see plan, Fig. 91).

Printed and bound in Great Britain by Biddles Limited of Guildford

In memory of Max, Agatha and Barbara,
and happy times at Nimrud

CONTENTS

ACKNOWLEDGEMENTS

Writing this volume has taken us back many years to what was both a formative and a very exciting period in our lives. We were both present at Nimrud for a number of the 1950s seasons (J 1952–53, 56–58; D 1955–58, 60–62); and David took over as Field Director in 1958, 1960–62, when Fort Shalmaneser was excavated. We are both especially grateful to Max, for tolerating and encouraging us on his dig staff, to Agatha, for making life on the dig unusually pleasant, to Barbara, for coping with everything and looking after us in Baghdad, and to all three for lifelong friendship. Without them our lives would have run a very different course.

We would also like to thank the British School of Archaeology in Iraq for the invitation to write this book and The State Board of Antiquities and Heritage in Baghdad for its very helpful cooperation. In this context we would like to thank especially Dr Rabi'a Mahmoud Al-Qaissi, Acting President of the State Board of Antiquities and Heritage, Dr Mu'ayad Sa'id Damerji, formerly Director-General of Antiquities and Heritage and now of the Ministry of Culture, for his help and assistance over many years, and Dr Donny George Youkhana and Sayid Muzahim Mahmud Hussein, for providing information about and photographs of the important Iraqi work at Nimrud. The book could not have been written without the help of Dr Lamia Al-Gailani Werr, who has not only provided new information but has also translated a number of Arabic reports for us. We are grateful to many others who have helped with the production of the book, and especially to those who have read parts of the manuscript, for their very useful comments and criticism, Dr Dominique Collon, Dr John Curtis, Dr Georgina Herrmann, Professor Nicholas Postgate, Dr Julian Reade. We hasten to add that the errors that remain are entirely our own. Others who have provided invaluable advice and assistance include Dr Jeremy Black, Dr Michael Müller-Karpe, Dr Jeffery Orchard, who was Field Director in 1963, Dr Paolo Fiorina, and Ms Helen McDonald, whose pottery drawings appear in Chapter 7. The book has been published with the generous assistance of the Al Sulaiman Faidhi Charity Foundation, to whom we wish to express our warmest appreciation.

Our gratitude to those who have helped us in a wider sense goes back over many years, especially to those who provided advice and assistance when we first worked in Iraq. It is not possible to list here all members of the dig staff over these years, whose labours are represented in this book, but we would particularly like to mention, and to thank most warmly, all our Iraqi representatives and the members of the Directorate-General of Antiquities whose friendship and support added greatly to the success of the work at Nimrud, and indeed our own subsequent work in Iraq. We must mention first of all, H.E. Dr Naji al Asil, who was Director-General during our early years at the site, and his successors, Dr Taha Baqir and Dr Faisal el Wailly; Professor Fuad Safar, then Inspector-General of Antiquities, and Sayid Mohammed Ali Mustafa, who were at that time the senior and greatly respected archaeologists of the Department; and Dr Faraj Basmachi, Director of the Iraq Museum. We not only valued their friendship but greatly benefited from their always helpful advice. Our official Iraqi representatives on the excavations were Dr Mahmud el Amin (1949), Sayid Izzet Din es-Sanduq (1950–51, 1953, 1955), Sayid Subri Shrukri (1952), Sayid (now Professor) Tariq el Madhloum (1956–58), Sayid Selim al-Jelili (1960–63); Sayida Selma al Radi (1963); to all of them we owe a great debt of gratitude both for their hard work and their good humour. Also of great assistance to us were Dr Behnam Abu al-Soof, former Director of Antiquities in the north, the Director of the Mosul Museum, Sa'id Daiwachi, and his staff, and Sayid Manhal Jabr, our Representative at Tell al Rimah in 1968 and now Director of Antiquities in Mosul. Among the members of the dig staff we must single out Tariq, now a university professor and a distinguished painter and sculptor, whom it has been our great pleasure to see recently in Baghdad, Selma, who has made her name in the archaeology of Yemen and has recently worked with us at Tell Brak, and Nicholas Kindersley (1957–63) and Julian Reade (1962–63), who continued with us to Tell al Rimah, where Nicholas was responsible for building the excavation house and for much of the photography.

We also wish to remember the trained pickmen from Sharqat, who worked loyally with us not only at Nimrud but also at Ain Sinu and subsequently at Tell al Rimah and Choga Mami, and especially our two foremen, Abdul Halaf al Angud, whom we had the pleasure of seeing when we visited Nimrud in 1987, and Mohammed Halaf al Musla.

15.i.01

INTRODUCTION

Nimrud is not the largest of the ancient capitals of Assyria, but it is undoubtedly one of the most beautiful archaeological sites in northern Iraq. Those who have seen it in the spring in particular have been struck both by its position and the extraordinary beauty of its flowers, especially the anemonies and poppies which, until recent times and the introduction of modern fertilizers and pesticides, blanketed the mound from late March until early May. Mallowan, in the introduction to his *Nimrud and Its Remains*, provides a highly evocative description:

> It is hard to decide what is one's strongest impression of Nimrud. I think of it in the winter as a lofty island in a sea of mud; in the spring as a green meadow gleaming in the sun; in the early summer as a torrid watch-tower, remote and proud, in a pitiless solitude. Across the fields flow the swift waters of the Tigris. From the town walls you can see the stream rushing past the steep mud-banks cracked and parched in the blistering sun, hemmed in on the west by cliffs of gypsum, mud and sandstone; downstream are islands of boar-infested scrub. Eastwards, less than a score of miles away, are the hills of Kurdistan edging back to the high mountains of Iran with their topmost peaks over the perpetual snow-line… Sometimes I have a picture of the golden-breasted bee-eaters flying down to their holes in the ruined walls at sunset, sometimes the pair of sheldrake which used to settle on the flanks of the S.W. Palace.

Our own memories add abundant hoopoes and rollers, large herds of gazelle roaming the fields below the tell, and the women of the local villages harvesting the spring crops by hand with the traditional sickle. It was an idyllic scene, worthy of its ancient monuments.

It is our intention in this introduction to identify those who have in the past contributed to our understanding of the history and archaeology of Nimrud both in the past and in the present. Nimrud was not one of the sites visited by early travellers from the west. In northern Mesopotamia that honour goes to Nineveh, easily accessible across the Tigris from Mosul, a city which like Nineveh itself lay astride the major routes both east–west and north–south, the latter by means of the river itself or along the foothills of the Zagros, the route of the famous 'Royal Road'. Moreover, despite Nimrud's appearance as biblical Calah,[1] the history of Nineveh was better-known, especially from classical sources. Nineveh was visited as early as the 12th century,[2] yet the first modern mention of Nimrud is by Claudius James Rich (1787–1821), an extraordinary young man with a precocious talent for languages, who was employed by the East India Company in 1804 and appointed a few years later to the Residency in Baghdad. In 1820 he spent four months in the north of what is now modern Iraq, the source of his *Narrative of a Residence in Koordistan, and on the site of Ancient Nineveh*, published posthumously by his widow in 1836. His survey of Nineveh, carried out at this time, set the precedent for the great expeditions of the 1840s. It was in 1820 that he also visited Nimrud, travelling down the Tigris by *kelek,* a local type of raft made from inflated goatskins lashed to a wooden framework, a method of transport attested also in ancient times. Indeed it was Rich's account of his four-month stay in Mosul that was to inform and inspire the succeeding generation, including both Botta at Khorsabad and Layard at Nimrud. The ancient fragments collected by Rich both here and in Babylonia were subsequently placed in the British Museum, at that time forming the principal, indeed virtually the only, collection of Assyrian antiquities in Europe. 'A case scarcely three feet square enclosed all that remained, not only of the great city, Nineveh, but of Babylon itself!'[3]

Austen Henry Layard (1817–95) is without question the best-known of the extraordinary, even heroic, figures who, in the 19th century, not only criss-crossed the Near East, ignoring the dangers and discomforts of their surroundings, but provided extraordinarily readable accounts of their travels and explorations. Layard in particular wrote with an enthusiasm and clarity that make his books still today a pleasure to read. In 1839–40 he and a friend traversed Asia Minor and Syria, 'free and unheeded', with neither guide nor servant, en route to Ceylon where Layard hoped to find suitable employment. They visited Nimrud, a mound

> of a pyramidical form which rose high above the rest… this was the pyramid which Xenophon had described, and near which the ten thousand had encamped: the ruins around it were those which the Greek general saw twenty-two centuries before, and which were even then the remains of an ancient city.[4]

Although Xenophon knew the place as Larisa, Layard records that local tradition attributed its foundation to the mighty Nimrod, and thus connected it 'with one of the first settlements of the human race', known from the book of Genesis. In the middle of April 1840 Layard left Mosul for Baghdad, travelling as had Rich by *kelek,* the site again catching his imagination:

> These huge mounds of Assyria made a deeper impression upon me, gave rise to more serious thoughts and more earnest reflection, than the temples of Balbec and the theatres of Ionia… It was evening as we approached the spot. The spring rains had clothed the mound with the richest verdure, and the fertile meadows, which stretched around it, were covered with flowers of every hue… My curiosity had been greatly excited, and from that time I formed the design of thoroughly examining, whenever it might be in my power, these singular ruins.[5]

Layard continued his journey eastwards as far as Hamadan, stopping to study the famous trilingual inscriptions of Bisitun, which again sparked his interest in the Assyrian mounds to the extent that he abandoned altogether his original intentions and remained in Persia, spending some time in the south-west among the Bakhtiari in Khuzistan. Finding himself again in Baghdad with no prospect of employment, he decided in 1842 to return to England. Layard's first-hand knowledge of Khuzistan, where border disputes between the Ottoman and Persian empires were affecting British interests, led the British Resident in Baghdad to take the opportunity to entrust to Layard letters concerning the dispute for Sir Stratford Canning, then British Ambassador to the Sublime Porte. Ironically, the boundary in question was that contested yet again in the 1980s. In Constantinople Canning at first refused to see him but finally agreed to a meeting that was to change not only Layard's future but the history of archaeology in Mesopotamia. Impressed by Layard's knowledge and experience, Canning engaged him as his unofficial (and unpaid) agent. But Canning was also a patron of antiquarian studies – indeed he was responsible at that time for the removal of the Halicarnassus 'marbles' to the British Museum – and Layard's enthusiasm for the mounds of Assyria struck a sympathetic response. In the meantime, the French had established a consulate in Mosul and, impressed by Rich's accounts and the antiquities in the British Museum, the new consul, Paul Emile Botta, was promised support for any archaeological work he might undertake. Encouraged both by Layard's enthusiasm and the spectacular success of Botta at Khorsabad, Canning was now to play a major role in the first excavations at Nimrud, agreeing to finance Layard for a brief season in the hope that comparable success would persuade the British government to match the generosity of the French. A memorandum in Canning's hand is of interest:

> I rely upon Mr Layard's obliging attention to the following points
>
> 1 To keep me informed of his operations, and of any objects of sufficient interest and curiosity which he may see or discover.
>
> 2 To keep clear of political and religious questions, and as much as possible of missionaries, or native chiefs in tribes regarded with enmity or jealousy by the Turkish authorities.
>
> 3 To cultivate the goodwill of the Pashas and others of the Sultan's functionaries by all becoming means.
>
> 4 To bear in mind that his professed character will be that of a traveller, fond of antiquities, of picturesque scenery, and of the manners peculiar to Asia. [The reason for such 'disguise' was that at this time Layard lacked the firman essential for excavation.]
>
> 5 Not to start on his return without a previous communication with me subsequent to his first inquiries and attempts at discovery.
>
> 6 In case of success to give me early and exact information as to the nature of the objects discovered, and the best means of removal etc. with an estimate of cost, doing what he can to obtain the necessary permission on the spot.
>
> … I reckon on Mr Layard's reaching Moussul towards the end of October [1845], and being able to complete a fair experiment of discovery in the most probable spots during the two ensuing months. Should he have reasons for adding another ten days, he is at liberty to follow his own discretion.[6]

Canning's initial advance, which he expected to be repaid, was of £60 for the journey and Layard's expenses, and £20 a month for two months for the excavations. By this means, and with the encouragement and assistance of Botta, who was unusually generous in sharing his knowledge and experience, Layard returned to Nimrud. Late in the autumn of 1845 the first trenches were cut in the mound, and on 8 November 1845 *The Times* drew attention to the occasion in a long article. On his first day of excavation Layard found not only a room in the North-West Palace (room A) but a wall of the South-West Palace as well, identifying in one day two of the more important buildings on the citadel. Among his early discoveries were the first

Fig. 1. Layard's drawing of the discovery of the head of a colossal human-headed gate figure at the entrance to the Ninurta Temple (1846), and the same head, re-exposed, in the spring of 1956. The gate figure, which had a lion's body (see Fig. 2), stood to a height of 5 m.

of the Nimrud ivories, some covered with gold leaf which persuaded the workmen that he knew what he was about and that now they understood clearly the real purpose of the excavations.[7]

Layard had his problems with the then Pasha of Mosul (as did the citizens of that city – on one occasion the Pasha feigned his death and then, as the citizens began rejoicing at the news, sent his men round the city seizing those who were celebrating, and especially those who possessed property which could be confiscated![8]). Not only did Layard have no formal authority to excavate, but the funds advanced to him were minimal indeed. In the beginning he could afford to employ only an extraordinarily small number of workmen, at first 6, then 11 and finally 31, a marked contrast to the 1950s when Mallowan employed as many as 250, working for the same length of time. For reasons of economy, and because it proved to be an easy method both of tracing the palace plan and at the same time finding the bas-reliefs which were the most exciting of the new discoveries, excavations were carried out largely by tunnelling along the stone slabs that lined the walls, leaving the central areas of the rooms unexcavated. For the same financial reasons Layard was forced to transfer excavated earth from one room to the next, thereby, regrettably, contaminating for future excavators the contents of the partially excavated rooms. Indeed the parsimony of his English sponsors, even in later seasons, forced a policy of obtaining 'the largest possible number of well-preserved objects of art at the least possible outlay of time and money.'

When work was resumed in the spring, the very large head of a human-headed lion colossus was found, causing amazement and terror among the workmen, and word spread like wildfire that Nimrod himself had been found.[9] Even today, for those of us already well-acquainted with such discoveries, to see the emergence from the soil of these extraordinary creatures continues to astonish (Fig. 1). It is not difficult to imagine the impact of these discoveries in the nineteenth century, not only in Mosul and Baghdad but in the western world. Here were discoveries not only remarkable in themselves but discoveries that lent credence to the evidence of the Bible, a matter of enormous importance in the Victorian world.

By now the friendly Botta had been replaced in Mosul by a less cooperative consul, and there developed a considerable degree of Anglo-French rivalry, one very important aspect of which involved the race to get the first Assyrian finds on display in Europe. Colonel Henry Creswicke Rawlinson, then British Resident in Baghdad, the position Rich had held many years before, now offered the East India Company steamer, stationed on the Lower Tigris, but rapids prevented the steamer getting up river as far as Nimrud. Thus both Layard and the French were forced to float their antiquities downstream by raft. The race was won by the French, with Botta's finds on display in the Louvre in May 1847. Layard's twelve bas-reliefs from Nimrud appeared in the British Museum in August. The good news, however, was that the British Museum now undertook to support the excavation at Nimrud with funding from the Treasury, but hardly on the scale of the French. The total allowed was £2000, from which Canning was reimbursed and Layard provided with an allowance, leaving only £1000 for the excavations, to say nothing of the cost of shipping the important discoveries back to England.

In 1846 Layard resumed work at Nimrud with more workmen and the assistance of Hormuzd Rassam, a Chaldaean Christian and brother of the British Vice-Consul in Mosul, as overseer and general agent. In the beginning Layard had had to do everything himself, including copying the inscriptions, drawing the reliefs, taking casts, removing and packing the reliefs. Now the Trustees of the British Museum sent out a succession of remarkably unsuitable young artists, most of whom unfortunately either arrived in poor health or immediately became ill. One rather stubborn young man (T.S. Bell), sent to record the famous Bavian reliefs, drowned while swimming in the Gomel against local advice, while F.C. Cooper, two of whose drawings are published here (Fig. 2), arrived in poor health and before long broke down completely.[10]

Layard left Mosul in 1851, never to return, Hormuzd Rassam thereafter taking over reponsibility for the excavations, perhaps not the wisest of choices since Rassam continued, even into the 1880s, an extensive and essentially unrecorded simultaneous looting of a large number of sites not only in Assyria but also in Babylonia, at a time when other excavators were beginning to act more responsibly. To Rassam, nonetheless, is owed the discovery of the Nineveh Library, the Balawat Gates and the famous Lion Hunt sculptures of Assurbanipal, all now to be seen in the British Museum. In 1853 overall charge of the British Museum excavations in Assyria was entrusted to Rawlinson. It was in fact Rawlinson who believed at first that Nimrud was ancient Nineveh, and was therefore responsible for the title of Layard's first book, *Nineveh and its Remains*, although he changed his mind shortly after the book was published. Rawlinson, who was one of the major contributors to the decipherment of cuneiform, was provided with considerably more money than had been placed at Layard's disposal and was now anxious that British excavations should continue in Assyria. He enlisted the help of the Assyrian Excavation Fund, a body supported in England by private subscription, which had appointed William Kennet Loftus to excavate at Warka in Babylonia. Loftus was a geologist and member of the Turco-Persian frontier commission, to which Layard had also been appointed during his time in Constantinople. Loftus worked at Warka in 1854, but was then requested by Rawlinson to continue the work in the north. He excavated at Nimrud in 1854–55, in particular tunnelling within what was then known as the South-East Palace (Ezida and the Burnt Palace of the 1950s excavations), where we were to come across his tunnels a century later, and extending the architectural plans recovered by Layard. Among his more important discoveries was a large collection of ivories, especially from the Burnt Palace, now known as the 'Loftus ivories'.[11] Regrettably, his work is recorded only in his reports to the British Museum.[12]

In 1855 the Crimean War put a temporary stop to exploration in Assyria, but by now the work of Layard had become widely known not only in Britain but generally in Europe. Layard's work at Nimrud and at Nineveh had made him, and even Assyriology, household names in England. His books, which recounted not only his excavations but also his travels throughout the Near East, became best-sellers, available on every railway station bookstall. Indeed, it would be difficult to exaggerate

Fig. 2. North and south entrances to the Ninurta Temple, drawn by F.C. Cooper (1850).

their impact on 19th-century England. The publication of his great *Monuments of Nineveh* (also in 1849) received no public funding, but was supported privately, the list of subscribers headed by the queen herself, Prince Albert, the King of Prussia and the Grand Duke of Tuscany. Perhaps surprisingly, in Victorian England the general public was far more aware of the archaeology of Mesopotamia than is now the case, and literary references to Layard and Rich were readily appreciated. Claudius Rich, for example, inspired a reference in Byron's *Don Juan*.

> … some infidels, who don't
> Because they can't, find out the very spot
> Of that same Babel, or because they won't
> (Though Claudius Rich, Esquire, some bricks has got,
> And written lately two memoirs upon't).[13]

In schools of Layard's day Nimrud and Khorsabad became subjects for prize essays, and a generation later references appeared in popular productions on the London stage, including *The Pirates of Penzance* (1880). Contemporary architecture and decorative arts were also influenced.[14] Layard was to end his life as a diplomat and politician, widely recognised in the political cartoons of *Punch* which depicted him as a winged bull colossus, often labelled 'Layard of Nineveh' or 'Baiting the Bull'.[15] However, his life in politics was not to be as successful as his archaeology, although he had the gratification of being appointed Her Majesty's Ambassador to the Sublime Porte, the post held by Canning when Layard arrived in 1842, impecunious and without prospect. In 1884 he and his wife moved to Venice, where his house, which survives as the Palazzo Cappello-Layard, retains its connection with Assyriology as the Oriental Institute of the University of Venice.

For almost a score of years no authorised excavations took place. Yet at Nimrud 'the sound of pick and shovel were not infrequently heard'.[16] All pretence of historical research had now been abandoned, and the place of the archaeologists had been taken by commercial speculators. Regrettably, this resulted in the 1860s in the dispatch by Baghdad merchants of at least two consignments of Assyrian sculpture to Europe. There is, however, one further name to mention in the context of serious 19th century investigation at the site, that of George Smith, an extraordinary cuneiform scholar who began his working life apprenticed to a firm of bank-note engravers. He devoted his spare time to reading everything he could find about the Assyrian excavations and studying the sculptures and inscriptions exhibited in the British Museum. His extraordinary interest in the subject drew the attention of an official of the museum, who found for him a minor post where he developed a particular genius for decipherment and was allotted the task of sorting and 'joining' the broken cuneiform tablets from the Nineveh Library. The story of his decipherment of an account closely resembling that of the Biblical Flood is well known, as is the offer by the London *Daily Telegraph* of £1000 (ten times Layard's initial budget) to equip an expedition to Nineveh in order to recover the missing piece of the Assyrian text. The most extraordinary part of this story is that on the evening of his fifth day at Nineveh (May

1873) he actually found a fragment which contained the missing part of the story, a remarkable piece of luck which any modern archaeologist would envy. During this time it is obvious that Smith also did some work at Nimrud, since tablets from the latter site are included in the Koujunjik collection at the British Museum, erroneously attributed to Nineveh (inter alia, Fig. 125, p. 208). Tragically, Smith died of dysentery in Aleppo at the early age of 36. Rassam returned briefly to Nimrud in 1878–80, under the auspices of the British Museum, but thereafter the site remained untouched, except for occasional robbing of the stone for purposes of building or the making of lime, until Mallowan's return in 1949, exactly a century after the publication of Layard's *Nineveh and its Remains*. Indeed during this time interest in Assyria had waned, with archaeological attention increasingly re-oriented towards Babylonia, now emerging as the more ancient cradle of civilisation. At the same time the discovery of the even older Sumerians, who had 'invented' writing and built the first cities, sealed the fate of the archaeology of Nimrud until Campbell-Thompson returned to Nineveh in 1927 and the young Mallowan joined him in 1931–32.

Mallowan's first introduction to the site had in fact taken place while he was working for Sir Leonard Woolley at Ur. At the end of his first season (1926), he drove north 'excited at the prospect of seeing the upper reaches of the Tigris in the spring.' Seeing Nimrud for the first time made a great impression on him, as it has on us all. 'Here I realised was an archaeological paradise where one day after I had done my apprenticeship, I might be privileged to enter. And from this intention I never faltered.'[17] This book is devoted largely to the results of his excavations in the 1950s and 1960s. Mallowan began work at Nimrud in the spring of 1949, the staff that year consisting solely of himself, his wife, Donald Wiseman, Robert Hamilton and their Iraqi Representative. The first four became the core of the expedition staff until 1953. It was Hamilton who found and rented the original British School of Archaeology in Iraq house in Baghdad; indeed the telephone in the Director's house when we lived in Baghdad in the 1960s, and the bank account, were still in his name. He also bought the ancient four-wheel-drive Dodge that formed the backbone of excavation transport for

Fig. 3. Ivory head from the rab ekalli*'s house in Fort Shalmaneser (p. 164), ht. 12 cm (ND 7561).*

many years (and ruined some backbones as well). He was responsible for the survey of the site and in the early years, the architectural plans; the later plans and reconstructions were drawn by John Reid and David Oates. In 1950 Robert Hamilton was succeeded as Secretary–Librarian of the British School by Barbara Parker, to whom all of us who worked at Nimrud remain deeply grateful, and who continued as a major figure on the dig staff throughout the seasons there and later at Tell al Rimah. Among many other duties she was the excavation photographer, and most of the photographs reproduced here were taken by her, in the early years on our enormous and splendid plate camera (Pl. 1b). She also acted as epigraphist, treated the sick and injured among the workmen, and in Baghdad looked after those of us who stayed in the BSAI house. My first acquaintance with Barbara (J.O., personal) was in the winter of 1951, when I stayed in the house in Baghdad and accompanied her to Nimrud to plant the peach and apricot trees demanded by Max for Agatha's terrace garden at the back of the dig house, with its early season view of the snow-covered Zagros (the house had been built by Barbara the previous year, when a serious financial crisis was ingeniously solved by the simple expedient of borrowing money from each individual workman to pay the next). We found Mosul both extremely cold and awash with heavy rains which had rendered the mud track to Nimrud virtually impassable. Barbara was not only fluently persuasive but one never to admit defeat, and she talked the Mosul police into taking us in one of their jeeps through the twenty miles of mud to Nimrud where the trees were duly planted, later of course to be consumed by the local goats.[18] We both worked with Mallowan in the 1950s; from 1958 onwards the excavations were under the direction of David Oates and, in 1963, Jeffery Orchard, who had succeeded Barbara as Secretary-Librarian in Baghdad.

Although the excavations of the British School in Iraq ended in 1963, work continued at Nimrud, the most important being the project of excavation and restoration begun by the Iraqi Directorate-General of Antiquities in 1956, while the British excavations were still in operation. In that year the decision was taken to restore and protect the northern façade of the North-West Palace throne room of Assurnasirpal II, work carried out under the direction of Sa'id Daiwichi, Director of the Mosul Museum. In 1959 and 1960 Dr Behnam Abu es-Soof cleared the throne room and excavated the rooms to the west. Further investigation and reconstruction of the North-West Palace in subsequent years, especially in the rooms surrounding the inner courtyard Y and in the domestic wing, was directed by Sayid Hazim Abdul-Hamid, then Director of the Mosul Museum.[19] The stone work on the north side of the ziggurrat was also investigated at this time. In 1973–74 work was carried out on the Ninurta and Šarrat-niphi temples.

From 1974–1976 a Polish expedition under the direction of Janusz Meuszynski began work at Nimrud, re-investigating the area of the Central Palace and carrying out some work in the North-West Palace, in particular in the wing west of courtyard Y. Regrettably, this work came to an end with the unfortunate death of the Director. In 1975 excavation and restoration continued in the North-West Palace under the direction of Myesser Said al-Iraqi. The most remarkable discoveries were those in well AJ, discussed on p. 92. Work was also begun on the restoration of the Nabu

Temple, carried out by Abdullah Amin Agha and Myesser Said and, from 1982, the latter together with Muzahim Mahmud Hussein who, from 1988 onwards was to excavate the extraordinarily rich tombs in the North-West Palace. Other fieldwork at Nimrud included three seasons of survey and excavation (1987–89), under the direction of Dr Paolo Fiorina on behalf of the Centre Scavi di Torino; 160 of the 360 ha of the outer town were topographically surveyed and an extensive programme of survey begun. At the same time excavation was carried out in the SW quadrant of Fort Shalmaneser and in the northern gate of the outer bailey. In the autumn of 1989 Dr John Curtis directed a British Museum excavation, also in Fort Shalmaneser. Further excavation and restoration under the direction of Muzahim Mahmud Hussein continued in the 1990s, including the investigation of another well in the south-eastern courtyard of the domestic quarters of the North-West Palace. Also excavated here were underground chambers thought originally to constitute a palace prison and the southern wall of the palace complex. The position of the palace of Adad-nerari III was also identified, and in the spring of 2001 further work in the area of the Ishtar Temple revealed a second monumental entrance to the temple complex.

To end on a personal note, we were fortunate to have known northern Iraq in the 1950s before the great changes wrought by the introduction of modern farming methods and machinery, and the rapid growth and modernisation of traditional cities like Mosul. This is not in any way to criticise the development that has taken place, only to note that our introduction to life in the countryside of the 1950s has been of enormous help in understanding the archaeology of this landscape. A single, and amusing, incident illustrates the point. In his introduction to the publication of the Governor's Palace texts, Mallowan refers to a cuneiform tablet dealing with the sale of a house 'together with its beams', remarking that specific mention of the wooden beams and the door in the sale of a house is a custom that still survives, and one of which he was ignorant in the negotiations for the purchase of a house from a watchman at Nimrud who, perfectly within his rights, simply carted them away.[20] A similarly specific sale is recorded in the documents belonging to the merchant official Šamaš-šarru-uṣur, who lived in the largest of the town wall houses. As Mallowan remarks, 'It may perhaps seem surprising that ancient Assyrian custom is often the wisest counsel for modern practice, but that is a truth which one is continuously learning with experience.'[21]

A final comment about the book itself. Nimrud is a large and complex site, excavated over two centuries, from which literally tens of thousands of objects have been recovered. It is impossible to do justice to such evidence in a book of this size. We have attempted to provide a readable general account, summarising much but far from all the important evidence. We recognise all too well that we have only skimmed the surface. For the benefit of the non-specialist reader we have supplied a short list of recommended general books; more detailed references can be found in footnotes listed at the end of the volume.

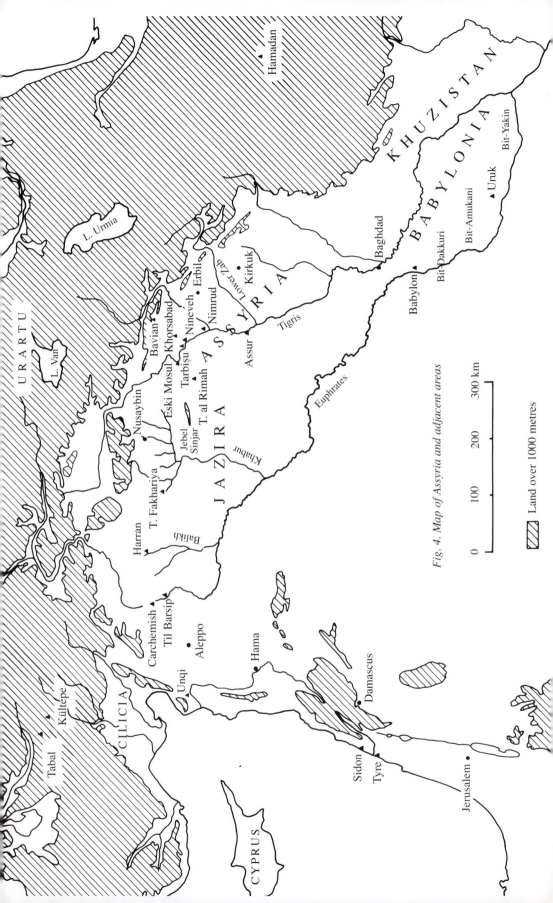

Fig. 4. Map of Assyria and adjacent areas

Land over 1000 metres

0   100   200   300 km

CHAPTER ONE

THE LAND OF ASSYRIA – SETTING THE SCENE

GEOGRAPHY AND SETTLEMENT

The homeland of Assyria was the eastern sector of the north Mesopotamian plain in what is now northern Iraq. It was bounded on the north and east by the foothills of the Anatolian highlands and the Zagros mountains and on the south and south-west by the sometimes variable limit of rainfall sufficient for agriculture; on the west there was no natural boundary (Fig. 4). The northern plain, unlike the flat alluvium of southern Mesopotamia (at this time known as Babylonia) is crossed by outlying ridges that run parallel with the foothills and intersected by two great rivers, the Tigris and the Euphrates and their tributaries. Even outside the rainfall zone their valleys offer intermittent basins of alluvial land that can be cultivated by simple irrigation, but the steppe between them (the Jazira or 'island') has throughout recorded history been the home of nomadic herdsmen, the present-day Beduin. They follow an annual pattern of migration, wintering in and around the Euphrates valley and moving north and north-east in the spring in search of pasture for their flocks. This has at times brought them into conflict with the agricultural communities of the rainfall zone who, unless they lived under the protection of a strong government, have tended to abandon their outlying land, on which sections of the nomad tribes have later settled.

This process is reflected in the tribal affiliations of present day villagers, and we cite one example because it may throw some light on the early history of the Assyrians themselves and their first capital, Assur (Qalaᶜat Sharqat). In the 18th century the great Shammar tribe migrated from northern Arabia and spent more than two centuries in the steppe, west of Sharqat, where Layard encountered them on more than one occasion.[1] A century later many of the tribe were settled villagers in the northern plain, and their paramount shaikh had built himself a mansion near Sharqat with gardens full of imported trees and plants, in unconscious imitation of the Late Assyrian king Assurnasirpal II, founder of Nimrud (Fig. 5). Like many Semitic peoples before them, the Assyrians too arrived as nomads. Although their earlier history remains obscure, we see an analogy in the Shammar tribe of modern times. Assur lies at the boundary of the 'desert and the sown' and, like the Shammar, the Assyrians came from the steppe west of the Tigris and established their first permanent centre at Assur, just 8 km south of the modern village of Sharqat.[2]

To the north there was much rich farmland in the plain around Mosul, and also to the north-east around Erbil, which was the best wheat-producing area. Such well-watered land was relatively limited, however, and the later Assyrians were heavily dependent on crops from the cultivable land south of Jebel Sinjar and, especially, in the Khabur plain north of the Jebel, areas west of their actual homeland. Grapes were grown to the north-east of Nimrud, and various types of fruit and nut were common, especially figs, pomegranates and pistachios; although palm trees flourished, the dates themselves, a staple food in southern Mesopotamia, did not normally ripen in

the north. Assyria itself lacked mineral resources, although its low hill ranges had good limestone for building and even fine-grained alabaster, known as 'Mosul marble', used lavishly by the Assyrians for their reliefs and monumental sculpture. The most accessible source would seem to have been near Eski Mosul on the Tigris 40 km north-west of Nineveh, from which the heavy stone could have been rafted downstream.

HISTORICAL BACKGROUND

Although the cities of Assur and Nineveh have long histories, and in the case of Nineveh, 'prehistory', they were not united in an Assyrian 'nation' until the 14th century BC. We remain uncertain who were the inhabitants of these cities before the arrival of the Assyrians, but recent third millennium evidence from the Syrian part of northern Mesopotamia suggests that they were speakers of a Semitic dialect that differed from both Akkadian and Assyrian. The Assyrian language is yet another distinctive dialect of Semitic Akkadian, and as such is related to more recent languages such as Aramaic (p. 217) and, later, Arabic.

Assur was originally a trading city, controlling both the river and a major east-west route following along the line of the hills to and from the west. Early in the second millennium BC there is evidence of a trading colony of merchants from Assur at Kültepe (Kanesh) in central Anatolia. Surprisingly, since Anatolia was rich in metals which Assyria lacked, this particular trade seems to have been a

Fig. 5. Limestone statue of Assurnasirpal II, found by Layard in the temple of Ištar Šarrat-niphi and now in the British Museum, ht 1.13 m.

commodities-for-profit venture for the Assyrians. The predominant traded goods were textiles, some made at Assur, some prestigious types imported from Babylonia, and tin which came to Assur from the east. Thus Assur functioned both as a producer and a 'middle man'. The history of Nineveh is less well-known, but it must always have been a, if not the, major city in the agricultural heartland of what was to become the country of Assyria.

In the second millennium BC another linguistic group is found, the Hurrians, whose settlements, like those of the modern Kurds, were distributed across the whole of the northern plain and south-eastern Anatolia. In the second half of the second millennium these Hurrian-speaking peoples were united under the Mitanni dynasty, at this time one of the great powers of the Near East, comparable in status with the Babylonians and the Hittites. The Mitanni ruled the area which was later to become Assyria, but in the 14th century BC the city of Assur under Assur-uballit I (1363–1328 BC) reasserted its independence; it was at this time that a 'kingdom' of Assyria first emerged. The city Assur gave its name to the national god; in order to distinguish the two in this book, the god's name is conventionally (and correctly) written Aššur. In Mesopotamia the transference of a city name to a god is unusual, and in this case may have originated in the fact that at an early period oaths were sworn in the name of the city as though it were a god. The fact that the national god had no family, i.e. no 'origins', is perhaps one reason for the later assimilation of the histories and symbolism of other gods with Aššur (discussed below).

A generation after Assur-uballit, an able succession of Middle Assyrian kings extended their control as far as the Euphrates to the west, incorporating the rich agricultural lands of the Khabur basin, and into the mountains to the north, both previously the territory of the Hurrian-speaking Mitanni. Tukulti-Ninurta I (1243–1207 BC) and Tiglath-Pileser I (1114–1076) were rulers of unprecedented power; both campaigned vigorously abroad, in Babylonia to the south and Syria to the west. It was at this time in Assyria that the principles of absolute monarchy were forged and the idea of imperialism given practical expression. Control of the areas to the west and south, as well as elsewhere on the homeland periphery, was to prove a major preoccupation of their successors until the final collapse of the Assyrian Empire in 612 BC.

A settlement existed at Nimrud throughout this period, but we know very little about it. The earliest material recovered from the tell consists of painted Ninevite 5 sherds of early third millennium date, but the excavations have nowhere even approached these deeply buried levels. Middle Assyrian occupation was reached in two areas of the excavations, but we cannot date this material with any precision. Although Assurnasirpal II tells us in the 9th century that the city had been in ruins since the time of Shalmaneser I (1273–1244 BC), Kalhu (the ancient Assyrian name of Nimrud, Biblical Calah) is listed as a provincial capital in texts from the reign of Tiglath-pileser I (1114–1076 BC).[3] In terms of the focus of this book, that is, the archaeology of the city of Nimrud, our story begins with this same Assurnasirpal II (883–859 BC), for it was he who moved the capital from Assur to Kalhu, where he built a magnificent new city (Fig. 5). In his inscriptions he gives no reason for the move but, as we have already noted, Assur lay at the southern boundary of rainfed agricultural land and a more central location would have been both strategically and economically desirable. Why Assurnasirpal rejected Nineveh also remains unexplained, but one can imagine that the abandoned Nimrud provided wider scope for his grandiose ambitions. Certainly he was one of the greatest builders of the Late Assyrian period, and the first part of this book is devoted to his palaces and temples and their rich contents. His military campaigns, again through Syria – he was the first Assyrian king since the 11th century to reach the Mediterranean, where he now established a corridor down the Levant coast – acquired for him the exotic items required for the construction and decoration of his new palaces and temples. Foreign labour was also transported to work on the new buildings. Indeed, it is to Assurnasirpal II that we can credit the establishment of the new imperial Assyria.

His son, Shalmaneser III, was a worthy successor to his father, completing his father's building projects, including the ziggurrat at Nimrud, and initiating his own, in particular the construction of the great arsenal in the outer town, referred to in the recent excavations as Fort Shalmaneser. A number of building projects were undertaken also at Assur, which remained an important religious and commercial centre. Indeed, the proper burial place for Late Assyrian kings was in its palace. Like his father, Shalmaneser continued the annual campaigns to the west, where Syria controlled both access to the Mediterranean and to the much-prized cedar forests. Among his opponents were both Aramaean and Neo-Hittite states, for example, Hamath (modern Hama), the name of whose Neo-Hittite ruler, Irhuleni, was found inscribed on a group of shells from Fort Shalmaneser (Fig. 6). Twice Shalmaneser failed to capture Damascus, but a third attempt against a new king, Hazael, was more successful, resulting in the submission of the king whose name, like that of Irhuleni, appears on the spoils stored at Nimrud (p. 181).[4] Although Assyrian troops did not enter the city, the 'victory' over Damascus led to the capitulation of Tyre and Sidon, and of Jehu 'the Israelite', whose submission is depicted on the famous Black Obelisk, found at Nimrud (Fig. 7). Shalmaneser's intervention in Babylonia is also illustrated at the site, this time on the great throne base from the arsenal (p. 173f). Although the supremacy of Assyria in the west was now secure, the states beyond the Euphrates were not as yet incorporated into the Empire.

Shalmaneser's lengthy reign ended in a rebellion, instigated by one of his sons and involving the cities of Assyria and as far west as the Khabur, a rebellion which his successor, Šamši-Adad V (823–811 BC), claims to have suppressed. Indeed there survives a treaty between Šamši-Adad and the king of Babylon, Marduk-zakir-šumi I, made at the time of this rebellion and before the former's accession.[5] This is the same Babylonian king who is shown on the Shalmaneser III throne base, having been reinstated by Shalmaneser (p. 174); in the later treaty the Babylonian repays his debt by supporting Shalmaneser's legitimate heir. We know relatively little of the activities of Šamši-Adad at Nimrud, but a large stone stele, dedicated by him in the Ninurta Temple and now in the British Museum, was found by Rassam in the Nabu Temple (Fig. 8). The apparent historical consciousness of this age, reflected in the revival of such famous Assyrian names as Shalmaneser and Šamši-Adad, the latter one of the

Fig. 6. Burnt shell ornament, incised with neo-Hittite hiero-glyphic signs recording the name of Irhuleni, king of Hamath (modern Hama). One of 14 examples found in Fort Shalmaneser, room T 10 (8.7 cm x 7.5 cm, ND 12518).

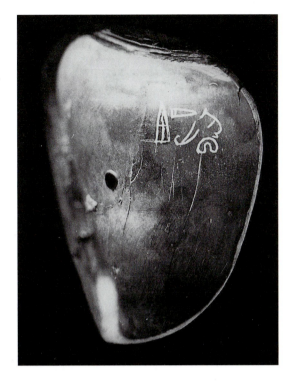

great kings of the earlier second millennium BC, is also reflected in the reign of Šamši-Adad V by the deliberate use of 'archaic' script on this stele.[6]

The main thrust of Šamši-Adad's campaigns was against Babylonia and Urartu, a vigorous new kingdom to the north-east of Assyria, in the vicinity of Mt Ararat (the same name), which had emerged in the 9th century and, protected by its high mountains and impregnable fortresses, was to plague the rulers of Assyria throughout the 8th and 7th centuries. It was particularly noted for the breeding of horses which were much desired by the Assyrians. Shalmaneser III marched twice to Lake Van, and his son campaigned in this area, but Urartu was too formidable and too well-protected for the contemporary Assyrian armies. Šamši-Adad V also campaigned against Babylonia, at that time controlled by various tribal coalitions. Indeed the invasion of Babylonia, in which he seems to have forgotten his debt to the Babylonian king, was the high point of his brief career. His stele inscription ends with the boast that he had even removed from the Babylonian king (Marduk-zakir-šumi's son) his 'pavilion, his royal tent and [even] his camp bed'!

Šamši-Adad V was succeeded by his son Adad-nerari III (810–783 BC), who continued the policy of regular military campaigns, most notably involving the actual capture of Damascus. He was responsible for extensive building activity at Nimrud, including a newly identified palace south of the North-West Palace, the (re)construction of the Nabu Temple, additions to Fort Shalmaneser and the building of an attractive palace north of the citadel. His reign is marked by two unusual

17

Fig. 7. The Black Obelisk of Shalmaneser III, found by Rassam outside the Central Building of Assurnasirpal II. a) The upper two friezes show the Gilzanite Sua and the Israelite Jehu, son of Omri, paying homage by prostrating themselves before the Assyrian king. The men from Gilzan (west of Lake Urmia) bring 'silver, gold, tin, bronze casseroles, horses and two-humped camels.' Jehu's attendants bring, 'Silver, gold, a gold bowl, a gold tureen, golden vessels, gold pails, tin, the staffs for the king's hand and spears.' b) Tribute from the land of Musri (Egypt) includes two-humped camels, a water buffalo, a rhinoceros, an antelope, female elephants, female monkeys and apes.' The obelisk is now in the British Museum.

18

aspects. The first was the extraordinarily high profile of his mother, Sammuramat, the legendary Semiramis, whose name appears with that of the king in royal inscriptions and who, remarkably for a woman, had her own stele at Assur. The second was the prominence of some royal officials who themselves acted as though their authority were equal to that of the king in extraordinary displays of *lèse-majesté*. This phenomenon began in the time of Adad-nerari and continued through the reigns of several relatively weak successors. Indeed some of these officials, most if not all of whom were eunuchs,[7] continued in their offices under more than one king. One of the best-known is Šamši-ilu, whose gold bowl, engraved with his name, was found in one of the recently discovered Nimrud tombs (p. 86). Most remarkable is a text inscribed on a stone stele found by the Orontes river near Antakya, recording the drawing up of a boundary along the Orontes. Here Adad-nerari III and Šamši-ilu, the eunuch *turtanu* (commander-in-chief), are recorded as jointly establishing this boundary line, and both men seem to be illustrated on the stele.[8] In a second text, engraved on two colossal stone lions at Til-Barsip (on the Euphrates), this same Šamši-ilu, who was not only commander-in-chief of the army but also a powerful governor of lands to the north and east of Assyria, describes in royal style his great victory in Urartu without reference to any royal name.[9] A number of stelae were erected by these powerful officials, often in connection with royal grants of territory. On one example, found by us at Tell al Rimah, the text begins with the campaigns of Adad-nerari III but concludes with the grant to one Nergal-eriš of a vast tract of land in the west, between the Khabur, the Euphrates and the Wadi Tharthar in the east.[10] The most interesting feature of this stele is that the portion describing the grant of territory had been carefully cut away, i.e. deliberately erased to remove evidence of the self-elevated position of Nergal-eriš.

There is a strong possibility that the extraordinary power of the eunuchs at this time may have been related to the dominant position of the queen mother, Sammuramat, who would herself have been unable, under the strict rules governing the behaviour of palace women, to deal directly with officials other than eunuchs, despite her position. Her unusual status is often attributed to the fact that her son succeeded to the throne as a child, but this has been disputed, and there is in fact no direct evidence to support this explanation. On one stele discovered in Turkey, on which her name is included next to that of her son, it is recorded that she had gone on campaign with him to the west, an event otherwise unparalleled in Assyrian history.[11] Three relatively weak monarchs succeeded Adad-nerari III, a situation which encouraged the governors to arrogate to themselves even greater power. Of these rulers, one stayed at home for most of his reign; under another there was both plague and serious rebellion. During this period a 'palace herald of the king', whose name appears before that of the king on the stele which records this event, founded a new city on the Wadi Tharthar, south of Tell Afar, not only named after himself but exempt from taxes.[12] Finally, in 745 BC, following a revolution at Kalhu in which Assur-nerari V was murdered, possibly at the instigation of Šamši-ilu, there came to the throne a ruler who during the course of his reign not only reshaped Assyrian administration, and indeed the map itself, but has been described as the true founder of the Neo-Assyrian Empire, his widespread reforms a 'watershed in the history of the Near East'.[13] This was Tiglath-pileser III (745–727 BC), who claimed no royal parentage[14] but revived the title first used by the great Naram-Sin of Agade, 'king of the four quarters', that is, 'king of the world'. Tiglath-pileser bore a second name, Pulu (Biblical Pul, the first Assyrian to be mentioned by name in the Bible).

No earlier Assyrian rulers had actually annexed territory west of the Euphrates, although Bit-Adini, its capital at Til-Barsip on the east bank of the Euphrates, was made an Assyrian province by Shalmaneser III. With the accession of Tiglath-pileser III this situation was completely altered, by conquest and annexation. Thus kingdoms from southern Anatolia to the Phoenician coast became vassals, expressing their dependence by both tribute and symbolic acts of obeisance. A gold statue of the Assyrian king was placed in Gaza, among the 'gods of their land'. Even Damascus became a part of Assyria. Local rulers no longer administered their own territories, providing only military assistance and tribute as tokens of their dependent status. Traditional provinces were broken up into smaller and more manageable units. Thus, although eunuchs were still appointed as local governors, the possibilities of self aggrandisement were much reduced. The Assyrian king conquered Babylonia and, 'taking the hand of Marduk' (the supreme god of Babylon) – a reference to the annual ceremony in which the legitimacy of the king was confirmed – assumed the throne of Babylon, the beginning of a southern policy that was to involve the Assyrian government in the expenditure of excessive time and money for the next century. At this particular moment, however, both the Assyrian intervention and the king's accession seem to have been welcomed in Babylonia, a territory which had long been unsettled by tribal rivalries. At Nimrud official letters concerning this event were found in the chancery offices of the North-West Palace (p. 197).[15] Tiglath-pileser III built a new palace at Kalhu, the so-called Central Palace, from which the stone reliefs were later removed by Esarhaddon for his South-West Palace (p. 73). Recent Iraqi excavations have exposed a large area of this building.

Tiglath-pileser's son, Shalmaneser V, succeeded to the throne without opposition, but reigned for only five years (726–722 BC). If one can rely on the testimony of his famous successor, Sargon II, Shalmaneser V's taxation policies provoked a revolution in which the throne was seized by Sargon. Whatever the cause of the revolt, the outcome was certainly to Sargon's advantage, and the latter, like Tiglath-pileser III, provides no genealogy in the surviving royal inscriptions. However, a glazed plaque records that he too is the son of Tiglath-pileser III,[16] although his name, 'the legitimate king' suggests that perhaps he was not. Sargon campaigned widely and successfully, his greatest triumph undoubtedly the defeat at last of the powerful kingdom of Urartu. The problem of Babylon rose again, but for a time Assyria directed its attentions elsewhere, leaving the able Chaldaean, Merodach-Baladan, in control in the south. This was the Merodach-Baladan of the Bible, whose inscribed clay cylinder was found in the North-West Palace (p. 198).

Fig. 8. Stele of Šamši-Adad V, which stood originally in front of the Ninurta temple; the stele shows the king himself with, before him, symbols of the gods. Found in the Nabu Temple by Rassam (p. 112), now in the British Museum.

Sargon lived at Kalhu and even spent considerable time and resources renovating major buildings, especially the North-West Palace. At the same time, indeed shortly after his succession, he chose to create a new capital named after himself, Dur-Sharrukin ('Fort Sargon'), modern Khorsabad, at the foot of the first range of hills north-east of Nineveh (modern Jebel Maqlub), but it was not completed until just before his death. Why he chose to abandon Nimrud, and why he selected this relatively remote location, remain unanswered questions. One possible reason is that he had problems with the old and well-entrenched families of Nimrud, but there is no suggestion of this in surviving texts. In 710 BC Sargon launched a major offensive against Merodach-Baladan, setting a trap for the Babylonian, who fled Babylon by night and tried to persuade his Elamite allies to attack Assyria. Sargon was invited by the priests and people of Babylon to enter the city where, like his predecessor Tiglath-pileser, he 'took the hand of Marduk', subsequently claiming the title 'viceroy of Babylon, king of Sumer and Akkad'.

Like his predecessor (? father) Tiglath-pileser III, Sargon was an unusually able monarch. By 705 BC Assyrian rule extended from the Arabian Gulf to the Mediterranean, in a sense fulfilling the imperial aspirations of Tiglath-pileser III, and establishing a precedent for many later Oriental monarchies.[17] Sargon was also dutiful in fulfilling his religious obligations. Yet, not only was he killed on the field of battle in 705 BC, but his corpse was not recovered, a serious matter in Assyria where a king's body required proper burial, with appropriate ritual, in 'his house' (the royal palace at Assur). The only direct reference to this unique event is in the *limmu* list (see below), which says simply, 'the king… against Qurdi the Kulummaean; the king was killed; the camp of the king of Assyria….'[18] His son Sennacherib makes a number of veiled allusions to the event, for the most part to deplore the obvious but unidentified offence that must have been committed by his father against the gods, the only possible explanation for such a terrible calamity. A unique but regrettably incomplete and difficult text, known to Assyriologists as the 'Sin of Sargon', provides some insight into the Assyrian mind, in the sense of how such events were later interpreted, and even perhaps exploited.[19] The sin which is alleged to explain the untoward death seems to have been against the god Aššur, that in taking Babylon Sargon had not kept a treaty (with the Babylonian Merodach-Baladan) 'of the king of the gods', that is, he had broken an oath sworn before Aššur. Yet at the same time Sargon is accused of neglect of the Babylonian gods. This seems to be rather clutching at straws, since it would seem from his own texts that Sargon paid all due respect to Aššur, and that at the same time the priests of Marduk in Babylon, tired of the tribal disputes of the Chaldaeans, had even encouraged Sargon in his acquisition of the city. More cynically, one could also argue that the text was a justification for the money and resources poured into Babylon by his son Esarhaddon.

Fundamental to the understanding of these difficulties is what has been called the 'Babylonian problem', essentially a conflict between the cultural dominance of Babylonia, with its ancient cities and scribal schools, and the military hegemony of 'upstart' Assyria, a cultural conflict visible already at the time of Tukulti-Ninurta I in the 13th century, when Babylon had its first taste of Assyrian rule, yet large numbers of cuneiform tablets were removed as booty by the Assyrians, hungry for Babylonian learning.[20] Sennacherib claims to have wrestled with the reasons for his father's god-forsaken death throughout his reign, ultimately coming to the most drastic solution, the capture and destruction of Babylon, but now the king was directly provoked by the kidnapping (and ultimately the murder) of his eldest son (694 BC). In his sack of Babylon the statues of the gods were destroyed and that of Marduk taken captive to Assur. Sennacherib also accelerated a theological shift detectable already in the time of Sargon, involving an attempt to subsume the Babylonian pantheon within that of Assyria.

From the perspective of Nimrud one of the most important decisions taken by Sennacherib was to select the ancient city of Nineveh as the new capital, rejecting Khorsabad, perhaps a superstitious choice owing to the manner in which Sargon met his death. This meant of course the rejection also of Kalhu, which was never again to achieve the status that it had held since the time of Assurnasirpal II. Sennacherib's distancing of himself from his ill-fated father is shown also in the fact that Sargon's name is not mentioned in his son's royal inscriptions. Sennacherib successfully ruled the most extensive empire the world had then seen and, in the 7th century version of Nineveh, built one of the greatest of ancient cities. In 681 he was murdered, probably by one or more of his own sons; it has even been suggested that Esarhaddon himself was the guilty party, but this seems less likely. Esarhaddon's version was that he was chosen by his father as heir to the throne, although he had elder brothers, who then plotted against him, while the Babylonian Chronicle reveals that the regicide took place during a rebellion.[21] There is one other remarkable individual who must have been involved in the choice of Esarhaddon as heir, his mother, Naqia (Zakutu), a formidable lady whose influence on palace politics was undoubtedly as great as that of Semiramis.

The one objective not yet achieved was the conquest of Egypt, and this was immediately undertaken by Esarhaddon, though at first unsuccessfully. On his second attempt Memphis was captured and the pharaoh Taharqa, whose inscribed scarab was found at Nimrud,[22] fled from his capital. In Babylonia Esarhaddon followed a successful policy of appeasement, and began an extensive (and expensive) rebuilding programme to repair the damage wrought by his father. He also officially reversed his father's attempt to 'Assyrianise' the Babylonian gods with the official recognition that in Babylonia Marduk reigned supreme; indeed his major project in Babylonia was the reconstruction of Marduk's temple, Esagila. He also announced his intention to repair Marduk's damaged cult statue, carried off to Assyria by his father. Yet at the same time, the process of repairing Marduk's statue, carried out in Aššur's temple, was characterised in one of Esarhaddon's texts as a 'rebirth', with Aššur now referred to as Marduk's father.[23] This was, of course, effectively a merger of the Babylonian and Assyrian pantheons in a manner similar to that attempted by Sennacherib. The roles in Assyria of Babylonian Marduk and his son Nabu will be met again in the discussion of texts from the Nabu temple at Nimrud (chapter 4).

At both Kalhu and Nineveh Esarhaddon rebuilt the arsenals – 'Fort Shalmaneser' at Nimrud – and at Nineveh he began the construction of a new palace, the so-called South-West Palace, which was provided with splendid columned halls. It has been suggested that it was his intention to return to Kalhu, but there is no explicit evidence to support this view, and the new palace for his crown prince Assurbanipal was built at Tarbiṣu, very near Nineveh. As to the king's character, he seems to have been unusually concerned with omens, in particular supernatural phenomena, and such matters form an important part of his royal inscriptions. An extraordinary number of astrological reports also survive from his reign; indeed it has been suggested that the king was ill.[24] On a third Egyptian campaign Esarhaddon died en route, an event that immediately brought his formidable mother into action once again.

After the uncertain circumstances of his own succession, Esarhaddon had tried to ensure that of his crown prince, Assurbanipal, by the imposition of a series of 'treaties' with his vassal kingdoms. A group of these vassal treaties, among the most physically impressive cuneiform tablets ever recovered (p. 204), survived at Nimrud in the Nabu Temple, where they had apparently been drawn up. Esarhaddon's carefully laid plans included not only the accession of Assurbanipal in Assyria but the equal appointment of his (older) brother, Šamaš-šum-ukin, in Babylon (discussed more fully on pp. 203–7). The latter's mother was herself a Babylonian, and not the mother of Assurbanipal; in fact, neither brother seems to have been a son of the queen consort. It was, however, the grandmother Naqia who safely orchestrated the well-planned succession, thereby increasing her already considerable influence at court.

The name Naqia is Aramaic, and the queen mother was obviously of Aramaean lineage; she bore also the Assyrian name Zakutu. Married to Sennacherib when he was crown prince, she became senior lady in the royal harem when her son Esarhaddon was designated crown prince, an opportunity she quickly exploited and by which she gained unprecedented authority. She now also acquired considerable wealth, for the lands of the then queen mother, now either deposed or dead, were transferred to her. She celebrated her new role by building a palace for the new king at Nineveh, commemorating this herself with a text 'exactly like a royal inscription.'[25] She dedicated cult objects, reports on cultic and military matters were directly addressed to her, a sculptor was commissioned to create her statue, and she appears behind the king on a royal stele,[26] activities that were not commonly the prerogative of women, even royal ones. Like Sammuramat, her character was the stuff of legends, and it is likely that her accomplishments as well as those of Sammuramat may have been assimilated in the later legends of Semiramis.

Thanks to Naqia/Zakutu the dual succession proceeded as planned. Indeed a further loyalty treaty was imposed by her on the royal family and the aristocracy at the time of Assurbanipal's succession, specifically referring to him as 'her favourite grandson'.[27] Her grandson Assurbanipal is one of the best-known kings of ancient Mesopotamia, collector of the famous library at Nineveh. From his reign there survive the greatest number of texts from any Assyrian or Babylonian monarch, but unfortunately the eponym list (p. 26 below), which provided the dating framework for the Assyrians and continues to do so for modern scholars, breaks off in 649 BC, while the Babylonian Chronicles are not preserved beyond 667. Thus, although we know a great deal about Assurbanipal, it is not possible precisely to date the events of the later years of his reign. We do know that he campaigned against Egypt, Taharqa having recaptured Memphis at the time of Esarhaddon's death. Memphis was recaptured in 667, and the fall also of Thebes in c. 663 BC marks the height of Assyrian success in Egypt. Although Esarhaddon had established good relations with Elam in south-western Iran, these collapsed after a revolt there sometime in the 650s. The new ruler (the man whose head hangs in a tree in the well-known Assyrian relief from Nineveh showing Assurbanipal and his wife feasting in the garden) joined forces with Šamaš-šum-ukin in an anti-Assyrian coalition. More serious was the actual rebellion of the Babylonian, with open warfare waging between the two brothers from 652–648 BC. The Assyrians laid siege to Babylon for two years until the city finally surrendered (648).

It is widely assumed that Assyria never recovered from the Šamaš-šum-ukin rebellion. Although Assurbanipal was victorious, it appeared in the end a pyrrhic victory. Such hindsight comments are of course easy to make, and it is unlikely that Assyria 'decayed' to quite the extent that is often suggested. Indeed building activities at Nimrud continued under the two sons who succeeded Assurbanipal, and numerous documents found there are dated to the time of the final king, Sin-šar-iškun (ch. 6). One reason for the 'decaying Assyria' view is that we lack the kinds of direct documentation for the years 649–612 BC that have guided us through the earlier history. Indeed, it is uncertain when Assurbanipal ceased to rule, beyond the fact that he was alive in 631 and appears to have died in 627. Some authorities suggest that he abdicated in 630; others that he reigned until his death, but the arguments are far too complex and ill-documented for this brief historical review.[28] It is clear, however, that Assurbanipal, perhaps then an old man, failed to guarantee the succession. Two sons did succeed him, but we know virtually nothing of the circumstances in which they gained the throne. And yet again a powerful eunuch is involved. This is the Assyrian Sin-šum-lišir, the 'chief eunuch' (GAL.SAG), whose protegé Assur-etel-ilani became king after the death (or abdication) of Assurbanipal, and who, even though a eunuch, was briefly recognised in Babylon in 623 BC as Assur-etel-ilani's successor on the Assyrian throne.[29] The Assyrians continued to contest the control of Babylonia at least as late as 616 BC, while at Nimrud there is evidence of two attacks on the city, one in 614 when, according to the Babylonian Chronicle, the Medes marched against Nineveh, captured Tarbiṣu and plundered Assur. Evidence from Nimrud demonstrates an attack on the city at this time, when the walls of Fort Shalmaneser were breached, and that the city fell and was sacked, as was Nineveh, in a second attack in 612. As the prophet Nahum foretells, her people were 'scattered upon the mountains', but remnants of the local population soon returned to Nimrud and settled within the ruins. A member of the royal family ruled for a further few years in Harran (near the city of Urfa in south-eastern Anatolia), Assyria itself now possibly coming under Median rule. To the west in Syria a surviving Assyrian 'political' authority is also attested in the early years of Nebuchadnezzar.[30]

A final comment on the sources themselves. As we have seen, from the time of Assurnasirpal onwards, we have, at least from his reign and those of his more distinguished successors, particularly the great builders, much more detailed historical evidence than has survived from earlier periods in Assyrian history. This is found largely in the form of royal annals, principally accounts of conquests which were inscribed on their sculptured wall reliefs and stelae and occasionally on stone or clay tablets as well. Moreover, from the 8th and 7th centuries, increasing numbers of cuneiform tablets have survived, including administrative records and correspondence between the king and his officials which can often be precisely dated because such documents bear the name of an annual official (*limmu*). We must not, however, overlook gaps in our knowledge which would not be acceptable to any historian of more recent times. We are told nothing, for example, of other members of the immediate royal family or collateral branches, whose ambition we assume to have caused many of the assassinations and disputes over the succession related above. The king, moreover, was dependent on the loyalty of high officials for his success and even at times for his survival. Many of these must have been members of eminent families with wide estates and probably, as in more recent times, considerable power in the cities where they lived. This local influence, and at Assur that of the dominant priesthood, may even have contributed to a particularly vigorous ruler's desire to found a new capital such as Kalhu or Dur Šarrukin, where he could express his own unfettered personality. Of such families and their feuds and alliances we know nothing. But their allegiance must have been vital to an insecure heir to the throne, and essential to retain thereafter by appointments to high rank at court or in the provinces, and by grants of land, many of which are attested in the texts. This may have contributed to the preference of some rulers for eunuchs in positions of power. They too doubtless coveted and exercised their own forms of patronage as they did under later Oriental monarchies, but at least their rivalries were not hereditary. Problems with the succession persisted throughout the history of Assyria, with powerful wives and mothers behind the throne, gaining or losing influence as their sons gained or lost precedence. At any one time there was a recognised queen consort, but, as in the case of Esarhaddon, it was never a foregone conclusion that the eldest son of the recognised consort would actually inherit the throne.

Dating by eponyms

The royal annals which provide much of our information concerning the history of the Late Assyrian Empire were dated by the year of the king's reign, but legal, administrative and business documents bore the name of the *limmu,* an annual official whose functions are unknown but are thought possibly to have involved some responsibility for the cult and shrine of Aššur. The office was already established in the early second millennium BC, when it was used to date the documents of Assyrian merchants at their colony of Kanesh (Kültepe) in south-west Anatolia and at Assur itself. References in the later second millennium imply that lists of *limmu* from the earlier period were known, though incompletely preserved, but the surviving consecutive record covers only the period from 910 BC to 649 BC, with other imprecisely dated names from the last years of the Late Assyrian Empire, the so-called 'post-canonical' *limmu.*[31]

Appointment to the office was formally made by lot, perhaps at the beginning of the preceding year. An example of the die used on one such occasion has survived, inscribed for the *masennu* Yahalu, who served as eponym three times, in 833, 824 and 821 BC.[32] We do not know how an apparently chance method of selection was manipulated but it was clearly not, in practice, left to the whim of the gods. The Late Assyrian list shows that the office was held in each reign by the king, the commander-in-chief and the highest court officials, followed by provincial governors in an order that presumably reflected the importance of their provinces and was substantially varied only when more and smaller provinces were created. Earlier departures from the standard pattern may reflect situations when the king was especially dependent on the loyalty of particular individuals or noble families. It can hardly be a coincidence that Yahalu's three terms of office in twelve years coincided with the last years of Shalmaneser III and the accession of his son Šamši-Adad V, when the notes to the Eponym List tersely record 'Revolt', referring to a disputed succession that is also recorded by Šamši-Adad himself.[33] Although we do not know with certainty the order of the post-canonical *limmu*, the adherence to relatively strict orders of precedence seems to have been abandoned in the last years of Assyria.

THE SITE OF NIMRUD

Nimrud lies some 35 km south of Nineveh in very fertile land on the eastern lip of the Tigris valley. In the time of Assurnasirpal II and his successors the river apparently flowed close by its western wall, but by 401 BC, when Xenophon and the 10,000 Greeks passed by the city, which he calls Larisa,[34] it had changed course to the west and is now some 2 to 3 km away. Still visible in the modern river bed NNW of Nimrud are the remains of a wall built of squared stone blocks fastened with iron clamps of which neither the date nor the purpose is known. It has been suggested that it was the retaining wall of a ford; Layard, who passed over it by raft in the spring of 1840 thought it was an Assyrian dam built to irrigate the land downstream[35] but, if it was indeed contemporary with the Assyrian city, it seems likely that it was intended to ensure that the river did not deviate from an easterly course beneath the city walls, thus affording direct access for river traffic.

The outer city wall encloses a rough square of some 360 ha. or nearly 900 acres, and has an overall length of 7.5 km, 4³/₄ miles (Fig. 9). Along the west and south sides it follows the irregular profile of the conglomerate terrace that borders the flood plain of the Tigris and its tributary wadis; outside the east wall is a watercourse now called the Wadi al Shauf (Felix Jones, 'Shor Derreh', Fig. 9) in which there is a bitumen well, no doubt the source of the material employed by the Assyrian builders to waterproof pavements and the lower parts of some mud-brick walls. The citadel, measuring approximately 600 by 400 m, stands in the south-west corner of the city and is founded on an earlier tell. The mounds of Tulul al Azar in the south-east corner cover the throne-room suite, ceremonial quarters and south postern gate of the arsenal, known to us as Fort Shalmaneser; the line of mounds enclosing Tulul al Azar on the west and north, which is shown by Felix Jones as a re-entrant sector of the city wall, is in fact the perimeter wall of the arsenal, enclosing a large outer bailey.

The defences of the city and the citadel

Unfortunately the survey of the outer city undertaken by Robert Hamilton and Sd. Izzet Din es-Sanduq was never extended to include the whole circuit of the walls, and their structure was only examined where they adjoined other areas of excavation on the south-east corner of the city around Fort Shalmaneser. On the north and east the line of the rampart is clearly visible as a prominent ridge with higher mounds representing towers at intervals; Layard observed 58 such mounds along the north wall, a distance of some 2100 m. There must have been a number of gates, but the positions of only two can be identified with fair certainty. On the north wall about 500 m east of the north-west corner is a prominent double mound that marks the principal north gate towards Nineveh; Layard dug here expecting reliefs or at least stone masonry,[36] but failed to find any plan because his workmen did not recognise mud-brick. It has also been reasonably assumed that the main east gate, leading to the crossing of the Upper Zab at Quwair and the Erbil road, was situated in a re-entrant angle of the wall just to the north of Fort Shalmaneser, on the line of the modern track that emerges from the Shalmaneser Gate of the citadel (Fig. 9). Assurnasirpal claims to have built the whole circuit of the defences, but it seems likely that it was completed, like others of his grandiose projects, by his son, Shalmaneser III. The structure of the wall where it passed over high, firm ground on the landward sides of the city was probably of mud-brick without stone foundations, which seem to have been used only

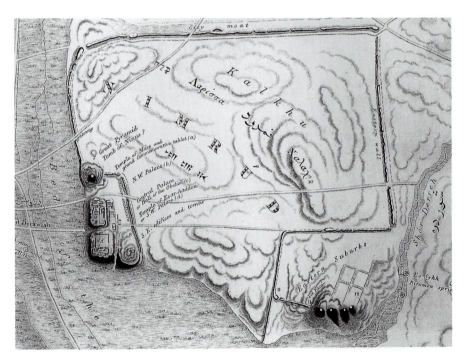

Fig. 9. The walls of Nimrud as surveyed by Captain Felix Jones in 1852; Fort Shalmaneser lies in the south-east corner.

Fig. 10. Plan of the citadel mound showing the excavations carried out by the British expedition in the 1950s.

Fig. 11. The 'Shalmaneser Gate' through which a stone-paved street leads from the outer town into the citadel; the stone lion bears an inscription of Shalmaneser III. The cap-stone of a gate socket and the central bolt hole are visible in the photograph.

where the ground was less solid or the face was exposed to erosion by water, as on the west side of the citadel. Its general aspect must have resembled closely the representations of city walls on the palace reliefs and indeed on a large terracotta vessel and a metal brazier found in Fort Shalmaneser (p. 152 and Pl. 12c).

In the south-east corner of the outer town, the mud-brick wall, which also formed the outer wall of Fort Shalmaneser, had been rebuilt in the seventh century by Esarhaddon, who constructed a new terrace in the corner of the building, adding a mud-brick revetment to the original outer wall, which extended some 270 m to the west and 60 m to the north of the south-east corner. To this was added a facing of six or seven courses of ashlar masonry. Over much of its length the revetment was 5 m thick and repeated the earlier pattern of interval towers, but at the west end it widened to a block of brickwork some 90 m long by 11 m wide, incorporating on its outer face a corbelled stone gateway (Fig. 95, p. 154) leading to a vaulted ramp that ascended to a postern gate in the upper wall, at the point marked 'Shalmaneser's Entry' on the plan (Fig. 91). The building of the ramp is dated to the reign of Esarhaddon by inscriptions on both jambs of the lower gate; the ramp itself opened into a long passage that led directly into the outer bailey of the arsenal and, through an intervening guard room, into the harem quarters (discussed in Chapter 5). It must have been an entry of some importance, for in the part of the passage leading to the outer bailey the walls still showed faint traces of paintings depicting a file of courtiers, a wheeled vehicle and possibly the king himself.

Mallowan examined the citadel wall in two places, in a narrow trench on the east side near the north-east corner where private houses (TW 53) were backed against it, and on the west below the North-West Palace (Fig. 10).[37] No interval towers were found, nor is their presence suggested here or elsewhere by the heavily eroded contours of the mound, but they are such a standard feature of military architecture at this time that they probably existed, if only at a higher level. Only one major citadel gateway has been identified, through which passed a roadway paved with irregular stone slabs. The gate was recessed into the citadel wall; the north side had been badly disturbed by stone robbers, but on the south side was found the lower part of an alabaster gate figure of a lion, bearing an inscription of Shalmaneser III (Fig. 11). Hence the designation 'Shalmaneser Street'. The gateway itself was 4.30 m wide, with one capstone of a door-socket against the south jamb and a bolt-hole in the middle, visible in the photograph, to secure the double doors; the paved roadway in places measures over 6 m in width. Rassam reports the discovery of a second minor entrance, which he says was near the south-east corner of the mound, but was more probably near the middle of the south side.[38] He describes it as 'an ascending passage, enclosed by stone walls, leading to an archway neatly built of kiln-baked bricks'.[39] This sounds remarkably like Esarhaddon's postern gate at Fort Shalmaneser, described above, but was not located during the Mallowan excavations.

The east wall of the citadel was built entirely of mud-brick, with a surviving height of 13 m and an apparent thickness of 37 m, perhaps including an external platform.[40] It sloped outwards at the base, and was skirted by a roadway surfaced with pebbles set in gypsum cement. On the west side of the citadel Mallowan made great efforts to obtain a picture of the wall, first in 1952 employing 60 workmen for three weeks to dig a deep trench against it and expose a part of its face to the foundations.[41] The work was continued in 1953 and finally concluded in 1955 by following the line of the wall some 200 m to the south with the assistance of a mechanical excavator generously lent by the Iraq Petroleum Company. The cross section at the north end of the excavation (Fig. 12) shows that here, as on the east, the superstructure of the wall was built of mud-brick, with a thickness of almost 15 m and a surviving height to citadel level of some 6.5 m. The natural conglomerate on which it rested was faced with squared limestone blocks set in bitumen, which probably extended westward to form a platform or quay in front of the mud-brick face. The stone had been heavily robbed at this point and we do not know the original width of the quay. A second sloping face of dressed stone some 6.8 m west of the upper wall was excavated to its full depth of 11 courses, 8.60 m. Against the lowest five courses was a layer of heavy clay which was thought to represent the ancient river bed, while a pronounced line of erosion 2.5 m higher up might mark the normal surface of the river. We may note that this trench was situated across one side of the great gully that runs through the north courtyard of the North-West Palace, where it has been suggested that there may

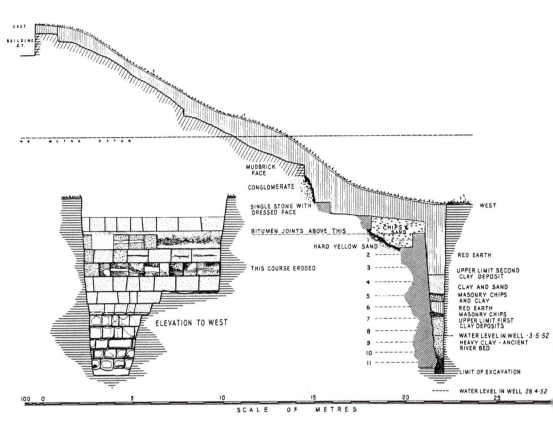

EAST

BUILDING Z.T.

MUDBRICK FACE

CONGLOMERATE

SINGLE STONE WITH DRESSED FACE

BITUMEN JOINTS ABOVE THIS

HARD YELLOW SAND

THIS COURSE ERODED

ELEVATION TO WEST

CHIPS & SAND

WEST

2 — — — — RED EARTH

3 — — — — UPPER LIMIT SECOND CLAY DEPOSIT

4 — — — — CLAY AND SAND

5 — — — — MASONRY CHIPS AND CLAY

6 — — — — RED EARTH MASONRY CHIPS

7 — — — — UPPER LIMIT FIRST CLAY DEPOSITS

8 — — — —

9 — — — — WATER LEVEL IN WELL -3·5·52 HEAVY CLAY - ANCIENT RIVER BED

10 — — — —

11 — — — — LIMIT OF EXCAVATION

— — — — WATER LEVEL IN WELL 28·4·52

100   0   5   10   15   20   25

SCALE   OF   METRES

Fig. 12. East-west section through the citadel and quay walls, on the western side of the citadel.

have been an approach from the quay to the palace; this question is discussed below (p. 42).

The profile of the wall and the quay was also observed some 50 m to the south. At this point the masonry had been even more severely robbed but it appears that, presumably owing to a local weakness in the underlying geological structure, it had been found necessary to reinforce the foundations with roughly trimmed blocks of limestone against which the outer wall was built. The whole structure may have been the work of Assurnasirpal II, but the use of rough-hewn blocks recalls the words of Tiglath-Pileser III who, referring to the river wall in the eighth century, says, 'I piled up heavy limestone boulders like a mountain to a depth of 20 cubits... arresting the flood'.[42]

Other rulers may have repaired or extended the structure, for in the course of over two centuries changes would inevitably have been needed, but we have no further epigraphic evidence. Access to the palace from the quay is very probable, if only for practical purposes. The large quantities of building stone for the river wall itself, and the very large alabaster slabs for the sculptures, neither of which were locally available, would best have been transported – as they were eventually removed in the 19th century – by water.

The Patti-hegalli Canal

In his Banquet Stele inscription celebrating the building of his new capital (p. 40) Assurnasirpal II says,

> I dug out a canal from the Upper Zab, cutting through a mountain at its peak, and called it the Patti-hegalli (Canal of Abundance). I irrigated the meadows of the Tigris and planted orchards with all kinds of fruit trees in its environs. I pressed wine and offered first fruit offerings to Aššur, my lord, and the temples of my land.

Then follows a long list of the trees and plants the king had seen on his campaigns, and from which he presumably collected samples for the gardens watered by the canal. He continues,

> The canal cascades from above into the gardens. Fragrance pervades the walkways. Streams of water as numerous as the stars of heaven flow in the pleasure garden. Pomegranates which are bedecked with clusters like grape vines... I, Assurnasirpal, in the delightful garden pick fruit like a squirrel...[43]

The course of this canal can still be seen over much of its length (Fig. 13). It is first visible as a deep cutting through a high ridge (the 'mountain at its peak') on the north bank of the Greater Zab opposite the modern village of Quwair,[44] but an unnaturally straight section of the river bank suggests that its original head was much higher. During the latter part of its existence it took its water through a rock-cut tunnel formed by linking two shafts sunk from the surface of a conglomerate bluff just below Quwair (Fig. 14); in it Layard found a stone slab bearing an incomplete inscription of Esarhaddon recording work done on the canal.[45] There is also evidence of an earlier tunnel now entirely filled with silt. Below the tunnel the canal continues parallel with the river to emerge into the low-lying plain south of Kalhu, then follows a sinuous course towards the city before disappearing at a distance of some 3.5 km south-east of the citadel. If it continued on the projected line shown on Fig. 13, it would have arrived about half-way along the south wall of the city, whence it presumably turned west to discharge into the Tigris. Although there is no surviving evidence for its course here, an unexplained feature on Felix Jones' map (Fig. 9) suggests an intriguing possibility. Continuing the line of the west wall of the outer bailey of Fort Shalmaneser he shows a ridge running out into the irrigable land to the south which cannot be a part of the city's defences. By a stretch of the imagination, we wonder whether this may have been an elevated channel, fed from the canal either directly or by means of some simple means of lifting water such as the *shaduf*, a bucket on a long beam which is certainly a very ancient device. This might explain Assurnasirpal's reference to the water 'cascading into the gardens'. The irrigated land served by the canal has been estimated as some 25 sq km. Part of this was occupied by gardens and orchards; the remainder was almost certainly used to feed some of the additional population of the new capital.[46]

In another inscription Assurnasirpal boasts of his zoological gardens. In a campaign as far as Mount Lebanon, where he 'cleansed his weapons' in the Great Sea, among the tribute he received from Tyre, Sidon and other cities along the coast he lists large and small female monkeys…

> I brought them to my land Assur. I bred herds of them in great numbers in Kalhu and displayed them to all the people of my land. With my fierce heart I captured 15 strong lions from the mountains and forests. I took away 50 lion cubs. I herded them into Kalhu and the palaces of my land into cages. I bred their cubs in great numbers. I captured live tigers. I formed herds of wild bulls, elephants, lions, ostriches, male monkeys, female monkeys, wild asses, deer, female bears, panthers, beasts of mountain and plain, all of them. In my city Kalhu I displayed them to all the people of my land.[47]

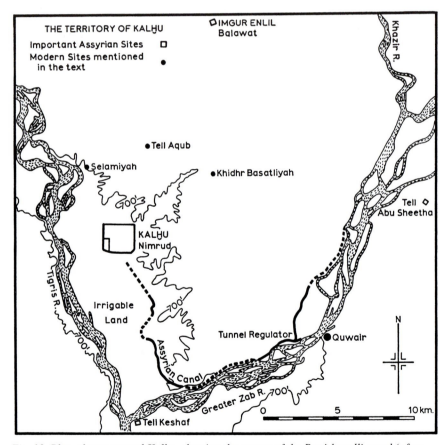

Fig. 13. Plan of area around Kalhu, showing the course of the Patti-hegalli canal (after D. Oates 1968, fig. 3).

34

Fig. 14. The Negub tunnel, which supplied water from the Greater Zab to the Patti-hegalli canal, photograph from the west.

CHAPTER 2

MAJOR PALACES ON THE CITADEL

THE NORTH-WEST PALACE

Mallowan began his excavations in the area of Layard's best-known and perhaps most important discovery, the famous North-West Palace built in the 9th century BC by Assurnasirpal II as the principal royal residence in his new capital. These excavations, sponsored by the British School of Archaeology in Iraq, began in 1949, exactly a century after the first publication of the building by Layard in *Nineveh and its Remains*. The North-West Palace is by far the largest of those identified on the citadel mound, measuring over 200 m from north to south and some 130 m wide (about six and a half acres in area). Although this building does not begin to compare in size with the 6th-century BC palace of Nebuchadnezzar in Babylon, it remains today one of the most impressive palaces in ancient Mesopotamia, owing largely to its attractive location and its decoration with large stone bas-reliefs and monumental stone gate figures of winged bulls and lions. The large-scale narrative reliefs were an innovation at the time of Assurnasirpal II, although the tradition of using orthostats as architectural decoration is found in earlier contexts, for example at sites to the west such as Carchemish and even earlier at Tell al Rimah.[1] No earlier examples, however, begin to compare with the lavish monumentality of the North-West Palace, or the imperial rhetoric of the throne room reliefs.

The North-West Palace complex consisted of three main units (plan, Figs. 15, 33). On the north was the *babanu* (entrance) courtyard, now largely obliterated by a deep gully marked 'ravine' on the Mallowan plans and visible in Pl. 2a. The main gate almost certainly lay on the east side, where the head of the gully has cut through the surviving buildings at an obvious point of weakness. The west side has been completely eroded, but there is some evidence, discussed below, to suggest that the administrative area was divided into two courtyards, on the east and on the west. The surviving buildings on the north and north-east were designated ZT (Ziggurrat Terrace) before their structural relationship with the palace had been established. In fact, as the name suggests, Mallowan originally thought that the northern wall of this area was actually the outer southern wall of the ziggurrat terrace. However, both the physical position of these rooms and the discovery in them of administrative tablets were eventually to identify them as the administrative or chancery wing of the palace itself. On the south the *babanu* courtyard was dominated by the towering façade of the throne-room suite (B, C, F) with its friezes of stone reliefs and colossal gate figures, designed to impress visiting dignitaries with the full grandeur of Assyrian kingship and which 'by their nature turn back an evil person'[2] (Figs. 16, 27). South of the throne-room block other ceremonial suites surrounded a second courtyard, Y, beyond

Fig. 15. Plan of the northern part of the North-West Palace (after Mallowan 1966, plan 3, and Paley & Sobolewski 1987, plan 2); the southern part of the plan can be found on p. 60.

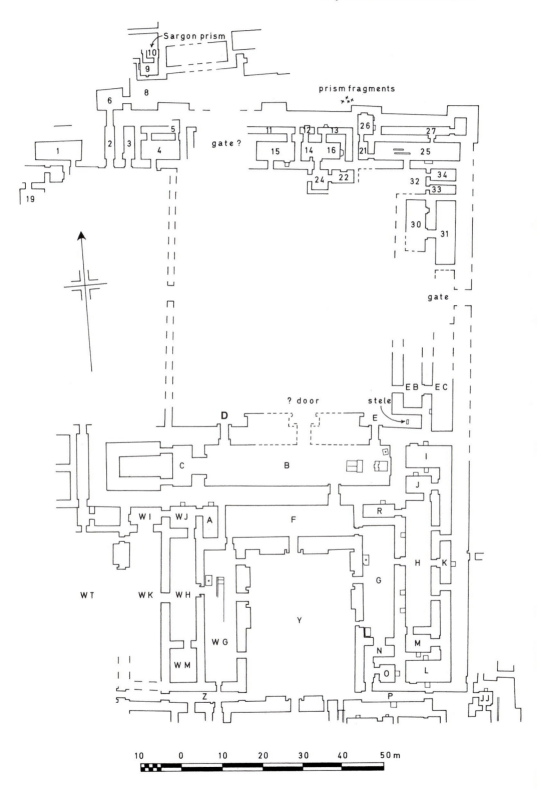

Fig. 16. Colossus gate figure from the main west doorway into room G, ht. 3.5 m, wt. c. 10 tons. BM 118873.

which lay the *bitanu* or domestic quarter where in recent years have been discovered the remarkably rich tombs discussed in Chapter 3. The *bitanu* is sometimes referred to as the harem, in Arabic the plural of *harma*, woman, meaning the '(place of the) women' and derived from the same root as *haram*, 'sacred' or 'forbidden'; *pace* Hollywood, there is no implication of licentious behaviour.

Layard dug much of the central block, the source of the extraordinary stone reliefs many of which now enrich a number of the world's finest museums, while others have now been restored to their original positions by the Iraqi Directorate-General of Antiquities. The plan of the palace as published by Layard showed the rooms with the stone reliefs enclosing a single central courtyard (Y), but more recent work has established that Layard's plan constitutes only part of a much more com-

Fig. 17. Head of a tribute-bearer, from the eastern procession on the throne room façade; the gesture of the hands is one of submission (see façade reconstruction, pp. 52–53).

Fig. 18. Upper part of banquet stele of Assurnasirpal II, now in the Mosul Museum. The inscription records the 10-day celebration of the refounding of Kalhu/Nimrud as the new capital; the inset panel depicts the king beneath the symbols of the gods (height of panel c. 47 cm).

plex building, extending both to the north (ZT) and to the south of his excavations. The rooms lettered A to AB represent the 19th century excavations; other 'lettered' rooms are those dug by Mallowan, with the exception of those prefixed with a 'W' which were partially investigated by Iraqi archaeologists (who used arabic numerals for these rooms) and later by the 1970s Polish expedition. The most recent Iraqi excavations, under the direction of Sd Muzahim Mahmud Hussein, have also returned to this area. Indeed the most extensive work carried out in recent years has been that of the Iraqis who have added substantially to the southern plan of the palace, to which we shall return.

The Banquet Stele

It is appropriate to begin a detailed account of the palace with one of the most interesting objects found by Mallowan, a stele of Assurnasirpal II, 127 cm in height, inscribed on the front and back with 150 lines of text (Fig. 18). It was erected to commemorate the founding of the new capital and the text provides extensive details of the ceremonies and festivities held to celebrate the formal consecration of the king's 'joyful palace'.[3] The stele stood within a covered alcove (room EA) which faced the great courtyard just east of the eastern entrance to the throne room, where both Layard and Rassam just failed to find it. At the top of the stele was an inset panel depicting the king surmounted by the symbols of the moon god Sin, the sun god Shamash, the star of Ishtar, the horned helmet of Aššur (the national god),

Fig. 19. Ivory carved in the Assyrian style depicting Assurnasirpal II in ceremonial dress. Found behind the stele, embedded in ash and mud beneath a fallen wall (ht 27 cm, ND 1082, now in the Iraq Museum).

the storm god Adad and the Sibitti (the Pleiades). The winged disc, here representing Shamash, is often attributed to Aššur, and would certainly seem to be his symbol when the god appears within the disc as on Fig. 25; the horned helmet was earlier the symbol of Anu, the father of the gods, and seems in the first millennium to have been transferred to Aššur, a god whose origins lie in the personification of the city itself.

The inscription relates in detail the refounding of Kalhu, the building of the palace and, perhaps most fascinating of all, provides a unique account of the food served at the ten-day-long celebration of the new metropolis. The inscription repeats the information known from other Assurnasirpal texts that the great city of Kalhu had lain in ruins since the days of Shalmaneser I (1273–1244 BC) and that in its rebuilding Assurnasirpal 'dug down as far as water-level and from there upwards filled in its foundation terrace with 120 courses of brick'. Not only are the materials used to build the palace enumerated – cedar, cypress, boxwood, terebinth, bronze, glazed bricks, doors of cedar fastened with bronze bands – but also the vast quantities of food brought in to feed, over the ten days of the celebrations, the 16,000 citizens of Kalhu, 5000 visiting dignitaries from as far away as Tyre and Sidon, 1500 officials and the 47,074 workmen and women 'summoned from all the districts of my land'. One notes with envy the 10 homers of shelled pistachio nuts, 10 homers of dates, 10 homers of figs, 10,000 jugs of beer, 10,000 skins of wine, and vast quantities of spices as well as the staple meats, fish, fowl and bread, all in extravagant abundance. Regrettably, the original translation of one entry as '10 homers of castor

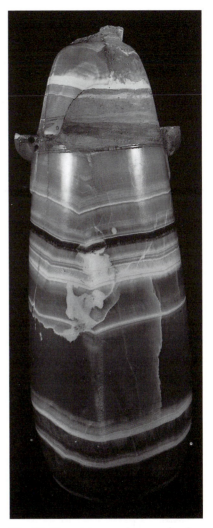

Fig. 20. Phoenician amphora made of Egyptian alabaster, found in the destruction debris of ZT room 25; a fragment of the top of the jar was recovered from the Town Wall houses (ht 47 cm, ND 3556, now in the Iraq Museum).

41

oil pods' remains uncertain. The stele inscription ends:

> For ten days I gave them food, I gave them drink, I had them bathed, I had them anointed. (Thus) did I honour them and send them back to their lands in peace and joy.

Assurnasirpal's son, Shalmaneser III (858–824 BC), continued his father's building work at Nimrud, also effecting repairs and some changes. His successors in the 8th century continued to maintain the North-West Palace, although Sargon II (721–705 BC), who founded a new capital at Khorsabad, was probably the last ruler to use this building as an official residence. An inscription of Sargon (below, p. 57) refers to huge quantities of plunder stored here, the remnants of which have been found in the palace. Indeed so much treasure of this date was recovered that Mallowan believed initially that the palace had been destroyed at the end of Sargon's reign. It became clear however that, although no longer the king's official residence after the time of Sargon, the palace continued in use as an administrative complex and a residence for court officials, and perhaps some members of the royal family, until the fall of Assyria in 612 BC. Its earlier role as the focus of royal administration had itself survived for over 150 years, but by the time of Sargon's grandson, Esarhaddon (680–669 BC), the diminished status of the building can be seen in the fact that the latter felt no compunction in removing many of the reliefs to decorate his new palace in the south-west corner of the tell.

Area ZT, the 'Ziggurrat Terrace': the Administrative Offices and Magazines

North of the alcove containing the stele, on the east side of the *babanu* courtyard, was a double range of rooms, eroded by the gully at the point where the main gate must have been situated. The walls of these rooms are markedly thicker than those on the north side of the courtyard and probably stood to a greater height to present an imposing façade flanking the gate-chambers. Along the north side of the *babanu* area were offices, abutting the outer wall of the palace which in turn faced the south side of the Ninurta Temple complex across a paved passage (plan, Fig. 15). It has been suggested that there was a second major entrance to the palace on the south side of this passage at the point where the buildings have been cut by a tributary of the main gully. The passage itself hardly suggests a formal approach for distinguished visitors, but the quantities of stores entering the magazines might well have justified a second wide entrance. We must emphasise, however, that there is no evidence whatsoever for such a gate. At the west end of the passage a doorway on the north side probably led into the magazines of the Ninurta Temple and conceivably also to a terrace on the west side of the ziggurrat. A second doorway on the west opened into a small 'guard-room' (6) from which a corridor (2) gave restricted access to the west end of the *babanu,* presumably for those who had day-to-day business in the offices.

It has also been suggested that there was access from the Tigris quay to a river gate on the west side of the *babanu.* The evidence for a quay on this side has been discussed above (p. 31), where we conclude that probably it formed part of the original plan and that there was access from it to the citadel at some point, but that

Fig. 21. Impression on clay bulla of the palace seal of Shalmaneser III, found in ZT 25. The inscription reveals that it had been attached to bales of cloth, part of the ilku-*dues levied on the nobility (d 2.7 cm; ND 3413).*

individual elements in its surviving structure cannot be securely dated and that any trace of an upper gate or the approach to it has been destroyed by erosion. The foundations of the roadway found between the inner and outer ashlar faces may be as late as the time of Esarhaddon, and there is no evidence for the configuration of the riverside structure in the 9th century. If there had been access from the river to the *babanu* at this time, it would have required a relatively narrow stair against and parallel with the quay wall, some 8 m high and at least 25 m long. There is no evidence for a gateway at the head of such a stair, beyond the presence of the gully itself which might imply here a weak point in the palace structure.

It is possible that the *babanu* area was divided into two courtyards. This is suggested by a stub of wall projecting from the west end of the throne room façade which, if it continued northwards, would have met the outer wall of room 4 just east of its doorway, but the wall face at this point is unfortunately eroded and the possibility cannot be confirmed. If the division existed, it would have provided separate courtyards for the rooms on the eastern and western sides which, as we shall see, seem to have housed different government departments. It would, moreover, have

Fig. 22. Surviving pottery in the storeroom ZT 15, destroyed in 612 BC.

provided a more central and focused position for the outer façade of the throne room.

Turning to the offices themselves, we observe that, opening off the north-east corner of the courtyard, was a porch with two small rooms (33 and 34) at its east end and, on the north, the entrance to a suite of five rooms, including a reception room 21 m long (25), with a vestibule leading to an ablution room (21 and 26). This arrangement reproduces on a small scale the plan of a typical Assyrian throne room, and the resemblance is heightened by the presence in the floor of the reception room of two parallel rows of stone blocks, known to us as 'tram-lines', and probably intended to carry a wheeled brazier (discussed below, pp. 48 and 58). This must have been the reception suite of an official of sufficient importance to be treated with considerable ceremony, and it may be worth remarking that the lobby (32) with its cubby-holes outside the door (33, 34), in a comparable office suite in more recent times, would have been the domain of his doorkeeper who admitted guests and provided the formal coffee or tea for their refreshment. The status of these apartments and their occupant is further emphasised by the discovery in them of a set of four unusually beautiful stone vases.[4] The most striking of these, in veined Egyptian alabaster, bore a pseudo-hieroglyphic inscription, almost certainly of Phoenician origin (Fig. 20). Most extraordinarily, the missing piece of the upper part of the vessel was found in a room in the Town Wall houses, some 150 m distant.[5] The ivories discussed in chapter 7 include many more objects carved in an 'Egyptianising' style that was very popular in Assyria. To the untrained eye such objects look Egyptian, but they were made elsewhere by artisans who did not fully understand the form or meaning of the motifs they employed. Room 25 also produced a cuneiform fragment from the Epic of Creation and a clay docket stamped with the royal seal, recording the delivery to Shalmaneser III of a number of garments in payment of dues from his nobles (Fig. 21). This is one of the earliest known examples of the royal seal type discussed on p. 221. Unfortunately we cannot prove that room 25 was the original provenance of these objects, since we know that Layard both disturbed and refilled this area.

Adjacent to this set of rooms was the palace oil store and perhaps the wine cellar (rooms 30, 31). In room 30 were 13 vast storage jars, partly set into the floor with mud-brick benches built around them. Cuneiform texts found here mention the issue of oil to various persons, receipts of grain, the loan of a large quantity of grapes, presumably for the making of wine, and the distribution of wine, grain and possibly sesame[6] to various temples at the site. One tablet (ND 3482) records 100 jars of oil of which 98 belonged to the palace herald (*nagir ekalli*); two of the most interesting documents record supplies issued 'from the pistachio wing of the palace and from the stables' for the maintenance of a substitute king (*šar puhi*), who 'stood in for' and thus served to protect the real king on two inauspicious days in different months of the same year.[7] The only tablet from this collection with a known date is a record of a loan of grapes (ND 3488), written in the last year of Sargon, 706 BC.

West of the reception suite were two more sets of rooms, each with its own entrance from the courtyard. The first included rooms 12, 14/16, 13 and 17, with a later addition of two small anterooms (24, 22), while the second consisted of two surviving rooms (11, 15). On the western side of the gap in the plan are two interconnecting rooms (4,5), a long room (3) which Mallowan believed to be a stair, passage 2, a rear entrance into the *babanu* and, in the north-west corner, three surviving rooms (1, 18, 19), evidently part of a suite corresponding in position and probably in function with that in the north-east corner. Indeed, the combination of offices and quarters for the official in charge of them, and possibly a further range of rooms or magazines along the eroded west side corresponding with the store-rooms on the east, strongly suggests that this block originally housed a second, separate palace department. It would seem that rooms 4 and 5 were scribal offices, for room 4 contained not only some 350 tablets, the greatest number recovered from any single room at Nimrud, but at its eastern end were two baked brick benches and box-like 'filing cabinets' for the actual storing of the tablets (Fig. 120, p. 197). Unfortunately, we were unable to determine the principles of the filing system, since the tablets themselves were found in a completely chaotic state, apparently thrown back into the room at some later period. Indeed, the room seems deliberately to have been filled in, as was the adjacent room 3 and part of the passage to the north. Mallowan was mistaken in believing this to have been the foundation for an extension to the ziggurrat terrace, but we have no better explanation since the rooms seem to have been burned after the infilling.

Many of the cuneiform documents recovered here were letters to the Assyrian king at the time of Tiglath-Pileser III and Sargon. These constitute the ancient equivalent of Foreign Office files, and have provided extraordinary insight into details of

Assyrian government at the time (see discussion in chapter 6). Together with the letters were found a group of administrative tablets, typical products of the Assyrian civil service.[8] Among these were receipts of valuable stores, including enormous stocks of grain, one tablet enumerating 3,050 homers from Nineveh composed of contributions from eleven districts, with further entries yielding a total of 14,000 homers – some 85,000 bushels (ND 3469). Another tablet records the receipt of 280 daggers, of which 97 were of iron (ND 3480).

The suites of rooms to the east were heavily burnt in the fire of 612 BC, yielding evidence at the time of their destruction of domestic activities in the form of carbonised wheat, barley and linseed, with mortars and grindstones, spindle whorls and loom weights, especially in room 15. In rooms 15 and 13 there was a wide variety of pottery types including water jars, plates, tiny oil bottles and lamps (Fig. 22). In one amphora of Levantine type (again found in room 15) was a large quantity of Egyptian blue, a material used, inter alia, in the decoration of the ivories. In room 12 a group of unusually fine 'palace ware' beakers was found stored upside down in a niche, perhaps originally a ventilation shaft (Fig. 23),[9] while in the corner was an elephant's tusk engraved with a guilloche pattern, which had broken into some 50 pieces (ND 2503). Rooms 11 and 13 were clearly storage magazines, with large jars, stacked plates and, in 13, much burnt wood, painted fragments of ostrich egg shell and part of a musical instrument, possibly a harp.

The larger set of rooms produced 61 tablets, of which all but 4 come from room 14/16; the fire had not only covered them with a deep deposit of ash but had conveniently baked and thereby preserved them. They are principally legal documents concerned with loans of barley and silver and sales of slaves, with two referring to a court case and a very interesting document detailing the lavish dowry given to 'the daughter of the *šakintu* of the new palace' on the occasion of her marriage to one Milki-ramu, possibly the *limmu* of 656 BC.[10] One text with no year date (ND 2345) is an administrative note concerning the despatch of a letter to officials in charge of the levy. Fifty-two of the room 14/16 documents bore *limmu* dates, two in the reigns of Sennacherib and Esarhaddon, the remainder in the time of Assurbanipal and his successors. At least three can be assigned to the reign of Sin-šar-iškun who, at least in the Sardanapalus legend, perished in the flames in the destruction of Nineveh.

Although no one person can be identified as the owner of these archives, of those named as principals or witnesses a number were officials or palace personnel. We believe from their association with the reception suite and the eastern range of offices, and from the character of other rooms in the north wing, that these rooms were originally built as offices, but that the character of the offices had changed by the late 7th century. Certainly at this time the bureaucracy of imperial administration had passed to Nineveh, and in the North-West Palace the focus of administration is now essentially local. Why some apparently unimportant tablets were kept for so long remains, here as elsewhere, a mystery. One of the interesting features of the later administration is the number of weights that were found here, inter alia a 10 mana basalt duck weight of Assurnasirpal II still in use in Room 14 (ND 2505) together with a bronze lion weight bearing an alphabetic inscription (ND 2163), a number of

Fig. 23. Palace ware pottery stored in a niche which served as a cupboard in the north wall of ZT 12. The fine beakers, which had very small bases, were deliberately stored upside down.

duck weights in room 24, and a large duck weight of Assur-dan III in room 19, found with the remains of a heavy, duck-footed, stone trough.

We have suggested that the buildings around the *babanu* housed at least two different government departments, together with the prestigious apartments of their chief officials. There is no substantial evidence of a major change in plan and, if we reasonably assume that the tablets from room 4, though found in packing, must have originated close by, they had a different history. The date-span of these tablets shows that the north-west department, dealing largely with imperial affairs and the receipt of taxes or tribute on a large scale, ceased to function at the end of Sargon's reign, while the north-east offices continued in use until the final destruction in 612 BC, though the documents in them reflect the essentially local affairs of the palace and its occupants. In short, the contrast between them reflects the change in status of the palace from imperial to local administration; it is interesting that the tablets from the Governor's Palace, formerly the centre of local government, bear no dates after 710 BC, and it is possible that some of its functions may have passed to the North-West Palace in the 7th century.

Fig. 24. The North-West Palace throne room façade was originally excavated by Layard; the photograph illustrates how it appeared when re-excavated by Mallowan in 1952.

The State Apartments

The core of the palace was the great central block, with the throne-room (B) to the north, a huge hall measuring 45.5 by 10.5 m. Re-excavation by Mallowan in 1951 revealed the enormous inscribed throne-base of the king still in position at the east end of the hall, the focal point of the room. It can now be seen in the Mosul Museum. Immediately in front of the throne dais the floor was paved with a rectangle of large stone slabs instead of the stone 'tram lines' commonly found in other throne rooms at the site. This must have served the same purpose, to carry a heavy object, which we suggest was a wheeled brazier of the type illustrated in Pl. 12c. Certainly some form of heating would have been welcome in the cold winters of northern Iraq.

The throne room itself was the focus of power, and its decoration reflected this role. Here the king received his subjects and foreign dignitaries in surroundings designed to impress. Carved bas-reliefs in the local alabaster depicted both ritual and historical narrative, including realistic scenes of battle, the bearing of tribute and the hunting of bulls and lions.[11] These constitute not only one of the earliest attempts at historical propaganda on a monumental scale but one of the most enduring, for their message remains clear not only on the site itself but in the great museums of the world. And for a population that could not read these were mighty visions. Much has been written about the content and meaning of the reliefs, and it is not our purpose here to add to the detail of these extensive publications.[12] But the patterns and distribution of different motifs provide clues to the use of the various state rooms and will therefore be commented on briefly.

We have already remarked that the king's throne room provides the focus of the palace. It was clearly the intention that the visitor should be impressed both with the scale of the chamber itself and of its public doorways, the latter marked by giant human-headed lion or bull colossi. Also flanking all formal doors were apotropaic winged genii, holding a 'fir cone' and bucket or occasionally a pomegranate branch, objects associated with ritual purification.[13] The external façade of the throne room bore at its western end a procession of tribute bearers, moving towards the western door where courtiers lead them to the king himself, a scene illustrating on a grand scale one important aspect of throne room ceremonial (pp. 52–3). Within the throne room itself, set in a shallow recess behind the surviving throne base, was a large stone panel illustrating the king flanking the many-branched 'sacred tree', above which was the winged disc of the god Aššur, originally the personification of the ancient city but by this time the supreme god of the emergent empire (Fig. 25). Depicted behind both representations of the king is the omnipresent genie with cone and bucket. This ritual scene was framed within the upper two-thirds of the large stone slab, revealing below and in front of it the king himself, seated upon his throne

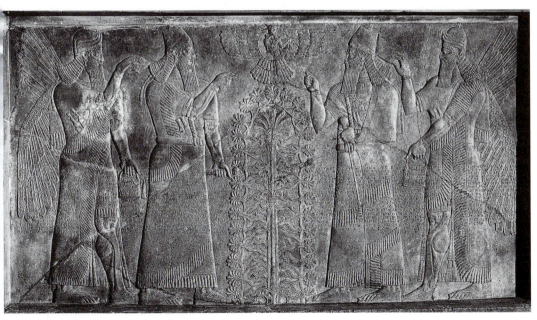

Fig. 25. This alabaster relief was situated behind the king's throne at the east end of the North-West Palace throne room. The relief shows the king on either side of the sacred tree, above which, in the winged disc, is Aššur, the national god of Assyria; at either side, protecting the king, a winged genie holds a ritual bucket and cone. Ht. 1.7 m; now in the British Museum.

before this symbolic representation of his authority. The symmetrical symbolism behind the throne is repeated in the centre of the south wall, though here no throne base has survived, if such was ever there. This repetition of the most important scene in the room has been interpreted to suggest the presence of an opposing door in the north wall, the evidence for which is discussed below. Moortgat has noted the psychological significance of the symmetry and centrality of this scene, which not only focus on the powerful symbolism of the god and the sacred tree but isolate and emphasise the figures in marked contrast with the movement and directionality of the narrative reliefs.[14]

The full-size reliefs, normally the king, his immediate attendants and the winged genii, stood as much as 2.7 m in height but almost certainly occupied only part of the full height of the wall, estimated at some 6–8 m. Across the centre of each of these large orthostats and the scene behind the throne was carved the so-called 'standard inscription', a condensed formulation of Assurnasirpal's titles and achievements. On the long north and south walls were 'narrative' reliefs arranged in two tiers, in this case with the band of inscription, 61 cm in height, inserted between them (as on Fig. 42, p. 74). These narrative reliefs depict a variety of military scenes, including the preparation of food in a military camp (p. 236); others portray the royal hunt, an event not only of symbolic importance but also of great antiquity (Fig. 26). Indeed the motif of the ruler killing a lion is one of the earliest to survive from ancient Mesopotamia, dating back to the 4th millennium BC, while throughout Mesopotamian history the king of beasts was viewed as the property of the monarch rather in the manner of royal swans in England even today.

The throne room reliefs appear to have been surmounted by brightly coloured paintings; indeed there is evidence elsewhere that at least some of the details of the reliefs were themselves emphasised by painting, especially the beard, hair, eyes (black) and sandals (red). Impressions of roof beams were found on the backs of some painted plaster fragments in the throne room, suggesting that ceilings were also decorated, producing what must have been a brilliant overall effect in an otherwise relatively ill-lit room.[15] In the centre of the room were numerous pieces of such painted plaster, the patterns in red and white and outlined in black against a sky-blue background. The surviving decoration included rosettes and fragments of a beardless Assyrian official, a eunuch, carrying a sword and, as on the reliefs, possibly introducing other officials or tribute-bearers into the presence of the king.

The Room B plan is that of a conventional Assyrian throne room, with entrances through the longer side walls, the so-called 'bent-axis' plan, which has a long history in northern Mesopotamia. At the western end is a stairwell, another standard feature of the Assyrian throne room suite. The stair (or ramp) was itself some 3.5 m wide, passing from its northern entrance around a solid mass of mud-brick which formed its central block.[16] In later throne rooms the presence of an ablution room formed a third element of the standard plan, but at the time of Assurnasirpal II such an arrangement seems not as yet to have become customary. However, an ablution slab was placed to the right of the throne both in room B and in WG, another formal reception room discussed below.

Much has been written about the access to Assurnasirpal's throne room. Indeed it is now widely assumed that the main entrance lay in the middle of the long north wall, opposite the central 'king and sacred tree' relief and in the manner of the later Khorsabad and Nineveh throne rooms. No actual doorway has been found here by any of the excavators of the throne room, but it is clear from Layard's account that the central area of the façade had been removed in antiquity.[17] Mallowan and Hamilton searched here for a central door in the early 1950s, finding only the niche that is indicated on the Mallowan plan. Circumstantial evidence for the presence of such a door includes part of a large stone door socket found by Behnam Abu al-Soof in 1959–60, fragments of a second socket and of a stone threshold and part of the paw of a gigantic lion colossus identified in the disturbed area north of the façade by Polish excavators in the 1970s.[18] As noted above, the presence in the centre of the south wall of the scene duplicating that behind the throne indicates another possible focal point in the throne room, which would make sense only if there were some direct visual access. But the surviving throne base is at the east end of the room, and it is clear that the North-West Palace throne room reflects the traditional, northern, 'bent-axis' plan, where the visitor enters a long chamber in which he must turn 90° to face the principal presence, be it a god or king.[19] The hypothetical central doorway seems more to reflect a formal, southern, Babylonian plan known to archaeologists as the *breitraum* type of reception room, suggesting that the North-West Palace central door, if it existed, served a special purpose, perhaps the state entry of the king himself. It must also be noted that at Nimrud no central doorway was found in the slightly later throne room in Fort Shalmaneser (p. 172), while in the North-West Palace evidence of public entrance at the west end and egress through the east door

Fig. 26. The royal lion hunt, an event of especial significance in ancient Mesopotamia; alabaster relief from the throne room of the North-West Palace; lions were the property of the king, and the bowman is the king, or perhaps the crown prince. Ht .98 m; British Museum.

51

Fig. 27. Reconstruction of the western portion of the façade of the North-West Palace throne room, either side of gate D (after Paley & Sobolewski 1994, pl. 4).

is suggested both by the façade reliefs (Fig. 27) and the fact that the lion colossi of the west gate hold offerings while those at the east gate exit were empty-handed, that is, bearers of gifts or tribute entered at the far end of the room and left by the east door. A similar non-central, bent-axis entrance is actually portrayed in wall paintings found in Fort Shalmaneser in the reception room S6, which literally illustrate the movement of the royal courtiers in a circuit around the room before approaching the throne (p. 186), strong evidence of the persistence of the bent-axis approach to the seat of authority even after the time of Assurnasirpal.

In the North-West Palace these doorways are flanked by colossal, winged, five-legged animals, either bulls or lions (Fig. 16, Assyrian *aladlammu*[20]). The five legs are a deliberate device to ensure the observer a 'fully-legged' view of the animal, whatever his position. Surviving evidence, including that of the Nineveh reliefs, indicates that unlike the reliefs, which seem to have been carved in situ, the colossi were hewn at the quarry. A letter to Sargon from a governor of Kalhu demonstrates also the installation at that time of such colossi at a central gate in Khorsabad:

> As to the bull colossi about which the king my lord wrote to me, I have worked out their positions at the … of the palaces and they are hewing them. We shall place the hewn colossi before the … residence; they will trim the big ones and we shall place them *before the middlemost gate*. As to the stone bulls of which I spoke to the king, they will modify them and turn them into bull colossi, and we shall place them *before the middlemost gate*.

Another Nimrud governor, who was *limmu* in 713, wrote to the king,

> Aššur-šumu-ke'in called me to help and loaded the bull colossi on the boats, but the boats could not carry the load (and sank). Now, although it cost me a great deal of trouble, I have hauled them up again.[21]

It would seem that not only was it obligatory for governors to dedicate expensive

monuments to the king (for example the statues in the Nabu Temple and the throne base in Fort Shalmaneser, discussed later in this book), but that at the time of Sargon they were obliged to make substantial contributions to the new palace in Khorsabad. Since Sargon's throne room at his new capital provides the classic example on the basis of which the Nimrud central door has been reconstructed, it provides at least food for thought that it was Sargon's governor at Nimrud who was busily installing bull colossi in just such a central gate.[22]

At the west end of the North-West Palace throne room is a further large door-way leading into chamber C and a large stairwell. The importance of this doorway is indicated not only by its width and the size of the winged bull colossi which faced the throne room, flanking the doorway, but also by the reliefs at the west end of the room, assuming that the suggested reconstruction is correct.[23] This group is thought to have depicted the standing king with cup and bow flanked by attendants and the ubiquitous genii; they face, of course, the king on his throne at the opposite end of the throne room. The precise function in court ceremonial of the stairwell leading to the roof remains unknown, but the association of stair and reception room is of great antiquity. Both the persistence of this plan and the extremely thick walls of the two rooms suggest not only their importance but also the possibility that some kind of ceremonial also took place on the roof (see also p. 185). The long chamber F, adjacent to room B, ornamented with carved reliefs of largely ritual character, completes the standard throne room plan, with a central entrance into a more private yet still official courtyard (Y). Two human-headed bulls of yellow limestone stood in the southern doorway of the throne room, leading into room F. These were badly damaged, and in raising them Layard discovered a collection of 16 bronze lion-weights, bearing the names of Assyrian kings from Tiglath-pileser III to Sennacherib; eight were clearly part of a single set, inscribed with the name of Shalmaneser V.[24] The Sennacherib weight is of particular interest, indicating that like ZT this area of the palace had remained in use in the 7th century, although perhaps for more mundane purposes.

53

Courtyard Y and adjacent areas

From this central courtyard, entrances lead east, west and south into further sets of public rooms accessible not only through the throne room via room F but also from the northern court by means of a passage which led behind the throne room stairwell into court WT, the 'river terrace' to the west, an arrangement also found elsewhere to avoid domestic traffic passing through the throne room. The long chambers to the east and west of court Y could also be entered directly from room F. Here too were elaborate stone reliefs and the pairs of long halls must have served other ceremonial purposes. On the eastern side the rooms were ornamented with carved reliefs of largely ritual character, as was chamber F. On the west were found the only narrative reliefs outside room B, suggesting that this western wing was second only in importance to the throne room suite. Here there were two possible reception rooms, one of which (WK) opened onto a terrace (WT) facing the river. As already remarked, this courtyard/terrace was also accessible from the western sector of the large court north of the throne room by means of a passage at the westernmost end of the throne room block; it could also be entered directly from court Y by means of passage Z, which ran through an area marked BB where Layard found a pair of lion-colossi. The overall plan of this western wing resembles triple-halled suites elsewhere, for example in Fort Shalmaneser and at Khorsabad and Nineveh,[25] which must have served some ceremonial purpose distinct from that of the king's throne room.

Unfortunately the western wing was poorly preserved, its reliefs having been

Fig. 28. Alabaster relief from the north end of room G, showing the seated king holding what was probably a gold cup (ht 2.03 m, British Museum).

removed for the decoration of Esarhaddon's South-West Palace (below, p. 75). A few
fragments and drawings have survived, however, including two relief slabs found by
the 1970s Iraqi expedition and now in the Mosul Museum. These include a two-reg-
ister relief showing a chariot scene recovered from WM, though it is not clear that
this was its original position.[26] Rassam also found reliefs depicting lion and bull
hunts, perhaps associated with room WK, but this is far from certain.

The position of the westernmost chamber, itself facing west, suggests the possibility that this may have served as a winter reception room, or even a secondary
throne room. This would be even more likely if there had been no original door from
WK into the bathroom WI. The western wall has only partially survived, but access
to this room would seem to have resembled that leading to hall WG from court Y.
Room WG was certainly a formal reception room, with its alabaster tram-lines and
ablution slab near the northwest corner of the room, comparable with a similarly
positioned stone slab in throne room B. WH seems to have been an intermediate
chamber, leading not only to the ablution room (WI) but to the relatively inaccessible strong-room A, the first room discovered by Layard in the North-West Palace. A
number of such 'strong-rooms' or 'treasuries' were found in the wings of the palace
adjoining court Y. These were small usually stone-paved rooms which were accessible only through several adjoining rooms; door fittings suggest that they were also
barred. Examples in the North-West Palace include rooms A and V.

In the Eastern Wing, rooms G and H were also formal reception rooms. It

*Fig. 29. Lower portion of an alabaster relief from room S; eagle-headed genii flanking
sacred tree, (ht. 1.03 m, Metropolitan Museum of Art).*

would appear that G represented another type of audience hall, also with the focus of the room on the short wall to the north, here marked by a central scene of bas-reliefs depicting the seated king with cup in hand (Fig. 28). The remaining reliefs here and in the adjacent room H consist of repeated patterns of king and genii and king and courtiers, while the other rooms in this sector display repeating patterns of genii flanking sacred trees (Fig. 29). The use of these repeating scenes has been seen as a 'resumé of the essence of order made explicit in the throne room',[27] that is, as a deliberate repetition of the symbols of order and authority. Because of the presence of the seated king with cup Mallowan suggested that this room had served as a banquet room, but there is no actual evidence to suggest the original purpose of the room and the representation of the king with cup undoubtedly bears some more esoteric symbolism. Both room G and the adjacent hall H were decorated with reliefs of unusually fine craftsmanship, especially the elegant 'embroidery' on the king's robes (Fig. 30);[28] similar elegance of detail is also found in passage P. Perhaps surprisingly, the small room K, situated virtually on the axis of the western entrance to all three rooms is not of obvious importance despite its central position, at least to judge from the lack of ornament.

Rooms I and L were relatively inaccessible and, despite the presence of carved reliefs, appear to have been used for the storage of valuable items, at least as a secondary function. Room L is fitted with stone slabs appropriate to an ablution room, which may also have been the original function of the comparable room I, but both are an odd shape for such a room and may therefore originally have served as 'treasuries'. Here too were the relatively inaccessible rooms J and M, with 'blind' doorways into room H, blocked only by carved reliefs. In room H was a hoard of smashed ivories, and in room I in particular Layard recovered a large number of valuable objects, including the famous Sargon glass vase (p. 238). Other discoveries there included a large quantity of scale armour, many iron helmets with bronze inlay, and large numbers of alabaster vases, some like the glass vase inscribed with Sargon's name. A quantity of glazed pottery was also found here. Whatever its original purpose, by the late 8th century this room clearly functioned as a royal storeroom.

Room S forms part of a further two-roomed reception suite, also decorated with the winged genii/sacred tree series, while at the east end of the room the reliefs depict a more warlike king with staff and sword, flanked by courtiers bearing weapons. This suite provided access to the more private parts of the palace, and in particular to court AJ, which could also be entered directly from court Y by a passage to the east of room S, which was later blocked. Room S also provided access to strongroom V, noted for its fine collection of ivories.[29] Two stone slabs forming the entrance to room U bore inscriptions of Sargon above those of Assurnasirpal, which describe the latter's great palace as having fallen into disrepair and boast that Sargon despite, or perhaps before, his construction of a new capital, made serious efforts to restore the building:

> At that time, the Juniper Palace of Kalhu, which Assurnasirpal had built before me – the foundation of that house had not been made firm, its foundation walls had not been set on bed rock, through rains and the downpours of heaven it became dilapidated and old,

Fig. 30. Detail of decoration of king's robe (after Layard 1849a, pl. 8).

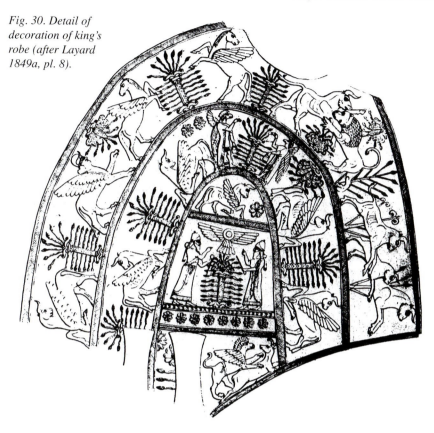

its 'footing' gave way and its joints became weakened...

Clearly Assurnasirpal's foundation terrace had not been quite as secure as he had boasted, but there is almost certainly an element of exaggeration in Sargon's claims as well:

> Upon great blocks of limestone I 'poured out' its foundation platform. From its foundation walls to its top I constructed, I completed it. A 'wind-door' I opened ... for my enjoyment.[30] The plunder of cities, acquired through the success of my weapons, I shut up therein and filled it to bursting with luxuries ... At that time I placed into that treasure-house 11 talents 30 minas of gold, 2,100 talents 24 minas of silver, out of the huge plunder which my hand captured from Pisiris, king of Carchemish.[31]

In the rooms south of courtyard Y Layard remarks that 'in all the chambers ... were found copper vessels of peculiar shape, but they fell to pieces almost immediately on exposure to the air.'[32] South of room S no further alabaster reliefs are found, but Layard comments on rooms decorated with badly faded wall paintings, including scenes depicting the king and his courtiers receiving prisoners and tribute. Similar observations have been made by recent Iraqi excavators.

Fig. 31. *Ivory carved in the Assyrian style showing details of a royal banquet. The king is seated with cup in hand, as in Fig. 28. An attendant holds a fly-whisk and a ladle to replenish his drink. At the left another holds the type of fan still used in the Near East today for fanning the charcoal when cooking kebab (it is very unlike the flywhisk held by the king's attendant), but here it would appear that it is the drinks that are being protected or cooled (see also Fig. 54). At the table to the right, the figure holding a shallow cup like that of the king and wearing a diadem is probably the crown prince. From room SE 9 in Fort Shalmaneser. (Length of strip 15.7 cm; ND 7576, Metropolitan Museum of Art).*

Before moving to courtyard Y itself, we would like to refer to a tablet from Nineveh, to which the late Leo Oppenheim drew our attention,[33] which describes the organisation of a royal feast (Fig. 31). It is not clear what kind of occasion this was, but it reflects details of domestic organisation which must have been common to many such ceremonies, both ritual and secular. Our immediate interest in this text is the use of the rooms we have been describing, and the explanation for the seeming lack of furnishings. The text is a long one and much of it deals with details of protocol which are not relevant to our immediate purpose. It opens with the instruction that the king's table and couch shall be brought in. The king himself enters, followed one at a time by court officials, then by the crown prince and the other princes. The duties of particular servants present in the chamber are prescribed, the ceremonial and practical observances appropriate to each stage of the feast are laid down, and the text concludes with a direction that the tables of the crown prince, the other princes and the nobles shall be removed. In this account are three points particularly relevant to the layout of the important reception suites as we know them in the North-West Palace and elsewhere. One of the servants whose duties are listed is required to stand with rake, poker and tongs in hand, ready to pick up ashes that may fall from the brazier, to control the heat of the fire, or to put on more fuel at the king's command. This passage obviously illustrates the provision, in the typical reception room where the floor itself was not paved with some hard material, of stone rails or dressed slabs to support the brazier, which could be moved towards or away from the king as his comfort demanded. The second characteristic element in the permanent furnishings of these rooms, always found unless there is an ablution room a few paces away, is the rectangular slab set in the floor and usually incorporating a drain. One use of this slab is illustrated here by the duties of an attendant at the feast who was placed in charge of the bowl of scented water with which the diners washed their hands. We may assume that it was the custom to carry water and napkins to the guests in the traditional Near Eastern manner. Yet another servant was responsible for the provision

58

of clean and the disposal of dirty linen. This custom survives still today among conventional society in the Near East, and indeed the ceremony of formally presenting the ewer and bowl of rose water at the end of a feast is still to be seen in certain Oxford and Cambridge colleges! The third point of interest in the text is that, at the beginning and end of the feast, the tables and the royal couch were brought into and removed from the room, implying that except in the special case of the throne room with a permanent stone dais, reception rooms were furnished in a manner appropriate to individual occasions. Space for the storage of furniture would thus have been needed close at land, an explanation for the well-guarded storerooms often found in the vicinity of reception room suites.

Courtyard Y is itself of interest. It is entered directly from room F through a central doorway with bull colossi facing the court.[34] This doorway has been restored by the Iraq Antiquities Department under the general direction of Sayid Hazim Abdul-Hamid of the Mosul Museum, and the glazed brick decoration, fragments of which were found scattered in the courtyard, replaced in its original position in the

Fig. 32. The north gate of courtyard Y, leading into room F, taken after restoration of the glazed brick surround by the Iraqi Directorate-General of Antiquities.

59

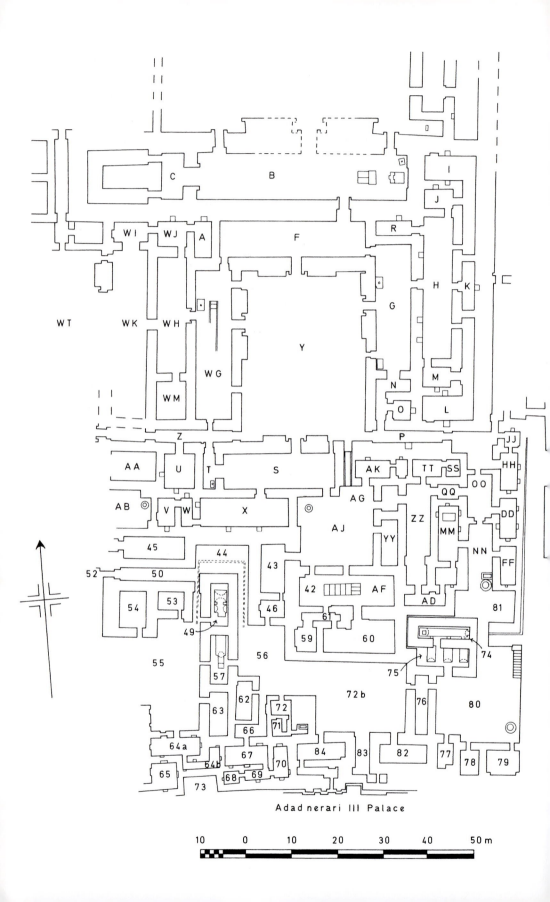

Adad nerari III Palace

10   0   10   20   30   40   50 m

arch over the gateway (Fig. 32). As elsewhere in the building, many of the glazed bricks bore mason's marks in black paint on their reverse surface to indicate their position in the design. The sides of the court were lined with inscribed (but not sculptured) stone slabs. Perhaps the most interesting feature of courtyard Y itself is the evidence it provides for monumental drains in the 9th century BC.[35] The pavement itself consisted of baked bricks and stone slabs, with bitumen used as a sealant as elsewhere in the palace. Beneath the floor was a remarkable drainage system operated by means of terracotta pipes which led from the adjacent rooms into stone-covered troughs in the centre of the courtyard; here the central holes in the stone covers provided for the drainage of the courtyard itself. The troughs led to further terracotta pipes which carried the water outside the palace walls to the west and presumably into the Tigris. Some of the baked bricks which formed the courtyard pavement had also been pierced with a circular hole in the centre; these were closed with mushroom-headed terracotta objects covered with bitumen, of which the purpose remains unclear. They resemble, at least superficially, the similarly-shaped glazed knobs (*siqqatu*) which were used as part of wall decoration (see Pl. 12b).

The Bitanu or Harem (private domestic quarters) (Plan, Fig. 33)

The private domestic quarters of the palace were separated from the more public areas by passages Z and P, which ran west-east across the building at the southern limit of courtyard Y. At their eastern end was a narrow entrance from outside the palace, apparently providing access to the *bitanu* without passing through the state apartments. Some of the most exciting finds made at Nimrud have come from this area, and we will look first at those discoveries made here by Layard and Mallowan. Passage P provides evidence of three periods of construction, with an original pavement laid at the time of Assurnasirpal, over which lay a second pavement with inscribed bricks of Shalmaneser III and a still later pavement in which the bricks were uninscribed but believed to date from the time of Sargon or Esarhaddon. The individual brick pavements were laid directly on one another with no intervening fill or debris; a ritual burial of a gazelle (?) was found beneath the uppermost pavement.[36] This passage led eastwards to an open court leading into a wing in which a number of grandiose apartments have been identified. The common pattern seems to have been a living or reception area, with wall cupboards and an adjacent bathroom, for example room MM, described by Mallowan as a well-constructed and spacious apartment, with water jars in a cupboard in the east wall. Room AK and bathroom AH provide another example. The unusually thick walls to the west and north of these rooms suggest the possibility here of an upper storey, but the only staircase so far identified in this part of the palace lies in the north-east corner of courtyard 80. Nor is there any evidence in the surviving building to explain why the east wall of the domestic quarter runs at a slight angle to the outer wall of the palace complex, but we suspect that this may reflect a narrowing of the building to conform to the

Fig. 33. Plan of southern part of North-West Palace (overlaps with Fig. 15); the plan of the domestic area has been redrawn on the basis of information supplied by Muzahim Mahmud Hussein (see also Hussein and Suleiman, in press, Arabic section p. 56).

Fig. 34. Ritual deposit of animal bones (?gazelle) beneath the lowest floor of room HH. Three successive floors are visible, above which was the destruction debris containing the ivories and dockets found here.

change in the line of the quay wall on the west (see tell plan, p. 29).

Immediately to the east of Passage P was another suite of rooms, JJ and HH, entered from the open court. In room HH were found iron spears stacked against the east wall, a large storage jar inscribed with its capacity (c. 99 litres),[37] a number of carved ivories, and a group of clay dockets, some inscribed, some sealed. One recorded a herd of 37 camels, another over a ton and a half of wool.[38] An intriguing discovery in this room consisted of a few trinkets, gold foil, beads and shells sealed into a wall cupboard, presumably by the occupant of the room. The collection was deliberately hidden, the cupboard itself masked with brickwork and plastered over.

Room HH is also important in providing one of our better-documented pieces of evidence concerning the stratification of the deposits in this part of the North-West Palace. Although Mallowan describes, and illustrates, what he interprets as three distinct occupation levels, the earliest of which is attributed to the time of Sargon,[39] this is very misleading. Indeed he himself remarks that 'in dissecting *successive* floors of at least three rooms (authors' emphasis), we found many examples of miniature pots, side by side with sheep bones', and continues, these votive deposits were 'part of the ritual when a new floor was laid'.[40] In Fig. 34 two earlier plaster surfaces can be clearly seen in section beneath the excavated floor, of which the lower lies just above the level of the foundation deposit. Unfortunately, the excavation records do not tell us whether the deposit was sealed by this floor, and it seems possible that it was asso-

Fig. 35. Limestone plaque, smashed in the 612 BC destruction; part of the plaque was found in room 00 and part in QQ, in the North-West Palace. The plaque was inscribed and bore on its back the figure of the demonic god Pazuzu, who seems to have played a beneficent role as a protector against Lamaštu, the female monster on the front of the plaque who is strangling two snakes and suckling a pig and a hound. Although her principal victims seem to have been newborn babies, she was also a bringer of disease. The purpose of the plaque is to expel the evil spirits which had possessed the sick man shown on his bed, Pazuzu's role being to force Lamaštu back into the underworld (on the back of the ass which carries her to the boat). In the upper register there is a row of ašipu *priests wearing lions' masks and reciting the appropriate spells through which the demons are exorcised. Protective Pazuzu amulets were placed in houses or, in the form of his head only, hung around the necks of pregnant women (12.5 x 9.6 cm; ND 484).*

ciated with one of the two later floors, perhaps contemporary with the gazelle burial in passage P which is said to have been inserted from the level of the latest pavement. Here the sequence of floors, where three baked brick pavements are identified each resting immediately on the previous one without intervening debris, is precisely that noted also in room HH. What is described by Mallowan in the preliminary reports as the original floor, in the burnt debris of which the ivories and dockets were found, is in fact the latest of the three floors illustrated in Fig. 34. Mallowan's Level II represents simply the upper surface of the 612 destruction debris, and at some time not long after the destruction, collapsed brickwork was levelled off to create a new (post-

612 BC) floor, his Level I.[41] These observations correspond with those of Iraqi excavators.[42] The 1950s evidence was not correctly understood until the identical sequence was identified some years later in Fort Shalmaneser. Moreover, unless a building was being completely reconstructed, the proper upkeep of a monumental building would have required the removal of rubbish before laying a new floor, the type of sequence which is illustrated here. Unfortunately, at Nimrud, it is only in the TW private houses that we have a reliable sequence of genuinely stratified material between successive Assyrian floors.

That these events are all closely related in time is proved by the discovery in room HH of dockets sealed by the same seal in both Mallowan's Level III and Level I,[43] while an inscribed sherd of the large jar is attributed in the excavation catalogue to Level I,[44] yet the jar itself is described as lying in 'another corner' of the room opposite the stack of spears, that is, Level III.[45] In the final report, these objects from Mallowan's original Level III are recognised as having been 'abandoned after the sack at the end of the 7th century'.[46] Moreover, in both its position and pattern of deposition Level I corresponds very closely with the so-called 'squatter level' identified not only in Fort Shalmaneser but elsewhere on the mound. This represents a re-occupation of the buildings not long after the destruction of Kalhu, presumably by the original inhabitants of the city, but lacking the royal authority represented in earlier repairs. The partial clearing and levelling off of the destroyed contents of rooms elsewhere on the site occasionally produced precisely the situation observed in HH,

Fig. 36. Courtyard 80, looking north; the recently excavated well is in the south-east corner, well NN can be seen in the background. Rooms 74 and 75 are in the north-west corner of the court.

that is, the presence of material from the destruction level within that of the squatter occupation (see also p. 165).

Further evidence for the 7th century date of this destruction is provided by the fragment of a prism of Assurbanipal (668–627 BC), as Mallowan observed at the time, 'at a surprisingly low level'.[47] This important piece was carefully recorded as having been found 23 cm above the 'original floor' in room OO, that is, in Mallowan's 'Level III' destruction debris. This debris also included a piece of a *lamaštu* plaque (Fig. 35), of which the other fragment was recovered from room QQ, clear evidence that the materials in these rooms had been thrown about by those who destroyed the palace. Moreover, as Mallowan remarks, it is highly unlikely that an Assyrian would have destroyed such a potent symbol of ritual magic, which was believed to dispel evil spirits, that is, this debris dates from the 612 destruction. In the adjacent room DD, and in MM, were found tombs, discussed in chapter 3. Also described in chapter 3 is the excavation of a well in court AJ by Layard, Mallowan and Iraqi archaeologists. Room ZZ seems at one time to have been a kitchen, with benches, water and cooking pots and a bread oven; it is also the source of the glazed vessel decorated with the amusing ostriches of Fig. 40.

The rooms at the western end of passage Z have unfortunately been destroyed by erosion, but to the south were a number of residential and other domestic rooms, many of which have only recently been excavated by teams of Iraqi archaeologists under the direction of Muzahim Mahmud Hussein. Particularly striking is the position of two rooms which form a central focus within the domestic wing, rooms 49 and, immediately to the south, 57. They lack the ablution rooms that normally accompany the residential suites but contain, beneath their floors, the two richest tombs discovered until now at Nimrud (again, described in chapter 3). The walls of these rooms, and in particular the large cross wall to the north, are noticeably thicker than the usual walls in this area. Tablets were found in room 57, crushed under a limestone slab (p. 202). Surrounding room 49, and presumably protecting the tomb against water seepage, is a brick-lined drain some 70 cm wide, which carries surface water into a sump in courtyard 56.

Undoubtedly the most prestigious set of rooms in the *bitanu* is that consisting of a large reception room (42) with ten dressed limestone slabs at its centre, together with a large inner room (60) and a bathroom suite (58, 59, 61). We believe this residence to be that of the queen, identified not only by its superior dimensions but also by the quality of the materials recovered here. The latter include the extraordinary ivories from the well in the adjacent courtyard (chapter 3) and large quantities of gold sheet from room YY. Moreover, on some walls the carefully smoothed plaster was decorated with paintings of human, floral and geometric motifs, subjects similar to those on the stone reliefs. An unusual part of the mural decoration in room 42 was a pillow-shaped object of copper sheeting which held a central knob in the manner of the glazed wall plaque illustrated in Pl. 12b.

In the south-east corner of the palace, recent Iraqi excavations (1992) revealed a further courtyard (80) with yet another well, this time full of ivories, seals and, more surprisingly, a large number of manacled 'prisoners' (Fig. 36). The finds from

Fig. 37. The long vaulted chamber beneath room 74, looking east.

the well are discussed on p. 100. It is uncertain whether the presence of the large number of prisoners, thrown into the well, is in any way related to the sack of the building, but this seems the most likely explanation, in particular since the bodies appear to be those of able young men aged between 18 and 30, possibly part of the household guard. Also associated with this courtyard were two further rooms, 74 and 75, which appear, at least superficially, to constitute another reception suite. Room 74 contained much ash, and in the western part of the room a number of remarkable finds were made. These included fine examples of glazed pottery, a collection of stamp and cylinder seals,[48] and an attractive, red, almost certainly Cypriote bottle, decorated with geometric designs.

Beneath these rooms is one of the most extraordinary structures to have been discovered in the North-West Palace. At the western end of the room, removal of stones from the unpaved floor revealed a deep, square, vertical shaft, which provided access to a low corbelled entrance and three steps into a long narrow chamber, 10 m long and 2 m wide, directly below room 74. This underground chamber had a very high radial vault (Fig. 37), and leading off it to the south, and at right angles to it, are three smaller vaulted rooms (plan, Fig. 38). In the centre of the northern wall is an arched niche, and identical niches are found in each of the walls of the smaller rooms. Their purpose was presumably to hold the lamps that would have been essential here (see Fig. 48, p. 88).

It was originally suggested that these rooms might have been the palace prison,

66

partly because of their distance from the main areas of the building but most importantly because of the obvious difficulty of escape. This interpretation was reinforced by the presence of the manacled bodies in the nearby well in court 80. Ironically, Assurnasirpal prays in one of his inscriptions that his palace shall not be dishonoured by being used for such a purpose (p. 104). However, some 271 objects were found here, including many of great beauty, suggesting that these secret chambers are far more likely to have been the treasuries of the royal ladies, also far from the general public and extremely difficult of access. Among the unique objects recovered here is an extraordinary glazed kernos, consisting of a stand which supports a central container together with eight surrounding bowls, rather like a branched candlestick (Fig. 39); other discoveries include a beautiful recumbent bull stamp seal, made from onyx with gold attachments,[49] a beautifully carved steatite spoon with three birds' heads carved at the sides (side chamber A), a carnelian necklace from room B, and a number of polychrome glazed vessels. An inscribed alabaster tablet of Shalmaneser III was also found in the long chamber. Also recovered here was an extraordinary collection of cylinder and stamp seals.[50] These were found both in the well itself and in the vaults and their overlying rooms; others came from room 77 in the south-west

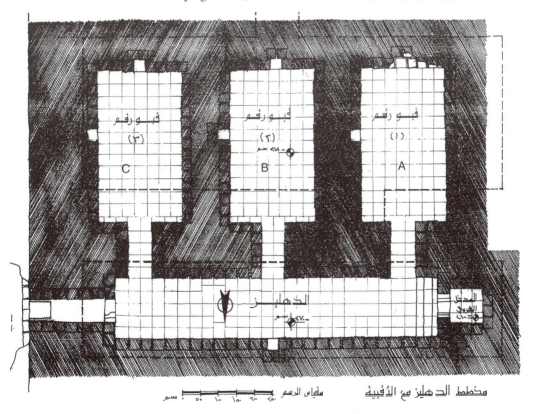

Fig. 38. Plan of vaulted underground rooms beneath rooms 74, 75 (surveyed and drawn by Muzahim Mahmud Hussein).

Fig. 39. Kernos *of 8 glazed cups surrounding a central bowl resting on a tall foot (broken on this example), from vault room C (ND 292-IM 127831). A similar but complete* kernos *consisting of six cups was found in the court 80 well (ND 294-IM 127833).*

corner of the court. Certainly the presence here of the harem strong room, if such these vaults prove to be, would have been more appropriate to the wishes of the founder of the palace.

In the 1990 season, again under the direction of Muzahim Mahmud Hussein, the southern limit of the palace was explored. Here were well-built rooms and court-yards lined with baked clay orthostats bearing inscriptions of Assurnasirpal II (for example, 65, 55 and 44).[51] A fourth tomb was identified beneath the block to the east of rooms 71, 72, its entrance leading down from 72 (Fig. 49). Further burials in ter-racotta sarcophagi were discovered under the floors of rooms 64b and 69, in the southernmost part of the building. Among the many accomplishments of the recent excavations has been the identification of the southern limits of the palace, with what was perhaps a service entrance leading into courtyard 72b via chambers 85, 84. Undoubtedly the most unexpected discovery here was the presence of a palace of Adad-nerari III, immediately adjacent to the southern boundary of the North-West Palace, its walls following the line of its northern neighbour, with only a very narrow passage, some 60 cm in width, separating the two. This space was filled with col-lapsed material and rubbish, including glazed bricks, plain alabaster slabs and a large number of objects including pottery and duck weights. This new palace is further dis-cussed below.

North-West Palace: historical summary
The history of the North-West Palace reflects the history of the city itself. Founded by Assurnasirpal II as the visible symbol of his, and the city's, status, the palace remained in use until the fall of Assyria in 612, although its importance was dimin-ished after the time of Sargon, when the capital moved first to Khorsabad and then to Nineveh. Its importance lies in the originality of its conception, in particular the

introduction of historical narrative in the alabaster reliefs, an innovation followed, though later modified, by subsequent Assyrian kings. It is likely that most of the original building was constructed during the reign of Assurnasirpal, although his son Shalmaneser III, who built the impressive palace-arsenal in the outer town (Fort Shalmaneser) may have completed unfinished work here. Certainly he made some additions to its original fabric, for example in passage P, where baked bricks stamped with his name directly overlay those of his father. The North-West Palace continued as the primary palace at the time of his successor Šamši-Adad V, but it is now clear that Adad-nerari III built a palace directly to the south of the North-West Palace, possibly associated with the so-called Upper Chambers, discussed below.

Tiglath-pileser III also built a new palace, on a grand scale, and also to the south of the North-West Palace and allegedly overlooking the Tigris. Little survives owing largely to the depredations of Esarhaddon in the 7th century. However, the North-West Palace certainly remained in use throughout this time, and royal burials of this date have recently been found in the domestic quarter. We know too that Sargon continued to use the North-West Palace, both as a residence and the focus of his administration, a building which clearly provided an important model for the new capital at Khorsabad. It was originally believed by Mallowan that the North-West Palace had been destroyed at the time of Sargon, since many of its storerooms contained valuable tribute and treasure bearing Sargon's name (the famous glass vase and the alabaster vessels in room I, for example). Many of the surviving tablets are also of this date, and in room U his inscription is added above that of the founder of the palace, telling us that he had used this room in order to store treasures captured from the king of Carchemish. Tusks and unfinished ivories were stored here, suggesting that work for his new capital was being carried out at Kalhu. Indeed the inscription on the writing boards from the well in chamber AB (p. 99) tells us that these were prepared for Dur-Šarrukin, while various letters reflect the part played by various governors of Kalhu in the provision of materials and finished sculptures for the new capital. Part of Sargon's administrative archives have survived in ZT, and also in the Burnt Palace.

Sennacherib took little direct interest in Nimrud, his grandiose plans involving only Nineveh, but there survives evidence for 7th-century use of the North-West Palace, at this time most convincingly the tablets from the administrative rooms in ZT and a fragment of an Assurbanipal prism in the domestic quarter. The ZT texts are dated for the most part to the time of Esarhaddon and Assurbanipal, but the names of many post-canonical *limmu* also occur here, down to the time of the fall of the city in 612 BC. In the 7th century the throne room seems to have lost its original purpose, however; for example, the set of sixteen beautifully cast bronze weights, including one inscribed with the name of Sennacherib (p. 53), suggest that this part of the palace, like the rooms to the north, now served some less ceremonial function. These also provide, of course, further evidence for the use of this part of the palace in the 7th century.

Despite such evidence for continuing use of at least parts of the palace and the renovations of his father, at the time of Sennacherib the building must have suffered some decay. The last Assyrian king to build extensively at Nimrud was Esarhaddon (680–669 BC), but he seems not to have been interested in the North-West Palace, tearing out the sculptures from the west wing and probably elsewhere for his new palace in the south-west corner of the citadel. The offices of Assurnasirpal's palace continued to function, however, and many of the rooms, especially in the harem area, continued both as storerooms and as residences. We have argued above that the palace was destroyed in 612 BC, as was the rest of the site; this is supported by the archaeological evidence which indicates not only that the destruction was severe but that objects were thrown from room to room and even dumped into the palace wells as gold was ripped from ivories and furniture, and other materials were deliberately smashed. The latest occupation in the palace lay just over a metre above the original floors and seems to represent a 'squatter' occupation, recognised elsewhere on the site. These were local residents of Kalhu, returning to the site after the 612 sack, at which time a remnant Assyrian government survived in the west. The final occupation was Hellenistic, and a number of tombs of this date were found above the palace.

THE PALACE OF ADAD-NERARI III AND THE UPPER CHAMBERS

Recent Iraqi excavations (1993) under the direction of Muzahim Mahmud Hussein have identified a new palace immediately to the south of the North-West Palace. A considerable area of this palace has been excavated, but there were no stone reliefs and little was found in it, with the fortunate exception of two doorway inscriptions revealing that it had been constructed by Adad-nerari III. The walls were thick, covered with white plaster, and painted with geometric and floral motifs. It was in this same area that Layard excavated the so-called 'Upper Chambers', consisting of a large hall and a suite of three small chambers, also with fresco decoration 'elaborate and graceful in design', depicting winged bulls, crenellated battlements and geometric patterns. Loftus also dug here, and the combined results produced a group of rooms forming the northern end of a residential suite, the main room of which contained alabaster 'tramlines' like those found in the major palace reception rooms.[52] Stone inscriptions of Adad-nerari III were also found here, apparently used as paving slabs in two of the doorways.[53] It has often been suggested that the Upper Chambers, which lay at a relatively high level – hence the name – were part of a building constructed by Adad-nerari III, a suggestion perhaps reinforced by the recent Iraqi discoveries although there are signs that the lower, original walls had been reused for some secondary purpose. The precise position of the Upper Chambers remains uncertain, but Layard observes that the rooms rested on a solid mud-brick platform and the remains of mud-brick packing were identified in area 73, to the south of the south wall of the North-West palace. This lies within the highest part of this area of the tell, and certainly represents the general location of the Upper Chambers, of which the surviving walls have now totally eroded. Whatever their date, it is clear that these remains represent a prestigious and attractive suite, on an upper floor and almost certainly with a fine view of the Tigris valley, perhaps, as Julian Reade has suggested to us, built by Adad-nerari III for his famous mother, Sammuramat. A tempting thought, at least.

THE CENTRAL PALACE

Until recently, the central area of the mound south of the North-West Palace had never been extensively investigated. Indeed, it appeared that relatively little had survived to be examined. Nineteenth-century excavations had revealed traces of monumental buildings approximately in the centre of the tell and, closer to the river, the so-called Upper Chambers and parts of an adjacent building to the south. Recent excavations by a Polish team under the direction of the late Janusz Meuszynski have further elucidated these structures and, in particular, identified the 'lost' positions of several 19th century monuments.

The oldest building in this area was found by Layard and further investigated by both Rassam and Loftus. It was erected by Assurnasirpal II and is now generally known as the Central Building ('R' on plan Fig. 41), in order to differentiate it from Tiglathpileser's Central Palace which lay just to the west. In the Central Building a south-facing façade with four surviving colossi and associated orthostats was identified. Perhaps the most interesting feature of this building was the apparent presence in the vicinity of the façade of at least three free-standing monuments, including the famous black obelisk of Shalmaneser III (p. 16), the 'Rassam obelisk', a very damaged obelisk of Assurnasirpal II, also black, and what seems to have been an unfinished or crudely carved statue of a eunuch courtier.[54] This fragmentary building was further investigated by the Polish expedition in the 1970s.[55] Just to the southwest Layard had also found a pair of colossal winged bulls, dating to the time of Shalmaneser III and referred to as the 'Centre Bulls'. These east-facing colossi must have formed one entrance to another palatial building, of which virtually nothing has survived. Like the Central Building, the Centre Bulls faced onto a large open space or plaza which may have extended as far south as the Governor's Palace and was perhaps approached from the east by means of the road leading from the outer town into the citadel through the eastern gateway, also built by Shalmaneser III (p. 30).

The location of these obelisks was not precisely recorded in the 19th century, and we should note that their position on the tell plan published in Mallowan 1966 is certainly inaccurate. In a close study of the 19th century sources, published in 1962, Falkner was able to rectify some of the most misleading information, but it was not until the Polish excavations of the 1970s that the related buildings were re-identified and accurately planned.[56] The original positions of the obelisks and statue remain unclear, but they were almost certainly situated in the open area south of the Central Building and east of the Centre Bulls. Layard tells us that the Black Obelisk was found over fifty feet to the north of the Centre Bulls, which would place it somewhere in the northwestern corner of this hypothetical plaza, while just to the east of the Assurnasirpal façade Rassam found a square block of limestone which had almost certainly served as a base for the Assurnasirpal obelisk, found shattered into many pieces around the surviving pedestal (the small square on the plan). Indeed, in 1952 Mallowan found a further piece of this black basalt obelisk in a small sounding in the middle of the mound near the modern track.[57]

It is generally believed that the 'Central Building' was one of the many temples constructed at Kalhu by Assurnasirpal II and listed in his Standard Inscription, a

Fig. 40. Hunting scene, decoration on glazed cylindrical, tub-like vessel from room ZZ in the North-West Palace. The decoration is in yellow and white glaze; the vessel itself is covered with blue glaze, inside and out (d 29 cm, ND 1355).

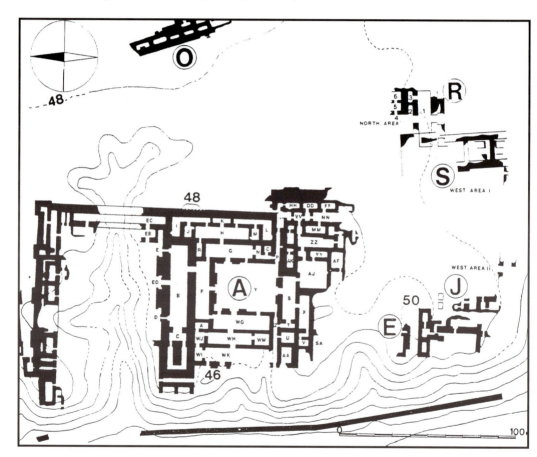

Fig. 41. Plan of Polish excavations in the area of the Central Palace, south of the North-West Palace (A); R = Central Building of Assurnasirpal II, S = Central Palace of Tiglath-pileser III, E = Upper Chambers, O = 1950 Building (after Mierzejewski & Sobolewski 1980, fig. 2).

suggestion reinforced by the presence of the obelisks, a feature of other temples at the site, for example that dedicated to Ninurta (chapter 4, and see Fig. 2, p. 7).[58] Several rooms within this building, to the north of the façade, were excavated in the 1970s, in one of which (room 5) were found some 300 pottery vessels, placed along the walls and, unusually, grouped according to their shapes.[59] The logic of this deposit, which is not paralleled elsewhere at Nimrud, remains a mystery.

The largest of the buildings in this area was the so-called Central Palace of Tiglath-Pileser III, 'the area of which was to be greater than that of the earlier palaces of my fathers' and a construction which involved enlarging a terrace on the river side by building up a wall 'out of the Tigris'... 'I piled up heavy limestone boulders like a mountain, to a depth of 20 cubits in the raging waters'.[60] Unfortunately, very little of this palace has survived and its limits remain ill-defined. Both the Central Building and that associated with the Centre Bulls had been savagely cut down, possibly at the time the Central Palace was built, while the Central Palace itself suffered a similar fate when Esarhaddon plundered its stone reliefs for the adornment of his new palace in the south-west corner of the tell.

The Polish excavators identified an extensive baked brick pavement west of the Centre Bulls, and it was in this area that Layard had found a group of some 20 Hellenistic tombs (see chapter 8). Five feet below the tombs he also discovered an extraordinary collection of approximately 100 carved orthostats, literally stacked up as though they were in a stone-carver's shop, 'lying against one another, as slabs in a stone-cutter's yard, or as the leaves of a gigantic book'.[61] It would seem that these were reliefs from Tiglath-Pileser's Palace which had been stacked up by Esarhaddon for removal to his new palace (Fig. 42). Although some of the Central Palace reliefs had already been transported to the south-west building, Esarhaddon never completed the new project.

We have already remarked that only small portions of these central buildings survive, indeed Layard remarks that the Central Palace had been 'so completely destroyed that its ground plan cannot be ascertained', a situation not helped by the fact that his workmen were not accustomed to the difficulties of tracing mud-brick walls, much preferring the ease of following the stone slabs of the better-preserved buildings. The precise area covered by this palace remains unknown, although observations made by the Polish team suggest that it overlay both the Central Building and the Shalmaneser bulls, and we are told by Tiglath-pileser himself that it stretched westwards to the Tigris, a situation now complicated by the discovery of the Adad-nerari III palace. Oddly, the reliefs were apparently stacked on the pavement associated with the building incorporating the Shalmaneser bulls, that is, Esarhaddon appears to have removed not only the reliefs but also the floors of the Tiglath-pileser building, providing good reason for Layard's difficulties. Some 70 m west of the Shalmaneser bulls Loftus found three further bull colossi forming a north-south gateway. This too was re-excavated by the Polish expedition, who found there a stone-paved gate overlaid with bitumen in which were preserved the wheel-ruts of the chariots which had passed through.[62] It remains unclear whether this too was in some way associated with the Central Palace, although the Polish team remark on the relatively

Fig. 42. Alabaster relief of Tiglath-pileser III showing, below, the king in royal procession and, above, the inhabitants of Astartu (in modern Jordan) being marched away from their captured citadel (originally from the Central Palace but found by Layard in the South-West Palace, ht 1.90 m, now in the British Museum).

poor quality of workmanship compared with the other surviving structures in the area. It is now of course possible that this gate is to be associated with the Adad-ner-ari III building, but this can only be established by further excavation.

SOUTH-WEST PALACE (plan, Fig. 43)
As its name suggests this building lies in the south-west corner of the citadel mound, south of the Central Palace. It was discovered on the first day of Layard's excavations at Nimrud (November 1845) and further investigated by both Rassam and Loftus. Its walls had been partly destroyed by fire and, as Layard first observed, 'the building had been destroyed before its completion.'[63] In 1951 Mallowan opened trenches to the east of the palace and also concluded that it was unfinished, 'for no

74

building remains were discovered in a place where they might obviously have been expected to extend.'[64] The date of the original building in the south-west corner of the citadel remains uncertain, but the surviving building was constructed by Esarhaddon, presumably at the same time that he was involved in rebuilding Fort Shalmaneser.[65] Although the palace walls were lined with stone orthostats as in the earlier palaces, these had not been carved specifically for the South-West Palace but had been removed in bulk from the Central and North-West Palaces. Indeed Layard correctly observes that

> the whole was panelled with slabs brought from elsewhere; the only sculptures express-
> ly made for the building being the gigantic lions and bulls and the crouching sphinxes.
> The slabs were not all from the same edifice. Some, and by far the greater number,
> belonged to the north-west, others to the centre palace. But there were many bas-reliefs
> which differed greatly, in the style of art, from the sculptures discovered in both those
> ruins…All the walls had been exposed to fire; the slabs were nearly reduced to lime, and
> were too much injured and cracked to bear removal. They were not all sculptured; the
> bas-reliefs being scattered here and there; and…when left entire, turned towards the
> wall of sun-dried brick.[66]

According to the Layard papers in the British Museum the reliefs were found not only with sculptured faces both turned to the wall and facing the rooms but with the relief decoration purposely shaved down by a sharp instrument; some slabs were upside down, some still lay on the floors, not yet placed in position along the walls.[67] In other words, the intention had been that these orthostats, removed from other buildings, should be recarved or perhaps even left plain. The stacks of stone bas-reliefs found by Layard in the area of the Centre Building (p. 73) were almost certainly destined for the South-West Palace, where of course they never arrived.

Esarhaddon's cylinder inscription, found at Nimrud and discussed below (p. 216), tells of the construction of a palace 'which was in the middle of Kalhu'. Owing to an original mis-reading of the term *ekal mašarti* (p. 145), this was once thought to refer to the South-West Palace, but it is now beyond doubt that the palace of the inscription is the building excavated in the outer town as 'Fort Shalmaneser'. That is, the inscription does not describe work in the unfinished South-West Palace of which, regrettably, little of the overall plan has been established. The most interesting part of the plan can be seen in Fig. 43. Here two long east-west antechambers with central doorways lead to a smaller central room in a third row of chambers, of which the south wall, which lay at the edge of the tell, was eroded. Oblong north-south chambers lay at either side of the complex, in the manner of Sennacherib's formal reception suites which flank court 19 at Nineveh. As in Sennacherib's palace, it is presumably this small room that forms the central focus of the Nimrud suite, which was apparently entered from a large courtyard to the north, itself over 60 m from north to south, with rooms to the west and a more public entrance on the north.[68]

The other new feature is the use of columns, a practice borrowed from northern Syria and an architectural convention for which in Assyria we have more textual than archaeological evidence. In the surviving suite the southern doorway 'a' is formed by a pair of gigantic human-headed winged lions, facing north. These are made of limestone not alabaster, and they have one feature that places them apart from the standard Nimrud repertoire. All the other winged bull and lion colossi have five legs, so that the viewer sees the appropriate number of legs whether the statue is viewed from the front or side (as in Fig. 16, p. 38). Uniquely, the Esarhaddon colossi have only four legs. But the most remarkable aspect of this doorway is that between the colossi are two crouching sphinxes, carved in the local alabaster, some 5 feet high. Supported by the wings and the back of the head is a circular column base.[69] The building had been severely burnt, and Layard found the whole entrance 'buried in charcoal', the sphinxes almost reduced to lime. Indeed, he had scarcely finished drawing the first sphinx when it fell completely to pieces. A small model of a sphinx column base was also found by Layard (Fig. 44).[70]

In doorway 'b' was a pair of much damaged winged bulls, and between them two double crouching sphinxes, forming even more elaborate column bases.[71] The

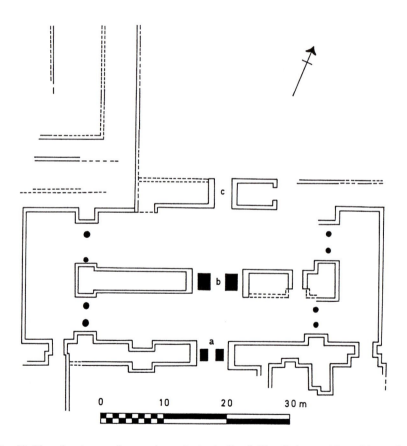

Fig. 43. Plan showing south reception suite in the South-West Palace, with positions of column bases (after Barnett & Falkner 1962, fig. 5).

northern doorway 'c' was flanked by a pair of winged bulls, but there seem to have been no column bases here, perhaps simply because the building remained unfinished. Also unusual were the columned doorways within the suite: 'In the narrowest part of each extremity [that is, in the side doorways] were two low spherical stones, flattened at the top,' that is, further plain column bases forming portico-like doorways to east and west. Such a columned suite would have been enormously impressive had it ever been completed. The columns themselves must have been of wood, and would explain the evidence of intense fires discovered by Layard.

Seventh-century kings refer to the construction of *bit hilani*, basically a columned portico, but the term seems also to have been used more generally for areas of the palace with columned entrances. In Assyrian sources the *bit hilani* is first mentioned in an inscription of Tiglath-pileser III – 'for my pleasure I built in Kalhu a *hilani*-portico like that of a Hittite [in the sense of North Syrian] palace.'[72] Sargon says that at Khorsabad he 'built a palace and enhanced its doorways with a *hilani*-portico',[73] and at Nimrud it would appear that the doorway colossi and column bases constitute the only original sculpture in the South-West Palace. No other Assyrian building has up to now produced elaborate column bases like those found in Esarhaddon's Palace at Nimrud,[74] although model column bases have been found elsewhere. In 1974 a similar suite of rooms was excavated by Sd. Manhal Jabr on the east side of Nineveh, south of the River Khosr, between Quyunjik and Nebi Yunus. Bricks inscribed with the name of Sennacherib were found here, as were circular stone column bases with a type of looped decoration found also at Khorsabad and characteristic of Syro-Hittite areas to the west. For the moment, however, the Nimrud sphinx-based columns remain unique in Assyrian architecture.

Fig. 44. Alabaster model of sphinx column base, heavily calcined, found by Layard in the South-West Palace (ht. 22.4 cm, British Museum).

77

CHAPTER 3

TOMBS, WELLS AND RICHES

For modern visitors, not only to Nimrud itself but also to the many museums which display in their galleries its massive gate-colossi and extraordinary relief sculptures, the state apartments of the North-West Palace provide the most immediately recognisable and impressive symbols of Assyrian power. It is perhaps surprising, therefore, that the domestic quarters of the palace have provided most of the spectacular small finds, both in the 19th century and, even more strikingly, in recent years. The domestic quarter is that area of the palace south of court Y and of passages Z and P, most directly entered via passage P to the east and presumably by means of the similar passage to the west (plan, Fig. 33), but the latter area of the palace, near the river, is now very heavily eroded and here we lack the equivalent plan. The term domestic should not be misunderstood. This is not simply a 'below stairs' area but the private living quarters of the royal family and their official servants. Indeed, we now believe that the large, central apartment, entered via room S and courtyard AJ, is that of the queen herself (above, p. 65).

Often referred to in modern literature as the 'harem', this area contains residential suites, storerooms and possibly areas in which some élite goods were actually produced. Raw materials were also stored here, at least in the later periods of use of the building. The term 'harem' is undoubtedly misleading in its most common usage (see p. 38). Textual evidence from the time clearly demonstrates the presence of a sufficient number of powerful women to indicate that the common interpretation of this anachronistic term is unsuitable (as, indeed, it is in Islam), despite the necessity also in Assyria that respectable women should be veiled in public. Women of ill repute and female slaves were actually forbidden the veil, which was clearly a sign of respectability.[1] One has only to recall the mothers of such powerful kings as Adadnerari III and Esarhaddon (pp. 19, 23), or to examine the official records of the *šakintu* in Fort Shalmaneser, to see that Assyrian women could wield both power and influence. Certainly the women of the palace lived in its southern quarter, however, and in that sense the word harem is accurately applied.

NIMRUD TOMBS
Undoubtedly the most exciting archaeological discoveries of recent decades have been made in tombs found in this domestic quarter of the North-West Palace. One of many interesting facts to emerge from these discoveries is that vaulted tombs were designed in advance for the burial of the royal women and were built beneath certain rooms in the domestic wing as part of the original palace construction. Many if not all Assyrian kings were buried at the ancient city of Assur, also beneath the palace, but the royal women of Nimrud were buried at home and the recent discovery in the North-West Palace of several of their unrobbed tombs has made headlines worldwide.

It was Mallowan who in 1951 found the first of the Assyrian tombs in the

North-West Palace. These however were relatively poorly furnished and the graves themselves appeared simply to have been inserted beneath the floor (room DD). Certainly it did not occur to him at the time that there were more to be found. His interests then lay largely in the wells, discussed below, from which exciting collections of objects were being recovered. The first burial found in room DD consisted of a terracotta bath-shaped coffin sunk five feet beneath the floor in the north-east corner of the room. A second, similar grave was found at the opposite end of the room, containing a well-preserved bronze bowl.[2] The position of the first burial seems to have been marked by small brick boxes, now empty, but which may have held votive offerings. The coffin was sealed by three large stone slabs, the two end ones of inscribed alabaster which proved to be re-used foundation tablets recording the building of the wall of Kalhu. Similar sets of stone tablets were found in Fort Shalmaneser, where they had been transported by Esarhaddon (681-669 BC) when he repaired the town gates (p. 165), suggesting a possible date for the room DD burial which in any case was stratigraphically no earlier than the late 8th century. The coffin contained the skeleton of a woman, her grave goods consisting of a necklace of semi-precious stone and glass beads, together with a pendant on a gold chain attached to a bronze fibula which had fastened a garment or perhaps a shroud at the shoulder (although in the tomb it lay across her wrist). This is the so-called 'Nimrud jewel', an engraved chalcedony seal set in gold and attached by links on a swivel to its gold chain.[3] A virtually identical 'jewel' was found in one of the wealthier tombs discussed below. In the adjacent room FF another bath-shaped coffin was discovered, against the north wall, perhaps a later insertion; the only recorded object was a bronze fibula.

An intriguing discovery in the adjacent room HH consisted of a large group of trinkets, a few strips of gold foil, and many beads and colourful shells sealed into a cupboard in the east wall, presumably by the occupant of the room.[4] The collection was deliberately hidden. Indeed, the cupboard itself, originally a ventilation shaft, had been masked with brickwork and plastered over. Mallowan suggests that this assortment of objects was 'a mixed bag of oddments such as I have watched fortune tellers using when they prognosticate childbirth before enquiring women outside the gates of Aleppo.'[5] Among these 'trinkets' were four ivory disc beads, one engraved with a palmette design, another with a stellar or radial sun pattern, of possible astrological significance. Three large shell beads bore engraved scorpions, a symbol of fertility also common on the seals of this period (Fig. 132, p. 220). It is relevant to the interpretation of the plan of this area that room HH with its adjacent bathroom (JJ), like rooms AK, TT, and perhaps MM, constituted residential suites of the type designed for persons of high status.

Tomb I

Mallowan excavated a number of rooms on the eastern side of the so-called harem court AJ, including room MM. The latter hardly merits mention in his final report, despite the fact that the same type of brick box was found here that marked the graves in DD. And indeed it was here that the first of the purpose-built burial chambers was later found. This remarkable discovery was made in 1988, during the extensive and very successful programme of excavation and restoration being carried out by the Iraqi Office of Antiquities and Heritage, at that time under the chairmanship of Dr. Mu'ayad Said Damerji. The Director of the excavations at Nimrud was Sayid Muzahim Mahmud Hussein.[6] In the course of clearing out the room it was noticed that the floor was uneven and that here the original bricks had been replaced. Further investigation revealed the crown of a vault beneath the floor. This proved to be part of a barrel-vaulted main room (Fig. 45) with an adjacent entrance chamber reached by means of a deep vertical shaft with a steep stair at its foot. Investigation of the tomb revealed remarkable wealth. On the lower steps stood alabaster and pottery vessels and at the west wall of the main chamber was a well-preserved terracotta sarcophagus (1.85 x 0.65 x 0.67 m high), its lid sealed with bitumen, containing the body of a woman lying on her back with a silver bowl beneath her skull; her age of death is estimated at approximately 50-55 years.[7] The unexpected and extraordinary grave goods included gold earrings of exquisite workmanship (Pl. 5); very large numbers of beads of gold and semi-precious stones from several necklaces; gold fibulae with Pazuzu, female, fish and eagle decoration;[8] armlets; rings (there were five on her left forefinger alone) and other jewellery including an even finer example of the 'Nimrud jewel' type of pendant (mentioned above). In addition to the objects of gold and precious stone there were also vessels of copper and bronze, and two frit (?faience) plaques with erotic scenes. In the antechamber was found a

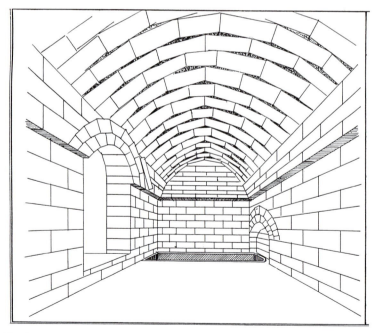

Fig. 45. Elevation of burial chamber, Tomb I (surveyed and drawn by Muzahim Mahmud Hussein).

second terracotta sarcophagus, but only the skeleton was found here, a female approximately 45-55 years old at the time of death.[9]

Tomb II
The discovery of the rich tomb beneath room MM received much publicity. At the same time, alerted to the possibility of further discoveries of this type, the Iraqi archaeologists began more closely to examine for evidence of disturbance the floors uncovered during their restoration programme. In April 1989 a second vault was identified beneath room 49, not far to the west of room MM but in a previously unexcavated part of the palace. This second tomb was also constructed of baked bricks with a barrel-vaulted roof but, unlike the first chamber which was filled with earth that had seeped through the top of the vault, the room 49 tomb chamber was empty of earth and completely dry. Like the first, this second tomb consisted of a main chamber and an antechamber reached by a vertical shaft with steps at the bottom, in this case on a direct line with the sarcophagus, but here the main chamber was roofed with a north-south vault while that of the ante-chamber ran east-west, at right angles to the main chamber (Fig. 46). As in all the tombs, the low entrance to the tomb

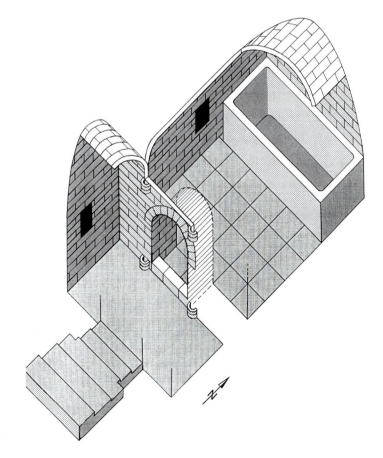

Fig. 46. Axonometric drawing of Tomb II (after Muzahim Mahmud Hussein , see also Damerji 1999, fig. 16).

chamber itself was closed with double stone doors which pivoted within stone rings, in this case secured with an iron bar. One of the most interesting features of the tomb was the presence of a vertical terracotta pipe, resting on the brick vault directly above the sarcophagus. This pipe had in fact served as the first indication of the tomb below, and almost certainly represents an unusual survival of the conduit through which the *kispu* offerings were made to the dead queen.[10] The pipe itself was concealed beneath the baked brick pavement of the floor of the room above.

On the floor of the antechamber was a large pottery vessel and an unusual bronze lamp;[11] similar types were found in tomb IV (Fig. 48). A stone funerary tablet had been placed in an alcove in the west wall, providing the first historical information pertaining to the Nimrud tombs and including the name of the tomb's occupant, a discovery of the greatest historical importance. The inscription reads:

> By the command of Shamash [the sun god and judge of the dead], Ereshkigal [queen of the Netherworld], and the Anunnaki, the great gods of the Netherworld, mortal destiny caught up with Queen Yaba in death, and she travelled the path of her ancestors. Whoever, in time to come, whether a queen who sits on the throne or a lady of the palace who is a favourite (concubine) of the king, removes me from my tomb, or places anyone else with me, or lays hands on my jewellery with evil intent, or breaks open the seal of this tomb, let his spirit wander in thirst in the open countryside. Below, in the Netherworld let him not receive with the Anunnakku, any libation of pure water, beer, wine or flour as a *takallu*-offering! May Ningišzida [the chamberlain of the Netherworld] and Pituh-idugallu [the doorkeeper of the underworld],[12] great gods of the Underworld, impose on his corpse and spirit restlessness for all eternity.[13]

In the tomb chamber itself the sarcophagus, made of a single massive block of stone, rested on the mud floor occupying the full width of the north end of the room. On the brick floor south of the sarcophagus lay more pottery, gold and bronze vessels, and an electrum cosmetics box with an electrum mirror as lid.[14] Both were inscribed. In the alcoves on the east and west walls were beautifully carved alabaster vases,[15] both of which contained burnt human bones and organic material, suggesting that they represent cremation burials (Pl. 2b). Surprisingly, in the sarcophagus itself were two skeletons. Found with them were truly spectacular grave goods. Indeed the objects found in the sarcophagus alone, a total of 157, made this tomb one of the most remarkable ever found in the Near East. Among these were a gold crown, a gold mesh diadem with a tasselled gold fringe and 'tiger-eye' agate rosettes, 79 gold earrings, 6 gold necklaces, 30 finger rings, 14 armlets, 4 gold anklets, 15 gold vessels, gold chain, etc. Among the most beautiful objects recovered were a group of rock crystal vessels (Pl. 8a). Of the gold anklets (Pl. 6b), one weighed almost a kilo, another over 1100 g, while the multi-coloured glass and stone inlay on some of the gold armlets was of a level of craftsmanship not previously attested (Pl. 6a). There was also a very large number of necklaces, perhaps as many as 90, of semi-precious stones. Interestingly, similar jewellery can be seen worn by the women portrayed in the many ivories found at the site, especially the ivory ladies of the Burnt Palace; compare, for example, the diadem Pl. 4b with that depicted on the ivory head illustrated on p. 128.

It was clear that a mass of delicate but badly decayed fabrics had been present, clothing or shrouding the bodies, or perhaps piled up over them. These were delicate, finely executed fabrics, 'befitting a royal burial'.[16] Low percentages of nitrogen and sulphur and a high cellulose content excluded the presence of any quantity of animal fibres such as silk or wool and confirmed the vegetable origin of the fabrics that were examined, that is, they were made of linen.[17] Small fragments of well-preserved material included embroidered linen and beautifully embroidered, small, attached tassels. Among the bones lay some 700 tiny gold rosettes, stars, circles and triangles which had been sewn onto these garments; these also included a large number of banded agate studs with borders of gold granules. Gold and carnelian beads lay in the folds of one layer of clothing, possibly also originally sewn onto the garment.

The two bodies lay one above the other. One of the most splendid objects lay on them, visible in the published photographs. This was a copper or bronze mirror with an extraordinarily beautiful and superbly crafted palmette handle made of ivory, gold, carnelian and other semi-precious stones. One of the gold bowls lay on the chest of the upper body; in it were 11 tiny gold flasks with, beside them, a larger flask on a chain.[18] The bowl bore an inscription around it, with an incised scorpion separating the beginning and the end, which tells us that it was the property of 'Atalia, queen of Sargon, king of Assyria' (Pl. 8b). Here now were two candidates for the two skeletons, but the interpretation of the tomb is further complicated by the presence in the sarcophagus of a gold bowl and the electrum cosmetics container, mentioned above, bearing the name 'Banitu, queen of Shalmaneser V' (726–722 BC). Fortunately, two of the gold bowls also identified the otherwise unknown Yaba, of the stone tablet and presumably the first occupant of the tomb, as the wife of Tiglath-Pileser III (744–727 BC), builder of the Central Palace (p. 73). Here therefore were treasures belonging to three different queens, all of whom were wives of kings of the second half of the eighth century BC. The question now became which two of these royal ladies were represented by the skeletons in the tomb.

Further evidence comes from the skeletons themselves, which have been identified as having died at approximately the same age, 30-35, at most 39, years.[19] However, and quite extraordinarily, on the basis of the condition of the bones it has been established that one burial followed the other after a gap of at least 20, perhaps as many as 50, years. Particularly notable is the fact that the body representing the later death had been exposed for several hours to a temperature of 150-250° C. This seems to represent some attempt at body preservation, and suggests that the younger of the two women may have died elsewhere and was then brought back to Kalhu for burial. The fact that the two bodies are in the same sarcophagus – despite the explicit prohibition in Queen Yaba's curse tablet – might also suggest that they are mother and daughter, or at least in some other way closely related. Also, that the circumstances of the second burial were in some way hasty or surreptitious, perhaps in some way associated with the inauspicious death of her husband. As far as the identification of the two ladies is concerned, the most logical explanation would seem to be that the first burial represents Yaba, for whom the funerary tablet was deposited; the second burial must then be Atalia, the wife of Sargon, who inherited or otherwise acquired property belonging to her predecessor Banitu. This conclusion, based simply on the logic of the written information, is supported by the position of the gold bowl belonging to Atalia actually on the chest of the upper of the two bodies. Among the other grave goods was a beautiful rock crystal bowl also inscribed with the name of Atalia, together with the electrum mirror bearing her name, which seems to have been converted from the cover for Banitu's cosmetics container,[20] another indication that Banitu's valuables had been acquired by Atalia. Interestingly, both Atalia's gold bowl and her mirror bear engravings of a scorpion, a symbol of fertility and one very closely associated with the women of the households of Sargon and his descendants. It is also found on three of the shell objects in the 'treasure cupboard' in room HH, discussed above (see also p. 62). Other heirlooms were also found in the tomb, including a carnelian bead inscribed with the name of a much earlier king of Babylon, Kurigalzu, presumably acquired as loot from Babylonia. The total weight of gold in the tomb was 14 kg.

One further comment should be made about these royal ladies. The names of two of them may be West Semitic, that is, they were of western, possibly of Syrian, origin, almost certainly a reflection of the widespread custom of diplomatic marriage, a tactic not unknown in more recent politics. Banitu is a good Assyrian name, but Atalia is certainly West Semitic and Yaba possibly also. A western connection is perhaps not surprising since for essentially economic reasons the Aramaean states of Syria had long been of interest to the Assyrian kings, and it was during the reign of Tiglath-Pileser that a number of vassal states beyond the Euphrates were taken over as directly-ruled provinces, that is, during the lifetime of the royal ladies represented in this tomb. Some of the Nimrud letters, discussed in chapter 6, reflect this situation.

Tomb III

The third tomb was found in August 1989, a vaulted crypt beneath the floor of room 57, immediately to the south of room 49 (Fig. 47). As in the other purpose-built tombs, access to the antechamber was by means of a shaft and a steep stair. But here the main chamber had been broken into in antiquity through a hole in the vault, which also provided access for the modern archaeologists. The tomb chamber was virtually empty except for the sarcophagus itself and the earth which had seeped in through the hole in the vault. The sarcophagus, set in the vault floor, measured some 2.38 and 1.32 and 1.25 m and, like that in the adjacent tomb, was of a size and weight that indicated its installation before the construction not only of the vault but also of the overlying room. It was covered with a heavy stone lid. Two large stone loops on the top would have allowed the attachment of ropes to let down the lid; stone knobs at either end fastened it, an Egyptian method of securing a box, and allowed the coffin to be sealed. The sarcophagus contained only a few bone fragments and a stone bead. Surviving in the tomb chamber, however, were a number of glazed *sikkatu*, large round-headed 'wall nails', commonly found in formal buildings of Late Assyrian date and here still in situ in the walls of the tomb at the level of the coffin lid.[21] Except for the fact that they obviously formed some type of wall ornament their function remains unclear, but it has been suggested that those in the tomb chamber may have held a cloth or canopy over the top of the sarcophagus.

Fig. 47. Elevation of Tomb III (surveyed and drawn by Muzahim Mahmud Hussein).

Most important was the 5-line inscription, carved lengthwise on the lid. It read:

Belonging to Mullissu-mukannišat-Ninua, queen of Assurnasirpal (II), king of Assyria, and (mother of) Shalmaneser (III), king of Assyria. No one later may place here (anyone else), whether a palace lady or a queen, nor remove this sarcophagus from its place. Whoever removes this sarcophagus from its place, his spirit will not receive the *kispu* (funerary)-offerings with the other spirits. It is the taboo of Šamaš and Ereškigal! Daughter of Aššur-nirka-da"ini, chief cup-bearer (*rab šaqe*) of Assurnasirpal, king of Assyria.[22]

Here then was the tomb of the wife of the king responsible for the refounding of Nimrud as the Assyrian capital and indeed the construction of the grand palace in which she was buried. Unfortunately, despite the curses in the inscription (and note again the prohibition of secondary burial), the grave had been robbed in the distant past, possibly not long after the queen's interment. Its modern excavators believe that this must have taken place surreptitiously, in poor light, and in a great hurry, since valuable objects were missed, especially on the floor of the antechamber. The door

85

between the two chambers was closed again, blocked with bricks and replastered, this action serving to conceal the overlooked objects, which included the gold base of an unusual type of frit beaker.[23] .

As in tomb II, the entrance to the tomb chamber was closed by a double stone door which had been blocked and could be opened only from the antechamber (Pl. 3a), forcing the Iraqi archaeologists to move to the entrance shaft to gain access to it. On removing the brick blocking of the stone doors the latter were found to bear an inscription very similar to but longer than that on the coffin, confirming the preparation of this tomb for the wife of Assurnasirpal II. The antechamber was found to contain another spectacular collection of royal treasure, surpassing even that of tomb II. The greatest surprise was the presence on the floor of two bronze coffins, standing next to each other, lengthwise in the room, and set against the blocked doors. A third coffin of the same type lay beneath the one on the east, and it was here that the mass of treasure was found (visible in Pl. 3a).

The bones of at least 13 individuals were recovered from the bronze coffins, all representing secondary deposition. Pottery, large bones and a round glass bottle lay outside sarcophagus 3, the one on the left of the door, that is, to the west. Of particular interest was an opaque turquoise bottle, inset with small squares of cobalt blue glass decorated with white rosettes. Around the stopper were rosettes and two figures in glass, while the stopper itself seems to have consisted of another figure enclosing an iron peg.[24] Coffin 1, the upper one on the eastern side of the antechamber, contained the bones of a 20- to 29-year-old woman together with a foetus and four children aged between 3 months and 11 years. The underlying coffin 2 yielded a breathtaking abundance of gold vessels and jewellery. These include the spouted ewer (Pl. 3b); a crown of extraordinarily delicate workmanship (Pl. 4a); the usual gold plates and jewellery, some inscribed; two cylinder seals, one carnelian, the other lapis lazuli, both with gold caps; and a second frit beaker with a gold base like that by the door. Traces of clothing included small, beautifully-made tassels like those in tomb II. The total number of objects in the tomb consisted of 449 separate items, the gold and silver alone weighing some 23 kg.

Among the inscribed objects are the seal of a eunuch courtier said to be of the time of Adad-nerari III (810–783 BC),[25] a gold bowl belonging to one Šamši-ilu, who was *turtanu* (commander-in-chief) under Shalmaneser IV, Assur-dan III and Assur-nerari V, covering the years 782–745 BC (and possibly under Adad-nerari as well), and a silver vessel with an inscription in hieroglyphic Hittite (p. 244). The most recent inscribed object in the tomb is a 15 mina duck weight of the time of Tiglath-Pileser III (744–727). In other words, the period of time covered by the grave goods themselves would appear to pre-date the ladies of Tomb II, but significantly post-date the time of the wife of Assurnasirpal. It is not clear from the available reports whether all the inscribed objects come from coffin 2, but some seem to have been found in coffin 3 as well. The coffins themselves are made of rivetted sheets of bronze and are a late 8th century type, rounded at one end and squared-off at the other, with double handles at both ends; they are surprisingly small, only 1.3 m in length.[26]

Bronze coffin 2 contained the almost completely preserved skeleton of a

Plate 1. a) View of the citadel mound and ziggurrat from the north.
b) The 1953 excavations in the area of the Town Wall houses, with the ziggurrat and Tigris Valley in the background. The photographer is Barbara Parker; Agatha Christie is at the left of the picture.

Plate 2. a) View looking south from the ziggurrat towards the North-West Palace; the excavation camp can be seen in the background, with Jebel Makhmur on the horizon.
b) The main chamber of Tomb II, with side of stone sarcophagus visible on the right, bronze and pottery vessels on the floor and an alabaster jar with petalled ornament, containing a cremation burial, in the west wall niche.

*Plate 3. a) The antechamber of Tomb III,
showing the double stone doors and its pitched
brick vault; the bronze coffin is burial no. 2,
the lower of the two coffins on the east side.
b) The gold ewer from Tomb III (IM 115618,
ht. 13 cm).*

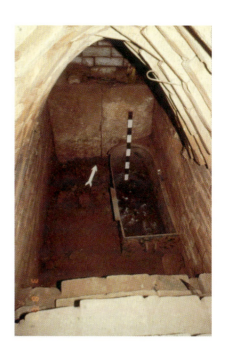

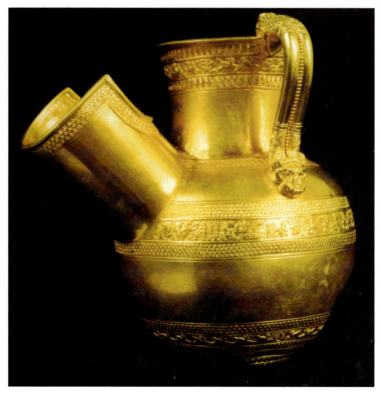

Plate 4. *a) The gold crown, which lay on the child's head in coffin 2, Tomb III; of exquisite workmanship, including fine granulation, the top consisting of a delicate pattern of vine leaves and bunches of blue grapes (IM 115598).*
b) Diadem of gold ribbon, 4 cm wide; the streamer measures 40 cm in length, inlaid with 'tiger-eye' agates. Found by the heads of the two women in the sarcophagus of Tomb II (IM 105696).

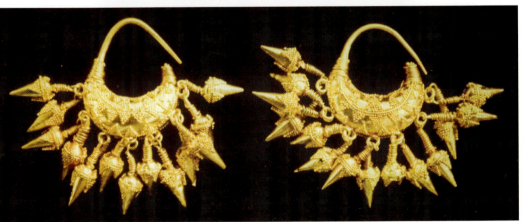

*Plate 5. Gold earrings from Tomb I, with delicate granulation (length of larger example,
over 6 cm; width of smaller type, c. 5.5 cm). At least four examples of the smaller type were
recovered (IM 108979, 108974).*

Plate 6. a) Gold armlets from Tomb II, inlaid with semi-precious stones and (?) glass (IM 105708, 105705).
b) Gold anklets, the larger example weighing over a kilo, from Tomb II (IM 105710, 115551).

Plate 7. a) Gold necklace, one of a number found in Tomb II (IM 105716).
b) Details from gold plate engraved with hunting scene depicting boats in a papyrus thicket;
in the centre is a crocodile with other animals. Phoenician style, Tomb II, inscribed with the
name of Yaba, wife of Tiglath-pileser III (d 17.7 cm, inside depth 3 cm; IM 105697).

Plate 8. a) Rock crystal vessels from Tomb II; the vessel on the upper right is inscribed with the name of Sargon's queen, Atalia, rim d 10 cm; the lower objects are a pomegranate and an elaborate spoon (IM 105930, 124999, 105921, 105917).

b) Gold bowls from Tomb II, inscribed with the names of Atalia together with a scorpion (rim d 20.4 cm, IM 105695), Yaba, wife of Tiglath-pileser III (rim d 20 cm, IM 105694), and Banitu, wife of Shalmaneser V (rim d 11 cm, IM 105698); the fourth bowl is IM 115548.

Plate 9. Ivory bowl from well AJ in the queen's residence, North-West Palace; probably the 'stopper' of a large ivory container such as Pl. 11b; two square perforations at the flat end lead into the lions' mouths, which 'pour' into the bowl. The rich brown colour is probably an effect of the well sludge; see also p. 102 (length 16.3 cm, IM 79511).

Plate 10. a) Bottom of elaborately carved ivory container from well AJ (for upper surface, see pp. 100, also 101) (length 24 cm; IM 79501).
 b) Detail of side of same container.

Plate 11. a) Three ivory plaques in champlevé style from SW 37, Fort Shalmaneser; all show traces of original glass inlay. The first shows a male figure attacking a griffin (ND 10449, ht. 5.1 cm, Iraq Museum); the second, a male figure and rampant lion (ND 10450, ht. 5.7 cm, British Museum, BM 132940); the third, a winged male holding papyrus flowers below a frieze of lilies (ND 10451, ht. 5.3 cm, Iraq Museum).
b) Large flask made from ivory tusk in four, possibly, five parts, decorated with four relief friezes depicting lions fighting griffins and grazing bulls; traces of gold leaf and paste or glass inlay survive. The large container is closed by a wooden piece to which a woman's figure is attached (see p. 96); the latter is hollow with a square perforation at the top, suggesting that a further piece, perhaps a bowl similar to Pl. 9, is missing (from well AJ, total length of convex side, 54 cm; IM 79506).

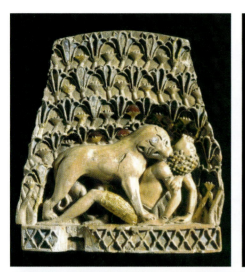

Plate 12. a) Chryselephantine ivory plaque depicting a lioness killing a Nubian in a field of lotus and papyrus plants, rendered in carnelian and lapis lazuli with golden stems and over-laid with gold leaf; the lioness has a lapis disc on her forehead while the Nubian's hair is made of blackened ivory pegs of which the tops had been gilded. From the NN well in the North-West Palace (ht 10.5 cm, ND 2548, now in the British Museum; an identical but better-preserved plaque, ND 2547, is in the Iraq Museum).
b) Glazed wall plaque bearing a text of Assurnasirpal II, from the Temple of Ishtar Kidmuri at Nimrud (width 28 cm, British Museum).
c) Iron brazier with bronze turrets and iron and bronze wheels, from the Italian excavation of storage magazine A2, Fort Shalmaneser (surviving width of brazier c. 80 cm; now in the Iraq Museum).

woman of c. 18-20 years, together with a 6- to 12-year-old child. The gold crown, which in view of its size must have been made for an adult, rested on the child's skull. Unfortunately we cannot identify either occupant. Coffin 3, the one on the west, contained the skeletons of five adults, three men and two women. One of these skeletons is a powerfully-built male who died between the ages of 55 and 65 years. It is very tempting to suggest that he may be Šamši-ilu, the *turtanu* whose gold bowl was found in the tomb. The fact that male skeletons are found with the women of the royal family strongly suggests that they too are either eunuchs (as was Šamši-ilu) or members of the family, or both.

The reasons for the sealing off of Mullissu's robbed tomb and the deposition not only of large quantities of valuable grave goods but also at least 13 bodies in the three bronze coffins in the antechamber remain unknown. All are secondary burials, but the green copper staining on the bones indicates that the original burial of at least some of the bodies had previously been in bronze coffins.[27] It is also impossible to establish whether Mullissu's body was re-interred in the antechamber, and if so, why. It is possible that some of the grave goods come from her tomb, but this seems unlikely. Certainly it is difficult to think of a reason why they should have been removed from one side of the internal door and redeposited on the other, especially since the original tomb was never re-used. It is also difficult to explain the secondary deposition of so many bodies. Epidemics are a favourite explanation for multiple interment, but these are not primary burials. It is possible that this apparently hasty and secret secondary interment may have had some connection with power struggles among the leading families, from whom the royal wives would have come. This might have occurred on a number of occasions in the history of Assyria, for example on the accession of Sargon or early in the 7th century, at the time of the disputed succession on the death of Sennacherib. Another possibility is that this event may in some way be associated with the position of Šamši-ilu (p. 19), but his burial too, if such it was, was secondary. Unfortunately we lack both the textual and the archaeological evidence to understand the rules and practices behind such burials, beyond the fact that these would seem to contravene normal practice. In terms of sheer spectacle, however, there has been nothing like this in Mesopotamian archaeology since the discovery of the royal tombs at Ur over 70 years ago.

The palaeopathology of the skeletons is of interest, and suggests a level of ill health surprising for the ruling class from which these skeletons obviously came.[28] Unfortunately we have no comparative material from the lower classes among the population of Nimrud. Within the tombs six of seven adults examined showed some signs of degenerative joint disease; only the 'child queen' in Tomb III, coffin 2, had healthy joints. Out of eight skeletons, four adults and one child showed characteristics indicating deficiency or persistent diseases in infancy. These included Queen Atalia (Tomb II) and the older female, probably also a queen, in Tomb III, coffin 2. It would seem also that the ladies of the palace ate extremely soft food, suffered severely from colds (perhaps not surprising in the cold, damp winters of Northern Mesopotamia) and were unaccustomed to exercise.

Room 57 provided other evidence both of interest in itself and of relevance to

Fig. 48. Bronze 'saucer lamp' from Tomb IV.

the dating of tomb III. This was a large group of cuneiform tablets, predominantly of an administrative nature. An older group of the time of Adad-nerari III included tablets belonging to a palace scribe; a younger group of the time of Tiglath-pileser III included tablets of the *masennu*[29] of the king, the 'treasurer' or 'steward of the royal household'. Both are officials of high standing, and the presence here of what was apparently their 'office' within the domestic part of the palace suggests that they too were either eunuchs or members of the royal family – certainly they were highly trusted officials. This evidence suggests that the tomb of Mullissu must have been emptied before or early in the reign of Adad-nerari III, and that the re-interments must have occurred later than the time of Tiglath-pileser III; the latter is of course suggested also by the inscriptions accompanying the burials. The fact that this room, overlying what must have been a purpose-built tomb, was used as an office in the 8th century seems strange to us; at the same time we lack evidence to explain why the wife of the builder of the palace should have been removed from her tomb.

Tomb IV

Yet another tomb, found in 1990 beneath a room south of courtyard 56 proved to have been robbed, containing neither a body nor especially valuable grave goods. The entrance was from room 72, leading down the narrow passage west of the tomb chamber; a pile of loose bricks blocked the entrance to the vaulted burial chamber, which was square in plan, with two niches in each of two walls containing bronze lamps (Fig. 48), small alabaster vessels and beautifully-preserved glazed pottery. The sarcophagus itself was of terracotta, decorated with shallow niches and horizontal bands; it was covered with four terracotta slabs (Fig. 49). In it were only a few amulets and stamp seals with gold surrounds together with the remains of a white textile. Two further burials were found, including a terracotta sarcophagus under the

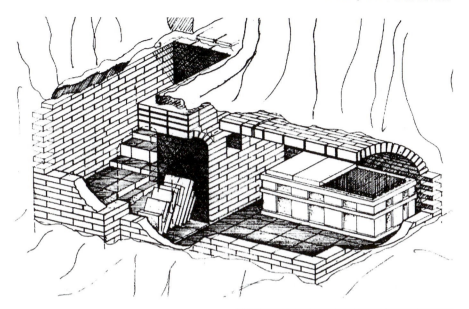

floor of Room 64b, in a cavity in the northern wall, and a second under the floor of room 69. The former contained human bones and pottery. The sarcophagus found beneath room 69 was decorated with geometrical motifs and six flat knobs, possibly used as handles; inside were human bones and a small number of funerary objects.

There can be little doubt of the importance of the recently discovered Nimrud tombs. It seems little known, however, that a very similar tomb, now to be seen reconstructed in the garden of the Mosul Museum, was found some 20 years ago near the village of Humaidat, close to the west bank of the Tigris some 16 km north-west of Nineveh and 2.5 km from the ancient and modern highway from Nineveh/Mosul to Nusaybin.[30] No other tombs or associated buildings are reported, but the excavation, carried out by Dr Jabr Khalil Ibrahim and Sd. Abdullah Amin Agha, was limited to the structure of the tomb itself, which seems to have been a slightly larger version of

Fig. 49. Isometric reconstruction of Tomb IV (surveyed and drawn by Muzahim Mahmud Hussein); the photograph shows the outer steps and the tomb entrance (to the left) which had been blocked with loose bricks piled in the doorway.

89

those found at Nimrud. It contained a large stone sarcophagus with a terracotta lid, in which were the bones of several individuals, and a small terracotta coffin with a child's skeleton; no gold was found, but the grave goods included an intricately decorated shallow bronze bowl, and a number of other bronze and pottery vessels, very similar to examples from Nimrud. The tomb would appear to have been a family vault, conceivably belonging to an important official or possibly a member of the royal family, who might well have had a country residence on his estates overlooking the Tigris valley not far from Nineveh. Generally similar tombs are also known at Assur, but these had been robbed of their grave goods long ago.

PALACE WELLS AND THEIR CONTENTS

It is not only the tombs of the domestic quarter of the North-West Palace that have produced exciting discoveries. The wells within this area have also yielded fascinating and unusually well-preserved objects, many made of ivory. During the 1951

Fig. 50. Ivory head from well NN; cut from a big tusk, the nose separately doweled by means of a copper peg (ht 18.8 cm, Metropolitan Museum of Art).

Fig. 51. Ivory mask-like head from NN well, known as the 'Mona Lisa'; cut from an unusually large tusk. The hair, eyebrows, and the iris and eyelids were stained black; the nose has been restored by Sd Akram Shukri (Iraq Museum) (ht 16 cm, ND 2250).

season, at the southern end of room NN in the south-eastern part of the domestic quarters, Mallowan identified a vast stone tank beside which was a well, the head of which stood about a metre above the floor of the room (visible in the background of Fig. 36, p. 64). It was well built, and the baked bricks, as is true of well bricks generally, were wedge-shaped in order to facilitate the curved construction, in this case some 80 cm thick; many of the bricks in the upper part of the well were inscribed with the name of Assurnasirpal II. The internal diameter of the well was 1.7 metres, which allowed two workmen to be winched up and down, but the rising water table which accompanied the spring floods in 1951, together with the excavation's lack of pumps, forced the abandonment of the investigations at a depth of about 18 m (245 courses below the well-head). However, in 1952, with a heavier tripod and winch, excavation of the well was again attempted. This time the rising water was bailed out by hand, and Mallowan instigated an extraordinary system whereby work began at

91

midnight, by the light of hurricane lamps, in order to empty the well of water. Thereafter, from dawn until sunset, for each oil drum of well sludge removed 40 gallons of water had to be drawn out. By this laborious method the sludge in the well was eventually removed, and the bottom of the brickwork was reached at a depth of 331 courses or 25.4 m (83 feet 4 inches). The well continued further into the bedrock, and another 1.3 m was excavated before a steel pulley snapped, crashing to the bottom just after the well excavator had been brought to the surface at the end of his shift. Work here was then abandoned, the water rising again to a depth of some 5 metres the very same day.

A great variety of objects was recovered from the lower deposits, including 70 water jars, some still tightly bound with frayed rope, fragments of ancient wooden derricks and at least three pulley wheels made of mulberry wood. Also in the deeper levels were many ornaments of ivory and shell (e.g. Fig. 154, p. 243), including some of the finest ivories recovered at Nimrud.[31] Among the horse-trappings were a splendid pair of ivory cheek-pieces and an electrum bit in the shape of a galloping horse.[32] Perhaps the best-known ivories from this splendid treasure are two female 'masks', the so-called Mona Lisa, an unusually large carved head (16 cm in height), coloured a rich brown, possibly by its sojourn in the well, and with black-stained hair and eyebrows (Fig. 51), and the 'Ugly Sister', to our eyes a more interesting piece (Fig. 50), together with two extraordinary chryselephantine plaques, depicting a lioness savaging a negroid figure against a brilliant background of lilies and papyrus flowers inlaid with lapis and carnelian and overlaid with gold (Pl. 12a).

A second well was discovered in 1952 in the corner of courtyard AJ, paved with baked bricks of Shalmaneser III and often referred to as the Harem Courtyard, almost certainly the courtyard which provided access to the queen's residence. Here the great well capstone was still in place, though badly broken (Fig. 53). The AJ well seems to have remained in use for a considerable time after the collapse of the Assyrian Empire, the well head at some later period having been encased in a heavy mud-brick surround and elevated by some two metres. In 1952 the well was found partially empty, presumably owing to the survival of the capstone, but the brick lining proved to be seriously worn, an observation which led, for reasons of safety, to the immediate abandonment of any thought of further excavation here. In 1975, however, the sides of the well were reinforced and its excavation completed by an Iraqi archaeological team under the direction of Sd Myesser Said al-Iraqi, bedrock being reached at a depth of some 26 m from the courtyard pavement. The riches contained within it were even greater than those found by Mallowan in the NN well,[33] almost certainly a reflection of the association of this courtyard with the queen's private apartment. The discoveries within the well included a truly magnificent group of ivories – *ajouré* plaques, elaborate carved ivory boxes with their lids (Fig. 54), and horse harness of types known elsewhere at Nimrud (Fig. 55), but also unique pieces such as a composite ivory statue of a eunuch (Fig. 56), natural tusks carved in low relief (Pl. 116) with, at the end, the likeness of a woman (Fig. 57), and a remarkable shallow oval dish with its base entirely covered with animal designs, also carved in relief (Pl. 10, Fig. 59). The objects made from the large hollow tusks were in four

*Fig. 52. Hollow pottery
stand in the form of a
woman, well NN (ht 23.7
cm, ND 1265).*

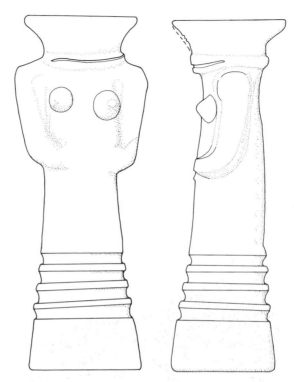

*Fig. 53. Well-head in
court AJ, showing the
steps leading up to it.
In the foreground is the
mud-brick casing which
surrounded the well in
the Hellenistic period,
when the well-head was
raised by some two
metres.*

Fig. 54. Ivory pyxis from well AJ. On the lid are four recumbent calves; the sides are deco-rated with three separate scenes in high relief. Of particular interest is the 'banquet scene' (see also p. 235). The decoration on the base consists of engraved rosettes and guilloche patterns. The box was overlaid with gold leaf, of which some survives, for example on the woman with the flywhisk. Its shape is oval (tusk-shape) (14 x 12.7 x 6.5 cm; IM 79513).

pieces, with the end and the main sections closed with a carved plug. An ivory lion's head cup was also attached to the top of the woman's head (missing in Fig. 57).[34] The purpose of these unique objects remains uncertain, although they must have con-tained some oil or other liquid. Also unique is the extraordinary limestone 'spoon' recovered here (Fig. 61). This is made of separate parts of limestone, onyx and ivory, with 'paste' inlay. A small wooden figure bearing an inscription of Assurnasirpal is also reported to have been found here.[35] Of particular interest in the context of the history of the site was a piece of horse harness that physically joined another from the well in room NN, 3 rooms and some 40 m away, an unequivocal indication of the random looting that was carried out in 612 BC, and which led to the discarding of these ivories, stripped of their gold, in the various palace wells and elsewhere in the building.[36] Well-preserved lengths of rope and bitumen-coated baskets were also recovered from this well, owing their survival to the excellent preservative condi-tions of the water-logged mud.

The third well excavated by Mallowan was situated in room AB, and had been

Fig. 55. Seven ivory 'cheekpieces' or 'blinders', decorated with the figure of a griffin treading on a fallen individual (?ruler) of Asiatic origin, were recovered from well AJ (this example is IM 79569, length 17 cm).

Fig. 56. This remarkable ivory head, found in well AJ, is part of a composite statue of a eunuch (total ht 53 cm). The head measures 18.2 cm in width; the feet (not illustrated here) are 11 cm in length (ND-7 IM 79520).

95

Fig. 57. This extraordinary 'flask' was made in five segments, of which one is missing. The largest, carved from a single tusk, is ornamented with gold inlay and four friezes carved in high relief, the latter depicting various scenes involving lions, griffins and bulls. The attachment at the small end of the tusk was carved separately, ending in a woman's head, the uppermost piece of which, probably a smaller version of the lion bowl (Pl. 9), is missing. The surviving end piece was attached to the larger 'horn' by means of a wooden disc, now badly worn. An ivory lid (9.5 x 7.5 cm) closed the large end of the tusk. Although this object superficially resembles a drinking horn, the connection between the two containers was blocked by the intervening piece of wood, suggesting perhaps its use for some valuable oil or perfume. The length of the container portion is 38 cm on the convex side of the tusk. (see also Pl. 11b; IM 79506, 79508-10).

first discovered by Layard in 1849. Within the room, possibly a small courtyard, Layard had found the most extraordinary collection of objects. Indeed, room AB came to be known as the 'Room of the Bronzes'. Among the objects piled up here were a throne and footstool with legs partly of ivory, and a remarkable collection of elaborately embossed and engraved bronze bowls of which some 150 were said to have been brought back to the British Museum. These had been piled up behind a number of enormous cauldrons, almost a metre in diameter. Two of these contained further bronze objects, which appeared to have been the remnants of horse harness and chariot decoration. These included a collection of 80 small bells with iron clappers, copper horse harness ornaments, several hundred studs and buttons in mother of pearl and ivory, and small metal rosettes. Two other cauldrons contained further vessels and bronze furniture mouldings. The rest were empty except for one containing only ashes and bones. In association with the cauldrons were found the badly rusted remains of at least 16 iron tripod stands supported by bronze bulls' hooves or lions' paws. Behind the cauldrons and around the bowls 'were heaped arms, remains of armour, iron instruments, glass bowls and objects in ivory and bronze'.[37] Among the weapons were swords, daggers, spears, shields and arrowheads. Several complete elephant tusks were found here as was an oval piece of rock crystal (4.2 x 3.45 x 0.64 cm), with one flat and one convex surface, originally identified as a magnifying lens but perhaps more likely to have been a piece of inlay. It would seem that this remarkable treasure, some of Assyrian manufacture and some presumably loot from military campaigns, had simply been stacked up and stored in room AB, where Layard found it. Other similar stores of valuable objects in the North-West Palace had contained objects inscribed with the name of Sargon, and it has often been assumed that the 'Room of the Bronzes' objects also date from approximately that time, but there is no direct evidence for their date.

Layard's workmen had emptied the well until they came to brackish water at a depth of some 20 metres. In 1953, after his success with the first well, Mallowan returned to the Layard well, this time with the help of a winch run by a diesel engine, a pump and the services of an Iraq Petroleum Company operator. As in Layard's day, water was reached at just over 20 metres, at which point bedrock conveniently replaced the brick lining. From about 18 metres a sludge deposit reminiscent of that in the first well was encountered. Here was made one of the most challenging and frustrating Nimrud discoveries, its interest far from immediately apparent. This consisted of literally hundreds of small fragments of burnt ivory. The pieces were flat and undecorated except for shallow cross-hatched incisions on the flat surfaces and occasional raised edging. Some fragments also bore the impressions of hinges. These hundreds of broken fragments constituted a jig-saw puzzle of impossible intricacy, since there were no designs to aid reconstruction, only the raised edges of some pieces, but these all looked alike. The fragments were spread out on all the available tables in the dig house (much to the irritation of some members of the dig staff), and it was only the perseverance of Mallowan's wife, Agatha Christie, that produced results. By the end of the season she had demonstrated that the basic component was a rectangular board with hinges and that each individual board measured 33.8 x 15.6 x 1.4 cm. Here, in fact, was what proved eventually to be a set of 16 hinged, ivory writing boards (Fig. 62), which together formed a polyptych, in a sense the earliest form of 'book'.[38] Wooden writing boards, later identified as walnut, were also recovered from the well at Nimrud, together with the ivory examples. Adhering to the hatched surfaces of the wooden boards were occasional traces of a thin yellow substance on which cuneiform signs were still preserved.[39] On analysis this proved to be a combination of beeswax and yellow orpiment, a sulphate of arsenic used to render the wax more fluid and malleable. The presence of repairs to the wooden boards sug-

97

gested that they had been used for some time. Writing boards are mentioned in cuneiform texts of second millennium date, but at the time they were found the Nimrud examples, dated not long before 705 BC, were the earliest that had been recovered. Since then, a diptych of Late Bronze Age date has been recovered from the Ulu Burun shipwreck, south-west of Kaş on the south coast of Turkey.[40] The Ulu Burun boards were considerably smaller than those from Nimrud, and were made of boxwood.

In the well with the writing boards was found the ancient equivalent of a title page. This was a single, flat piece of ivory, the cover to the set of ivory boards. It bore a cuneiform inscription providing both the name of the king who had ordered them and the text with which they were inscribed:

> Palace of Sargon, king of the world, king of Assyria. He caused *Enuma Anu Enlil* to be inscribed on an ivory tablet and set it in his palace at Dur-Šarrukin (Khorsabad).

Enuma Anu Enlil is the opening phrase of a long astrological text which comprised omens taken from celestial observations of the sun, moon, planets and stars. The reading of such astral portents was of particular importance to the life of the king, and Sargon had obviously had this text prepared for his new capital. Indeed we actually know that a copy of the text series *Enuma Anu Enlil* was being made at Kalhu in 707 BC, perhaps this very 'book'.[41] However, it would appear that for some reason, perhaps the king's death in 705 BC, this set of boards was never taken to Khorsabad. Who threw it into the North-West Palace well remains unknown, but it is likely to have been destroyed in 612 BC, together with the other contents of the North-West Palace. It had been deliberately dismantled, the hinge fittings consistently broken. No actual hinges survived, conceivably owing to the use of gold, although there is no direct evidence to suggest this. It is also possible that the boards were fastened together with leather hinges; had this been the case, however, one would have expected at least some of the leather to have survived. Indeed, part of a leather shoe was preserved in the well in room NN. Fragments of other ivory writing boards were subsequently identified in the Burnt Palace, the Nabu Temple (NT 13) and in ZT.

As in the case of the NN well, the AB well excavation nearly ended in disaster. One of our Sharqati workmen, Hassan Abdullah, who had been Andrae's tape boy at Assur in 1913, had volunteered to excavate the well on the grounds that he had clearly enjoyed a long life and was therefore the most expendable member of the expedition. The excavation of the well involved descending literally in a bucket, and send-

Fig. 58. Ivory flask in the shape of a woman with unusually long fingers, holding her breasts. The style is Egyptian, especially the wig. Like the flask at the small end of Fig. 56, the woman's head bore a further ivory attachment, literally plugged into the top of the head, in this case a small bowl surrounded by a lion's head and forelegs (not illustrated here). It is suggested that the flask was filled from the top of the head; clearly the contents were poured into the attached bowl. The bottom of the flask was closed with an ivory disc, to which was attached a wooden disc, its sides wrapped in leather or cloth (ht of flask 28–31 cm, ND-7 IM 79505).

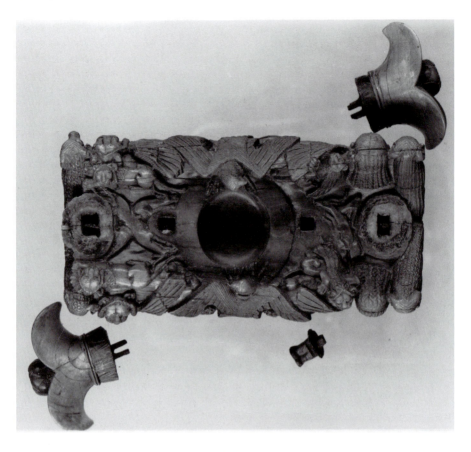

ing up the well sludge, which contained the objects, in a second bucket, with two workmen operating the pulley at the top. A pre-arranged signal of two short pulls was to indicate danger, and a quick ascent, please; fortunately the workmen on the pulley were fully focused when the signal came, and the old man rose to the surface just as the sides of the well below crashed in. Thus he lived to visit us at Tell al Rimah over twenty years later. However, the incident served to discourage any further well excavation in the 1950s.

WELL 4 AND THE 'HAREM TREASURY'

Yet another well was found during the recent Iraqi programme of excavation and restoration under the direction of Sd. Muzahim Mahmud Hussein. The new well is situated in courtyard 80, in the very south-east corner of the domestic wing (Fig. 36, p. 64). It contained more than 130 objects, including 20 seals, a number of interesting ivories, and over 180 manacled bodies, all of relatively young males. A mass of clay covered the mouth of the well, perhaps placed there when the bodies were thrown in. The well itself was 1.7 m in diameter, with 300 courses of brick resting on the rough limestone conglomerate. The upper part of the well was filled with rubbish, ash,

Fig. 59. Large carved ivory container for cosmetics, or perhaps salt (?). A unique piece and one of the most elaborate objects found in the AJ well. The small central bowl of bird's nest type (left; d 5 cm) and the elaboration and density of rich ornament suggest some special, perhaps ritual, use. The photograph of the upper surface includes as separate pieces three of the four objects (flower buds and perhaps a lion's paw) which had been inserted into the square holes. The other photographs show one side and the base of the object (see also Pl. 10; 24 x 11.5 x 9.5 cm, IM 79501).

sherds and the large quantity of human bones. At a depth of 11.8 m the finds became more concentrated, including glazed pottery, objects of gold, semi-precious stones, a complete copper mirror, polished on both sides, with remains of a wooden handle, and other objects in bronze and iron. Of particular interest were 23 small cylindrical ivory containers, described by the excavator as possibly kohl pots; cosmetic pencils were also found in the well, which would have fitted into the small holes bored in the lids of the containers. These were decorated in the incised Assyrian style. Most bore very simple geometric designs; a few, however, were more richly ornamented, with the usual genii or gazelle flanking stylised trees, and in one case a banquet scene. The

101

Fig. 60. The top and base of this bowl can be seen in colour on Pl. 9. Fig. 60 illustrates the side and the front of this extraordinary vessel, which had originally been attached to some other object, perhaps a larger version of the long tusk-like container illustrated in Fig. 57. Certainly the associated flask was much larger than Fig. 57, with which a small version of this type of cup was associated (there are on the flat end of Fig. 60 two rectangular holes for attachment). As in the case of the lion's head on the small cup attached to Fig. 57, these lions' tongues are extended as though they were tasting whatever liquid was involved; in this example it would appear that a small circular hole led from each of the square holes, by which this object was attached, from the liquid source actually through the lions' mouths into the bowl. A number of ivories from the Nimrud wells have acquired a comparable brown colour, but this is one of the finest examples of what may have been a natural staining process in the context of the well sludge (16.3 x 13 x 5 cm; IM 79511).

102

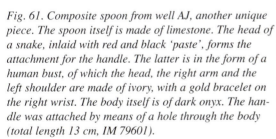

Fig. 61. Composite spoon from well AJ, another unique piece. The spoon itself is made of limestone. The head of a snake, inlaid with red and black 'paste', forms the attachment for the handle. The latter is in the form of a human bust, of which the head, the right arm and the left shoulder are made of ivory, with a gold bracelet on the right wrist. The body itself is of dark onyx. The handle was attached by means of a hole through the body (total length 13 cm, IM 79601).

containers vary in height between 4.7 and 11.3 cm.[42] Among the pottery was a six-cup version of the kernos type found in one of the side chambers of the underground 'treasury' (Fig. 39). Undoubtedly the most interesting of the seals was a cylinder seal made of a bluish-green stone (amazonite?) with gold caps at either end, a gold cross-like ornament at the top, the lower cap bearing the design of a horse.[43]

We have already mentioned that the contents of the well also included at least 180 human skeletons, many of whom were fettered with iron manacles. Their presence seemed at first to support the original interpretation of the vaulted chambers beneath room 74 as a 'prison', but we now think this interpretation unlikely, and that the bodies probably represent Assyrian prisoners executed in 612 BC (pp. 65–68). If

Fig. 62. Three leaves of the set of ivory writing boards found in well AB, reassembled to show the method of folding. The sunken surfaces were originally covered with wax, on which the cuneiform text was inscribed (single panel 33.8 x 15.6 cm; ND 3557).

'prison' were to prove the correct interpretation for these vaulted chambers, it would provide an ironic end to the magnificent palace of one of Assyria's greatest kings, who prays in one of his inscriptions that his palace shall not be dishonoured by being used in this way:

> I founded (in Kalhu) a palace as my royal residence and for my lordly pleasure for eternity … May a later prince repair its weakened portions and restore my inscribed name to its proper place. Then Aššur will listen to his prayers. He shall not forsake my mighty palace, nor abandon it in the face of enemies … He shall not clog the outlets of its rain spouts, nor block its door.
>
> *For his treasure house he shall not appropriate it, nor shall he consign it to be a house of bondage. Men and women who are captives, he shall not confine therein in darkness and solitude.*[44]

CHAPTER 4

TEMPLES, MINOR PALACES AND PRIVATE HOUSES

THE ZIGGURRAT

The Ziggurrat (a staged temple tower) is the most prominent feature of the Nimrud landscape and can be seen from a considerable distance. It stands before the North-West Palace, at the north-west corner of the citadel mound, immediately adjoining the Ninurta Temple on the south and east. Its remains now appear as a pyramid of heavily eroded mud-brick, with a base some 50 metres square, rising some 34 m above the level of the plain (Pl. 1; Fig. 63). It was first and most extensively explored by Layard, who exposed foundation walls of ashlar masonry decorated on the north and west sides with shallow niches and, in the middle of the north face, an engaged

Fig. 63. View of the citadel at Nimrud looking south, with the remains of the ziggurrat in the foreground and showing the line of the old river bed on the west side of the tell. Traces of Layard's 19th century excavations of the temples of Ištar Šarrat-niphi and Ninurta can be seen just to the left of the ziggurrat.

105

column c 5 m wide (Fig. 64).[1] The ashlar walls, which stood originally to a height of 6 m, rested directly on the stone conglomerate of the river bank and were surmounted by crenellations of which pieces were found in the debris against them. They must have presented an imposing façade to the lower city and to river traffic on the Tigris. Similar walls facing the citadel and completing the square are mentioned as undecorated and were probably no more than a shallow footing for the superstructure, the base of which was level with the floors of the Ninurta Temple and the North-West Palace courtyard. This superstructure consisted of a core of mud-brick with a baked brick face set back slightly from the stone revetments below. Some baked bricks bore inscriptions of Shalmaneser III, showing that he completed the construction begun, or at least planned, by his father Assurnasirpal II. At ground level and on the east-west axis of the mud-brick core, Layard found a vaulted mud-brick chamber 30 m long, 1.8 m wide and 3.6 m high. It had been broken into in antiquity, some time after the fall of Kalhu, and was entirely empty. Its function remains unknown. Layard's original suggestion that it was intended as a king's tomb was undoubtedly influenced by Rawlinson's early, and mistaken, belief that Nimrud was in fact Nineveh, the city which, according to classical tradition, was the site of the tomb of Sardanapalus. The chamber may have contained foundation deposits, which would explain its later robbing.

No evidence survives for the proportions of the upper stages of the ziggurrat or the means of access to them, although George Smith in 1873 claimed to have

Fig. 64. The north side of the ziggurrat, showing the large engaged column and the ashlar wall with its shallow niches, as re-exposed in the early 1970s by the Iraqi expedition.

observed traces of a stairway on the south side.[2] The approach must have been from the east or the south and almost certainly gained the first stage by way of an internal stair within the Ninurta Temple precinct, as in the case of other, earlier, ziggurrats in the north, at Tell al Rimah, for example, and in the Anu-Adad temple at Assur. There has been little further investigation of this impressive structure, with the exception of work by the Directorate-General of Antiquities in 1971–72 under the direction of Sd Hazim Abdul-Hamid, who re-exposed part of the stone façade on the north and confirmed the findings of Layard, including the presence of the central engaged column.

TEMPLES IN THE VICINITY OF THE ZIGGURRAT

Assurnasirpal claims to have built (or restored) nine temples at Kalhu. Of these, three have been identified in the north-west corner of the citadel, the most important of which was the temple of Ninurta, a warlike god whose name may have been transformed in the biblical accounts to Nimrod, presumably the source of the modern name of the site (plan, Fig. 65; see also Fig. 2, p. 7). Although the Ninurta Temple abutted the ziggurrat on its south and east sides, their precise relationship remains unknown; however, the ziggurrat too seems to have been dedicated to Ninurta. To the north-east of the Ninurta temple, the northernmost temple was dedicated to Šarrat-niphi (an aspect of Ishtar)[3] and was entered through a door flanked by colossal lion sculptures. In the spring of 2001 excavations were reopened here by Muzahim Mahmud Hussein, to the east of Layard's trenches and north of the modern track. The discovery of a second entrance flanked by lion colossi has been reported.

Both temples were entered through large doorways with massive gate figures, were decorated with both reliefs and painted walls and were distinguished by the lengthy inscriptions installed in them. These inscriptions constituted the king's record of his reign and his justification to the god, those from the Ninurta temple being among the longest Assyrian royal inscriptions known from any reign. In both temples a recess at the end of the sanctuary was paved with a single enormous inscribed alabaster slab. In the case of the Ninurta temple this measured 6.4 by 5 m, and 33 cm thick. The surface alone held 325 lines of text, with a further three columns on the back. As in the case of the palace inscriptions, the stone orthostats were also inscribed on the back, where of course the god could read them without difficulty.

Outside the northern entrance to the Ninurta temple was found a splendid stele depicting Assurnasirpal surmounted by the symbols of the major gods (Fig. 2). This too bore a lengthy inscription (the so-called Great Monolith inscription, some 568 lines of text).[4] A three-footed limestone altar was placed before it. A stele of Shalmaneser III's son, Shamshi-Adad V, must also have stood here, according to the text inscribed on it; it was found by Rassam in the Nabu Temple, to which it must have been moved at some later time (Fig. 8, p. 21). Unfortunately nothing survived of the gold and lapis lazuli ornament or the 'wild ferocious gold dragons by (Ninurta's) throne', of which the Banquet Stele tells us.[5] Even the roof beams were covered with gold, as we learn from a letter to Esarhaddon found at Nineveh which reports the arrest of a night watchman, a lamentation priest and other accomplices

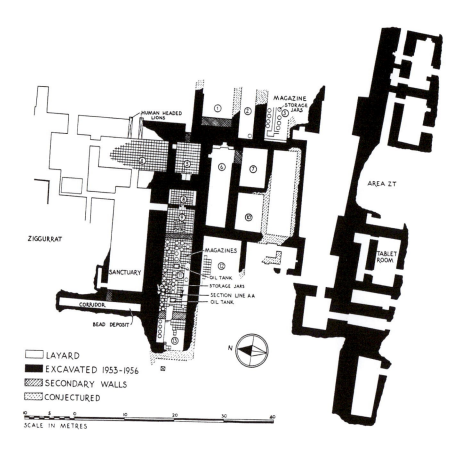

Fig. 65. The area of the Ninurta temple, as excavated in 1953. It remains unclear to what buildings rooms 1-3, 6, 7 and 10 belong; the south-western rooms seem to represent a further extension of the ZT offices.

after gold and eight silver bands had been stolen from the roof and walls of the Ninurta temple in Kalhu; it is also remarked that this was not the first time the temple had been so robbed:

> In the time of the father of the king, my lord, the priests of the temple of Ninurta cut off three fingers worth of golden appendages (?) at the head of Ninurta.... [Now] they cut off .... X spans wide and eleven cubits [5.5 m] long, and they removed eight silver bands (?) from the walls. The eunuch of the king should come and investigate... The lamentation priest and the temple guard were in charge of the cutting. They should be interrogated and their accomplices brought out.....

They have been taught a lesson but still they don't keep their hands off the temple. When in the time of your father they didn't keep their hands off the temple, some of the men were killed. The king, my lord, should do as he deems best.[6]

At either side of the door of the Ishtar Šarrat-niphi temple stood two altars, virtually identical with one found by us at Tell al Rimah in the 1960s.[7] Glazed bricks decorated the façades of both shrines. Royal statues were also found in both temples, broken fragments of a Shalmaneser statue in the Ninurta temple, a statue of Assurnasirpal in the other (Fig. 5, p. 14). Both the Assurnasirpal statue and stele can now be seen in the British Museum. It is this very specific association of stelae and statues with temples that has led to the suggestion that the Central Building too is a temple (p. 71), probably one of those named by Assurnasirpal and yet to be identified.[8]

One of the oddities of the Ninurta temple is that in his inscriptions Assurnasirpal states that he built a temple to Ninurta and Enlil, yet the dedication text in the sanctuary of the temple mentions only Ninurta. It has been suggested that either room 5 or room 6, both of which had the customary niches at one end, could be the missing Enlil sanctuary, but neither seems of sufficient importance, either in size or position. It is possible, however, that Enlil's shrine, if it was ever built, may have been situated on the south side of the large central courtyard around which this group of shrines was arranged, but the room excavated by Rassam (Mallowan's room 1, Fig. 65, plan) seems, again, too insignificant, despite its position, for a temple of one of Mesopotamia's most important gods. Enlil is said to 'dwell in the temple of Kidmuru'[9], the third of the shrines situated east of the ziggurrat. But this too is a temple of Ishtar. There is a complex theology involving Ninurta, Enlil and Aššur, and it must also remain possible that at least the first two are in some way subsumed within Ninurta's shrine.

The third temple, the 'temple of the goddess Ishtar, mistress of the divine Kidmuru', was excavated by Rassam in 1878. It is located about 100 m south-east of the Šarrat-niphi shrine and seems to have been entered from the north, possibly from the same large courtyard onto which the other temples also opened. It is clear from Assurnasirpal's inscription that a temple dedicated to this goddess had already existed at Kalhu in earlier times, and that Assurnasirpal had renovated the building which had 'crumbled and turned into ruin hills'.[10] He also says that he created an image of the goddess Ishtar out of red gold and settled it on her dais, an object regrettably but not surprisingly missing by the time Rassam found the reconstructed temple. The interior was decorated with glazed wall plaques (see Pl. 12b). We know too that the temple had its own well, since inscribed well bricks of the Kidmuru temple were found in the North-West Palace well room AB.[11]

To return to the Ninurta Temple, Mallowan excavated its storage magazines to the south of the sanctuary towards ZT. He also re-excavated the west end of the Ninurta shrine dug by Layard where he 'caught sight of the great [inscribed] stone paving slab, now badly broken'.[12] At the back of the sanctuary Mallowan found a blocked door leading into a vaulted north-south corridor, the purpose of which remains a mystery. Here he found a large cache of beads concealed under the floor, consisting of many hundreds made of frit, faience, rock crystal, carnelian and other varieties of semi-precious stones. In addition there were over two dozen cylinder seals, including a number of heirlooms dating as far back as the 16th century BC. Whatever the original purpose of this room, it must have been blocked off at the time the temple was constructed, since an operative doorway in this position in the main sanctuary is most unlikely.[13] The most probable function of the narrow, north-south corridor, would have been as a repository for votive or foundation offerings.

The remainder of the rooms south of the sanctuary were temple magazines. The largest of these was originally a single room 32 metres in length (Fig. 66). Here a series of large pottery jars, each with a capacity of some 300 litres, was arranged in four rows down the length of the room. Each jar was supported by a mud-brick bench and stood on a drip-stone with a bung in the base. Some jars were inscribed with their capacity in terms of the *homer, sutu* and *qa*, the standard measures then in use. In room 3 the storage jars were arranged on either side of a central bench. Although the temple and its subsidiary rooms had been sacked – indeed, as in ZT, the rooms were filled with ash and fallen mud-brick – both Layard and Mallowan found a number of fragmentary objects suggestive of the value of the treasure that had once been kept here.

Fig. 66. Ninurta temple magazine (room 11), showing oil jars, drip stones and two stone tanks, bearing inscriptions of Assurnasirpal II, who built the temple.

110

THE NABU TEMPLE

Among the nine temples that Assurnasirpal II claims to have built at Nimrud, the Nabu Temple is for the archaeologist by far the most important. It has been restored by the Directorate-General of Antiquities and, together with the North-West Palace, is a building well worth a tourist's visit. Nabu was the god of writing, the scribal god, whose cult centre was in Borsippa, not far from Babylon. He was of especial importance in Babylonia where he was believed to be the son of Marduk, the god of the city of Babylon, who had come to be worshipped not only as king of all the gods but as virtually a monotheistic deity incorporating the other gods as aspects of his own persona. In Babylonia during the first millennium BC Nabu the son became of increasing importance, ultimately perhaps even threatening his father's supreme position. During the 8th and 7th centuries his cult was also to become popular in Assyria, a situation reflected in the attentions paid to the maintenance of his temple and library at Nimrud. A number of the Nimrud texts mention Marduk, usually in association with Nabu, for example Fig. 75,[14] and there are even hints of a shrine in Ezida possibly associated with this Babylonian god.

The Nabu temple complex, Ezida (a name adopted by the Assyrians from Nabu's home Temple in Borsippa), lies on the east side of the citadel mound. It is bounded on the east by the broad citadel wall, on the north by the street leading up from the Shalmaneser Gate and on the west by a second street separating it from the Burnt Palace (plan, Fig. 67) The east wall of the complex was separated from the inner face of the citadel wall by a narrow alley, providing passage here without entering the limits of Ezida. A short cross wall, which apparently blocked the alley, may have served to support a stairway leading to the ramparts. With the exception of the ziggurrat, the south-east corner of the tell was the highest area on the citadel, presumably reflecting the conformation of the earlier tell beneath. Here there was also a considerable slope in ground level, represented by a drop of some five metres from the southern boundary of the citadel mound to 'Shalmaneser street', south of the dig house, while the Nabu Temple floors lay three metres above those in the Burnt Palace, just across the street to the west. Considerable post-Assyrian material was excavated in this area (discussed in chapter 8), above which the 19th century excavation dumps, at times surviving to a depth of 5 m, posed considerable, to say nothing of expensive, problems to the modern excavator.

The entrance to Ezida was directly from Shalmaneser Street through what is referred to as the Fish Gate owing to the presence of limestone 'mermen', unfortunately headless but with scaly bodies and fins, mounted on stone podia in deep recesses on either side of the entrance, itself approached by steps leading up from the street.[15] An interesting but unfortunately incomplete text from Fort Shalmaneser actually gives the measurements for the Nabu Temple fishmen (and women!) and calculates the amount of gold needed to cover them with gold leaf.[16] The Ezida plan consists of two large courtyards on the east, the shrines themselves facing onto the inner court, together with two smaller but no less important courtyards within the north-western quarter of the building, referred to in the earliest excavation reports as the South-East Building (SEB). The complex itself had been investigated by all the

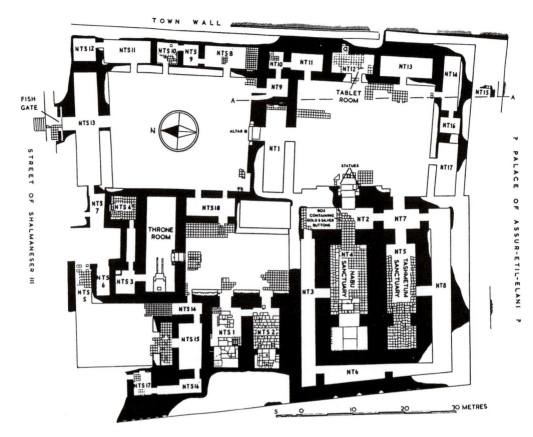

Fig. 67. Plan of Ezida, the temple of Nabu (Oates 1957, pl. 2, revised after Hussein 1995, 33).

19th century excavators, in particular Loftus and Rassam. Their excavations had identified the temple of Nabu itself, and revealed several statues including two dated to the reign of Adad-nerari III.[17] On either side of the entrance to the temple gate-chamber (NT1) Rassam had found colossal figures with folded hands, measuring almost 4 m in height (11 feet), presumably divine attendants of the god, now to be seen in the Iraq Museum. Also in front of the entrance was a much-weathered lime-stone altar. The mud-brick walls of the gate-chamber were set on a plinth of three courses of drafted ashlar masonry which continued along its outer, northern façade (Fig. 68). Within it Rassam discovered the Šamši-Adad V stele which had originally stood in the Ninurta Temple (Fig. 8, p. 21).[18]

The west side of the temple courtyard was occupied by two large shrines (NT 4 and 5), each with a raised podium at its western end, approached by two flights of steps of unequal width (Fig. 69). The shrines were paved with stone slabs, and each had an ante-chamber separating it from the courtyard (NT 2 and 7). These central rooms were surrounded by a corridor leading from the ante-chambers and accessible also from the shrines themselves. NT 4 can be identified as the shrine of Nabu himself, while the smaller NT 5 must have belonged to his wife Tašmetum. A large slab at the foot of the podium steps in the northern shrine bears a broken inscription of Adad-nerari III, obviously re-used although this version of the Nabu temple was clearly built during his reign. Small box-like cavities, lined with clay, had been cut into the top of the platform beneath the building, three in Nabu's shrine and one in its ante-chamber. These had been carefully sealed with stone covers, cemented flush with the paving. Three of these foundation boxes were empty, but apparently undisturbed, suggesting that their contents had consisted of some organic material, perhaps apotropaic figurines of wood. Unusually, the ante-chamber box was sub-divided diagonally into four segments, each containing a gold or silver 'button'.[19]

Two inscribed statues now in the British Museum faced east on either side of the entrance to Nabu's ante-chamber, while two further statues depicting attendants bearing rectangular offering trays faced each other across the entrance.[20] The inscriptions record the dedication of the former in 798 BC by Bel-tarṣi-iluma, then governor of Kalhu, for the life of Adad-nerari III and his mother Sammuramat, the famous Assyrian queen known in classical sources as Semiramis. The prominence of Nabu

Fig. 68. North entrance to the long chamber NT 1, which gave access to the southern courtyard and the shrines of Nabu and Tašmetum. The lower courses of ashlar masonry were surmounted by mud-brick; before the façade are an altar, stone podia and the lower part of the statue of an attendant of the god. The large statues found by Rassam, now in the Iraq Museum, stood in the reveals on either side of the entrance.

113

Fig. 69. Shrine of the goddess Tašmetum, wife of Nabu, looking west across the antechamber.

is clearly indicated in the final command: 'Whoever you are, after me, trust in the god Nabu! *Do not trust in another god!*'[21] (see also Fig. 75). The essential unity of plan of the temple group and the rest of the southern courtyard suggests that this wing was (re)built as a coherent unit at the time of Adad-nerari III, although the original version of the Nabu Temple was almost certainly of earlier 9th century date. Later repairs and alterations included the rebuilding of the outer, western wall, which had been demolished, a new stone foundation inserted and the new upper wall decorated with recesses and rows of engaged columns in the style of the Nabu Temple at Khorsabad, built by Sargon II.

The eastern range of rooms along the inner court is of especial interest, since it

Fig. 70. Inscribed tablet which records a grant of land in perpetuity, as an act of piety, for the life of Sin-šar-iškun and his queen; dated by the limmu Bel-iqbi, *sometime around 620 BC. Found embedded in ash behind the Fish Gate. The design on the seal impression depicts a bearded male clutching two human-headed ostriches, below which are two priests wearing fish-cloaks (ND 5550).*

housed the scribal god's library from which a number of important cuneiform texts have survived (see p. 207). NT 12 has been identified as the *scriptorium* or 'tablet room', a long chamber with an unusually wide door-way which would have provided additional light for the scribes, though presumably they would have worked also in the courtyard. This room contained a small well in a recess in its rear wall, providing the water essential both for storage and for keeping the clay suitably damp to be inscribed. In NT 12 was found a sizeable part of the temple library, unfortunately in some disorder, disturbed in or after the 612 destruction, probably both. Indeed the adjacent chamber to the south (NT 13) had been occupied by squatters after the 612 destruction, leaving no evidence of its original function, although a cache of beads and seals was found in rubbish in the south-east corner of the room. Interestingly, a number of tablets was recovered here by Iraqi excavators in the 1980s. Some of these may have come from back-fill, the earth for which was taken from the 19th century dumps. The southernmost rooms around this court had also been badly damaged by 6th century settlers, who had dug a wide trench along the line of these chambers presumably to rob their pavements and such of their contents as remained. Here also, debris thrown back into the pit after the rooms had been ransacked contained considerable numbers of contract tablets dated between 699 and 661 BC, suggesting that these rooms too may have formed part of the scribal quarters.

The line of rooms on the east side of the north courtyard may have served as temple offices, and it was here that traces of an earlier 9th century structure were found. Inscribed bricks recovered here also attest repairs effected by the penultimate Assyrian king, Assur-etel-ilani, while a tablet of the time of Sin-šar-iškun found

Fig. 71. The private 'throne room' in the north-west sector of Ezida, showing the stepped mud-brick dais and the stone tramlines. Traces of the deep bed of ash in which were found many ivories and cuneiform tablets are visible in the photograph.

behind the Fish Gate records a grant of land in perpetuity to the god Nabu (Fig. 70). On the west, Iraqi archaeologists have identified a second entrance into room 18, directly opposite the door into NTS 8.[22] Here an apparently unobtrusive entrance gave access to a separate complex which formed the third of the three units composing Ezida. The walls of this complex are not bonded either on the south with the Nabu Temple itself, which is earlier, or with the gate-chamber of Ezida on the northeast which, although its façade had been rebuilt, was also probably part of the original plan.

The most important rooms in the north-west wing of Ezida are clearly the reception suite, which seems to have served as a private throne room of the temple. This lay to the north of the courtyard and the two small shrines (NTS 1 and NTS 2), which appear to be almost exact but smaller replicas of the Nabu and Tašmetum shrines. The throne room contained the usual stepped dais and tram lines, above which there was evidence of fierce burning (Fig. 71), the lowest levels of ash containing large numbers of burnt ivories which had clearly decorated 'royal' furniture and hundreds of fragments of unusually large cuneiform tablets, discussed in chapter 6. Interestingly, the throne room suite, unlike that in the earlier North-West Palace, includes adjoining ablution and perhaps robing rooms (NTS 4 and 3), to

Fig. 72. NTS 1 and NTS 2, small shrines in the north-west sector of Ezida, associated with the small, private 'throne room'.

which access was essentially private. Equally, the very limited access from the great north courtyard to this complex itself suggests the admission of only small numbers of people.

In the north-west angle of the throne room courtyard, between the shrines and the throne room, a doorway led to a passage, NTS 14, a fourth small courtyard and a range of rooms (NTS 15–17) which were also accessible from the main gate-chamber.[23] This north-west corner clearly constituted an important part of Ezida, and it is unfortunate that the plan has been almost completely obliterated by a series of later occupations. Since the publication of the original plan in 1957, however, Iraqi excavators have made a significant addition to it, identifying in the middle of the north wall of NTS 15 a massive stone doorsill with twin doorsockets that define a doorway 2 m wide opening into the portico and the small courtyard beyond.[24] In the 1950s an isolated mud-brick pier and, in the vicinity, a round column base of limestone were found here, perhaps part of the northward-facing portico and presumably a 7th century addition. Thus rooms NTS 15–17 can be seen as a small version of the principal throne room suite just to the east, and clearly designed for some high official, whose business required access both from within Ezida and from the main gate by way of the passages NTS 7 and 5. A text concerning the rituals associated with an *akitu* festival celebrated in Ezida (quoted on p. 121) suggests that this official may have been the 'mayor', who was required not only to attend the royal banquet but later to 'sit by' while the gods 'remained in their bedchamber'. The only find of importance in

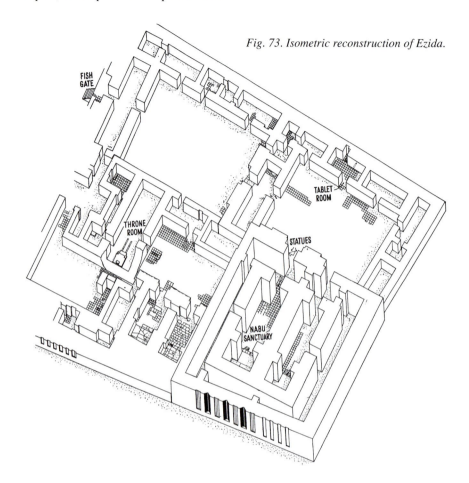

Fig. 73. Isometric reconstruction of Ezida.

this suite was a very fine alabaster tablet of Shalmaneser III,[25] found by Iraqi archaeologists in NTS 17 and obviously a relic of earlier times.

The façade of the shrines (NTS 1 and 2) was decorated with engaged columns
on a plinth of finely dressed limestone,[26] similar to but not identical with work possibly carried out by Sargon elsewhere in Ezida, while the stone pavements of the
shrines had been damaged and patched with burnt bricks, probably in the reign of
Assur-etel-ilani, whose inscription appeared on some examples found in the fill just
above the floor. In each shrine the podium was approached by two flights of steps,
as in the larger sanctuaries, the smaller versions having been cut from a single block
of stone (Fig 72). Boxes for foundation deposits were an original feature; these were
empty, their contents presumably again organic. On the west of the shrines a very
thick wall of solid mud-brick, 6.75 to 8.50 m in thickness, carried this wing out to
the prescribed boundary of Ezida along the street and aligned with the western façade
of the Nabu Temple itself. This northern stretch of wall was decorated with a simple
system of niches on a plain pediment, unlike the more elaborate Nabu Temple wall

118

to the south (p. 114), further suggesting the slightly later date for this rebuilding (Fig. 73).

A fragment of a glazed bowl from the Nabu temple bore on its rim the inscription 'Temple of the Sibittu…', a temple as yet unidentified. The locations of the other temples referred to in Assurnasirpal's inscriptions remain unknown.

FINDS IN THE NABU TEMPLE

When we review the history of Ezida, it is clear that it continued to flourish throughout the period of Assyrian hegemony, texts dated to the reign of virtually every Assyrian monarch having been recovered here. Ezida was heavily burnt and pillaged in the 7th century sack of the city. Indeed ash to a depth of up to 80 cm was found in the throne room. However, this heavy destruction preserved for us some of the most interesting objects found by the Mallowan expedition. The most important Nabu Temple finds include two classes of object, cuneiform tablets from the temple library and the carved ivories which decorated the furniture and other objects used in the building. The destruction debris in the library rooms contained fragments of tablets including literary texts and a substantial collection of royal inscriptions of various rulers. Further work on the Nabu Temple by Iraqi excavators, working in particular on the restoration of the shrines and the tablet room, produced many more important texts, including a number of Assurbanipal prism fragments in which he claims also to have restored the Nabu Temple and, in room NTS 17, the complete alabaster tablet of Shalmaneser III, referred to above.

Perhaps the most impressive tablets found at Nimrud, at least in a purely physical sense, were the Esarhaddon treaties found in the north-west wing throne room. In the ash above and around the dais, and associated with the ivories, were hundreds of fragments of unusually large cuneiform tablets which proved to be a series of treaties made by Esarhaddon with various princes of western Iran in the year 672 BC, the purpose of which was to secure the uncontested accession of his son Assurbanipal; these are discussed in detail in chapter 6. The ivories, which had been heavily burnt, were found even on the surface of the dais, and at least some of this extraordinary collection must have decorated the throne itself. These included two ivory chair arms and a number of panels which had originally been set on wooden backing. They were carved in the Assyrian style appropriate to royal furniture, and illustrate the king himself receiving processions of tribute bearers, much in the manner of the North-West Palace throne room reliefs, and indeed the ivories also recovered there (Fig. 74). Two large ivory heads of women may also have been furniture components; both had been overlaid with hammered sheet gold.[27]

An Akitu/*Sacred Marriage Festival*

Some hint of the function of the group of rooms in the north-west wing of Ezida is given in an interesting series of letters, dated to the reign of Esarhaddon, and written by three officials of the Nabu Temple, who describe the ceremonies at Kalhu on the occasion of an *akitu* festival.[28] One of these officials, Nabu-šum-iddina, addresses the Crown Prince Assurbanipal:

On the third day of the second month (Iyyar) the bed of Nabu will be prepared in the city of Kalhu, and Nabu will enter the bed-chamber. On the fourth day will occur the wedding night (*quršu*-ceremony) of Nabu....the god will go forth from the threshing floor (*adru*) of the palace, from the threshing floor of the palace he will go to the park. A sacrifice will be made there. The charioteer of the gods will come with the team of horses of the gods. He will then take the god forth and cause him to pass in procession, he will then bring him back....Of the apprentice priests, whoever has a sacrifice to make will do so. Whoever offers up even one *qa* of his food may eat in the house of Nabu.[29]

This passage defines the successive events in the *akitu* ceremony: first, the statue of Nabu was taken from his sanctuary to the 'bed-chamber', which had previously been prepared, and where, the next day, the 'marriage' of the god takes place.[30] The statue then goes to the 'threshing floor of the palace', and thence to a garden where a sacrifice is performed. The statue was transported by a chariot and horses of the gods. At the conclusion of the ceremonies it was brought back to the temple, the ceremony ending with further sacrifices and a ceremonial meal. Interestingly, the letter ends with an appeal to both Marduk and Nabu to protect the life of the crown prince. Another letter reports specifically on the transfer of the statues to the 'bed-chamber' and says that orders have been given for the offerings of the royal family to be made before them there:

On the fourth day of Iyyar, Nabu and Tašmetum shall enter into the bed-chamber. At the beginning of your reign, I performed the sacrificial offerings before Nabu and Tašmetum which have given life to the king, my lord ... I have (now) given instructions

Fig. 74. Reconstructions of scenes engraved on a series of ivory panels found near the dais (Fig. 71). The first (top) shows the king, with his attendants, receiving a procession of foreign tribute bearers. (68 x 8 cm, ND 4193, Iraq Museum).
b) (lower left) Another panel fragment, perhaps illustrating bearers of offerings to Nabu (24 x 10.7 cm, ND 4204, Iraq Museum).
The panels had been attached to wood and almost certainly formed parts of furniture; several decorated chair (?throne) arms were also recovered with this group.

about the offerings for Assurbanipal, the great crown prince, for Šamaš-šum-ukin, the crown prince of Babylon, [and for other sons of Esarhaddon]. I will bring their offerings before Nabu and Tašmetum and will perform them in the bedroom. May they allow them to live 100 years.[31]

A third provides a more specific timetable:

On the fourth day, in the evening, Nabu and Tašmetum will enter the bedroom. On the 5th day they will be served the royal banquet, and the *hazannu*-official[32] will attend. They will bring the lion-head rhyton and a *tallakku* [a cult object] to the palace. From the fifth day to the tenth the gods will remain in their bed-chamber, and the 'mayor' will sit by. On the eleventh day Nabu shall go out and 'stretch' his legs. He shall go to the game park. Wild oxen he will slay. He shall then return and dwell in his house.[33]

A governor of Kalhu also writes to Sargon that 'The festival has been celebrated; the god…came out and returned in peace. May Nabu and Marduk bless the king,' while several letters from another governor to the same king refer also to this festival, 'On the 8th the gods are going to get up and take residence in the *akitu* chapel (*é.akitu*); they will stay there until the middle of the month.'[34] Another letter refers to an *akitu* festival of Tašmetum:

Tomorrow is the 'party' of Tašmetu. Tašmetu, the beloved, will go out and take up residence in the festival (*akitu*) chapel. Sacrifices will be offered before her….In the evening she will come back in and take up her seat. May she bless the king, my lord. May she give to the king, my lord, long days everlasting years, happiness and good health. The king, my lord, should know about this.[35]

The god Nabu was closely associated with the New Year ceremony in Babylon, when he was brought from his cult centre, nearby Borsippa, to visit his father Marduk

Fig. 75. Red pebble, perforated longitudinally, bearing cylinder seal-like decoration, depicting a priest before the symbols of Nabu (stylus) and Marduk (spade). The inscription invokes trust in Nabu (translation in note 14); (8 x 7 x 4 cm, ND 4304, from the corridor near the side (north) door of the Nabu sanctuary).

in Babylon. The Babylonian ceremonies consisted of a sequence of rites including celebration of the spring harvest, the ritual enthronement of Marduk and the reception and enthronement in Babylon of Nabu.[36] The ceremonies also included a procession to the *bit akitu*, which lay outside the city. The information from these Nimrud letters tells us not only that a 'sacred marriage' took place in the Nabu Temple itself, but that in Assyria an *akitu* festival could be performed at various times during the year, indeed that there were possibly several types of *akitu* festival. That is, it was not of necessity a New Year festival. We learn also that not only did the god (or goddess) proceed to the *akitu* shrine, but also that the ceremony required the god's presence in a garden or park, almost certainly in the outer town.

The Nabu temple plan as excavated in the 1950s provides a secluded throne room, apparently designed for temporary and occasional use, closely associated with two small replicas of the shrines of Nabu and Tašmetum, and another formal suite to the north-west. It seems more than likely that this relatively restricted part of the temple complex constituted the 'palace' in which these ceremonies took place. This suggestion does not of course imply that this was necessarily the only function of this suite of rooms, but it is perhaps no coincidence that the treaty tablets of Esarhaddon, designed to ensure the succession of his son Assurbanipal, are found in a throne room associated with the *akitu* festival's yearly legitimation of the king's position on his throne.

One further letter concerning the affairs of the Nabu Temple at Nimrud merits mention. And again, the complaint concerns a lamentation priest, this time running riot in the temple, replacing ancient gold work with new, tampering with ancient rites, etc:

> Now Pulu, the lamentation priest, has been acting arbitrarily in the temple of Nabu. Without the permission of the king, he tore out doorposts, fastened others, and cut down the ….in the *akitu* house of Nabu and the *akitu* house of Tašmetu. As for the golden table

122

of Marduk, which Sargon had made, he assigned a goldsmith to it. He removed the old work and replaced it with the new. Furthermore, the dragons upon which Nabu stands.... [are in some way interfered with]....No one has authority, and no one says anything to him.

He has appointed officials of his own choosing in the temple. Moreover, the king's father set up golden bottles....with royal images on them. They would fill with wine the one in front of Marduk and the one in front of Nabu. They would be decanted. The wine was the palace allotment. Now this has been stopped. He himself measures out the wine and carries it in. And formerly, when my father supervised the 'house of the first fruits',[37] ordinary beer from groats was decanted, and he used to inspect new and old beer at the same time. ... Pulu is the one who is to blame for.....all the treasuries are under his supervision. He is the one to open and seal them. He enters the ritual bath house of Marduk and Nabu. There twice a year the lions of Marduk are ungirded. All the precious stones and jewellery are under his custody; he does not show them to anybody. He also does the work of the woman who carries out the 'polishing' ceremony for Tašmetu. Nobody with him sees her.

There follows a complaint about the inappropriate management of the sheep offerings and an objection, that may sound familiar, to the 'modernising' of ritual:

No one can do anything; there is an order to remain silent. But they have changed the old rites![38]

The importance of this letter in the context of the Nabu Temple is that it strongly suggests that the *akitu* house is actually in Ezida, and that there is a separate 'house' for Nabu and for Tašmetum. We would propose that the throne room (with its accompanying ritual ablution room) is the 'bedroom', the scene of the sacred marriage, and that the two small shrines nearby are the *akitu* 'houses'. A generally similar conclusion was reached some years ago by Nicholas Postgate, largely on the basis of an administrative text actually from the throne room of the Nabu Temple.[39]

The Temple of Nabu and the Horse Letters from Nineveh

A number of 7th century letters found at Nineveh but written at Nimrud are concerned with the delivery of large numbers of horses and mules to Nabu-šum-iddina, the 'mayor', described as the '*hazannu* of the temple of Nabu' (presumably the mayor of Kalhu).[40] These letters, probably dated to a single year in the time of Esarhaddon, suggest some close relationship between the temple and the affairs of the *ekal mašarti* or arsenal (chapter 5), where many of the horses are transferred. The 'mayor' receives and reviews the horses, forwarding reports to the king at Nineveh on their numbers, breeds, origins and eventual disposition. The horses, some 3000 in this single year, came from as far away as Parsua in Iran and Damascus, and were destined to become either cavalry mounts or 'yoke horses'. These texts also tell us that the *ekal mašarti* at Kalhu still functioned as a military arsenal and the scene of an annual 'muster' at this time;[41] indeed we know from his own inscriptions that it was rebuilt by Esarhaddon. Unfortunately the precise relationship between these deliveries and the Nabu Temple remains unclear.

PALACES ON THE SOUTHERN PART OF THE TELL
The Burnt Palace and its stratigraphic relationship with Ezida

The building now known as the Burnt Palace was first excavated by Loftus in 1854–55. Unfortunately he died at sea on his way back to England in 1858, and no account exists of his work other than letters and brief reports. Perhaps his best-known contribution to the work at Nimrud was the excavation of a collection of burnt ivories, now in the British Museum and known as the 'Loftus ivories', in a building then described as the South-East Palace but now referred to as the Burnt Palace in order to distinguish it from other buildings in the south-east area of the tell. As was the practice of other excavators at this time, Loftus dug by tunnelling along the walls, and we were amused when digging there to come upon his tunnels and find in them broken pieces of the Turkish pipes of his workmen.

The building itself, which has been only partially excavated, lay to the west of Ezida, across the north-south street which ran between the two (Fig. 76). It must have had an entrance on Shalmaneser Street, but this has not been identified. The plan consists of an entrance court, beyond which was a large courtyard from which, in its final phase, one entered directly into the reception room. As in the North-West Palace, a

Fig. 76. Plan showing relative positions of Ezida, the Burnt Palace and the Governor's Palace. The Shalmaneser Gate lies at the north-east corner of Ezida, leading into 'Shalmaneser Street' which runs east-west between the Governor's Palace and the other buildings.

paved stone strip provided an alternative to the more usual tram lines. This led up to a mud-brick dais at the east end of the room, on which were found large numbers of heavily burnt ivories, lying in ash up to 60 cm deep. The room was decorated with geometric designs painted in green, red and blue, which were replaced in its latest phase, probably at the time of Assur-etel-ilani, with simple painted red bands on the white background. In the south-east corner of the throne room one of Loftus' tunnels led to a stone cist grave of the 18th century BC, over 5 m below. This contained three bodies, a bronze axe, knife and spear head.[42]

The building histories of both the Nabu Temple and the Burnt Palace were investigated in 1955.[43] The latter has provided the longest 'historical' sequence as yet clearly identified at Nimrud. Nine phases of occupation were defined (A–I). Unfortunately the earliest phase cannot be dated with any precision beyond the general attribution 'Middle Assyrian' (late second millennium BC). Phases A through C were in fact found only at isolated points, but they were characterised by common alignments and construction techniques. There is, moreover, an extraordinary piece of heavily buckled pavement in Phase B, strongly suggesting damage from a powerful earthquake sometime well before the 9th century.[44]

Phases D to F represent successive versions of the Late Assyrian palace plan, D being the original palace. These phases show a radical change in alignment, type of building and building methods in comparison with the earlier structures. Phase G represents a post-612 BC squatter level, present in both buildings, H seems to have been an attempt to rebuild the palace structure, and I identifies a Hellenistic level in which important kilns and glass cullet were found (p. 241). These levels were originally numbered in the Mallowan reports; the chart below relates the two numbering systems:

A–C		pre-ANP II
D	1A	earliest version of BP (9th century)
E	1B	palace dismantled and rebuilt; 'box level' (? Adad-nerari III)
F	2A	final version of palace, destroyed by fire; 'ivory level'
G	2B	squatter level (room 39 repaved as thoroughfare)
H	3	levelling and refurbishment, pavement raised 1.2 m (? Achaemenid)
I	4	Hellenistic kilns, ash and glass cullet

Although only isolated pieces of evidence exist for Phases A–C, it is clear that the earlier buildings were in no way comparable with the monumentality of those that followed in the Late Assyrian refounding of Kalhu. In Phase B traces of an east-west street were identified, clearly marked by its edging stones.

The foundations of the 9th century (Phase D) building are cut deeply through the earlier walls and pavements to rest on the Phase A platform. At this time the layout of this area of the site was completely altered, and the original east-west street abandoned for the north-south version, passing between the Nabu Temple and the Burnt Palace. The principal focus of the building erected in Phase D, presumably by

Assurnasirpal II or his son Shalmaneser, was its long reception room, approached through an ante-chamber which lay to the north. One interesting feature of the construction is that in the north-west corner of the courtyard the inner wall of the west wing is carried over a pre-existing well by means of a brick relieving arch.[45] In Phase E the original residence (D) was dismantled and rebuilt from ground level but in general to the same plan. Of particular interest in this phase is what seems to have been a new feature of the building, the practice of burying small clay images of guardian spirits in clay boxes at the corners and beside the door-jambs of the rooms, here often inserted into the surviving Phase D mud-brick (p. 253 and Fig. 77).[46] One wonders whether some disaster occasioned the rebuilding of the palace, and that subsequently greater attention was paid to the protection of its occupants.

In Phase F, the standing walls, with the exception of the throne room, appear once again to have been razed. The lay-out of the building remained essentially the same, although the ante-chamber to the throne room was now abolished. The partitions of the east wing were also rearranged to provide two new rooms with a slightly higher floor level and only indirect access from the courtyard. These included an ablution room with a bitumen-coated pavement and accompanying drain, accessible from the throne room through the 'ivory room'.[47] Such a change in use and access to the throne room may suggest a change in court ceremonial, but unfortunately we cannot precisely date this final renovation.

The phase G post–612 squatter level is found in both the Nabu Temple and the Burnt Palace, as elsewhere on the site. It is identified by ash, bread ovens, pottery and trodden floors in the palace itself. In Phase H was found an inhumation grave, about 6 m south-west of the south-west corner of NT 17, containing a fine glazed jar with polychrome chevron decoration which must be considerably earlier than the

Fig. 77. Foundation box, Burnt Palace, from beneath the Phase E floor of the long chamber south of the 'throne room'; the mud-brick box contains a set of seven protective figurines (lahmu, p. 255; ht of figurines 13.5 cm, ND 3606-09, 3628-29).

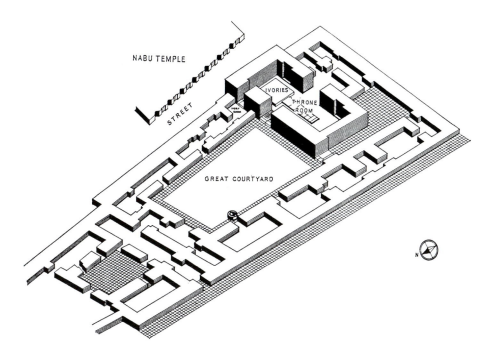

Fig. 78. Isometric reconstruction of the Burnt Palace as it existed in the late 8th and 7th centuries. The well in the courtyard doorway was dug from a much later level.

apparently Hellenistic date of the grave.[48] In Phase H in both buildings there were attempts to rebuild, identified by stone foundations for mud-brick walls associated with a trodden earth floor; Phase I is Hellenistic. These late occupations will be considered further in chapter 8.

A narrow street separated the Burnt Palace from Ezida, and a section was excavated here in order to determine the relationships between their different building phases.[49] In Phase D the reverse impression of a stone facing-slab was discovered along the street façade of the Burnt Palace, suggesting that stone slabs had formed the original outer face of its eastern wall. Unfortunately little survives of the earliest (Phase D) Nabu Temple, but the Adad-nerari III structure was built in Phase E, at which time the stone slabs had been or were removed from the Burnt Palace façade. It is perhaps no coincidence that many re-used stone slabs were incorporated in the floors of the Nabu Temple itself. In Phase E the palace wall was rebuilt and reduced in width, while the Phase D version of the Nabu Temple was obliterated by filling up the rooms to the level of the palace floor. A clay band was laid over the whole area to provide a base for the temple platform, a massive construction 15 courses high which elevated the floor of the south-western quarter of Ezida, where the sanctuaries lay, by some 3 m above the floor levels in the palace. The plan of the new Phase E building (that built at the time of Adad-nerari III) had been outlined in dressed limestone blocks on the top of the platform, a procedure that serves no practical function

Fig. 79. Ivory heads from the Burnt Palace: a) 2 views of a blackened head from a room north of the central courtyard (room 23, ht 4 cm, ND 2102, Metropolitan Museum of Art), b) ivory head found by Loftus in the 19th century (ht. 5.7 cm, British Museum).

in a mud-brick building. The reason for this remains unknown, but one suggestion has been that it may represent the use of foreign workers more accustomed to building in stone.

Phase F marks the final form of the Burnt Palace, while in the southern half of the Nabu Temple the same level continued in use. At some time, however, the western façade wall had been completely rebuilt. The section excavated here shows that the stone foundations were trenched into the edge of the platform and capped by a single course of limestone blocks. The mud-brick wall which rested on the stonework was decorated with panels of three small semi-columns alternating with rebated niches, a pattern also found on the collapsed north façade of Ezida flanking the north gate. It resembles closely the decoration of the temple of Nabu built by Sargon at Khorsabad, and is probably of the same date. Similar engaged columns surmounted a plinth of dressed stone on the façade of the two small shrines NTS 1 and 2. The large scale destruction, by fire, can only be explained by a common disaster which destroyed both buildings at the same time. The Phase G squatter level, re-using the Phase F structures, is also common to both buildings.

Thus, by analogy with Ezida where there survives some written documentation for the various phases of building, a similar sequence can be identified in the Burnt Palace, with two reconstructions dated approximately to the time of Adad-nerari III and Sargon. Letters addressed to Sargon were found in the formal reception room, and elsewhere the debris included baked bricks inscribed with his name (again of a type used in the Khorsabad Palace). It is clear that Sargon resided at Nimrud while he was building his new capital, and it is certain that he used both the Burnt Palace and the North-West Palace, where we know that he renovated parts of the building and where some of his official correspondence and adminstrative records were found. We have dwelt at length on the sequence of building in the Burnt Palace, since it provides one of the few instances where evidence has been found of the earlier city.

Similar though less detailed evidence was found also in the 1950 Building (p. 135). Regrettably, we lack the accompanying sequence of material culture that would enable archaeologists to date less well-defined structures elsewhere, a common problem in the context of well-maintained monumental buildings.

Finds in the Burnt Palace

As noted earlier, it was here in 1854–55 that Loftus found the immense collection of ivories that bear his name. Many more were excavated by Mallowan, especially in the throne room and, as in Ezida, literally on the dais. Outstanding among these was a variety of elaborately costumed ladies' heads, most of which had been burnt in the fire, resulting in an extraordinarily beautiful, and apparently unintentional, shiny black surface (Fig. 79).[50] There were also caryatid ladies forming the handles of objects such as mirrors and a number of beautifully carved bulls and calves, the latter probably originally the ornaments on the lids of small ivory boxes (Figs. 80, 81; see also Fig. 54, p. 94).[51] Among the other finds were many items of glass, including two pieces of the second millennium variety of core-moulded glass vessel decorated with chevrons drawn as threads into the body of the vessel (see p. 237). Also found here was a fragment of a beautifully carved rock crystal bowl (Fig. 151, p. 239), and of course the cuneiform letters mentioned above. The final destruction of the building can probably be dated to 612 BC, as elsewhere on the site and contemporary with that in Ezida. There is some evidence for occupation of Achaemenid or Neo-Babylonian date (Phase H).

Fig. 80. Fragmentary ivory pyxis from the Burnt Palace, depicting musicians playing a lyre, drum and flute; found near the entrance to the 'throne room' (ht of box 6 cm; ND 1642, Iraq Museum).

129

Fig. 81. Ivory bull found on the floor of the Burnt Palace 'throne room' (11.5 x 8 cm; ND 1088, Iraq Museum).

SOUTH-EAST PALACE (ASSYRIAN BUILDING AB)

We have already remarked on the confusion caused by the indiscriminate use of the term South-East Palace to denote several different buildings on this area of the tell, including Ezida and the Burnt Palace. It is now preferably used solely for a building which lies to the south of the Nabu Temple, originally identified by Layard beneath the Hellenistic tombs which he excavated on this south-east corner of the tell. The building was reached again in 1957, in the lowest level of the trenches dug in the investigation of the Hellenistic village (chapter 8). We have preferred the term Assyrian Building (AB), which was originally used simply to differentiate it from the overlying Hellenistic material.[52] The walls run at a different alignment from those of the Nabu Temple, though the earliest versions of both buildings probably date to the time of Assurnasirpal or, perhaps more likely, Shalmaneser III, whose stone inscription was found leaning against the north wall of room AB 6. This was not in situ, however, and had perhaps been left there by Layard's workmen.[53]

The AB 'palace' is yet another formal building which contained a long reception room or audience hall of the usual throne room plan. Indeed the rooms excavated form a characteristic throne room suite. The main audience chamber (AB 3) is the largest of the eight rooms investigated, and is identified by the mud-brick dais at the west end and the limestone 'tram lines' leading up to it (Fig. 82). The audience chamber was approached by two doorways in the south wall. An eastern door gave access to two stone-paved rooms, at least one presumably an ablution room; both had a limestone dado and in the corners of both rooms and in the niche in AB 1 were small foundation boxes closed with tightly fitting stone lids. On investigation all proved to

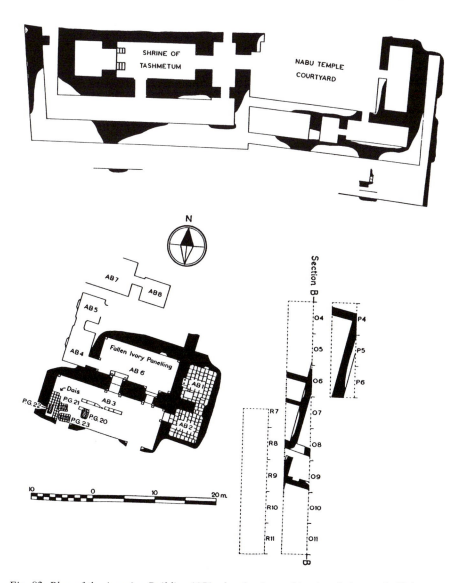

Fig. 82. Plan of the Assyrian Building (AB), showing its position in relation to the Nabu Temple and the Hellenistic trenches dug in 1957.

be empty. In the larger of these rooms (AB 1) there was a ventilation shaft in the north wall, an ancient and very practical form of air-conditioning still in use in the Near East. On the north side of the audience chamber was another long hall, entered by two doors both of which were originally double-leaved, the large pair being set in the stone sockets visible on the plan. Opposite the smaller doorway was another ventilation shaft, also in the north wall, and apparently masked by a screen composed of undecorated ivory panels set on wooden struts. George Smith noted wall decoration in the form of red, green and yellow horizontal bands, remarking that where the lower parts of the chambers were panelled with small stone slabs, the colour continued over these.[54] In the fire that destroyed the building – again almost certainly in the destruction of 612 BC – the combination of the ventilation shaft and the hollow-backed ivory screen would have provided a forced draught, the heat from which literally fused the bitumen-coated wall plaster into a molten mass. The two rooms found by Layard west of AB 6 were not re-excavated in 1957. Beyond them are two further rooms originally excavated by Loftus.

The latest phase of the building is characterised by a series of small clay-lined boxes, covered with single bricks, which had been placed on either side of the doorways and in the corners of the room. These are generally similar to the large number of foundation deposits found in the Burnt Palace and dated to the time of Adad-nerari III; indeed the same type of *lahmu* figure is found but there were none of the *apkallu*-figures or the multi-figure boxes of the Burnt Palace (p. 126). A late 7th century date is suggested for the AB deposits by the unusually small size of the covering bricks in the two reception halls, of which the only inscribed examples elsewhere on the mound date from the reign of Assur-etel-ilani. Indeed it seems clear that Assur-etel-ilani refurbished the earlier building that had existed here.

Whose residence this was remains to be established, although it could have been built for a minor member of the royal family or even the Crown Prince. Work was not continued here owing to the mountainous dumps left by Layard, some five metres of which had to be cleared to reach the building. Again there is some evidence for occupation of Neo-Babylonian or Achaemenid date, while Hellenistic tombs were dug into the building, some even into the dais in the audience chamber (Fig. 167, p. 262). In one of the richest of these tombs (PG 21) was recovered a collection of Neo-Assyrian cylinder seals, presumably the occupant's personal collection, which even included a serpentine seal of late third millennium (Akkadian) date.[55]

GOVERNOR'S PALACE

This building, known originally as the 1949 Building, lies to the north of Shalmaneser Street, opposite Ezida and the Burnt Palace. It was probably built by Shalmaneser III, whose bricks are found in its pavements (though they are bricks made for the construction of the ziggurrat, which has led some authorities to date the building to his grandson, Adad-nerari III). It was only partially excavated, but the recovered plan includes a large central court flanked by long audience chambers to the north and south (Fig. 83). These rooms were decorated with attractive geometric frescoes.[56] An unusually well-preserved ablution room lay in the south-west corner of the building. It was water-proofed with bitumen and had the usual double floor slabs, rounded at one end, between which was a central drain-hole leading into a well-built drain which ran under the wall into Shalmaneser Street; a 'man-hole' had been constructed in the wall over the drain, for ease of access.[57] A lamp was found in the room which would certainly have needed some artificial source of light. The building is noted particularly for the tablets found within it, in three of the rooms north of the central court (rooms K, M and S), and also for a mud-brick platform or table covered with almost 100 cups, plates and bottles, many of the very finest palace ware, known to the dig staff as the 'governor's dinner service' (Fig. 84 and p. 251).

There is no evidence to show that this building was actually the residence of the governor of Kalhu, although there have been found here cuneiform documents

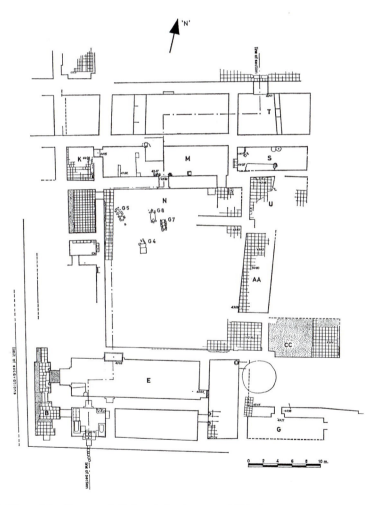

Fig. 83. Plan of the Governor's Palace (after Postgate 1973, fig. 1).

Fig. 84. The 'Governor's dinner service', nearly 100 palace ware vessels and other pottery found on a mud-brick bench or 'table', in the corner of room S, Governor's Palace.

relating to the affairs of several governors. But the records of a great many other types of official have also been preserved here, and there are no governor's archives as such. In fact it seems not to contain a personal archive, but a store of administrative records of a variety of types and dates. The designation Governor's Palace may not be wholly inappropriate, however, and we can assume that it was the office and/or residence of a series of individuals important in the administration of Kalhu. Several tablets date from the time of Bel-tarṣi-iluma, the governor who dedicated the Nabu Temple statues for the life of Sammuramat and her son, Adad-nerari III. One document is dated very early in the reign of Adad-nerari III, to a time when some authorities have suggested that the king was still a minor and his powerful mother, who was the legendary Semiramis, was acting as regent,[58] a view now disputed.

No tablets were found dated after 710 BC, and we lack the evidence to establish with certainty the date of the final use of the building. However, the pottery found on the table in room S is not unlike that from the 612 BC destruction level both in the town wall houses and from Fort Shalmaneser.[59] The likelihood is that, like the other buildings on the citadel, the Governor's Palace continued in use throughout the 7th century, though possibly no longer as the prestigious administrative residence of the 8th century. The quantity of palace ware preserved here, however, indicates that the building had certainly remained an upper class establishment, this pottery being the Assyrian equivalent of modern porcelain. As in Ezida and the Burnt Palace, there is a squatter level following the destruction of the building, in or not long after which some of its inhabitants were buried within the building. At the end of the 3rd century BC the great courtyard was used as a burial ground by the Hellenistic inhabitants of Nimrud.

1950 BUILDING

This large residence is situated midway between the North-West Palace and the eastern citadel wall. Its west wall may have bordered the north-south street which passed adjacent to the Governor's Palace. The building, which was over 65 m long, with walls 2.5 m thick, was only partially excavated. Like the Governor's Palace, it was decorated with geometric wall paintings of the type common in the lesser palaces. Bricks of Shalmaneser III were found in the courtyard, perhaps reused; a very small number of undateable tablets was also recovered. Little was established of the plan, but a large hall was identified, at the north end of which mud-brick steps led up to a raised podium. To the south was an ablution room, suggesting that here was yet another formal reception suite. The southern court was flanked by storage magazines on its western side, where many large jars were found, possibly for the storage of oil. In one of these rooms was found a burial containing two equids; regrettably, its date is not known.

A trench was dug to the east of the published plan and in a sounding here 'lying in confusion in a burnt stratum was a collection of black, green and yellow faience rosettes' which were almost certainly of Middle Assyrian date.[60] A deep sounding in this trench also produced, at a depth of 6 m below the 9th century pavement, second millennium pottery painted with red stripes.

TOWN WALL HOUSES

The buildings described up to now have all been of a formal, public nature, that is, palaces, temples, administrative buildings and/or residences of very senior officials. In 1949 a trench was excavated across the north-eastern part of the mound running up to the citadel wall. Parts of what appeared to have been more simple houses were found in this area, identified further in a second trench in 1950, at which time the so-called 1950 building was investigated. Mallowan returned to this area in 1953 and excavated a group of houses which have provided not only the sole non-palatial residences investigated at Nimrud but also the only area where there was a genuine sequence of archaeological levels with in situ material, especially tablets and pottery. Several deeper soundings were carried out within these trenches, in which were identified a total of eight levels of occupation from Middle Assyrian in the lowest level to Neo-Babylonian or Achaemenid and Hellenistic at the top. Considerably earlier levels, including those of Ninevite 5 date, have been identified at Nimrud on the basis of surface or other out-of-context potsherds, but it has not been possible to investigate such earlier occupation owing to the extremely deep deposits of late- and post-Assyrian materials overlying them. Surface sherds of Ninevite 5 pottery seem to have been concentrated especially at the south-east corner of the tell.

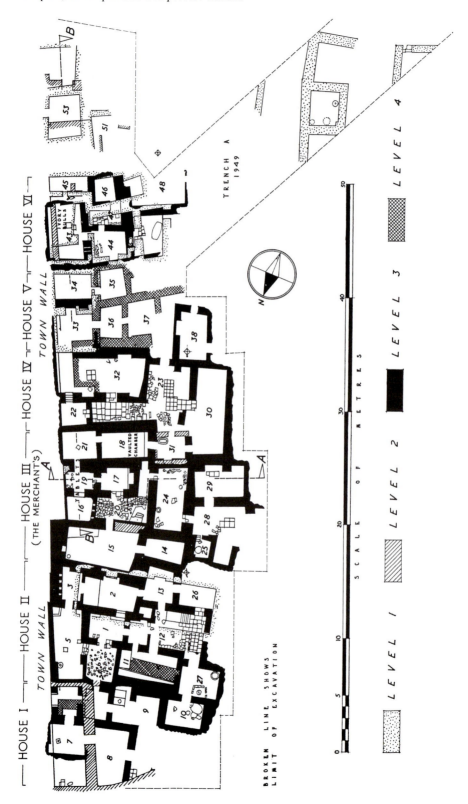

The 1953 Town Wall houses were excavated over a frontage of some 70 metres, the backs of the houses abutting directly onto the town wall on the east. None of the house-fronts was identified, but access must have been from a street or passage not far to the west. A curving wall at the northern limit of excavation suggests a passage here leading to the outer wall itself. Of the upper four levels, that is, those more extensively investigated, the earliest (4) can be dated to either the late 8th or the early 7th century; Level 3, the best-preserved, covers a period from, at the latest, early in the reign of Assurbanipal to the fall of Assyria, while the upper two levels, which are less well-preserved, include a 'squatter' or perhaps Neo-Babylonian occupation with overlying Hellenistic houses. These post-Assyrian levels are best-preserved within the southern area of the Town Wall excavations.

The Assyrian houses consisted of irregular groups of rooms (over 50 in all) situated around paved courtyards, the latter either square or oblong (Fig. 85). Mallowan identified six different houses (as indicated on the plan), but it is more likely that we have here the remains of only two large establishments (rooms 1–13, 26, 27 on the north, and a large central house, rooms 14–25, 28–32), with part of a further house represented by rooms 43–48. The large central structure may originally have consisted of two separate houses, but in its surviving form it was clearly a single large establishment belonging to Šamaš-šarru-uṣur, a eunuch and court official who was also a well-to-do merchant, landowner and money lender. Another of his concerns seems to have been the provision of birds for temple divination. This information is derived from the 47 tablets recovered from his storeroom (19), which perhaps even tell us of the purchase of the southern part of his house.[61] His surviving business documents reveal an extraordinarily long life, indicating that he was active throughout the reign of Assurbanipal, while various post-canonical limmu attest a further period of business, perhaps even as late as the 612 BC destruction, that is, over a period of perhaps 50 years.[62]

Storeroom 19 also contained a variety of other objects, including large storage jars, decayed sacking (?) and wood, all jumbled together. It was the fire that consumed these objects which baked the tablets, ensuring their preservation. There were also traces of copper nails, heavily corroded iron and a fragment of an iron bill-hook. The storeroom was entered through three very low doorways, only 60 cm wide, through which the access could only have been by crawling. (Such secure storerooms, with low doors, can still be found in contemporary mud-brick villages.) It is possible that the three entrances were not in simultaneous use, but rooms 16 and 21, on either side, were also relatively inaccessible. Preservation was unusually good, since both rooms 16 and 19 had been very heavily burnt. Room 16, which could be entered only from storeroom 19, was also used as a strongroom, where oil, vegetables (?), grain, metal and wooden objects had been kept; it also provided an excellent collection of pottery types which could be unequivocally dated to the latter part of the 7th century.[63]

In room 25 four steps led down to a bread oven, entered from a more public

137

Fig. 86. Ivory bull from destruction debris in room 43, Town Wall houses (length 7.5 cm, ND 3586. Metropolitan Museum of Art).

courtyard towards the front of the house. Room 21, to the south of the two store-rooms, was approached through what seems to have been a separate wing of the house by means of a long chamber (18) which was roofed by a corbelled vault. Indeed a number of chambers in this residential area would appear to have been vaulted, suggesting perhaps an unusual number of storerooms. The latter included room 34, originally excavated by Layard and mistakenly thought by him to have been a kiln owing to the presence of vitrified bricks, the result of the intense fire that had destroyed these houses.[64] Further interesting evidence of the activities of those who sacked the site can be seen in one of the more attractive objects found in ZT, an alabaster vase of which a joining fragment was recovered from the Town Wall hous-es, some 150 m away (Fig. 20, p. 41).[65] A burial beneath this vaulted chamber, exca-vated in 1951, contained two palace ware vessels including a very beautiful ram's head rhyton lying at the feet of the skeleton (Fig. 158, p. 253). An iron dagger lay nearby.

The northern house produced a small number of cuneiform business texts, of which one was a contract involving the sale of a house, specifying the inclusion of its roof beams and two doors (see p. 11). Tablets in room 11, like those in the house of Šamaš-šarru-uṣur, were dated to the time of Assurbanipal. As in the first house, a vari-ety of objects, including palace ware vessels and ivories were found here. In the paved courtyard 12 was a stair providing access to the roof, a common feature of mud-brick houses, even today. Many household activities were carried out on the roof, which would also have provided a cool sleeping area in the summer heat. However, there is no evidence to suggest a second storey, as Mallowan suggests. Room 11 provided one of the areas where the earlier level 4 was clearly distinguished, but regrettably little was recovered from this level; in Level 3 were found ivories, objects of bronze and more late tablets. In both houses a variety of iron tools and weapons was recovered, including scale armour; there were also weights reflecting the commercial interests of their inhabitants and considerable quantities of pottery. The one level 4 tablet recovered is unfortunately not dated; it deals with remission by the *rab ekalli*, the palace chamberlain, of *ilku* dues owed by a group of charioteers.[66]

Very little of the southernmost house was excavated. Room 43 provided its most interesting discoveries, a collection of ivories and other objects, which had been removed from their original Level 3 contexts and redeposited in Level 2. Most striking were a group of five ivory bulls,[67] which had originally been attached to an inlaid circular ivory frame (Fig. 86). Among the more intriguing pieces from the room 43 deposit were engraved scenes of royal processions and fragments of an ivory pyxis depicting the king outside a fortified city with women clashing cymbals on the battlements (Fig. 87).[68]

Post-Assyrian settlement at Nimrud is discussed in chapter 8, but it is more convenient to comment here on Level 2 in the Town Wall houses not only because much displaced Level 3 material was found here, both in room 43 and elsewhere, but because some of the Level 2 features are actually indicated on the published plan, in rooms 10 and 20 for example. Level 2 lay generally at 60 to 90 cm above the latest Assyrian floors,[69] and is characterised by large numbers of water jars (e.g. rooms 5, 10 and 53) and other pottery including several glazed vessels of 'Neo-Babylonian' type, and a number of very fine seals, also of Neo-Babylonian types. Although the Level 3 walls were often re-used, in courtyard 12 the stairs were actually cut off from Level 2 by a layer of ash. In room 8 at this level was a shell-shaped iron lamp with a chain for suspension. There were a number of burials of this date, and a saluki skeleton lay on the floor of room 29. We remain uncertain of the precise attribution of these levels. They must fall not long after the 612 destruction, however, since many of the Level 3 walls are re-used.

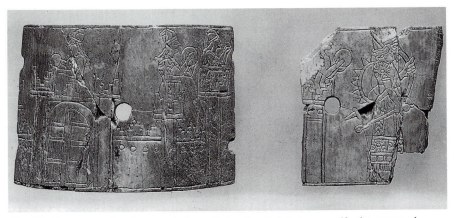

Fig. 87. Fragments of an ivory pyxis from destruction debris in room 43; the engraved design illustrates crenellated fortifications on which women are shown clashing cymbals, apparently in celebration of the arrival or departure of a royal figure (ht 4.8 cm, ND 3599, Metropolitan Museum of Art).

139

PALACES IN THE OUTER TOWN
The PD 5 palace
In 1953 Mallowan excavated a series of soundings in the outer town to the north of the ziggurrat. In the first two the natural conglomerate was found to be close to the surface, and the trenches were abandoned. Some palace ware was recovered from the first, and bread ovens were identified in the second. In the third trench two levels of small houses were identified, with inhumation burials beneath the floors. In the fifth trench (PD 5), some 30–40 m south of the north-west corner of the outer wall, at a point where the course of the river turned slightly to the east, was found an impressive palatial structure, its thick walls just beneath the surface, their tops cut away by modern ploughing. Like the houses in the outer town, it was built directly on the natural conglomerate, its walls cut deeply into the bedrock (in room 3 to a depth of 8 courses of brick). Relatively little of this building has been excavated, since it was identified only two weeks before the end of the 1953 season. It is clear, nonetheless, that it was built by Adad-nerari III, whose name is stamped on the bricks in the original floor of the well-preserved ablution room (9).[70] All the rooms appear originally to have been paved with baked bricks, but most of these pavements had been

Fig. 88. Bathroom with wall paintings in the palace built by Adad-nerari III in the outer town; a number of water jars survive, and in the upper part of the wall can be seen the remnants of two ventilation shafts. The wall decoration includes cushion-shaped patterns and kneeling bulls.

dismantled. In the bathroom (9) a stone slab with a curved end lay in the south-east corner of the room, and a dozen large water jars leaned against the walls (Fig. 88). Of architectural interest are the two wind-shafts still surviving on the east wall of this room.

One of the most interesting features of this building was its brilliantly painted decoration. As on the acropolis, a variety of colours and patterns was used. The designs were outlined in black, and the patterns coloured in red, blue and white. In room 9, where the walls still stood to a height of 4 m, a frieze 85 cm high had been painted around the room 1.4 m above the pavement. The design on the east wall was particularly well-preserved, consisting of a central panel of young bulls rampant, with heads turned back, on either side of a solid disc. On the adjacent projecting piers were concave-sided, cushion-like patterns. Painted murals also decorated the oblong hall 11, with brilliant blue striding bulls outlined in black, cushion patterns, and stylised red flowers used as filling motifs at the corners. In the south-west corner was a stylised tree with interlaced branches terminating in pomegranate and lotus buds, very like the 'sacred trees' of the North-West Palace bas-reliefs (also found in the corners of rooms).

The ablution room had survived in its original state, but the pavement of room 11 had been torn up and carelessly relaid. This would appear to have been the work of the ubiquitous post-612 squatter population, a conclusion suggested not only by the presence of a Neo-Babylonian tablet, found in the doorway connecting rooms 2 and 3, between the original pavement and that of the second phase of occupation, but by the presence there also of faience seals of relatively late date; moreover, several Neo-Babylonian stamp seals were found in graves dug into the palace.[71] There were painted friezes also in room 13 – cushion patterns alternating with bunches of lotus buds, above which, in red and blue, was a crenellated design and below, festoons of black and red stylised pomegranates. As in the bathroom there was also a bitumen dado around the room, with white lime (*juss*) plaster between the dado and the painted frieze.

The latest occupation level, some 2 m above the original pavement, lay still within the original walls. Graves of Neo-Babylonian or Achaemenid date were dug from this level, of which one, against the west wall of room 13 and about a metre below the surface, contained a considerable collection of seals, beads, cosmetic items and jewellery.[72] Another dug into room 11 contained an iron dagger and 8 small iron lance heads.

The 'Town Wall Palace'

This building was found accidentally in 1956, when a modern canal was cut on the south side of the outer town, between the citadel and the arsenal (Fort Shalmaneser), coinciding inadvertently with an ancient Assyrian canal bed, almost certainly part of the old Patti-Hegalli Canal (p. 33). The new cut revealed the mud-brick face of the ancient city wall in which was observed, in a high-lying part of the outer town some 400 m to the east of the citadel wall, a vertical baked brick drain leading from what had obviously been an important building, which proved to be over 60 m wide from

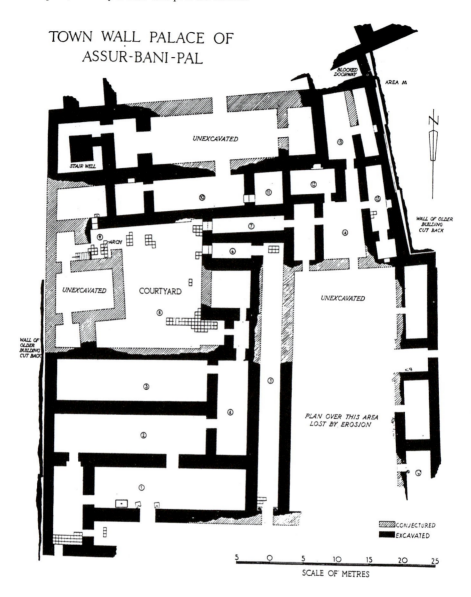

TOWN WALL PALACE OF
ASSUR-BANI-PAL

Fig. 89. Plan of the 'Town Wall Palace of Assurbanipal'.

west to east. The excavated area (referred to in the excavation records as DD) extended some 80 m to the north, where the principal feature was a large ceremonial reception suite with a stairwell, of the type common in the royal palaces (Fig. 89). The
main approach to this suite must have lain on the north through an outer courtyard.
To the south of the reception suite lay a small inner courtyard, probably part of the

domestic quarters which also extended to the north-east; here some of the rooms and corridors were decorated with simple frescoes, unfortunately in poor condition. In the south-east corner of the palace was another larger courtyard, separated on the west by a corridor from a suite of three chambers, each over 20 m long and 6 m wide and apparently intended for ceremonial involving large numbers of officials.

Mallowan suggested that this palace, lying between the citadel on the west and the arsenal on the east, may have been the official military headquarters of the king himself when in Kalhu, or of the *turtanu*, the commander-in-chief, but there is no evidence for its occupant's identity. On the east side the building cut into an earlier structure; to the west the palace had also cut back the walls of an older building, suggesting a concentration of important residences along this southern outer wall, unlike the area of relatively impoverished houses north of the ziggurrat. Here, of course, they would have looked out over the irrigated gardens and orchards below. In one of the few rooms excavated in the earlier building to the west was a fragmentary deposit, under the floor, in the form of a bird's head of sun-dried clay, inscribed with the name of Assurbanipal. Two other bird figurines were found under the floor of the same room, together with a bifrons figure which had a human body and heads of a lion and a man.[73] The Assurbanipal inscription, under the floor of the west building which was cut by the 'Town Wall Palace', implies a date for the construction of the latter no earlier than his reign, or possibly even later, in the time of one of his successors.[74] The plan of this building with its large reception suite of royal type provides important evidence of the continuing status of Kalhu and its outer town in the second half of the 7th century BC.

CHAPTER 5

FORT SHALMANESER: THE EKAL MAŠARTI

The first survey of the site of Nimrud and its surrounding landscape was carried out in 1852 by an English naval officer, Felix Jones (p. 28). In the early years of the Mallowan excavations part of the outer town was again surveyed, this time by Robert Hamilton with the assistance of Sd Izzet Din es-Sanduq, our Iraqi Representative (Fig. 90). Both surveys indicate the presence of an unusually large building in the south-east angle of the site, a building that lay beyond the outer wall as reconstructed by Felix Jones and that was clearly visible on the surface of the outer town. The two high mounds on its southern perimeter, known locally as Tulul al 'Azar, suggested also the presence of massive defensive towers. The apparent towers and the very visible character of the building itself, with its enormous courtyards, had long led us to speculate about the possible presence here of a large military establishment,

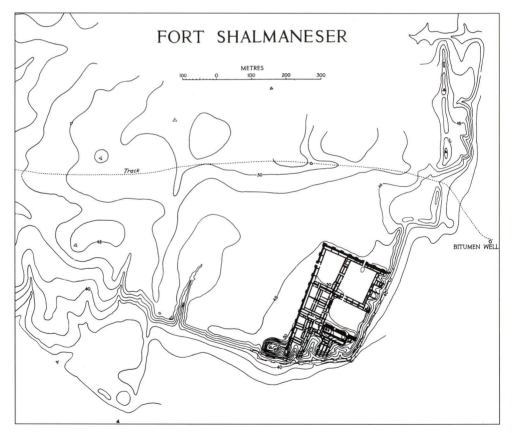

Fig. 90. Plan of south-east corner of outer town, showing position of Fort Shalmaneser.

144

but it was the discovery by Jørgen Læssøe early in 1957 of an inscribed brick of Shalmaneser III near the north gate of the south-eastern 'enclosure', in a wall that proved later to have been the outer bailey of just such a military establishment, that led to the adoption by the dig staff, before any excavation had taken place, of the name 'Fort Shalmaneser'. Although work began here later in 1957, its identification as the *ekal mašarti* was only confirmed in 1958 by texts from the *rab ekalli*'s house (below), including inscribed cylinders of the 7th century king Esarhaddon describing in some detail his renovation of this building.[1] Other inscriptions, found in later seasons, further confirmed this identification, including, in 1963, two inscribed door jambs at the entrance to room R 1.

The functions of an *ekal mašarti* are best described in a hexagonal prism of this same Assyrian king found in 1955 at Nineveh, in the mound now known as Nebi Yunus (claimed locally as the site of Jonah's tomb):

> The preparation of the camp (equipment), the mustering of the stallions, chariots, harness, equipment of war and the spoil of the foe of every kind.....May I – every year without interruption – take stock (there) during the New Year's Festival, the first month, of all stallions, mules, donkeys and camels, of the harness and battle gear of all my troops and of the booty taken from the enemy.[2]

These various functions are reflected in the different translations that have been suggested for the term *ekal mašarti*, *ekal* itself being simply the general word for 'palace', literally, a 'great house'. In addition to 'fort', which was never a serious intention, 'inventory palace', 'review palace' and 'arsenal' have been proposed. We prefer the translation 'arsenal', in its widest sense a term inclusive of these other functions. Although at the time of Shalmaneser III the original building seems to have been referred to as a 'palace', the basic form and conception of this vast arsenal can be attributed to this 9th century monarch. And indeed a 'palace' could be any building that was a royal residence and/or repository for the king's property, both of which functions are served in Fort Shalmaneser.

From 1958 onwards Fort Shalmaneser became the major focus of the work at Nimrud, which continued until 1963.[3] Within the south-east corner of the outer town the outline of the large enclosure already referred to defines the limits of this massive building, some 200 x 300 m (Fig. 91), its regular division into four quadrangles clearly visible on the contour plans. It is bounded on the east by the city wall south of the Erbil Gate, and on the south lies Tulul al 'Azar, the pair of high mounds referred to above, which stand some 20-25 m above the level of the plain. The NE, NW and SE sectors appeared to be courtyards surrounded by ranges of chambers, while the ground level in SW, as also in the S sector west of the corner tower, lay at a higher level. Here we expected, and eventually found, more extensive structures around smaller courtyards. The southern wing of the building contained the throne rooms, treasuries, residence and other reception rooms of the king; in area S with its elaborately guarded access was a second household of the queen, comparable with that in the North-West Palace on the citadel.

The contours of the land surrounding Fort Shalmaneser suggest that the build-

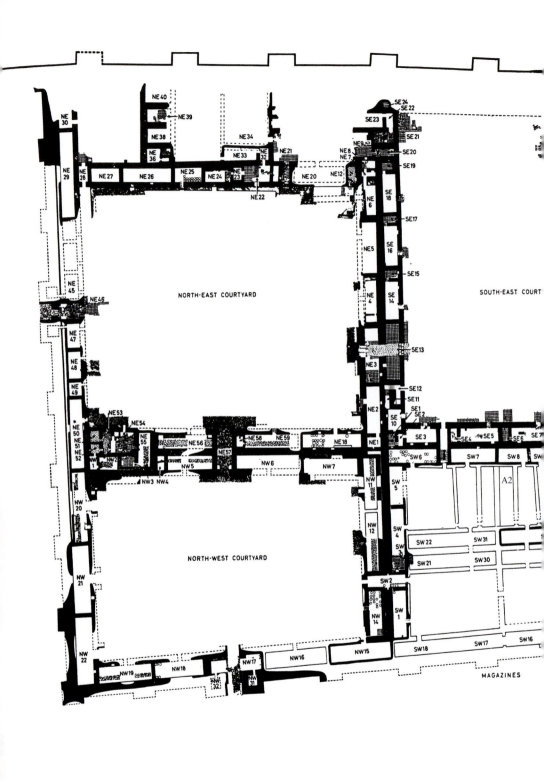

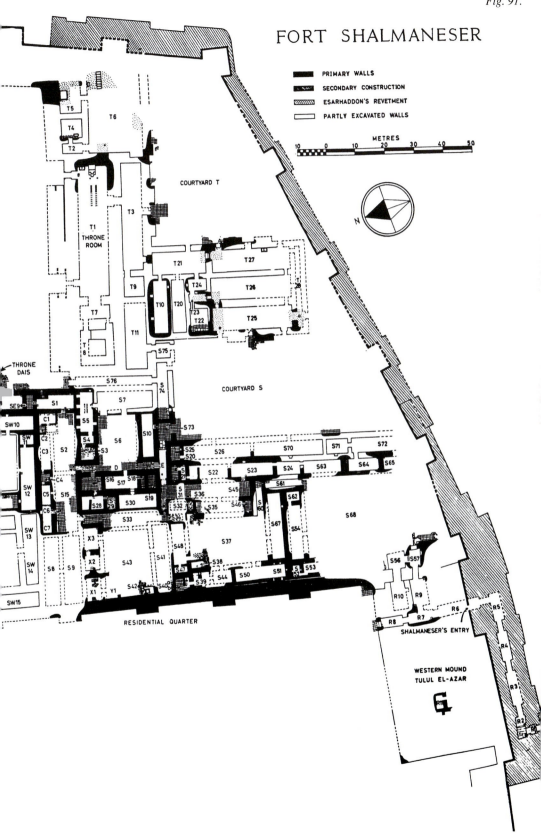

Fig. 91.

FORT SHALMANESER

PRIMARY WALLS
SECONDARY CONSTRUCTION
ESARHADDON'S REVETMENT
PARTLY EXCAVATED WALLS

METRES
10   0   10   20   30   40   50

N

COURTYARD T

T5
T4
T6
T2
T3
T1 THRONE ROOM
T9
T21
T27
T24
T26
T10 T20
T23
T22
T25
T7
T11
T8
S75

THRONE DAIS
S76
S74
SE9
S1
S7
COURTYARD S
SW10
C1
S5
S73
SW11
C2
S4
S6
S10
S25
S26
S70
S71
S72
C3
S2
S3
S20
D
E
S22
S23
S24
S63
S64
S65
SW12
C4
S16 S17 S18
S
S61
C5
S15
S30 S19
S31
S36
S45
S62
S60
S68
C6
S28 S29
S35
S46
S67
C7
S33
S34
S54
X3
S37
X2
S48
S56 S57
S43
S41
S38
S51
S
S53
R10
R9
SW13
S8
S9
X1 Y1
S42
S40
S39
S44
S50
S
SW14
S47
SW15
R8
R7
R6
R5
SHALMANESER'S ENTRY

RESIDENTIAL QUARTER

R4

WESTERN MOUND
TULUL EL-AZAR

R3

R2

ing discussed here was no more than the nucleus and headquarters of a much larger establishment. On the west and north sides the arsenal is surrounded by an open space, extending over 200 m to the north and 450 m to the west, in which there is neither surface pottery nor any sign of walls. This seems to have been a great exercise or parade ground, which would obviously have been essential for the annual muster of the levies and the training of cavalry and chariots (frontispiece). This open space is itself enclosed on the north and west by further massive ridges, obviously covering a considerable range of buildings enclosed by an outer wall, which wrongly appears as the city wall itself on Felix Jones' plan (Fig. 9, p. 28). One might expect to find here the stores, especially granaries, stables and other large structures which did not require the greater security of the inner fortress.

The north gate of this enclosure or 'outer bailey' was investigated in 1989 by the Italian expedition under the direction of Paolo Fiorina. Here they found a number of foundation boxes, most of which were empty, but two had clay figurines and a third contained many miniature bronze symbols and weapons accompanying, unusually, a wooden apotropaic figure.[4] Associated with this box was a brick of Shalmaneser III, approximately in the position where the first brick had been found in 1957.

Unlike the tell itself which, as we have seen, was extensively explored in the nineteenth century, Fort Shalmaneser had survived virtually untouched. Only a few pits and tunnels on and near the high eastern mounds of Tulul al 'Azar bear witness to brief soundings by Layard and Rassam, who failed to identify the buildings (there were no alabaster reliefs!) and were soon discouraged by the mass of brick-work and debris.[5] A consequence of this was that the finds here were richer and far more numerous than on the citadel mound, and we faced almost overwhelming problems in coordinating the attempt both to clear the building in order to obtain coherent plans and to allow for the infinitely slower work of treating properly the enormous quantity of small finds, themselves of extraordinary importance.

The history of the building is relatively straightforward. Built in the ninth century by Shalmaneser III, it was extensively renovated in the seventh century by Esarhaddon.[6] Some rebuilding seems also to have been carried out by Shalmaneser's grandson, Adad-nerari III (810–783 BC). Information was also recovered here relating to the fall of Assyria, in that the building provided evidence of two 'final' attacks, confirming the account of the 'Babylonian Chronicle' which mentions two major invasions of Assyria, one in 614 BC when the Medes advanced on Nineveh, captured Tarbiṣu (not far from Nineveh and the site of Assurbanipal's palace as Crown Prince) and then marched down the Tigris to Assur, and the second and final destruction in 612.[7] Kalhu is not mentioned in either entry, but the city lies on one possible line of the Median attack and it certainly suffered a major assault not long before the final destruction.

THE WALLS AND GATES OF FORT SHALMANESER
On the west side the arsenal is bounded by a single defensive wall, 290 m long and buttressed at intervals by large towers. Assyrian building inscriptions which relate to

the construction or restoration of city walls inform us that the usual height is some 120 brick courses (c. 15 m), which seems a reasonable approximation for the external height of the walls at Nimrud. The use of enfilading towers is a basic principle of military architecture at this period, and the west wall of Fort Shalmaneser reproduces almost exactly the arrangement and dimensions of the east wall of the North-West Palace, built on the citadel by Shalmaneser's father, Assurnasirpal II. This same towered pattern was repeated on the other three sides of the arsenal, but the projection of the towers and the distances between them were less regular.

The defences on the south side proved to be the best preserved because here, in the seventh century, Esarhaddon had reinforced those originally built by Shalmaneser III. Wherever the south face was examined, it proved to consist of mud-brick surmounting a base of massive, finely dressed ashlar blocks, the bottom course resting on an earth scarp (see p. 153).[8] In the south-east corner of the building the junction between Esarhaddon's wall with its relatively shallow buttresses and the line of Shalmaneser's projecting towers provides a sharp contrast on the plan. It is possible that the Patti-Hegalli, the Zab canal dug by Assurnasirpal II (p. 33), ran along at least part of the south side of Fort Shalmaneser. This would have added to the defences of the arsenal, and could suggest that Esarhaddon's gate (R1) may have connected with a 'water gate' at some lower level.

From the outer town, access to the arsenal was through two gates, in the north and west walls. The West Gate was comparatively well preserved and yielded important evidence for the architectural reconstruction which can be seen in Fig. 92. The gate arch, which spanned an opening just under 4 m wide and about 4 m high, was a barrel vault consisting of two concentric, unbonded rings of radiating voussoirs, only a few of which had survived. Its only structural peculiarity is a slight convergence of the opposing faces of the piers below the spring of the vault, which gave it the semi-elliptical profile characteristic of the gates depicted on the sculptures. The lack of bonding may explain the paucity of surviving remains of these large arches. The gate itself was originally closed with double doors. A flagged stone roadway led through the gate into the north-west courtyard, and both the NW and NE courtyards had originally been paved with the same rough limestone slabs. The gate had been severely damaged in the attack of 614, and it would appear that repaving was actually in progress when the city was finally captured and destroyed in 612 BC. Indeed the evidence here is important in our reconstruction of the last years of Kalhu, since it is clear that a major attack on the city had been followed by an attempt to repair the damage, and that these repairs had not been completed before the final sack in 612 BC. For example, a pile of stone awaiting re-use was found outside the south tower, while the south socket of the main gate was found with the capstone in place yet on the north side, although a pit had been dug for it, the capstone had not as yet been reinstalled. Moreover, the bitumen on the flagstones of the unfinished roadway had wheelmarks running in many different directions, revealing that they had been relaid. It is also clear that the fallen brickwork associated with this phase was the result of deliberate demolition and that it can be stratigraphically distinguished from the weathering and decay that followed the Median assault of 612. Thus, there is

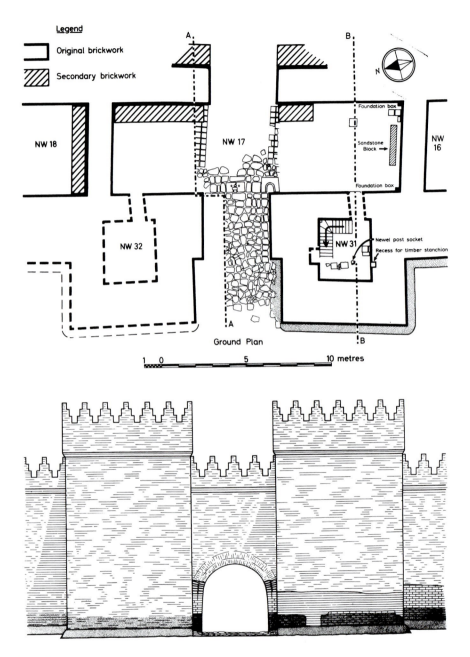

Legend

☐ Original brickwork

▨ Secondary brickwork

NW 18

NW 17

NW 16

NW 32

Foundation box

Sandstone Block →

Foundation box

NW 31

Newel post socket

Recess for timber stanchion

A

B

Ground Plan

1 0   5   10 metres

Fig. 92. Plan, elevation and reconstruction of the west gate.

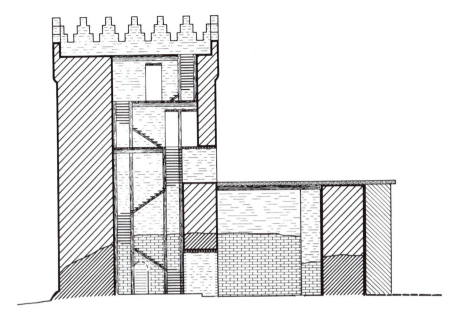

unequivocal evidence for two separate assaults, relatively close together in time.

The gateway was flanked by massive towers 7.5 m wide, projecting 3.60 m from the outer face of the wall. Only the south tower, within which was the small room NW 31, was completely excavated. The reconstruction shows a flight of stairs ascending within this room to give access to the top of the outer wall and to the tower roof. Sufficient indications of the actual treads remained for both the gradient and the width of the stairs to be estimated, and it was on this evidence that the height of the *chemin de ronde* was calculated.[9] The fragment of a pottery storage bin found in the debris against the west gate provides some idea of how these walls would have looked (Fig. 93). As elsewhere in the building, foundation boxes containing *lahmu* figures (p. 255) were found in two of the corners of the gate chamber.

By contrast, the structure of the North Gate survived only to the height of a few courses above pavement level. As in the case of the West Gate, its demolition seems to have been a deliberate act of the Assyrians themselves, but here the reconstruction had only begun. The plan of this gate differed from that in the western wall not only in the absence of a gate chamber but in the fact that at some time the gate had been narrowed, perhaps to prevent the entry of wheeled vehicles. Indeed the absence of wheel marks on the bitumen surface of the latest pavement indicates the lack of such traffic in the latest stage of its use (Fig. 94). It has been remarked that it seems extra-ordinary that the Assyrians had left one of their major fortresses defenceless 'at a time when their empire was crumbling'. Such comment is made with the wisdom of hindsight, for it would appear that in 613 BC, between the period of the two attacks, the Assyrians were sufficiently confident of their position to mount a campaign against the Babylonians in the south.[10] Certainly they would have repaired one of

Fig. 93. Fragment of a pottery storage bin decorated with the crenellations and 'glazed brick' rosettes of a city wall (ht of fragment 52 cm; ND 10931). An even larger fragment was found depicting a second, upper storey, also with crenellations and rosettes.

their major fortresses more quickly had they anticipated the repetition of the 614 BC attack.

The presence of evidence for post-612 BC squatter occupation has been mentioned in connection with all the major buildings on the site, and especially with reference to the Burnt Palace and Ezida. Fort Shalmaneser was no exception, and here, in the North Gate, a levelled roadway had been constructed for a narrow, stone-paved entrance some 90 cm above the original pavement. We know from historical sources that an Assyrian government survived for some years after 612 BC in Harran (near modern Urfa), but it would appear that in Assyria also some semblance of local authority must have persisted, or been revived.

We know very little of Shalmaneser's southern entrance to the arsenal, because much of his construction in this area was either dismantled or covered over by Esarhaddon. In room R 6, however, the remains of a barrel-vaulted doorway were found, totally buried within Esarhaddon's brickwork. An interesting feature of Shalmaneser's wall is that it had been regularly studded with ventilation shafts, closed by plain perforated bricks. These were perhaps to allow drainage or expansion of the brickwork, or both. But the south wall as one sees it today was the work of Esarhaddon, a great revetment extending the whole length of the south wall and some 60 m along the east wall. Here a footing of six or seven courses of ashlar masonry was surmounted by a massive mud-brick wall, in one place surviving to a height of some seven metres. Below this, the stone rested on a steeply sloping glacis. It is possible that Esarhaddon intended to extend this new outer wall around the whole of the building, but there is no actual evidence to suggest this. In fact, the northern limit of the eastern sector coincides almost exactly with the line of the repairs to the throne room suite and includes the area rebuilt by him in the south-easternmost sector, suggesting that the external repairs were solely to that part of the building that had either already subsided (p. 180) or was in need of reinforcement along the canal or river bank conglomerate on which this part of Fort Shalmaneser was constructed.

Fig. 94. North gate of Fort Shalmaneser, looking north, showing the narrowed gate and the unmarked bitumen surface on the paved roadway. The outer east wall of the city is just visible in the background.

Fig. 95. Esarhaddon's postern gate; his inscription is preserved on ashlar blocks on either side of the corbelled gate.

A glance at the plan will show that the new wall widens at its south-western limit. The widening of the defences along this stretch was for the purpose of containing a new postern gate, leading to a series of narrow corridors, which provided both a more secure approach to (or exit from) the official quarters of the arsenal and an entrance to the outer bailey, by-passing the building itself. The corbelled outer gate is illustrated in Fig. 95; a text describing Esarhaddon's work, in phrases virtually identical with those of the cylinders, was inscribed on either side of the entrance. Both the inner and outer doors of the stone entrance chamber had been fitted with a single-leaf door, with a multiplicity of locking mechanisms and bolts. Access through the rest of the entrance passage was along an upward-sloping passage, through arched mud-brick doorways.[11] In R 7 faint traces of wall paintings were discernible, including the usual procession of courtiers, a wheeled vehicle and perhaps the king. It was in this room that the entrance passage divided, continuing straight ahead into the outer bailey west of the arsenal or turning right into R 9, a paved room which led through a bolted door into a further vestibule (S 57) and on into the south-western courtyard of the building (S 68). Here there existed a considerable difference in level between Shalmaneser III's courtyard floor and the sill of the exterior door of S 57, indicating a rise of some two metres as a result of Esarhaddon's rebuilding. This per-

154

haps implies some form of ramp or terrace in the area of the throne room (below, p. 180).

THE NORTH-WEST QUADRANT

Entrance to this quarter was by means of the formidable towered gate in the west wall, already described. Around the courtyard were a number of large magazines and workshops. As elsewhere in the building, it was impossible fully to excavate these large rooms, one reason for the limited areas of cobbling and brick paving indicated generally on the plan. But in the workshops benches abutted the long wall, the cobbled or paved floors extending only some 1.5. m in front of them. In other words, only what has been excavated is shown, but in some cases the cobbling was actually deliberately restricted. Only one of the workshops, of which there were originally at least eight opening off the main courtyard, survived in its original form until 612 BC. The rest were adapted to other uses after Kalhu yielded place, first to Khorsabad and then to Nineveh, as the centre of government and the headquarters of the army.

The surviving workshop was NW 20 (Fig. 96). Its principal feature was a long mud-brick workbench about 80 cm high and 60 cm deep, running most of the length of the wall opposite the door. Interestingly, this almost precisely paralleled the working areas in our modern dig house, made of course of the same very flexible building material, mud-brick. A series of plastered holes in the wall above the bench again resembled our own primitive but very convenient system of storage shelves supported by pegs in the wall. The floor in NW 20 was roughly paved for a distance of 1.5 m in front of the workbench, but patches of a more regular cobbled surface probably represent the original floor. There was a ventilation shaft in the south wall,

Fig. 96. Workshop NW 20, showing the mud-brick workbench, the partially paved floor surface and the peg holes in the wall.

beneath which was a rectangle of baked bricks, clearly a footing for some piece of equipment. Such features were not standard fittings but seem to have been installed where needed.

The doors of the northern workshops in this quadrant were unusually wide, as much as 3 m in breadth. On the west jamb of the doorway of NW 22 we found the stub of an arch from which we could calculate that the crown of the arch was originally c. 3.40 m above floor level. Obviously these particular workshops were intended to accommodate very large objects, perhaps chariots, the repair of which is attested in some of the Fort Shalmaneser tablets.[12] Another interesting point of design is the provision for a porch in front of each of the south-facing doors, obviously intended to shield the interior from the sun.

Most of the other workshops had been adapted for use as storage magazines. NW 19 had been used as a granary, and at the time of the final sack it was evidently a pottery store, for it yielded fragments of a number of bowls, at least 24 lamps and literally hundreds of potstands. Large quantities of bronze horse harness were found in two rooms, the largest collection, in NW 21, consisting of caps, studs, beads, embossed plaques and rosettes, again suggesting that these rooms might have accommodated chariots. A notable number of lamps (26) came also from NW 22. Large storage jars were found at one end of some of these rooms (see plan); those in NW 18 must have contained oil, judging by the ferocity of the fire that raged here. NW 15 contained ivories, and a quantity of armour and weapons, including iron daggers, spears and an iron snaffle-bit, while a small docket from NW 21 recorded the inspection of an extraordinary number of bows, a total of 36,242.[13] In other words, this courtyard seems to have been devoted specifically to the maintenance and repair, and ultimately the storage, of military equipment and supplies, and especially equipment associated with the use of chariots and horses (see also the horse texts, discussed on pp. 159, 215).

THE NORTH-EAST QUADRANT

The NE courtyard was considerably larger than that to the west, measuring some 95 x 80 m. The surrounding chambers again consisted of workshops and magazines and, in the north-west corner, an official residence of some size and status. As described above, a towered, cobbled gateway in the north wall provided one of two main entrances to the building, and there was a second means of access to the NE quadrant from the courtyard of the NW sector, a wide cobbled gate through the west wall, closed on its western side by double doors, the pivot holes of which survived. Long storage magazines occupied the south side of the courtyard where there was also a cobbled approach to a wide gate-chamber (NE 3), with a bitumened roadway leading into the SE quadrant.

The southern gate-chamber (SE 13) was virtually identical with its counterpart in the NE courtyard, the bitumen-surfaced road passing through both. The outline of the original gate towers, cut back at the time of Esarhaddon's renovations, was still visible in the limit of the cobbles which abutted them. Large socket-holes were identified on either side of both gates, in which the double-door posts had once revolved,

Fig. 97. Pile of door sockets in the north-east corner of the gate chamber SE 13, stacked here after the 614 BC sack and awaiting reinstallation.

but the stone tops had been removed. The sockets themselves were probably among the number we found stacked in both gate-chambers, presumably for reinstallation after the first sack when looters had ripped out the metal shoes (Fig. 97). Of the recovered door sockets, the largest may have been made for an external or nearby city gate; certainly they were too big for any of the inner gates of Fort Shalmaneser.[14] Other evidence of repair came from Room NE 26. Here, leaning against the south wall of the chamber, were six limestone tablets, five of which bore an inscription of Assurnasirpal II and one of Shalmaneser III.[15] The removal of these large stone tablets (the largest measured some 66 by 42 cm) from their original positions, almost certainly as foundation deposits in the city wall that enclosed the building on two sides, may date to the 614 BC sack or possibly to the time of Esarhaddon, who repaired the walls of the arsenal. Interestingly, two similar stone tablets, possibly also removed from their original location when repairs to the walls were being effected (in this case presumably the citadel walls), had been used to seal the grave in room DD of the North-West Palace, the grave which contained the so-called Nimrud jewel (p. 79). Also in NE 26 were a very large quantity of shell inlay (some 3-4000 pieces), large numbers of assorted metal bindings, heavy bronze sheathing, often in the form of bulls' hooves or lions' paws and two open work copper panels; these were clearly the component parts of several pieces of furniture which had been stacked against the end wall (Figs. 145, 146, p. 233).

Although a number of rooms in this courtyard had originally been designed as workshops, NE 50 seems to have been the only one to have retained its ninth century function. It was here that was found an alabaster statue of Shalmaneser III, just over a metre in height, dedicated to the god Adad of Kurbail. The statue, on which traces

Fig. 98. Alabaster statue of Shalmaneser III, in situ in the workshop NE 50, where it had been brought for repair (ht 1.03 m; ND 10000).

of paint survive, had clearly been in the process of repair; indeed holes had already been dowelled to mend a fracture across its bottom corner (Fig. 98). The statue had obviously been brought to the arsenal for repair, possibly from Kurbail itself or from Assur where there was also a temple of this god.[16] An extraordinary iron frame-saw found nearby, over a metre and a half in length (p. 249), must have been part of a stone-cutter's equipment. Similar stone-cutting saws are shown being carried by workmen on the series of reliefs from Nineveh showing the quarrying and transport of the bull colossi.[17] Stone fragments found in NE 50 suggest either the making of pigment as a colouring agent or, conceivably, the smelting of iron, although there is no evidence of foundries within the boundaries of Fort Shalmaneser and iron is far more likely to have arrived in the form of already smelted metal.[18] NE 56 and 59 had also been built as workshops, but 59 was later converted for residential use, the paved workshop floors having been plastered over and a bathroom added.

NE 48-50 yielded a large number of cuneiform tablets. In NE 48-49, however, these were contained within packed debris of the 612 sack, re-used by the post-destruction squatters to raise the floor level by some 70-80 cm, that is, the tablets were no longer in their original contexts. Many of those from rooms 48 and 49 are records of wine rations issued to members of the royal household, from the queen down to the mess attendants, and to government and army officials. They are very similar to the SW 6 wine lists (p. 213), but their original provenance remains uncer-

Fig. 99. Ivory two-horse chariot and charioteers, from SW 37 (11.3 x 6 cm, ND 10316, British Museum).

tain.[19] Those from NE 50, found scattered in the floor debris, are more varied in character. An important category consists of records of musters of men, horses and mules, registered under their commanders or under the names of provincial cities. The totals involved are often considerable, over 2000 horses and 67 mules detailed on the obverse of a single tablet.[20] Other texts from NE 50 deal with very large quantities of copper, tin and lead in the hands of the *masennu*, a powerful administrative official perhaps best translated as the 'treasurer'.[21]

NE 51-55 together with NW 1-3 constituted the nucleus of the largest residence in this part of the building. Here there was an internal, private courtyard (NE 53-54), in which were at least two workshops (NW 2 and NE 55). In NW 1 was a painted frieze of horizontal black and white chevrons, hardly a feature of barrack rooms. The thickness of the outer walls suggests an upper storey where the principal living rooms would have been situated. In this instance the stairs themselves were discovered, rising from the internal courtyard and providing an estimated height for the upper storey of rather more than four metres above the courtyard surface.[22] Unfortunately we have no tablets to tell us directly of the occupant of this apartment, although one of the horse lists (ND 10079) was recovered from NW 3, a paved room which adjoined workshop NE 55, perhaps having fallen from the upper storey. The so-called horse lists (found largely in NE 50) relate to the annual muster, held at Fort Shalmaneser (p. 215), and it must remain a possibility that the official whose residence this was played an important role in this aspect of the administration. Indeed all the so-called horse lists came from rooms opening onto the north-east courtyard, and information from these tablets suggests that all incoming items, whether foodstuffs, metals, chariots or horses, were recorded as they entered the arsenal, conceivably under the direction of the official who occupied this residence. An inscribed brick bearing the name of Adad-

Fig. 100. Ivories from the cupboard in NE 2, probably belonging to the rab ekalli. *a,b) front and back views of ND 9301, Nubian carrying a baboon on his shoulders and leading an antelope (ht of figure 13.2 cm, Iraq Museum); c) ND 9302, Nubian carrying a monkey and leading an oryx; he carries a badly damaged leopard skin over his right arm (ht 13.4 cm, Metropolitan Museum of Art); d) back view of ND 9306, the figure carries a goat on his shoulders and holds an ostrich by the neck (ht 13.3 cm, Iraq Museum). This group is from a set of six ivories carved in the round and set on an ivory plinth (see also Fig. 140).*

nerari III in the pavement of NW 3 suggests that its construction dates to his reign. As the plan also indicates, the long rooms along this section of the north wall were not bonded with the outer wall itself. This does not necessarily mean that they were not part of the original building, only that the various sectors were built separately.

NE 6-8, in the south-east corner, formed another residential suite, which was rebuilt at some time linking it with rooms to the east, surrounding court NE 9, in order to provide larger accommodation, again presumably for an official of some standing. Fibulae, arrowheads and armour scales were found here, including an unusual copper object that seems to have been some type of doorlock.[23] There is no direct evidence of the date of the alterations, but the east side of the courtyard

provides interesting confirmation of the extent to which Fort Shalmaneser had been allowed to decay at some period in its history. Here the whole of the courtyard wall had to be reinforced by the addition of an almost equal thickness of mud-brick along its outer face. The renovation was very competently executed, in a manner quite unlike the hasty improvisations after the first sack of the building.[24] It was also accompanied by the insertion of new foundation deposits, consisting of boxes for the usual apotropaic figurines, and the repaving of considerable areas. This is a situation which undoubtedly matches that described on Esarhaddon's cylinders, strongly suggesting that these and other alterations, particularly to the eastern side of the building, were carried out by him. Beyond the eastern wall were three further blocks of buildings separated by small courtyards. Unfortunately these barrack-like structures were heavily eroded, and their plans could not be traced further to the east.

In NE 2 and NE 1 were found tablets and other objects, including ivory and glass, some possibly fallen from the upper storey of the *rab ekalli*'s house, discussed below, p. 164. However, an unusual group of ivories appear actually to have been stored in NE 2, since these were recovered not only from the burnt debris on the floor but actually from the eastern cupboard in the south wall. These ivories comprised a unique and very beautiful group of statuettes carved in the round, arguably the finest ivories found in Fort Shalmaneser. They depict Syrians and negroid types, perhaps Nubians, carrying animals across their shoulders or leading them on the rein (Fig. 100). Monkeys, ibex, goat, gazelle, ostrich and lion are represented. The figures had originally been attached to an ivory plinth. That they had genuinely been stored in NE 2, rather than the rooms above, is confirmed by the fact that the two figures found in the cupboard had been shielded from the fire, while the others had been burnt. These constitute the only set of ivories from Nimrud carved fully in the round, and the craftsmanship is quite remarkable.[25] Indeed their quality suggests that NE 2, like the wine cellar SW 6, was actually part of the *rab ekalli*'s establishment, despite the apparent lack of direct access.

SOUTH-EAST QUADRANT

Like the northern quadrants this was constructed around a very large open space, here some 80 x 100 m, designed to accommodate military and other traffic. Its north gate (discussed above in the context of the parallel NE gate chamber) was some 4 m wide, and on the west two passages led into the smaller courtyards that formed the SW quadrant. The size of the north gateway shows that it was designed to permit the passage of vehicles, probably military chariots and wagons either coming to unload outside the SW magazines or involved in some way in the annual muster, or both. Indeed the marks of their studded wheels can still be seen on the bitumened roadway which was laid across the gate-chamber to protect the brick pavement.[26] To the south lay the entrances to the ceremonial and domestic quarters. The double wall on the south side of the court is discussed below, p. 172, in the context of the throne room suite.

Along the west side, set in a shallow niche in the east wall of SE 8, but not in its original position, was a throne dais which may have served as a royal 'saluting base' for the review and inspection of troops. The throne base, which bore an inscription of Shalmaneser III, may have been installed originally in some other position within the courtyard, or even elsewhere in the building, although we have found no surviving niche of the appropriate shape.[27] Along the north and west sides of the court were groups of rooms, three along each side, each group consisting of a single long chamber with attached bathroom. The latter were paved, with the usual ablution slab and provision for drainage. These suites of rooms were clearly residential, perhaps barracks for the king's household troops. As in the quadrant to the north, the corner suites were the residences of more senior officials, that in the north-west corner already identified as the house of the palace chamberlain, the *rab ekalli*. The rooms numbered SE 20-24 constituted a second residential suite, but here barely 30 cm of soil covered its floors, and no objects remained to provide a clue to its former occupant. The unusual size of the bathroom (SE 21) is, however, some index of his status.[28]

Among the more interesting objects from the barrack rooms was a small cache of iron tools and weapons in SE 16, resting on a low brick-built shelf;[29] these included a crescent-shaped sickle blade, a dagger and what may have been the blade of a short sword. In the adjoining bathroom a water jar was found still standing in position in the niche behind the drain-hole, which remained as it had been aban-

Fig. 101. Entrance to the harem quarters from the SE courtyard: room S 1, looking south-west through doorway into S2 (the figure stands against a baulk).

doned, closed with its stone plug. In the next chamber, SE 18, a large collection of pottery including pot stands, bowls and small beakers identical with the small glasses (*istikanat*) in which tea is drunk today in the Arab world, lay in a heap in rubbish at one end of the room. Of interest in the context of the military establishment which was housed here was a small clay tablet, found lying on the pavement at the eastern end of the courtyard, recording 784 bows from the city of Arpad in northern Syria, dated to 683 BC, late in the reign of Sennacherib.

On the west side, SE 5 yielded a large number of fragments of small apotropaic figurines. In Fort Shalmaneser the type represented most commonly was the *lahmu* (referred to as the bearded spearman in the preliminary reports), but an unusual quantity and variety of types were found here.[30] Conspicuously lacking, however, were the *apkallu*, common in the late 9th century boxes in the Burnt Palace. Also found in SE 5 were two examples of the miniature copper symbols, a crescent pole and a spear, that sometimes accompany these figurines. The most likely explanation for this unusual collection is that it had been stored here during the 614 repairs and had never been replaced (see also p. 256).

A long passage from the SE courtyard led through the ante-chamber S 74 into courtyard S and the more private quarters of the building. Here too the northern door was protected by figurines in foundation boxes, of which only two miniature copper spears had survived. Originally a door led directly into S1, thence into the inner royal quarters (Fig. 101), but this had subsequently been blocked, leaving a more

163

restricted access through SE 8, which now served as a guard room. In SE 8 were found a number of Assyrian style ivories, an iron knife, two blades, an armour scale and some 20 arrowheads, eight of which were stored in a small jar embedded in the original floor. In the courtyard outside SE 8, and running over the throne base, was a patchwork brick pavement, again representing rebuilding during the post-612 squatter occupation. It is of most interest for the small oblong clay bead with a circular hole at the top for suspension, found on its surface. This bore a votive inscription of Merodach-Baladan, the Babylonian king whose inscribed cylinder was found in ZT (p. 198). This label (ND 7084) must originally have been attached to an object dedicated in one of the temples in Babylon and later removed to Kalhu, perhaps at the same time as the cylinder. Whatever the actual object was, it seems to have been looted once again in the 612 sack, at that time losing its dedicatory label.

HOUSE OF THE *RAB EKALLI* (ROOMS SE 1-3, 10-12; AND SW 6; NE 1,2)

West of the gate-chamber, in the north-west corner of the SE courtyard, lay the residence of the senior official in charge of the *ekal mašarti*. It consisted of a large ground floor room with access to a small ante-chamber and bathroom (SE 1-3) and a second chamber with an alabaster-floored ventilation shaft and an arched cupboard-niche (SE 10). There was in addition a stairwell with its own entrance, leading to an upper storey (SE 11, 12). That this was a single suite, despite the lack of internal communication between its rooms, is shown by its more palatial character, expressed also in the traces of painting on the walls of SE 1-3 and the ornamental reveals on the doorways of SE 10 and 11; such decoration stands out in stark contrast to the severely utilitarian aspect of the barracks. At some time during the history of the building the doorway to SE 3 was enlarged and against the new north jamb was set a limestone block, presumably intended as a seat for the *rab ekalli*'s doorkeeper.

The *rab ekalli*'s residence had been ravaged by fire, and many of the valuable objects which had been kept in the upper chambers had cascaded down into the rooms below. These included unusually fine ivories, metal tools and weapons, and cuneiform tablets. Similar items were also recovered from the adjacent wine cellar (SW 6, discussed below), suggesting that the residence extended over this room as well. In SE 1, burnt ivories and charred wood were found from a depth of 50 cm below the surface literally down to the floor, while the whole of the floor of SE 10 was covered in burnt debris to a depth of over a metre. The small room SE 11, which was situated at the foot of the stairs, had served as a kitchen and contained a wide range of cooking and drinking vessels. A set of ten stone duck weights was found, seven of them in an alcove under the stairs. Also found here was a broken stone lion-weight inscribed with the name of Shalmaneser, together with a badly calcined alabaster vase bearing the inscription 'Palace of Esarhaddon'.[31] One of the tablets recovered here was an incantation with ritual instructions concerning the washroom, perhaps connected with the building of a reed privy,[32] in the context of which should be mentioned the small lavatory (SE 24), situated in the north-western part of the court and apparently on the western wall.

Among the most historically significant documents from the *rab ekalli*'s residence were fragments of four baked clay Esarhaddon cylinders which had obviously been stored in one of the upper rooms. Indeed joins were made between SE 1 and SE 10, and further fragments were subsequently recovered in NE 2. The text was much the same as that on the cylinder recovered from Nimrud village (p. 216), although the Fort Shalmaneser fragments were dated to 676 BC, that is, four years earlier.[33] Both recorded repairs to the 'gate-walls of the great buildings of Kalhu', and it is likely to have been at this time that the large limestone tablets found in NE 26 had been removed from their original positions in the walls of the building. Other documents from the *rab ekalli*'s rooms, recovered in 1958, were the first to identify the building as the *ekal mašarti*.[34] It is conceivable that the long chamber NE 2 was also part of the *rab ekalli*'s establishment, not only because his rooms obviously extended over it but because of the remarkable quality of the group of figures leading animals, carved in the round, perhaps the finest ivories recovered from the *ekal mašarti*, which had obviously been stored here (Fig. 100).

At some time not long after the 612 sack squatters occupied the *rab ekalli*'s house, as elsewhere in the arsenal. On the citadel, and especially in the North-West Palace and the Nabu Temple, we had occasionally observed that a piece from the floor of a room joined one from the squatter level above, demonstrating the degree to which the burnt debris had been shovelled about after the sack. In this part of Fort Shalmaneser it was an ivory from SE 10, in the *rab ekalli*'s house, that joined a piece found in the squatter level.[35]

SOUTH-WEST QUADRANT

Of the four sectors of the outer building this was the only one that lacked a large central area. It was instead sub-divided into four courtyards, themselves of no small size, each lined with enormous storage magazines. SW 37, for example, measured some 30 x 4.3 m, with walls still standing to a height of up to 1.80 m. Access to these well-protected magazines was through two long passages from the SE courtyard or, more directly, from the NW quadrant via passage SW 2. Interestingly, in the latter passage were four large water jars set up to their necks in a massive mud-brick bench. A hole had been pierced near the bottom of each jar and connected by a bitumen-lined channel with one of a row of bitumen spouts on the outside of the high bench, about half a metre above the floor of the passage. The spouts must originally have been closed with removable plugs, the jars presumably serving as butts for drinking water, replenished from a well or even rainwater from the roof. Enclosing these water jars in mud-brick must also have served to keep them cool.

Although an overall plan has been established, largely by partial excavation of the walls, we were able to investigate only a few of the rooms in this sector owing to the extraordinary quantities of objects contained in some of them. The excavation of the carved ivories found in SW 7, 12 and 37, for example, occupied us over five seasons, in fact throughout the remainder of our time at Nimrud. Further excavation may well modify that part of the plan which has been reconstructed largely from surface scraping (unblackened walls).[36] However, with the exception of the *rab ekalli*'s wine cellar (SW 6), relatively little was found in the other rooms along the north and east

sides of the eastern courtyards. Unusual objects found in this quadrant are the bronze and iron wheeled brazier, discovered by the Italian expedition in room A2 and illustrated in Pl. 12c, and the ostracon from room SW 1, inscribed in Aramaic with what appears to have been a list of personal names.[37] SW 3 and 4 had originally been a single magazine, but at some later time a partition wall was inserted to convert this into the usual residential suite, living room plus bathroom. Of interest here are the baked bricks found in the vicinity of the bathroom drain (SW 3) which bore a lion stamp, possibly to be associated with Esarhaddon's renovations (see also p. 220).

As already noted, SW 6 was the wine cellar above which lay part of the upper storey of the house of the *rab ekalli*. Thus many of the objects recovered from SW 6 came from the house above and were not originally associated with the wine cellar. However, the majority of the tablets recovered actually refer to entitlements of wine, and in one case beer, to members of the royal household, officials and dependants of the palace, and to distinguished visitors, and suggest that the *rab ekalli* was himself responsible for the administration of these issues. At either end of SW 6 were groups of large storage jars set in the usual low platform of mud-brick. A number of these jars were almost intact, and some had been inscribed after firing with a measure of capacity expressed in homers, *sutu* and *qa*. We attempted, in 1957, both by calculation and by experiment, to determine the volume of the two best-preserved jars,

Fig. 102. Ivory table leg terminating in a lion's paw, identical with that illustrated on Fig. 147, p. 235; the smaller ivories were probably used as appliqué ornament. From the SW 6 wine magazine (ht 47.5 cm; ND 6383).

166

Fig. 103. Ivory chairback from SW 7, the only example with a geometric design. The mould-ing of half cylinders must originally have been combined with some other material, perhaps the wood of the frame (overall width 54.5 cm, ND 7910, Metropolitan Museum of Art).

and thereby the true value of the Assyrian homer, assuming that the measure record-ed referred to the full capacity of the jar. Unfortunately, the results differed, though the capacity of the *qa* was reasonably accurately calculated at 1.84 litres. Our prob-lem in attempting to establish the volume of the homer was complicated by our igno-rance of the precise meaning of the expression "in the *sutu* of x *qa*", which seemed to define recognised variations in the larger measures. The capacity of the wine jars themselves was just over 300 litres, and it was calculated that altogether the wine store could have held as much as 4000 gallons at any one time. Among the other finds in the room were a number of ivories, including a table leg of Hepplewhite pattern (Fig. 102), originally assumed to have been a chair leg. These, together with large chunks of Egyptian blue found on and among the jars, must have fallen from the upper storey.[38] Lying beside the wine jars in the north-west corner of the magazine was a human skeleton, one of very few found in the building, killed possibly by the collapse of the upper storey. The reader can perhaps imagine the speculation of the younger dig staff as to whether he had been trying to balance on the ivory chair on top of a wine jar. It is certainly possible that the contents of the wine cellar had helped to render him insensible to the danger without.

In the east wall of SW 7 was a ventilation shaft; seepage in the mud-brick

Fig. 104. Detail from the cross-piece on one of the large ivory chair backs, depicting a bull hunt (width 27.5 cm; part of ND 7904; Iraq Museum).

Fig. 105. Cloisonné *ivory panel, goddess in 'Egyptianising' style. One of the most beautiful ivories found at Nimrud (from SW 7, 15.9 x 5.2 cm; ND 7580, Iraq Museum).*

around the bases of a pair of shattered storage jars at the north end of the room suggested the storage of oil. The northern part of the room was covered by a corroded mass of both bronze and iron scale armour. Large fragments were preserved, lying in layers up to 35 cm thick interspersed with broken brickwork, to a height of 1.40 m, suggesting that the armour had either been stored above or, perhaps more likely, given the presence of oil in the room which could have been used for its maintenance, actually in the room, either on high shelving or in some way suspended from the walls or roof. The south end of the room served for the storage of objects of a very different nature. Here, over a depth of some 2 m from the ground surface to the floor, was one of the richest series of ivories recovered from the site. During 1957 we were able to remove only the upper levels of this deposit, but in 1958 we uncovered many more pieces in position, as they had been left at the abandonment of the building. These proved to be large panels of ivory veneer which had originally ornamented the backs of chairs or perhaps the heads of couches (Fig. 103).[39] These remarkable discoveries are discussed at greater length in chapter 7. Other types of decorative inlay were also found in this room, most notably five small glass plaques, two of which were almost complete. Each was very delicately painted in black with traces of blue on a white background, depicting a sphinx of Phoenician type advancing towards a papyrus plant (p. 239).[40] Together with four further examples from SW 37, these provide some of the earliest known examples of painted glass.

In our preliminary examination of the SW sector of the building we had determined that rooms SW 12 and 37 also contained large quantities of ivories. Our limited staff and facilities permitted us to undertake the excavation of only one such room at a time, so it was necessary to complete first the excavation of SW 7 before undertaking the other ivory rooms. Thus in 1958, after completing the work in SW 7, we embarked on the extraction of the ivories from SW 37 and in that year, in the uppermost metre of soil alone, we removed over 150 pieces. Indeed the excavation of SW 37 was only completed in 1961 and SW 12 occupied us for the remainder of our time at Nimrud. Both rooms produced some of the finest objects recovered from the arsenal (including Fig. 105).

Whether the objects in these rooms were simply booty and tribute deliberately stored here or valuable furnishings from the residential apartments cannot be established. The occurrence of ivories throughout the fill of these rooms, from top to bottom, suggests that they had been stored on shelves along the walls, but the entirely haphazard disposition of the decorative components led us to conclude that at least some had been either violently dismembered before being placed in the store or in the sack of 612 BC. In general the style of the ivories is considered to be older than the seventh century, but that does not prove either when they were actually brought to the site or when they were placed in store. A plain strip of ivory found in 1961 in SW 37 bore an inscription of Šamši-Adad V, grandson of Assurnasirpal II, but again, this dates only the manufacture of the object on which this inscribed veneer appeared. Other inscribed fragments from this room bore in Aramaic the name of the ancient city of Hamath (modern Hama) (Fig. 131), and three lines of 8th century BC Hebrew, constituting one of the finest examples of ancient Hebrew cursive script.[41] Over 2000 ivories were ultimately recovered from this room, including some 200 pieces of ornamental horse harness.[42] Not only did their excavation require much time and effort in the field, but the work of conservation and repair occupied for some considerable time the laboratory staffs of the Iraq Museum and the Institute of Archaeology of the University of London.

Not only ivories were found here. Lion's head finials, rosettes and petals of white limestone were probably also furniture ornaments. Small pieces of inlay, of glass, frit, shell and rock crystal may originally have been set in *champ-levé* ivory plaques or in a wooden matrix. Nose and cheek pieces from horse harness, fashioned in fine-grained white stone, obviously echo the more ornate examples in ivory. Other finds included a variety of beads.

SW 12 was excavated in 1962 and 1963. During this time some 500 pieces were cleaned and catalogued, but it proved impossible to complete this work during the excavation seasons and many were taken to the Iraq Museum in Baghdad for

Fig. 106. Curved ivory plaque, probably from a pyxis; cow of Egyptian Hathor type suckling its calf; the background papyrus thicket is inlaid with blue and green glass; from SW 37 (ht 5.6 cm, ND 9412, Iraq Museum).

treatment and recording, a task that remains unfinished. The same is true for the enormous numbers of ivories excavated from T 10 (below). Those from SW 12, as in SW 37, included many plaques that almost certainly served as decoration for furniture. Many glass inlays were also found in SW 12, and a quantity of scale armour.

Further excavation of the SW quadrant of the arsenal was carried out in 1987-89 under the direction of Paolo Fiorina for the Centro Scavi di Torino. Here another storage magazine (A2) was investigated. This is the long east-west chamber indicated on the plan between the northern ends of SW 8 and SW 37. Black and white frescoes were found here, facing onto a small paved courtyard in the corner abutting SW 8, and possibly to be dated to the time of Esarhaddon. Ivories, bronze and iron weapons, glass and stone vessels, and cylinder seals were among the objects discovered. Undoubtedly the most unusual discovery was part of a well-preserved bronze and iron wheeled brazier, referred to earlier (Pl. 12c).[43] The Italian excavations also demonstrated that at the time of Esarhaddon the remainder of the south-eastern part of the SW quadrant was further divided into smaller chambers.

THE STATE APARTMENTS

It was remarked earlier that the high, steep-sided mounds in the south-eastern corner of the outer wall, Tulul al 'Azar, had been thought to indicate the presence of massive towers, part of the defences of the outer city. However, detailed investigation in 1962 of the area furthest to the south-east revealed not a defensive tower but the state apartments of a royal palace of which area S to the west constituted the private and domestic wing. The unusual height of the mound here reflected no more than the great thickness and height of the walls, particularly of the throne room (T 1), which had been erected by Shalmaneser III on a scale as grand as that of his father in the North-West Palace and provided the focal point of this part of the arsenal. Its walls

Fig. 107. An 'Egyptianising' piece from SW 12; figures of pharaoh facing a sacred tree are surmounted by a winged disc and a row of cobra/ uraei (12.3 x 7.4 cm; ND 11035, Iraq Museum).

were thicker than those elsewhere and doubtless towered over the remainder of the building. It is their collapse that accounts for much of the accumulation constituting this area of Tulul al 'Azar.

The throne room block was divided into two sections of unequal width by a massive longitudinal wall. The wider, northern section housed the throne room (T 1), a small lobby (T 7) and a stair-well (T 8), a plan closely comparable with the throne room suite in the North-West Palace. On the south lay an ante-chamber (T 3), with a small square room (T 9) at its western end. A third room (T 11), approached from courtyard S, had no internal communication with the other rooms in the block. The throne room was 42.10 m long and 9.8 m wide, almost as large as that in the North-West Palace. As in the North-West Palace, two doors, one at either end, provided access directly from the SE courtyard while a third led to the ante-chamber on the

171

south. The ante-chamber in turn could be approached directly from courtyard T by means of a monumental entrance flanked by projecting towers, or from T 21 in the south wing through a smaller doorway which was blocked at a later period.

The thickness of the throne room walls, 4.40-4.80 m, suggests not only that they originally stood to a greater height than the surrounding structures but that they may even have stood higher than the outer wall of Fort Shalmaneser, which had a maximum thickness of 4.40 m. Indeed the volume of mud-brick that had fallen into the throne room from the upper parts of the walls suggests that they originally reached almost double their present height of just under 6 m. (The minimum height of the outer wall to the *chemin de ronde* was more than 7 m, and it may have been considerably greater, p. 151.) This great height was clearly intended to enhance the visual importance of the throne room, both internally and externally, but it probably also had a practical purpose in providing clerestory lighting.[44] The north wall, facing the SE courtyard, was at some time rendered even more massive by the addition of a baulk of mud-brick, 5.60 m thick, along the length of the façade, interrupted only by wide recesses framing the entrances to the throne room and to the corridor S 76, which linked the SE court with courtyard S to the south, thus providing access without passing through the throne room suite, an arrangement that can be seen also in the North-West Palace. This massive baulk was built in two stages, marked by a vertical joint in the brickwork, and is structurally separate from the wall of the throne room. It remains uncertain whether it was an early feature, and it has been suggested that this revetment masks the presence of original towers flanking the doorways. We found no trace of them, but it must remain possible that they existed, as in the North-West Palace. However, the outer baulk is certainly a continuation of the wall separating the south-east corner of the SE courtyard from rooms T 2, T 4 and T 5, east of the throne room, which were part of the original plan.[45] Its function may have been to support an upper terrace below clerestory level, which would have extended along the whole length of the façade on the north and also over rooms T 3, T 9, T 11, on the south. Access to the terrace would have been gained by the stairwell, T 8, at the west end of the throne room. These rooms are further discussed below.

There has been much discussion here, as in the North-West Palace (p. 51), of a possible central entrance to the throne room from the SE courtyard. The known doorways stood to such a height that their tops were not preserved, that is, to more than 6 m. We therefore realised that if there had been a central door, it too should appear if the line of the north wall were further investigated, even if the wall were not exposed to pavement level which would have been extravagantly expensive. As shown on the plan (Fig. 91), the line of plaster marking the outer face of the original wall was traced on the surface for a distance of 20 m from the east doorway, well beyond the midpoint between the two entrances, and a corresponding middle stretch of the inner face of the wall was found by surface scraping and confirmed by shallow excavation. No opening was found.

Within the original throne room block only the east end of the throne room was excavated to floor level, again for reasons of expense. In the fill were found the remains of two of the original timber beams, each a massive 45 cm in diameter, but no small objects of any significance came to light. However, on the floor of the throne room at the east end was found one of the most splendid single objects to have come from the recent excavations. This was the original throne base of Shalmaneser III, installed by the then governor of Kalhu, Šamaš-bel-uṣur, and set in the rebated niche in the east wall, approximately though not precisely on the axis of the room (Fig. 108). Two stone 'tram-lines' with shallow grooves in their upper surfaces were set in the conventional position before the throne; these extended to within 3 m of the

Fig. 108. Yellow limestone throne base of Shalmaneser III, set in a rebated niche at the east end of the Fort Shalmaneser throne room (T 1). The throne base itself is in two pieces and measures 3.82 x 2.29 m; it is now in the Iraq Museum. The large postholes almost certainly date from a post 614 BC repair.

throne base but their full length was not exposed. These rails almost certainly supported a brazier of the type found in Fort Shalmaneser in 1989.[46] Beside the throne base in the north-east corner of the room was the requisite alabaster ablution slab, with a raised rim and a rectangular drainhole with a stone plug. Unusually, the drainhole was situated in the middle of the side adjoining the east wall, rather than in the centre of the slab, the more usual position for the drain. This arrangement is particularly puzzling because a slight concavity in the upper surface of this slab would have caused water to flow towards the central depression rather than the drain. In the excavated corners of the room were small foundation boxes, cut in the mud-brick platform, lined with clay and covered with fragments of brick sealed beneath the plaster of the floor. The boxes contained clay figurines of the *lahmu* type (p. 255), coated with white gypsum plaster and inscribed with a short apotropaic text.

The throne base itself consists of two slabs of yellowish limestone, 2.28 m in width and 3.82 m in overall length (Fig. 109). The upper surface of the dais is divided by a single step into two levels, each with a projecting tongue on the axis of the throne. The throne occupied a blank space in the middle of the rear of the slab, in which are three sets of symmetrically disposed circular indentations marking the positions of three successive thrones of slightly different dimensions, each with its foot-stool, as depicted on the reliefs. On most of the upper surface of the dais is a geometric pattern of rosettes, originally picked out in white, but the most interesting part of the decoration lies in the sculptured friezes in low relief which line the sides of the throne base. A long inscription of Shalmaneser III occupies part of the upper and lower surfaces of the dais, while four shorter passages identify the relief scenes; on the south face is a note recording the erection of the dais for the king by Šamaš-bel-uṣur.[47]

The reliefs themselves illustrate events in the reign of Shalmaneser as described in the inscriptions (Fig. 110). The most remarkable is the picture of the king grasping the hand of Marduk-zakir-šumi, whom he had reinstated on the throne of Babylon following a rebellion. The gesture, unique in contemporary sculpture, is reminiscent at a lower level of the annual ceremony in which the Babylonian king 'takes the hand of Marduk', his divine overlord, and is thereby confirmed in his royal authority.[48] To 'strike away the hand of another' signified the formal rejection of a preferred alliance, and it is reasonable to suppose that the clasping of hands, like the modern handshake, marked the acceptance of an agreement.[49] It seems unlikely, however, that in this instance it implies equality between the protagonists, for the pre-eminent position of the scene on the throne-base is obviously intended to emphasise one of Shalmaneser's greatest achievements, which is further described in the accompanying text, setting out the Assyrian view of events.

> Shalmaneser, king of Assyria, marched to the aid of Marduk-zakir-šumi. He felled Marduk-bel-usate [the rebellious brother] with the sword and confirmed Marduk-zakir-šumi on his father's throne. I (Shalmaneser) marched about justly in the extensive land of Karduniaš [Babylonia]... I went down to Chaldaea and gained dominion over Chaldaea in its entirety. I received tribute from the kings of Chaldaea as far as the sea and imposed my powerful might upon the Sealand.[50]

Fig. 109. View of throne base showing position of reliefs.

The tribute of the Chaldaeans is illustrated with that of other vassals elsewhere on the throne base (Fig. 110b) and, in general, the emphasis of the text on military might seems intended to show where real power lay rather than to express good fellowship between rulers of equal standing.

Shalmaneser's son Šamši-Adad V later concluded a treaty with the same Marduk-zakir-šumi of which a partial text survives, which must be dated in the last years of Shalmaneser since Šamši-Adad does not bear the royal title. It is thought that the treaty was made in consequence of Marduk-zakir-šumi's assistance in suppressing the wide-spread revolts in Assyria at this time, no doubt connected with the anticipated succession, and indeed a clause requiring the king of Babylon to 'indicate', presumably to hand over, refugees from Assyria suggests such a situation.[51] However, any obligations that Šamši-Adad might have felt were not of long duration, for among the proudest achievements recorded in his own annals as Šamši-Adad V (823–11 BC) were his victories over Marduk-zakir-šumi's successor.

To return to the throne base, the remaining scenes are reminiscent of those on the North-West Palace reliefs, and show the king and his courtiers receiving bearers of tribute, including gold and silver, ivory tusks, horses and even large cedar logs.[52] The epigraphs identify these scenes as tribute from a Syrian ruler, Qalparunda, and from shaikhs of the Chaldaean tribes Bit-Amukani and Bit-Dakkuri.[53] As can be seen on the throne base, the tribute of the Chaldaeans (south side) included silver, gold, tin, bronze, ivory, elephant hides, ebony and sisoo-wood, while from the west (north side of throne base) came also silver, gold, tin, bronze and ivory, together with ebony, logs of cedar, coloured cloths, linen goods and yoked horses.

175

*Fig. 110. Details of throne base decoration. a) central panel: Shalmaneser III (on the left),
with his attendants; on the right, the Babylonian king, Marduk-zakir-šumi, clasps the hand
of the Assyrian king, who had reinstated him on the throne of Babylon. b) (left) Tribute of
the Chaldaeans: at the head of the procession walks a Chaldaean ruler and his son, followed by tribute including a model city, a tray of jewellery and ingots, elephant tusks, metal
vessels and valuable logs (? ebony). c) (below) Tribute of Qalparunda of the land of Unqi
(the Amuq in northwestern Syria); the photographs illustrate part of this tribute including
elephant tusks, metal cauldrons, a trident, and large logs of cedar.*

177

Fig. 111. The great raising of the throne base, with the very welcome assistance of the Iraq Petroleum Company (1962).

The extraction of Shalmaneser's throne base from its original position and its transfer to the safe custody of the new Iraq Museum, then under construction, was an operation worthy of brief description. It lay at a depth of over 6 m below the top of the steep-sided mound that covered the ruins of the throne-room suite, and we had calculated that, if our estimate of the density of the stone was approximately correct, the larger of its component slabs weighed about eight tons. The Directorate-General of Antiquities, on our behalf, requested the loan of equipment from the Iraq Petroleum Company, based in Kirkuk, who had helped us generously in the past, though never with a task of this magnitude. The IPC sent a crane, their two largest trucks, a bulldozer and, most important, their most experienced foreman. First, the bulldozer was used to construct a long ramp against the east end of the mound to provide access for the crane and two trucks. Next, the crane had to be sited on top of the mound and far enough from the end of the excavation where the throne base lay that its loaded weight would not cause it to slide into the throne room, carrying with it the ground on which it stood as well as the east wall. This minimum distance proved to be the full length of the crane's jib. It then transpired that the breaking strain of the jib at its maximum extent was approximately eight tons, and we could only hope that we had not greatly underestimated the weight of our priceless slabs. Meanwhile, transverse channels had been cut in the floor beneath each slab, using long pointed iron bars borrowed from our workmen and called by them *saif* (sword); into the channels were inserted iron girders which were then bolted together to form cradles on which the slabs could be lifted. Finally, two ropes were attached to each cradle, to be held at the far ends by the Director and another member of the dig staff stationed on platforms against the side walls of the throne room, whose function was to control any lateral movement of the load. Each slab in turn rose slowly into the air, supported by its cradle and the audible prayers of a hundred men, and was deposited gently and with consummate skill on a bed of earth in one of the two trucks (Fig. 111); the only unscheduled delay was caused by our epigraphist, who was with difficulty persuaded that it was inadvisable to stand directly under each slab to copy any inscription that might appear on its lower face. With inexpressible relief we watched the trucks depart for Baghdad with an impressive escort kindly furnished by the Chief of Police in Mosul. When they reached their destination we received a telegram saying that the slabs were too large to pass through the doors of the new Museum but, though sympathetic, we felt that this problem could be left to others, and it was indeed solved by temporarily cutting away the bottoms of the doorjambs. After forty years the whole operation remains a terrifying memory, but coupled with great satisfaction that we were able to contribute this unique monument to the glories of the Assyrian Gallery.

One further comment should be made about the condition of the throne room at the time of the sack of Kalhu. In common with the majority of the unburnt rooms in Fort Shalmaneser it seemed to have been virtually empty at the time of its abandonment. Also suggestive of the abandonment of the room before the final sack is the presence in the plastered floor just in front of the throne dais of two large circular sockets, lined with fragments of brick and stone, which were obviously designed to receive the bases of wooden posts supporting the roof. One of them was directly in front of, and very close to, the north-west corner of the throne dais, an arrangement that would scarcely have been tolerated if the throne room still served its ceremonial purpose. The asymmetrical insertion of these posts was clearly a practical measure to reinforce a weakness in the roof above, carried out at a time when the internal appearance of the room was no longer a matter of great concern. This would suggest that, as elsewhere in the building, the damage had been effected in the attack of 614 BC.

East of the throne-room block a series of trenches revealed the partial plan of a courtyard, T6, with a range of rooms on the north side – T 2, a small ante-room leading into T 4, which was stone-paved and contained an ablution slab, and T 5, also with a large slab against the north wall. Indeed courtyard T 6 was itself a terrace, bounded by a retaining wall identified in its south-west corner, and with a pavement some 1.50 m above that of courtyard T. It may even have opened directly onto the city wall. In T 4 was identified an earlier pavement of bricks of the size used by Shalmaneser III, with the later stone floor some 25 cm above it. A dado of plain limestone slabs, 1.15 m in height, which lined the excavated sections of the walls, seemed however to be an original feature.[54]

There were probably other rooms on the south and possibly the east, but here the walls had been heavily eroded, a danger which the builders had anticipated by the use of stone blocks in their foundations. The plan of T 6 and the rooms along its north side, including an ablution room, suggests that they formed part of a residential unit, raised on a terrace adjoining the city wall, that was part of the original palace but was refurbished and possibly extended by Esarhaddon who, in his cylinder inscription recording repairs to Fort Shalmaneser, says,

> The *ekal mašarti* which Shalmaneser, king of Assyria, ...had built had no base terrace and the site was small. To me, Esarhaddon, king of Assyria, exalted prince, the capacity of the sage Adapa was in my understanding as concerns that terrace, and I brought his thought to it. Undeveloped land I took for an additional site, with bonding of mountain stone I filled the terrace, I raised it from a depth of 120 brick-courses. I built palaces (rooms) for my royal dwelling on it.[55]

This describes very precisely the additions made to the south-east corner of the original building.

The identification of T 2, T 4, T 5, and T 6 as a part of this 'royal dwelling' is supported by the plan of Esarhaddon's outer revetment, built against the city wall on the east side of Fort Shalmaneser. Here the revetment terminates in an unusually large bastion, projecting up to 10 m rather than the normal 5 m beyond the original wall, and almost exactly spanning the combined width of courtyard T 6 together with the ranges of rooms that opened off it to the north and probably also to the south. We conclude that the bastion was specifically intended to support Esarhaddon's enlarged residence, possibly with a terrace on the city wall looking out over open country to the snows of the Zagros, as we have so often done.

COURTYARD T AND THE SOUTHERN SUITE

Evidence of ancient subsidence was observed in Courtyard T immediately to the south of the throne room block, further confirmation of Esarhaddon's description of 'Shalmaneser's Palace'. Indeed most of this courtyard had been washed away, and its position is now marked by a deep gully as is the principal courtyard of the North-West Palace. In the area between the southern door of T 3 and the entrance to the southern block of rooms, however, the courtyard remained intact.[56] The southern extension consists of a suite of three long reception rooms, of the same general type as the western wing, between courtyard Y and the river terrace, in the North-West Palace, but much closer in plan to similar suites in Sargon's Palace and the *ekal mašarti* (Palace F) at Khorsabad. With the possible exception of the North-West Palace, where the plan is lost, these triple suites opened onto a spacious terrace overlooking the river and/or the wider countryside. T 25 and T 27 were important reception rooms, the first identified by the shallow niche which framed the place of honour at the north end of the room, the second by its painted decoration and the ablution slab set in the south-east corner. All three rooms were paved with *juss* (gypsum) plaster. At Nimrud, as in the palace of Sargon, there is here the triple entrance which characterised the later reception suites. The main doorway from both courtyards (T and S) was flanked by projecting towers and, on the west, was approached by a bitumen roadway. There was a wide door at the south end of T 25, and other evidence suggests the presence of a comparable external door just to the south.[57] The south wall of the triple suite has been restored by analogy with the very similar plan at Khorsabad, but we have no independent evidence of this at Nimrud other than the suggestion of a second door south of room T 25. It must be emphasised that owing to the great depth of the room deposits here only small areas of the principal rooms were excavated to their floors.

Between this reception suite and the throne room block was a complex of six smaller rooms, T 10 and T 20-24. Of these T 21 originally served as a vestibule with doors leading to the other rooms in the wing and the adjacent suites. T 22 was a bathroom associated with the reception suites, while T 10 and T 20 were storage magazines. The only considerable collection of objects found in this area during the 1960s excavations came from T 10, in which there had been a fierce conflagration during the sack of the building. Only the ends of the room were excavated in 1962 and here, among the debris on the floor, were not only bronze fittings and ivory decorative elements but parts of the wooden members of various pieces of furniture, which had perhaps been used in the adjacent reception rooms (see p. 58). Elements of horse harness were found here, including limestone forehead and cheekpieces. Decorated shell segments like those from the North-West Palace well NN were also recovered (Fig. 153). Other finds included bronze and iron armour scales, fragments of a shell bowl with decoration carved in low relief and the long bones of an elephant. Found also in T 10 were a large number of ivory fragments engraved with alphabetic inscriptions, on one of which was the name of Hazael, king of Damascus,[58] presumably part of the spoil that included large numbers of chariots, horses and military equipment captured from him by Shalmaneser III and recorded in the inscription on the statue found in NE 50. Fourteen shell fragments with the name Irhuleni inscribed in Hittite hieroglyphs were also recovered (Fig. 6, p. 17). The central part of room T10, in which many more ivories were found, was excavated in 1963.

In the passage T 23, which had also been gutted by fire, the remains of the south door were found, lying on the pavement. Meticulous recording by Olwen Brogan enabled us to reconstruct the general appearance and approximate dimensions of the door, an important addition to our knowledge since it is the only relatively complete example of the wooden fittings of the building that has come to light. Approximately 1.30 m wide, the door was composed of vertical panels c. 20 cm wide, inset between ribs of approximately cylindrical section, 6 cm in diameter, which projected from both faces of the door. Each panel was apparently two planks thick, the planks held together with some form of adhesive. The ribs of the door were made up of alternate cylinders of wood and ivory, the overall effect perhaps resembling the papyrus thicket motif depicted on the *champ-levé* ivories. The presence of what may have been a representation of a papyrus flower suggests the possibility that the overall decoration of the door may have been a deliberate copy of this motif.[59]

In room T 20 the upper metre of deposits was examined in 1962, but the room was not further excavated until the autumn of 1989 when a team from the British Museum under the direction of John Curtis returned to the site.[60] Evidence of two floors was found, the upper of white plaster and the lower, 10 cm below, of yellow clay. In the fill between them were found items of horse harness and small glass inlay plaques, together with several objects of iron, including a spearhead, blade and arrowhead. Also from the earlier deposit were 170 small bronze bosses of the type that can be seen decorating bridles on the stone reliefs; more than 1000 of these have been found in Fort Shalmaneser alone. As in T 10 there had been a fierce conflagration at the time of the final sack, associated with the upper, plaster floor. Here were found a number of metal objects, including a complete iron dagger, and an ivory plaque in the Assyrian style. An unusual discovery, of particular interest from an ethnographic point of view, was a stone roof roller, together with part of the roof on which it had been stored. This is a type of object still common in the countryside of Iraq today, used in the maintenance of mud-plastered roofs. A number of glazed bricks were also recovered here (further discussed below).

Of importance in determining the architectural history of the arsenal are the doorsill inscriptions in this south wing, referred to earlier, which demonstrate beyond any question that in its original form this part of the building had been constructed by Shalmaneser III.[61] In other words, the triple entrance, triple room ceremonial plan dates from the ninth century, and must serve some purpose separate from that of the throne room itself.[62]

MURAL DECORATION OF THE STATE APARTMENTS

Little survived of the original decoration of the throne room. The existence of wall paintings could be inferred from the very faint outlines of a 'cushion' frieze, but the paintings must have been badly faded before the collapse of the walls, suggesting that the throne room lay for a time empty and roofless. Some notion of the original character was obtained when the throne dais was lifted, since brightly painted fragments lay beneath it. This suggests, rather surprisingly, that the walls had been decorated some time before the installation of the throne base or, perhaps less likely, that the original throne base had been reinstalled when the throne room was renovated, a formidable undertaking. Among the surviving patterns were geometric examples and fragments of representations of the king and his attendants, of which a surviving archer measured c. 60-70 cm high. Painted decoration was also employed in the south wing. T 24 had a simple dado of red stripes, as in the Assur-etel-ilani renovation of the Burnt Palace, but in the doorway connecting T 21 with T 27 were figures c. 1.50 m high, dressed in fish cloaks of which the tail descended to the knees. The legs were encased in scales, and the raised right hand held the conventional 'cone', the left hand the bucket, characteristic of the genii figures on the North-West Palace reliefs. Traces of the sacred tree were also discerned nearby. In the north-east doorway of T 27 was the genie figure with three-flowered branch and on the north jamb of the doorway, c. 2.0 m above the sill, a standing bull, facing outwards.

The more durable glazed baked brick was employed on external walls, commonly above doorways as in the North-West Palace.[63] As Esarhaddon says of the Nineveh arsenal, 'All the doors I crowned with vaults and a *matgiqu* like the rainbow,'[64] a clear reference to the brilliantly coloured bricks. Contemporary representations of large buildings suggest that glazed bricks were also commonly used as a frieze, with simple floral or geometric patterns on the upper part of the façade imme-

diately below the crenellation, as indicated on the decoration of the pottery bin illustrated in Figure 93 and the metal brazier, Plate 12c. No wall has survived to such a
height, but when the south-east corner of the SE courtyard was excavated in 1958, a
number of bricks bearing parts of brightly coloured rosette motifs in blue, yellow,
black and white glaze were found. Here we know from the components recovered that
each rosette was comprised of three brick courses. In the preliminary report it is suggested that this glazed brick decorated 'the face of the tower'; we now know this wall
to be the north wall of the throne room suite. Layard had also found glazed bricks in

*Fig. 112. Reconstruction of glazed brick panel above the south doorway of Fort
Shalmaneser Room T 3. Shalmaneser III is shown beneath the winged disc of Aššur. Original
ht of panel 4.07 m; now in the Iraq Museum.*

this area of the *ekal mašarti*, depicting scenes of battle and the bringing of tribute.[65] Unfortunately we do not know their precise location, but courtyard T is a possibility.

The most splendid example of glazed brick decoration, however, was found collapsed and lying on the pavement of court T outside the south doorway of the ante-chamber T 3. Over 300 glazed bricks were recovered here, a total weight exceeding three tons. This fallen mass was both protected and damaged by the even greater weight of the mud-brick of the wall that had collapsed on top of it. During the 1962 season Julian Reade, assisted by other members of the expedition, began the task of reconstructing the design, a jig-saw puzzle of the greatest complexity which was only completed after a further three months' work in the Iraq Museum. Fitters' marks, which had been painted in thin glaze on the upper sides of almost all the bricks as a guide to assembly, proved an invaluable aid to reconstruction.[66]

The bricks had originally been set in the face of the wall above the doorway, itself almost certainly covered with a flat lintel. The original height of the doorway is not known, but it was certainly above the surviving door jamb, more than 4 m above the pavement. The panel (Fig. 112) is itself just over 4 m high (38 courses of

brick), with a maximum width of c. 2.90 m. and a semi-elliptical profile resembling that of an Assyrian gate arch. Below the central inscription is the winged disc of Aššur and two opposed representations of Shalmaneser himself in ceremonial dress. Together with the throne base, this splendid piece now adorns the Assyrian gallery in the Iraq Museum.

In 1962 fragments of glazed brick were found in and near the uppermost surviving walls of the stairwell T 8. The presence of bricks at such a high level in this part of Fort Shalmaneser suggests the possibility of a formal, decorated entrance to the stairwell from the roof terrace. Such a decorated entrance would strengthen the view that some form of royal ceremonial was carried out on the roof, a suggestion already proposed in the context of the North-West Palace throne room. Further evidence of glazed brick ornament of the time of Shalmaneser III was found nearby in T 20, some 80 polychrome bricks discovered in the western part of the room, lying *directly* on roof debris. Like those in front of the T 3 doorway, they must have decorated some external door, but it is not clear where this would have been unless it too was on the roof, perhaps even the stairwell door, since the tell here slopes downward to the south. As well as the inscription of Shalmaneser III, the surviving decoration from T 20 consisted of part of a winged disc together with floral and geometric patterns. Of considerable interest are the fitter's marks which, like those referred to above, would have aided the builders in assembling the bricks. Rather surprisingly, they are always upside down when viewed from in front of the glazed face, that is, they appear the correct way up only from the back, perhaps suggesting that they were stacked and handled from the back and that the fronts were covered for protection

Fig. 113. South-east corner of the small throne room (S 5) in the queen's residence, Fort Shalmaneser, showing the south entrance, the tram lines and the beginning of the procession of eunuch courtiers, which ornamented the walls.

until they were set in place. The marks were of two kinds, painted black in Aramaic or Phoenician letters and various symbols painted in white.[67] The association of West Semitic letters with the cuneiform inscription of Shalmaneser III dates them to the 9th century BC, incontrovertible evidence of the early use of this alphabetic writing in Assyria. Of course the use of such script by builders and masons would have been much simpler than any attempt to incise or paint cuneiform.

The Queen's Household (Area S)

A residential area in the south-west corner of the arsenal constituted the official quarters of the queen and her household. It was overseen by a female official, the *šakintu,* some of whose archive was recovered (p. 213). Presumably the queen was in residence in Fort Shalmaneser whenever the king was present; indeed it is possible that she maintained there her own military unit.[68] The most important suite of rooms in area S was that surrounding courtyard S 6, on the north side of which was a 'throne room', entered from its ante-chamber S 7 and containing the usual 'tram line' fittings in stone (Fig. 113). As in Ezida there are two small private rooms associated with the throne room, including a bathroom (S 3, Fig. 114), but no associated stair. No dais was found here, although it would have been situated against the east wall. The inscription on a door sill leading into the bathroom bore a shorter version of the inscription found on the SE courtyard throne base,[69] clearly indicating the original construction of this wing by Shalmaneser III.

The most interesting feature of this throne room was the procession of life-size eunuch courtiers depicted on the painted walls above a bitumen dado some 45 cm in height. Sufficient traces survived to permit a reconstruction although no single section was complete enough to warrant its removal, an extraordinarily difficult task even when wall paintings are well-preserved (Fig. 113). The procession of figures passed from the ante-chamber doorway along the south wall of the room, where the best-preserved fragments remained, and thence along the west and north walls as if making a circuit of the room before approaching the throne. Unfortunately the figures on the north wall, facing the sun, have been almost entirely destroyed, but immediately after exposure it was possible to see the faint remains of a bearded figure facing the approaching file at the point where the foot of the dais would have been. Only his sandals were well-preserved; these were much more elaborately worked than those of the other figures, and painted in red and blue. The usual pillow patterns, rosettes and pomegranate buds and flowers were painted on the upper walls, creating a total decorated height of over 2.60 m. At least the lower registers of the decorative frieze were carried around the walls of the two small, adjoining chambers S 3-4, but there is no indication of human figures here. It seems likely that the frescoes themselves date to the time of the Esarhaddon renovation.[70] One may ask what was the function of a throne room adjacent to if not within the harem, but the king must have had his own quarters here, as in the North-West Palace; thus the eunuchs illustrated in the wall paintings are those of the *bitanu,* that is, the private household.

In the throne room also were five large ventilation shafts, four in the north and one in the south wall, perhaps suggesting summer use or that the circulation of air here may have been impeded by the height of the main throne room block. Foundation boxes containing *lahmu* figurines were found in the north-west and south-west corners of the room.[71] Finds here included a quantity of decorated ivory. Of especial interest is a large collection from S 4-5 in the Assyrian style, including processions of tribute bearers, small engraved plaques for inlay, *ajouré* plaques and many other pieces from ivory furniture, including a group of small, elegant, ornamental columns with papyrus capitals.[72]

The evidence for our assertion that this part of the building contained the queen's household comes from the archive belonging to the *šakintu,* the comptroller of her household, found in room S 10. At first glance S 10 appears to be part of the suite of rooms, including the throne room, surrounding court S 6, but close examination of the plan reveals that it had no access from that area except by means of the heavily barred passages D and E (Fig. 115). Indeed one of the more interesting aspects of this sector is the care that was taken to prevent unauthorised entry. From the main areas of the arsenal the only entrances were through passage S 76, which led to courtyard S and passage E, or originally through S 1 which gave access to the

Fig. 114. Stone-paved bathroom (S 3) associated with private throne room, showing ablution slabs and drain-hole.

Fig. 115. Corridor E, looking west toward the citadel mound.

small courts S 2 and S 15 and passage D (Fig. 101). This entrance was later altered to require the visitor to pass through an additional guard-chamber, SE 8. Both corridors D and E were heavily bolted and barred. In addition to the usual bolt socket in the stone threshold, a recessed stone slab was set in the pavement behind both ends of D and the east end of E, to receive the butt end of a beam braced against it. By closing these doors access to the formal reception rooms surrounding court S 6 was completely cut off. Protection was also offered by the unusual number of boxes of apotropaic figurines, hidden guardians of the ladies of the household. Of particular interest from corridor E was a collection of small bottles, some of which were painted, perhaps used for some type of cosmetics or unguents.[73] Among the other objects found in the ash and rubbish which covered the floor at the east end of corridor E was a burnt section of elephant tusk with a splendid double register of bulls (ND 7560).

In S 10 itself the marks of a fierce blaze were apparent on the walls, and the south wall had buckled until its face overhung the floor at a dangerous angle, supported only by the cohesion of the brickwork and the mass of burnt debris which filled the whole room to a depth of 1.50 m. In this debris was a quantity of charred ivories so vast that we could only carry out the most essential work of cleaning and sorting on the dig, and were forced to leave the task of reconstituting the bulk of the material, consisting largely of broken plaques, to be carried out in the museum laboratory. However, more than 70 pieces were identified and catalogued at Nimrud that year, including fragments of the 'lady at the window' type, many plaques in the Phoenician style, parts of human and animal figures and a particularly attractive

Fig. 116. Ivory bowl of 'bird's nest' type, probably used for cosmetics or perfumed oils. From S 10, where the šakintu's *documents were found. The very beautiful and consistent polished black surface suggests that the colouring was done deliberately (see p. 227) and was not an accidental result of the fire that ravaged the store-room.*

cosmetic palette (?salt cellar) (Fig. 116).[74] Interestingly, there were here no ivories in the Assyrian style, frequently found elsewhere in royal contexts, especially in throne room suites, including that in area S and also in SE 8 and SE 9, which had become the formal entrance to the domestic quarter.[75] Other finds in S 10 included terracotta figurines and a bronze figurine of the Egyptian god Bes, originally attached to some wooden object.

It is not clear how such a collection of valuable objects came to be incinerated in S 10, but a group of tablets discovered in the room and nearby in corridor E provide the information that the room was a storage magazine in the queen's household and that the official in charge was a female official, the *šakintu*. Moreover, there was a female scribe and some of the documents refer to court cases in which the decision seems to have been handed down by a female *šanitu* magistrate. It is apparent that S 10 had been deliberately adapted for the storage of valuables, since the original doorway had been blocked, leaving a narrow entrance only about 1.50 m high (Fig. 117).

In marked contrast to the military workshop areas to the north, this sector

contained a number of luxurious apartments, grouped in rectangular blocks around inner courtyards. The most palatial suites were the two most closely connected with the throne room and protected by corridor D (rooms 16, 28, 29 and 17, 18, 19, 30). The latter was a particularly elegant double suite, and in S 30 was found one of the finest of the Nimrud ivories (illustrated on the back cover), possibly from a piece of furniture. It had been stripped of its gold overlay, of which a small fragment survived, by those who looted the building in 612. Further Assyrian style ivories were also found here. Other residential suites were identified around courtyards S 37 and S 43, the rooms around the latter courtyard producing a large collection of women's items in the form of literally hundreds of beads, many of frit and glass, amulets, fibulae, a bone comb and in particular a number of alabaster and rock crystal vessels of the types designed to hold cosmetics. In 1958 an exploratory trench (X) was dug from the corridor west of S 28 to the west outer wall. The east end of this trench produced yet another fine ivory, the very beautiful winged boy, in the Egyptianising style, with a Horus hawk perched on a lotus bud between his extended wings, in which some of the blue frit inlay was still preserved (Fig. 118). At the west end of the trench we observed an interesting sequence of late 7th century squatter occupation. Among the other discoveries south of the throne room area are large quantities of pottery found up to a height of c. 15 cm above the floor of both S 20 and S 21.

It is possible that the chambers around S 37 were the residences or offices of eunuch officials: at least they are more likely than the ladies of the palace to have needed the fine sword found in S 67.[76] This area was also directly accessible from the outermost courtyard S 68, by means of yet another passage, S 60-61. It was also less directly connected with what were clearly women's residences to the north. Unfortunately, on the south and the south-east corner of the building the underlying

190

conglomerate drops steeply to the alluvial riverain land, and here the walls of the building have been destroyed beyond recovery.

As elsewhere, this part of the building had clearly been remodelled by Esarhaddon, and evidence discovered in S 35 and neighbouring rooms permits a reconstruction of the architectural course of events leading to the final abandonment of the arsenal. Here the earliest pavement contains an inscribed brick of Adad-nerari III, suggesting the possibility that the southern part of sector S may originally have been built by him. Certainly he carried out some renovation here, including the

Fig. 118. Cloisonné *ivory, winged boy holding papyrus plant, with a Horus hawk between his wings and resting on a lotus bud, from room X3 (ht 25.7 cm, ND 8068, Iraq Museum).*

191

installation of the only Fort Shalmaneser foundation box with prophylactic figurines comparable with those in the Burnt Palace (seven *apkallu,* p. 253). Further evidence that renovation was carried out by Esarhaddon is demonstrated by the presence of his inscribed bricks in the pavement of the small inner courtyard S 31/45.

SUMMARY OF HISTORICAL EVIDENCE

The *ekal mašarti* was built by Shalmaneser III (859-824 BC). Evidence of baked bricks and stone door sills inscribed with his name is found throughout the building, clearly indicating that the concept and main layout of the arsenal must be attributed to him. We do not know whether in his time the building was referred to as the *ekal mašarti,* since only the word *ekal* ('palace') appears in his inscriptions, but both the plan and the contents reveal that its function differed little if at all from the later 'arsenal'. Indeed the presence of an ivory plaque inscribed with the name of Hazael, probably the king of Damascus, and shells inscribed in neo-Hittite characters with the name of Irhuleni, king of Hamath, prove that Shalmaneser was already using the building as a storehouse for booty and tribute, while the military associations of the building are clear from its earliest plan. The establishment continued in use under Shalmaneser's son and grandson, and the evidence of inscribed bricks and thresholds reveals that the latter, Adad-nerari III, carried out some rebuilding and renovation. There is little evidence for any further renovation in the 8th century, but both the cuneiform records and the contents of the building indicate that during that century the building continued to serve both military and administrative purposes, the latter largely concerned with the administration of taxes. It seems to have continued in use as an arsenal and repository at least until the time of Sennacherib who, as we know, neglected Kalhu for Nineveh. It must be at this time that the building suffered at least some of the depredations evident by the time of Esarhaddon. Further evidence of the use of the *ekal mašarti* at the time of Esarhaddon and Assurbanipal is found in the so-called 'horse letters', reports written to the king from Kalhu concerning the delivery of large numbers of horses from all over the empire to the Nabu Temple.[77] Some of these horses are reassigned for military use to the arsenals of both Kalhu and Nineveh.

We have seen how well the building excavated as Fort Shalmaneser fulfills Esarhaddon's description of the *ekal mašarti* at Nineveh, 'for the ordinance of the camp, the maintenance of the stallions, mules, chariots, weapons, and the spoil of the foe of every kind.' Esarhaddon's Nimrud cylinder inscription tells us of his renovation of Fort Shalmaneser; indeed it was he who introduced there the term *ekal mašarti.* The excavations attest that the building had fallen into disrepair,[78] and substantiate Esarhaddon's claims to have 'brought much thought to it' and to have filled the subsiding terrace with mountain stone. Mallowan suggests that it was Esarhaddon's intention to restore the city to its former position as capital. But there is nothing in the actual inscriptions to confirm this, and we know that he also renovated the arsenal at Nineveh. In fact it was the proper responsibility of an Assyrian king to carry out repairs, even to build anew, in all the ancient cities.

By far the greatest number of dated tablets preserved in Fort Shalmaneser belong in the period after 649 BC, the time when, after the death of his brother in

Babylon, Assurbanipal ruled the whole of Mesopotamia, to say nothing of much of the world beyond; this phase includes too the reigns of his two successors. A number of Nimrud texts date to the time of Sin-šar-iškun, and demonstrate what seems obvious also from the archaeological evidence, that the arsenal of Kalhu continued to function until the fall of the city in 612 BC. In this latest period, however, there is less documented evidence for regular military activity, although such evidence is not entirely lacking (for example, in the *rab ekalli*'s archive). The archaeological evidence reveals that the building suffered severe damage not long before the final attack in 612 BC, and that the walls and gates were undergoing substantial repairs at that time. Even the throne room seems to have suffered. The most likely explanation is that the damage was the result of the Median attack in 614, attested in historical inscriptions. The reinstallation at this time of foundation boxes with their apotropaic figurines was a pious hope, unanswered. After the sack of 612, the population did not simply disappear, but returned to reoccupy the sad remnants of the once glorious city. A mass burial containing skeletons of some of the slain was found at the south end of S 42 (Fig. 119), presumably given hasty burial after the sack of 612 BC. These

Fig. 119. Mass burial at the west end of S 42, looking south (612 BC). A slightly later and equally hasty burial of six further bodies lay precisely above the original grave; the line of the later grave pit is visible in the far section. Beneath the original floor is a vaulted drain.

193

bodies were subsequently covered by debris which accumulated to a height of nearly two metres above the original floor. The memory of the position of the original grave clearly remained, however, for in this debris, and at precisely the same place as the original burial, six further bodies were interred with equal haste and lack of ceremony. It seems likely that this second burial contained victims of a later raid, carried out perhaps by tribes from the hills to the northeast.

CHAPTER SIX

THE WRITTEN EVIDENCE

One of the most extraordinary facts about the 19th century excavations at Nimrud is that only one cuneiform tablet was recorded as coming from the site.[1] This sounds quite unbelievable, especially given the fact that since 1949 tablets have been found in every building that has been excavated. The problem was a simple one, that those digging at Nimrud at that time were not accustomed to identifying unbaked clay, whether a mud-brick wall or a cuneiform text. The great cuneiform library at Nineveh was found without difficulty because the tablets had accidentally been baked in the fire that consumed the city in 612 BC. Similarly baked tablets have, of course, been found at Nimrud, and were recovered in the 19th century by George Smith, although there is no mention of them in his brief account of the site. These were subsequently catalogued with the Kouyunjik (Nineveh) collection in the British Museum, see for example Fig. 125. Unfortunately for their excavators, by far the majority of cuneiform tablets at Nimrud have survived in their original unbaked state. These are often crumbly, and full of salt, and are not easy to excavate even with the techniques of modern archaeology. The surfaces, moreover, are often damaged and extremely difficult to clean without causing further loss. For this reason a large kiln was built at Nimrud in 1952, for the purpose of baking tablets on site so that they could be cleaned and read more safely. At the same time, with the very helpful coop- eration of the Iraqi authorities many were also brought back to the British Museum, where they could be treated in the conservation laboratories which had long experi- ence in dealing with the tablets which had come to the museum in the 19th century.[2]

The poor condition of the unbaked cuneiform tablets is in marked contrast to the well-preserved and lengthy historical inscriptions carved on the orthostats that lined the palace walls. The discovery in the 19th century of these remarkable monu- ments, and the eventual decipherment of the cuneiform inscriptions which they dis- played, provided an exciting new window into the past. In the context of the mid- 19th century, when this ancient writing was first deciphered, perhaps the greatest impact was made by the identification of names known from the Bible, the earliest of which was Pulu, identified as Tiglath-pileser III.[3] Subsequent study of the remark- able stone reliefs has occupied generations of art historians, while definitive transla- tions and historical analyses of the inscriptions themselves continue to appear, pro- viding an increasingly detailed framework within which the archaeological evidence can be examined. It is not our purpose to repeat these specialist studies, but simply to introduce them as background to a discussion focused specifically on the archae- ology of ancient Kalhu. At the same time we hope that sufficient information is pro- vided in the footnotes for those who are interested to pursue these subjects further. We cannot ignore, however, what were, in a wider historical sense, unquestionably the most important discoveries from the site, the monumental versions of the royal annals. In particular the stone inscriptions of the founder of the new Kalhu, Assurnasirpal II, provide an extraordinary picture of the military and political strategies of the period. Even today it is the legacy of this king that provides among the longest and earliest historical annals.

There is little doubt that it was the systematic military campaigns of Assurnasirpal II that in the ninth century BC established Assyria as the new power in the ancient Near East, a position emphasised by the monumental buildings of his new capital. The fact that his royal inscriptions, in which we today can trace the details of these achievements, were also combined with a pictorial record of his campaigns, visible on the walls of his great palace, is important not only as a ninth century innovation but as a new architectural format the impact of which can still be felt by the visitor to the site itself or to the many museums in which these bas-reliefs are housed. It is true that both historical texts and pictorial representation on orthostats existed long before Assurnasirpal II; indeed his father's texts contain records of campaigns related in annalistic style. But it was Assurnasirpal who established the written models for preserving a king's 'true version' of his own accomplishments and initiated the lavish use with such inscriptions of carved orthostats illustrating both ritual and historical motifs. These physical monuments, and those of his successors, especially Sargon at Khorsabad and Sennacherib and Assurbanipal at Nineveh, must undoubtedly be counted among the most successful exercises in propaganda ever attempted.

Perhaps the most important of Assurnasirpal's surviving texts is that inscribed on his stele and on stone slabs in the Ninurta Temple (see also p. 107), which remain among the longest Assyrian royal inscriptions. His famous Banquet Stele, commemorating the refounding of Kalhu (Fig. 18), is discussed on p. 40. Also referred to in earlier chapters is the so-called 'Standard Inscription', a much shorter version of the royal annals, which was engraved across the stone slabs of the North-West Palace. As can be seen on Fig. 28 (p. 54), this passed across the carved decoration on those slabs on which the figures filled the full height; often the back of the slab was also inscribed. The annalistic inscriptions begin with an invocation to the gods and continue with an account of the king's campaigns, year by year, often in brutal detail and including long lists of the loot carried away. Detailed descriptions are also provided of the king's building enterprises. Treaties and dedicatory inscriptions end with often lengthy threats to anyone who violates them. Thus, an inscription found on limestone tablets known as the Nimrud 'wall inscription' ends:

> I inscribed this stone tablet and deposited it in its wall. May a later prince restore its weakened portions. May he restore my inscribed name to its place. Then the god Aššur, the great lord, and the goddess Ištar, mistress of battle and conflict, will listen to his prayers. As for the one who removes my name: May Aššur and the god Ninurta glare at him angrily, overthrow his sovereignty, take away from him his throne, make him sit in bondage before his enemies, and destroy his name and his seed from the land.[4]

Translations of these formal inscriptions are readily available,[5] and it is our intention here to focus on the large collections of clay tablets recovered at Nimrud during the 1949 to 1963 seasons of excavation. Among the most historically important cuneiform documents found at this time are those from the ZT area of the North-

West Palace, from Ezida in which was situated the temple of the god of scribes and writing, and from the *ekal mašarti* or arsenal (Fort Shalmaneser).

ZT TEXTS

Many of the ZT texts are chancery documents and represent most clearly among the Nimrud texts the official functioning of government both at home and in the provinces. Indeed the large number of tablets from the tablet room, ZT 4 (Fig. 120), includes letters to Tiglath-pileser III, Shalmaneser V and Sargon which are especially valuable for the insight they provide into both local and international affairs. These texts are soon to be published in their entirety. Our intention here is simply to provide a few examples as a foretaste of their historical importance. Among these documents, for example, are letters to Tiglath-Pileser III from his governors in the west. Others deal with affairs in Babylonia. The latter include contemporary accounts of a late eighth century rebellion led by a Babylonian tribal chieftain, Mukin-zeri.

Relations with Babylonia to the south, a region with a lengthy and distinguished history, had long posed problems for the kings of Assyria. The long tradition there of literate urban civilization was much respected in Assyria yet, perhaps not surprisingly, the Assyrians were wary of any suspected threat to their new-found authority, especially within their border territories. In the eighth century inter-tribal rivalries in Babylonia had caused Tiglath-Pileser III to intervene in what he perceived as an unstable situation. In consequence, the Babylonian Nabonassar, was placed

Fig. 120. The scribal room ZT 4, its 'filing boxes' lined with baked bricks, in process of excavation. Some 350 tablets were found in the rubbish which filled this chamber, including diplomatic archives of the late 8th century BC.

Fig. 121. Baked clay cylinder inscribed for the Chaldaean shaikh Merodach-Baladan, boasting of his victories over Assyria. Removed from the Babylonian city of Uruk (Warka) and found in ZT 4, broken into three pieces. Sargon later substituted an 'improved' version at Uruk, retaining the original in his archives (length 15.7 cm, ND 2090).

under the protection of the Assyrian king, subsequently to enjoy a long and prosperous reign. On Nabonassar's death, however, southern rivalries broke out once again and a rebellion in Babylon led to the murder of Nabonassar's son, forcing yet another intervention by Tiglath-pileser.

The Nimrud letters reflect this period, and the conflict of loyalties within the cities of northern Babylonia is strikingly revealed in letters which tell of intrigue and conspiracy among pro- and anti-Assyrian factions. One letter even reports a public debate between official representatives of the Assyrian king and the citizens of Babylon, with an official of the Chaldaean usurper (Mukin-zeri) standing by. In this debate the Babylonians are reminded that their privileges as citizens are recognised by the Assyrians, to which they reply that they would submit to the Assyrian monarch if he came in person, though 'they did not believe the king would come'.[6] This Tiglath-Pileser proceeded to do, and after a successful campaign in which many Babylonians chose to side with him, the Assyrian king placed Babylonia under his own administrators, at the same time elevating himself to the kingship of Babylon and thereby inaugurating the policy of dual monarchy followed also by Esarhaddon and Assurbanipal in his later years. Another letter actually reports the forcing of the gates of Babylon and the final crushing of the Mukin-zeri rebellion:

> We have engaged within the great gates (of Babylon)...Mukin-zeri is killed and his son is killed; the city is as good as taken.[7]

Such Nimrud documents are remarkable in bringing these extraordinary events to us in the actual letters of contemporary officials.

Another of the many important texts found in the ZT archives is a baked clay cylinder of another important Chaldaean shaikh, a certain Marduk-apla-iddina II, whom the Assyrians had recognised as King of the Sealand, an independent area of southern Babylonia and who was the first Babylonian mentioned by name in the Bible (as Merodach-Baladan).[8] After the death of Tiglath-Pileser's son, Shalmaneser V (726–22), Merodach-Baladan had seized the Babylonian throne, provoking the intervention of the new Assyrian king, Sargon II. At some point during or after the ensuing conflict, Merodach-Baladan's clay cylinder (Fig. 121) had obviously been removed from the southern city of Warka by one of Sargon's officers, probably during Sargon's restoration work there. From the Babylonian point of view Merodach-Baladan had been highly successful in uniting the country and holding out against Assyrian intervention. Perhaps not surprisingly, however, much space in the official *Assyrian* annals recounting this event was devoted to the Babylonian's 'submission' and the itemising of his wealthy tribute: expensive gifts of gold, gold ore in quantity ('the dust of his mountains'), precious stones, exotic woods and plants, frankincense, cattle, sheep…'.

The interest of this historical story for the archaeology of Nimrud is that Sargon later substituted his own 'improved' version of events, as a blatant piece of propaganda, in a document directly modelled after that of Merodach-Baladan and replaced in the same temple in Warka. Indeed the final lines of the 'substitute' cylinder read, 'copy of a foundation-text sent (?) to/from the palace in the land of Aššur; *copied and revised*'.[9] Sargon retained the seditious original in his archives, where it was found by Mallowan in 1952, literally over a period of three days, the cylinder itself having been broken – ?deliberately – into three pieces in antiquity.[10] At the same time several fragments of inscribed clay prisms bearing historical texts of Sargon II, found in the passage between ZT and the Ninurta Temple, include, inter alia, a remarkable passage concerning Sargon's campaign against Merodach-Baladan and the Assyrian king's subsequent restoration of Babylon (Fig. 122).[11] An inscribed

Fig. 122. Eight-sided prism of Sargon II, inscribed with a chronicle of his campaigns and describing his victory over Merodach-Baladan. Fragments found over two seasons in the corridor north of ZT; the largest piece (ND 2601, ht 23 cm) came from north of the corridor in room 10 (see Fig. 15).

199

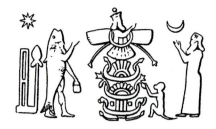

Fig. 123. Sealed tablet from ZT room 17. The seal belongs to Gabbu-amur, who sells a slave for 53 shekels of silver. The contract contains a clause protecting the purchaser's right to claim if the man contracts epilepsy (?) or another recurrent disease within 100 days. The tablet is dated in the limmu-ship of Milki-ramu (656 BC). On the seal impression are a bearded worshipper, a monkey and a priest in a fish robe before an artificial tree above which is the winged disc of Aššur (8.4 x 4.6 cm, ND 2328).

barrel cylinder of Sargon II was also found in ZT room 4, the archive room.[12] Unusually, this was written in Babylonian, suggesting that this text too may have been intended as one of the Assyrian king's propagandist exports. Unfortunately the end of the text is missing, so we cannot be certain that this was the original intent. We know too that Sargon, like (his father) Tiglath-Pileser III, made a determined effort to win over the citizens of the Babylonian cities, and indeed one of his Nimrud inscriptions recording his restoration of the North-West Palace (p. 56) was written in the Babylonian dialect of Akkadian.

Among the many other letters from ZT 4 was a group addressed to the Assyrian king, in particular Tiglath-Pileser III, from his governors in the west.[13] Under earlier kings many of the states of western Syria, when defeated, had remained under local administration but bound to Assyria by treaty. Where direct rule by provincial governors was imposed, some among them had on occasion remained overlong in office without adequate control and even came to regard their provinces as personal fiefdoms in which they were able to usurp royal privilege. This changed at the time of Tiglath-Pileser III, when more and smaller provinces were brought under more effective central control. Assyria's foremost political competition in this later period came from Urartu in eastern Anatolia, and with the Assyrian king's attention diverted north-eastwards, anti-Assyrian sentiment broke out in Syria and Palestine, ranging from open military action to the withholding of tribute. Of interest in this context are letters from an Assyrian official troubled by dissent in the cities of Tyre and Sidon, especially with respect to the payment of taxes. The particular problem seems to have involved timber from Mount Lebanon which had previously been exported to Egypt but was now required by the Assyrians. The situation was not improved by the killing of the Assyrian tax-collectors in Tyre; in Sidon a more fortunate colleague was merely impounded. A senior Assyrian official reports to the king that he had sent a contingent of police who 'made the people grovel',[14] a treatment which seems to have been successful, at least from the Assyrian point of view. Other letters refer to the restoration and development there of the water supply. Still others deal with the transportation and resettlement of Aramaeans who had been moved to Assyria. They were provided with food, oil, clothes and shoes, presumably provisions for the journey, and were encouraged to marry, though there was some dispute as to who would pay the *nudunnu* (dowry). Such letters show the Assyrian policy of deportation in a somewhat different light from that in which it is popularly portrayed. Indeed it would appear to have been the intention of the central government that such groups should be efficiently and contentedly resettled.[15]

Still other letters refer to affairs in Urartu. In the longest of the letters found in 1952 Sargon instructs the Crown Prince Sennacherib to convey his pleasure to one Mita, the king of Phrygia (the legendary Midas), who had intercepted an embassy sent to Urartu from Cilicia.[16] Sargon proposes an alliance and the exchange of embassies between Assyria and Phrygia, the accompanying gifts perhaps the source of the bronze situlae of Assyrian origin recovered from the famous Midas tomb at Gordion. The final section of the letter seems to return to Babylonian affairs, with another possible reference to Merodach-Baladan (written *Aplaya* or possibly Apla-iddina, but now thought 'hardly likely' to be Merodach-Baladan despite the apparent similarity of the written name[17]) and the request that he and his people, 'whether citizens of Babylon, Borsippa, Kish, Nippur or...', be brought to the Assyrian king.

Room 4 also produced a great variety of administrative tablets.[18] One records over 3000 homers of grain received from Nineveh and cities within its administrative district (ND 3469); other memoranda concern vessels from the palace wine-store and large quantities of grapes. Another text refers to writing boards of 2 to 5 leaves (ND 2653), suggesting that these boards were normally bound together in smaller sets than is indicated by the 16 ivory boards found in the room AB well in the North-West Palace. Many of the tablets found with the letters were typical products of the Assyrian civil service: inventories of valuable objects including 280 daggers of which 97 were iron, lists dealing with captives and subject peoples, lists of personnel and appointments, and lists of state revenues in yearly tribute and taxes.

Another suite of rooms in the same area (11–17) also contained documents, including some administrative texts.[19] The most notable tablets from this area are the private agents' accounts from ZT 16. These contain a number of the names that appear also on the tablets from the town wall houses (below). One of the most interesting tablets from this room is the marriage contract of a daughter of the 'šakintu of the new palace',[20] which lists her dowry on the occasion of her marriage to a man who is probably rich and perhaps elderly if he is the Milki-ramu who was *limmu* in 656 BC (Fig. 123 illustrates a text dated in the eponymy of Milki-ramu). Among the many expensive items listed are gold plate, numerous silver objects and jewellery, a great variety of garments, many objects of copper including chairs and a bronze bed. At the end of the contract is a series of clauses which spell out the wife's position if she is childless and the husband exercises his right to take a concubine, and the obligations if there is a divorce. Three other texts in this group (ND 2310–12) list loans of grain and silver, expenditure on the hire of a goldsmith and a purchase of jewellery and other goods including wine and food, some in Assur and Nineveh as well as Kalhu. It has been plausibly suggested that these concern preparations for a wedding, perhaps the same as that referred to above, and that all belong to the archive of the *šakintu*.[21] From room 30 came tablets relating to the issue of oil, grain and wine. One tablet (ND 3482) records 100 jars of oil of which 98 belonged to the palace herald (*nagir ekalli*); two other interesting texts, written by the same scribe, record supplies issued for the maintenance of a substitute king (*šar puhi*) (see p. 45).

Although the texts from the archive room 4 date to the latter part of the 8th century, those from room 14/16 clearly belong to the 7th, including a number dated with post-canonical *limmu*, at least a few of which can be attributed to the time of Sin-šar-iškun. The survival in the North-West Palace of many valuable objects dating from the time of Sargon II, who is known from his inscriptions to have stored large quantities of 'treasure' in the 'Juniper Wing' (p. 57), led Mallowan originally to the view that the sack of these buildings had taken place at that time. But it is now clear from the late post-canonical dates of many of the documents found over the whole of the site that the major buildings continued to be occupied until the fall of Assyria in 612 BC, and that many of the surviving tablets date from that time. It was the tablets from ZT found in 1952 and 1953 that first suggested this possibility. The survival of unbaked clay tablets is a matter of pure chance, but it is also clear that some tablets were kept deliberately, while others were not. Unfortunately we have no idea of the criteria exercised by the ancient scribes, except in the obvious case of unfulfilled contracts.

OTHER TEXTS FROM THE NORTH-WEST PALACE

One of the most intriguing groups of texts from the North-West Palace is that recently found in room 57, the room above Tomb III in which were discovered the bronze coffins filled with gold grave goods (p. 84). These texts were basically business documents of various palace officials of the time of Adad-nerari III together with a later group of the time of Tiglath-pileser III. The texts themselves are perhaps of less intrinsic interest than their presence in the room above the tomb of the wife of Assurnasirpal II. The officials included a palace scribe of the time of Adad-nerari and a chief cupbearer or steward of the time of Tiglath-pileser.[22] The tomb itself contained a gold bowl which belonged to Šamši-ilu, *turtanu* under Shalmaneser IV, Assur-dan III and Assur-nerari V, and eponym in 780, 770 and 752 BC,[23] and the seal of a *rab šaqe* of the time of Adad-nerari III. The tablets were found on the north side of the room, lying crushed under a limestone slab. It is not clear whether they were part of the original contents of the room, or part of deliberate infill. The inscriptions found in the tombs are discussed in Chapter 3.

A small number of tablets was found by Mallowan elsewhere in the North-

West Palace and in particular in rooms in the domestic quarter. Interestingly, room FF produced fragments of both lexical and literary texts, while tablets and inscribed bullae were recovered from rooms HH, OO, AH, M and S. A single tablet from DD was a text concerning women's rights on divorce, including a clause excluding her from responsibility for her husband's subsequent debts, one of the few documents that seems appropriate for the residents of the harem,[24] but it is clear that officials of the *bitanu*, presumably eunuchs, carried out their business here, as in room 57. The HH dockets, dated 717–715 BC, listed large quantities of wool, sheep and grain; another mentions a herd of 37 camels (ND 805). Yet these were found in a room that had obviously been occupied by one of the palace ladies (p. 79). Undoubtedly the most important discovery in this area was part of a prism of Assurbanipal recovered from the destruction debris in room OO.[25] The significance of the HH dockets for the dating of the destruction of the North-West Palace is discussed on p. 64.

TEXTS FROM EZIDA (THE NABU TEMPLE)
Among the most fascinating historical texts from Nimrud are the vassal treaties of Esarhaddon, found in the private throne room in the north-west wing of Ezida. These were formal records of a treaty made by Esarhaddon in 672 BC and enforced by oath on nine vassal princes from states bordering the modern frontier of Iraq/Iran. The treaty tablets were found in 1955 within the destruction debris and along with a num-ber of ivories and furniture fragments, smashed and burned by the looters in 612 BC. Some 350 fragments of these tablets were recovered from the north-west corner of the room, between the throne dais and the door leading to NTS 3, with further frag-ments in the adjacent courtyard. With the generous permission of the Iraqi authori-ties these were taken to the British Museum for treatment and reconstruction, where the large tablet illustrated in Fig. 124 was made up from 75 joins and at least 8 fur-ther copies identified.[26] The former is a treaty with a Median chieftain, Ramataia, while the remaining tablets were duplicate texts recording treaties with other chief-tains or governors.

The treaty represents an attempt by Esarhaddon, who was younger than his brothers, to avoid for his sons the dangers he himself had faced on his accession after the patricide of his father Sennacherib.[27] It is the longest Assyrian treaty yet discov-ered and one of the largest tablets, measuring 45.8 x 30 cm and containing 674 lines of text. As far as can be determined, the lay-out and content of each of the treaties is identical. The same three seals are used on all copies – one Old Assyrian, one Middle Assyrian and one Late Assyrian: on the left a seal dedicated by Esarhaddon's father – Sennacherib's 'Seal of Destinies' (Fig. 124), in the centre an 18th century BC seal of the god Aššur and, on the right, a Middle Assyrian impression (such a chronolog-ical division looks deliberate, but it must be remembered that this terminology reflects only modern convenience). Unfortunately the inscription on the third seal, the Middle Assyrian example, is very poorly preserved, but recent studies have demonstrated convincingly that these are all seals of the god Aššur, which at the city of Assur were kept not, as one would expect, in the god's temple but in the *bit alim* ('City Hall');[28] later, at Nimrud, it would appear that they were kept in Ezida.[29]

Fig. 124. Obverse of vassal treaty of Esarhaddon with Ramataia of Urukazabanu in western Iran. It is one of the largest clay tablets known (674 lines in length). The accompanying drawings illustrate two of the three seals of the god Aššur, found on the treaty. The seals themselves were almost certainly made of rare materials and ornamented with gold caps. On the right is Sennacherib's 7th century 'Seal of Destinies'; below, a Middle Assyrian seal, with the kneeling king being introduced by a minor god to (?) Aššur, while the storm god Adad looks on. The tablet measures 45 x 30 cm (ND 4327, Iraq Museum).

The seals were rolled before the text was inscribed, in fact even before the columns were ruled, the 18th century seal in each case having been the first applied. In using these earlier seals Esarhaddon was not only enlisting the authority of the god but also following customary procedure in validating documents requiring the weight of precedence. The long inscription on the seal reads:

> The Seal of Destinies, with which Aššur, king of the gods, seals the destinies of the Igigi and Anunnaki of heaven and underworld, and of mankind. Whatever he seals he will not alter. Whoever would alter it may Aššur, king of the gods, and Mullissu [Assyrian Ninlil, Aššur's wife], together with their children, slay him with their terrible weapons! I am Sennacherib, king of Assyria, the prince who reveres you. Whoever erases my inscribed name or alters this, your Seal of Destinies – erase his name and his seed from the land.[30]

As the inscription implies the deities depicted on this seal are the god Aššur and his consort, standing on their associated animals, the *mušhuššu* dragon, symbol of the Babylonian god Marduk, and the lion, more commonly an aspect of Ishtar but in Assyria the animal of Mullissu. It would appear that the dragon symbolism was brought to Assyria by Sennacherib after his conquest of Babylon in an attempt to reattribute the mythology of the supreme Babylonian god to Aššur who, as a personification of the city, lacked such identifying symbols (see also p. 15). The god Aššur is unusual within the Mesopotamian pantheon in his derivation from the city, the

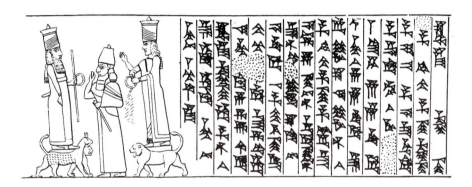

205

existence of which is attested before the 'creation' of the god. The Old Assyrian seal was inscribed briefly, 'Seal of Aššur, of the *bit alim* (the 'City Hall'). The Middle Assyrian seal depicts the kneeling king being introduced by a minor god to Aššur, while the storm god Adad looks on. Unfortunately the lengthy background inscription is largely illegible. It was once thought that this was a lapis lazuli seal of a 13th century Kassite king, taken as booty and recut by Tukulti-Ninurta I of Assyria,[31] but the argument that all are seals of the god Aššur now appears more convincing.

The text of the treaty itself begins with a two-line heading describing the seal(s) of Aššur:[32]

> Seal of the god Aššur, king of the gods, lord of the lands – not to be altered; seal of the great ruler, father of the gods – not to be disputed.

Then follows:

> The treaty of Esarhaddon, king of the world, king of Assyria,
> son of Sennacherib, king of the world, king of Assyria,
> with Ramataia, city-ruler of Urakazabanu,
> with his sons, his grandsons, with all the Urakazabaneans
> young and old, as many as there may be from sunrise to sunset,
> with all of you, your sons, your grandsons
> who will be born in days to come after this treaty,
> all those over whom Esarhaddon, king of Assyria, exercises
> kingship and lordship, on behalf of whom he has concluded this treaty
> with you concerning Assurbanipal, the crown-prince designate,
> son of Esarhaddon, king of Assyria.

This introduction is followed by a long list naming the gods who witness the treaty. Then follow 33 clauses, each of which the vassal swears to keep. Inter alia, the vassal princes swear in agreement that 'When Esarhaddon, king of Assyria, dies, you will seat Assurbanipal, the crown-prince designate, upon the royal throne. He will exercise the kingship and lordship of Assyria over you....You shall fight and even die for him. You shall speak with him in the truth of your heart...You shall not depose him nor shall you seat one of his brothers, older or younger, on the throne of Assyria instead of him. You shall serve only Assurbanipal, the crown-prince designate' (lines 46–59). Surprisingly, the other provision of the treaty is not even referred to before line 86, which adds 'help Šamaš-šum-ukin, (Assurbanipal's) 'equal-brother', the crown-prince designate of Babylon, to ascend the throne of Babylon.' The treaty deals almost in its entirety with the rights of Assurbanipal, and there is even an adjuration that should Esarhaddon die in the minority of his sons and Assurbanipal be killed, '(You swear) that you shall await the woman pregnant by Esarhaddon, king of Assyria or the wife of Assurbanipal, the crown-prince.'

It has been suggested both that Šamaš-šum-ukin and Assurbanipal were twin brothers ('his equal brother'), and that the former was the elder of the two. It is indeed the position of Assurbanipal that seems to be in question, and it must be more than a coincidence that Esarhaddon's queen died in February 672 and the treaties are dated to May of that year. The queen's first born son died young, and she was not the mother of the twins, if such they were. Her death would almost certainly have provoked maternal family pressures and jostling for position in the succession, in which it would appear that Esarhaddon's mother favoured Assurbanipal (p. 24). Recent opinion favours the view that the two brothers were not in fact twins, nor were they born of the same mother. Certainly Assurbanipal's mother remains unidentified in the texts, and the mother of Šamaš-šum-ukin would appear to have been Babylonian.[33]

One of the most extraordinary aspects of this document is the final section in which the curses invoked upon anyone breaking any of the sworn obligations or altering or destroying the text itself occupy over 150 lines. The wrath of over 20 individual deities is invoked upon any transgressor, followed by a further forty curses based on similes from everyday observation, a type of curse little known in Akkadian literature:

> May they treat you as a fly, caught in the hand; may your enemy squash you.
>
> May the gods make you, your brothers, your sons and your daughters go backward like a crab.
>
> Just as the noise of doves is persistent, so may you, your women, your sons, your daughters, have no rest or sleep.
>
> Just as the inside of a hole is empty, may your inside be empty.
>
> Just as gall is bitter, so may you, your women, your sons and your daughters be bitter towards each other.
>
> Just as the water of a split waterskin runs out, so may your waterskin break in a place of thirst and famine, so that you die of thirst.' And so on.

The full text remains incomplete, although much has been restored from the fragments of other copies that have survived. Nonetheless, the Ramataia treaty remains the most impressive single cuneiform tablet to have been found at Nimrud, perhaps even the most striking found at any Assyrian site.

The Nabu Temple library lay in the south-east court of Ezida, where room NT 12 would appear to have served as the archive room, with its wide door for light and its associated well (plan, p. 112). Tablets were found in most of the rooms surrounding the south-eastern court, and rooms NTS 9 and 10 may also have been scribal offices. Regrettably, although some 300 tablets were found here, their primary contexts had been much disturbed not only by the succeeding squatter occupations but also by Layard, Rassam, Loftus and Smith in the 19th century. Indeed many of the tablets came from the disturbed fill of later pits. The literary texts found in the 1950s, which would have been part of the temple 'reference library', have recently been published.[34] These include tablets from poetic compositions such as the Gilgamesh Epic and *Enuma eliš*, proverbs, and a number of omen lists, magical and medical texts, prayers, hymns, and ritual and lexical texts. Indeed the largest part of the collection is devoted to divination, magic and medicine. These texts were acquired over a long period, from the time of Assurnasirpal until the late 7th century, and the surviving collection includes not only some previously unknown sections of known texts but also some that were entirely unknown. Also in the library were fragmentary

Fig. 125. Fragment of reverse side of a lexical text from Ezida, inscribed in 4 columns, part of the standard list of Late Assyrian cuneiform signs (Syllabary A), with fanciful drawings of the pictures which the scribe imagined to be the original pictographic forms of the signs. It would seem that he had little knowledge of this early period since the signs bear little resemblance to those actually found on the pictographic texts from Uruk. The other interesting observation is that this piece, found in the Ezida throne room by Mallowan in 1955, actually joins a fragment found in the 19th century and at that time thought to have come from Nineveh (original size c. 11.7 cm in width; ND 4311, Iraq Museum).

prisms and barrel cylinders of Esarhaddon and Assurbanipal.

A limestone tablet of Shalmaneser III was found during the Iraqi excavations of 1985–86 in the courtyard to the north of NT 15.[35] In addition to the stele of Šamši-Adad V referred to on p. 107, a fragmentary tablet apparently of the same king's annals was also recovered,[36] together with at least six tablets of the annals of Tiglath-Pileser III, two of which had been found by George Smith in NTS 10.[37] We have already remarked that tablets found at Nimrud by George Smith had been catalogued at the British Museum as though they had come from Nineveh. A particularly nice example of this is provided by two pieces of the lexical text illustrated in Fig. 125, one from the Mallowan excavations and one found in the 19th century.[38] A number of tablets dated in the reigns of Sargon and Sennacherib and now in the Kouyunjik collection also bear colophons which state explicitly that they were written at Kalhu, while letters from the reign of Esarhaddon refer to an *akitu* festival of Nabu at Kalhu (see p. 119). Unfortunately nothing can be said concerning the organisation of the library, since virtually all the tablets would appear to be in secondary or even tertiary contexts. A pigeon-hole system was in use for the storage of tablets at a number of sites in Babylonia, at Nineveh, in the North-West Palace (Fig. 120) and in the Nabu Temple at Khorsabad, but no evidence has as yet been found for the presence of such a system in Ezida.

Also from the Nabu Temple are a small group of 7th century economic and legal texts, the first collection of Late Assyrian temple documents of this type to have been discovered.[39] Two tablets record gifts of land and slaves, including Fig. 70 (p. 115). Some 30 are dockets, largely heart-shaped, recording debts of grain owed to the temple. The god Nabu is named as creditor, while the debtors include a cultivator, a fuller, a night watchman, three of the governor's gem cutters and a man of the queen's guard. The amount of the debt is usually very small, and rates of interest, which vary widely, seem to depend on the security of the debtor in relation to his debt. In three cases the Nabu Temple seems to have been acting as a bank for providing business capital.

Another interesting feature of the Nabu Temple texts is that a number of scribal names are recorded in the colophons of some of the surviving texts. It is possible that these represent at least six generations of the same scribal 'family', a family also with Babylonian connections, the youngest a scribe of Adad-nerari III, descendant of an official of Assurnasirpal II.[40]

TEXTS FROM THE GOVERNOR'S PALACE

The texts recovered in the Governor's Palace were among the first discovered by the Mallowan expedition. More than 200 tablets and fragments were found here, dealing largely with administrative and legal matters, land sales, marriage transactions, official inventories, etc. The activities of farmers, smiths, textile and leather workers and many other trades are attested. The tablets were found largely in three rooms north of the courtyard (plan, p. 133). Those in rooms K and M were largely legal in nature and can be dated for the most part to the first half of the 8th century; those from room S included letters and administrative texts. The latter are undated but may perhaps belong in the latter half of that century. It would appear that there are no tablets dated after 710 BC, and it has been suggested that at approximately that time whatever aspect of the royal administration is represented here moved to some other building, perhaps the 1950 building where the recovered tablets are of 7th century date, or even the North-West Palace, this change probably coinciding with the transfer of the royal administration to the new capital at Khorsabad. This is only speculation, however, as is the suggestion that the so-called Governor's Palace was actually a governor's residence.[41]

That this building had some connection with the activities of local governors is based on the presence of tablets concerning their affairs. Indeed five governors' names are mentioned in the texts, as are persons who appear to have belonged to the individual governors' households. Much interesting information can be gained from these texts, some purely social, some concerning affairs of state. Among the documents found in room S is a group of administrative letters addressed to two of these governors, at least one of whom was an official of the time of Tiglath-Pileser III. Another governor whose documents were found here is Bel-tarṣi-iluma, donor of the statues dedicated in the Nabu Temple to queen Sammuramat (Semiramis) and her son Adad-nerari III. The latter had possibly succeeded to the throne as a minor, and one of the earliest texts from the Governor's Palace, one which is sealed by this same governor, can be dated to 808 BC, when in the view of some authorities Adad-nerari's famous mother reigned as regent.[42] This was a time when the power of provincial governors had grown immensely and some were beginning to exceed their authority. A stele found at Tell al Rimah in 1967, for example, also dedicated by an Assyrian governor for the life of Adad-nerari III, bore an inscription detailing the achievements of the governor himself, a serious case of *lèse-majesté* (p. 19).

A brief sample of subjects may give some indication of the great variety of the Governor's Palace documents. One mentions the import of Sissoo wood (*Dalbergia sissoo*) from Makkan in Iran (text 189). Another from the governor of the province of Assur to his counterpart at Kalhu complains that subjects of the province of Kalhu have set fire to the desert and thus destroyed the grazing in his own area ('eaten up the whole desert', text 188). In another document detailing a transaction involving a large area of land the penalties threatened against anyone instigating litigation against the new owner (an official of Adad-nerari III) include several rather bizarre punishments from the (relatively common) dedication of four white horses at the feet of the god Aššur to eating a mina of carded wool and gathering 'with the tip of his tongue' cress (?) seed all the way from the gate of Kalhu to the gate of Assur (some 80 km as the crow flies) (text 17). A number of tablets from Room S list various equids, including horses of different colours, mules and donkeys, the property of various officials, apparently the responsibility of a 'village-inspector' (texts 125 ff).

TABLETS FROM THE TW 53 HOUSES

Forty-seven tablets come from a private residence belonging to Šamaš-šarru-uṣur, eunuch and government official (LÚ.SAG), prosperous landowner, merchant and

Fig. 126. Two heart-shaped grain dockets recording loans of grain, from storeroom 19 in the house of the merchant Šamaš-šar-uṣur. a) 5 x 3.5 cm, ND 3447, the semi-circular marks remain unexplained, although they may represent the six witnesses (see p. 225); b) the stamp seal impression shows a very popular Kalhu motif of a cow suckling a calf; post-canonical limmu, i.e. after 648 BC, 5.2 x 3.5 cm, ND 3464, 666 BC, Metropolitan Museum of Art.

money lender. This is the only non-palatial archive found at Nimrud, though it is clear that such officials also enjoyed private wealth. The dated business documents of Šamaš-šarru-uṣur and his scribe Samedu range over at least 40 years, from 666 to approximately 622 BC, while tablets dated by later post-canonical *limmu* suggest that their commercial activities may well have continued as late as the sack of Kalhu in 612, that is, over a period of more than 50 years.[43] The names of other officials, perhaps his neighbours, appear as witnesses on contracts; penalty payments are made to the Ninurta temple treasury, suggesting that Šamaš-šarru-uṣur and his scribe may have been officials of this temple. Many of his transactions are sales of slaves or loans of silver; an unusual feature involved dealing in birds. For example, 230 doves were loaned in February–March to be returned in May–June. More valuable were the KUR.GI birds (geese), of which two were loaned to be returned six months later. In default, 120 doves were to be exacted. Even ordinary advances of silver required 2 KUR.GI birds as part of the payment of interest.[44] It is not clear whether these birds were sought as food or as instruments for the taking of omens, but augury is hardly attested in Assyria. The late 7th century texts from Fort Shalmaneser, discussed below, are also notable for their preoccupation with the keeping and feeding of birds.

THE TABLETS FROM FORT SHALMANESER[45]

Many important collections of cuneiform documents were recovered from Fort Shalmaneser. These span a considerable period, largely from the late 8th century to the fall of the city. The royal annals, of which a number of copies were also found here, tell of the rebuilding and restoration of areas of the arsenal, discussed further in chapter 5. The tablets themselves have provided considerable information about the actual function of the various parts of this vast building. Of particular interest is the presence here of a household of the queen, supervised by a female official, the *šakin-tu*. The remainder of the building was run by the *rab ekalli*, the 'palace manager'. Parts of the 7th century archives of both these officials have survived.

During the 9th and 8th centuries the building served many military purposes; indeed the tablets of this date also include muster lists of men and horses, chariots and armour. The late 8th century cuneiform documents indicate that it was at the same time a centre for the administration of taxes. The military functions of the arsenal, though still attested in its equipment, are less well documented in the dated post-canonical tablets, which are largely concerned with loans and other financial transactions, certainly a reflection of the greater importance at this time of the arsenal at Nineveh but probably also a matter of chance survival and discovery. Nonetheless, among the post-canonical texts there are some which do refer to military matters, for example ND 7010, dated to the time of last king Sin-šar-iškun,[46] while 7th century letters from Nimrud found at Nineveh clearly indicate the continuing importance of Kalhu in the training of horses, cavalry and chariotry.[47] One letter also refers to the annual muster.[48] It should also be noted that the sealed dockets in the *rab ekalli*'s house, discussed below, which refer to the review of troops, cannot actually be dated, that is, that they could equally well be contemporary with ND 7010 from the same archive.[49] Certainly other dated records from the same room can be attributed to the time of this last Assyrian king.[50] Notable among these later texts are documents dealing with the keeping of birds, attested also in the contemporary Town Wall tablets. Among the other post-canonical tablets from SW 6 are letters written from one palace official to another, a type of correspondence virtually unknown elsewhere.[51]

The archive of the rab ekalli[52]

This group of tablets was found in 1958, scattered in rooms SE 1, 8, 10, 11. In rooms 1 and 10 large parts of inscribed cylinders of Esarhaddon were also found, of which further fragments were recovered several years later in the adjacent NE 2, the distribution of these cylinder fragments confirming the presence here of an upper storey where they had been stored. A massive sealing with royal seal impressions of the time of Esarhaddon was also found here (Fig. 127). The *rab ekalli* was the senior official in charge of the arsenal and responsible for its internal organisation, as clearly indicated in his full title: *rab ekalli ša ekal mašarti ša ᵘʳᵘkalha*. Several holders of this position can be identified, and their texts gave us for the first time, in 1958, confirmation of the identification of the building as an *ekal mašarti*.

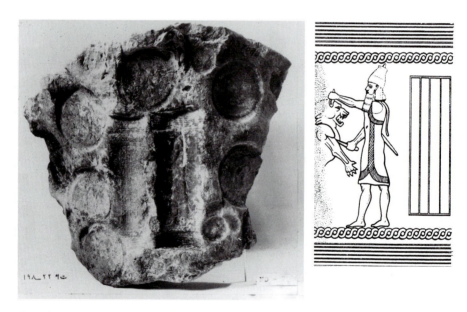

Fig. 127. Impressions of a cylinder seal bearing the inscription 'Palace of Esarhaddon, great king, king of the universe, king of Assyria, son of Sennacherib, king of Assyria, son of Sargon, king of Assyria'. The seal bore end caps, almost certainly of gold and probably comparable with those preserved on a seal recently discovered in the North-West Palace (p. 103). Here the cylinder seal was simply 'stamped' on the clay, as though it were a stamp seal, while the gold cap on the bottom of the seal was almost certainly also the 'stamp seal' which produced the larger of the two circular impressions. Both the cylinder and the stamp seals are examples of the 'royal seal' type, depicting the king stabbing a lion. Found in the rab ekalli's *residence (size of surviving sealing 13 x 6 cm, ND 7080, Iraq Museum).*

The documents fall into two main classes: letters, contracts and legal records dealing with both public and private affairs, in six of which various holders of the office of *rab ekalli* are mentioned, and more than 30 dockets, bullae and jar sealings dealing with the specific issue of goods or their recipients. Among these are several dockets referring to the review of troops and, in one case, stamped with a scaraboid seal, the delivery of stakes (?) 'before the campaign' (ND 7065).[53] With the exception of the Esarhaddon documents, all the *rab ekalli*'s dated tablets are post-canonical, that is, after 649 BC (p. 27) and can be attributed to a period during the later years of Assurbanipal or the reigns of Assur-etel-ilani or Sin-šar-iškun; a number can be dated with certainty to the time of Sin-šar-iškun. This fact alone emphasises the likelihood that the two dockets referred to above,[54] which read 'soldiers of the king, reviewed', followed by the name of the officer in charge, are to be dated in the 7th century. Also of interest is the fact that these are stamped with the royal seal and appear to seal flat surfaces with wood impressions, possibly the wooden boards on which the muster was recorded. Another small docket, unfortunately found on the excavation dump but found at the same time as the *rab ekalli*'s rooms were being excavated, records the delivery of 'an iron coat of Damascus mail'.[55]

Tablets from the Queen's Household[56]

These tablets were also found in 1958, largely in storeroom S 10, mixed together with ivories and other objects among the burnt debris which represented the destruction of the arsenal. Many of them deal not only with the queen's affairs but with other household matters, and it is reasonable to assume that they had originally been stored in the office of the *šakintu*, the comptroller of the queen's household (p. 187). Again the tablets are all of post-canonical date. Tablets from the office of the *šakintu* identify also the queen's scribe and the *šakintu*'s deputy, the *šanitu*. It is of interest that the witnesses for documents relating to affairs within the queen's household are all men; indeed women rarely act as witnesses. On these tablets, however, the male witnesses, although they include two *rab ekalli*s, are drawn largely from the queen's household, for example the doorkeeper, the bolt keeper, the surveyor, etc. The queen's scribe seems to engage in the lending of silver. In one document she lends a large sum (52 shekels) to Ṣalmu-šarru-iqbi, whose name is synonymous with that of a *turtanu* who held the office of *limmu* at the time of Sin-šar-iškun. The silver itself came from the temple of the goddess Mullissu (Ninlil).[57] Figure 128 illustrates a docket from S 10, dated to the *limmu*-ship of Bel-iqbi, of the time of Sin-šar-iškun.

The wine ration texts

These texts deal exclusively with daily rations of wine and are unique among documents of this period. Specifically, they deal with entitlements of wine within the royal household which, on the basis of the evidence of the texts, can be estimated at approaching 6000 persons. Technically, the tablets are not records of 'issue' but of the daily rations owing to various members of the household. They are records from a single administrative department within Fort Shalmaneser, under the direction of a *rab karani*. They date from the 8th century, and we have no indication why these par-

213

Fig. 128. Tablet covered with unopened clay 'envelope', from the šakintu's archive (S 10). This is an unusual grain loan which requires that the contracted grain be delivered 'on the day of the king's entry into Nineveh', perhaps for some religious festival. The tablet is dated limmu Bel-iqbi, *that is c. 620 BC, in the time of Sin-šar-iškun (see also Fig. 70; 5 x 3.5 cm, ND 7074).*

ticular records should have been kept over the next 100 to 150 years, as it were, in the files. Although only some 30 in number, the texts are of especial importance in the unique information they provide concerning the administration of imperial Assyria.[58] All aspects of the government are represented, in the sense that the king's 'household' encompassed officials of all varieties and ranks. Information concerning the relative status of different types of official is clear from the quantity of wine allotted to each, the highest ranks of course receiving the largest entitlements.

The first group of wine tablets, found in 1957, literally came from the 'wine cellar', room SW 6, found on and amongst the large wine jars (further described on p. 166). A larger group of related tablets was found in 1961, in rooms NE 48–49, but these were in secondary packing in the rooms and thus not in situ. Other texts dealing with wine were found in the North-West Palace wine store (room 30 in area ZT). Deliveries as well as entitlements are recorded, for example on dockets from SW 6 which account over 37 homers of wine from the town of Yaluna, presumably somewhere in the hills northeast of Kalhu, the homer being 100 *qa* or, very approximately, 184 litres, a figure derived from calculations based on the inscribed wine jars from SW 6.[59] For ease of receipt and delivery, storage magazines such as SW 6 were invariably situated with direct access to the large open courtyards.

It is not possible in this very general book to describe the wine tablets in detail, but a few examples may give some sense of the great variety of information they provide. In particular, the relative rank of various officials is clear not only from the quantity of wine allotted but from the order of their positions on the tablets themselves. Among the 'lower classes' the amount of wine seems very small. It would appear that 1 *qa* of wine (estimated at 1.84 litres[60]) was the modest daily ration for 10 men; for skilled workmen the same amount was allotted to 6 men. As Mallowan remarks, 'There would seem to have been little opportunity for drunkenness on this ration'.[61] The nobility fared much better, with daily allotments amounting to the ration of perhaps 5 men. The rations were also calculated in terms of the *šappu*-jar, with a capacity of 5 *qa*. The rations themselves seem to be allotted to individuals, groups or specific 'houses'. Concerning the recipients, there is, inter alia, much information about the eunuch officials, apparently specifically assigned either to the *babanu,* the public area of the palace, or the *bitanu,* the private household. There was also a 'boy's half-ration' for the *mare šaqe,* sons of the 'cupbearers', who were presumably adopted since these officials were eunuchs. A 'cup' (*kasu*) was also used as a measure, apparently one tenth of a *qa*.

The tablets confirm the presence of a queen's household in Fort Shalmaneser (ND 6218, 6219). Indeed the 'lady of the palace' seems to have had a considerable taste for wine. A number of different groups of musicians are recorded in the wine lists, our favourite being the Kassite choir (ND 6219).[62] Two groups of female singers are also listed. Among the professions found on the wine tablets, in addition of course to the senior government officials and 'nobility', are the king's brewers and bakers, his messengers and the 'escorts' of the postal service, charioteers, officials of the royal stables, dove-keepers, physicians and diviners, and large numbers of foreigners and interpreters. Indeed the presence of Egyptian scribes and of Ethiopians or Nubians in a text probably to be dated two years after Tiglath-Pileser III established overseers in Egypt (ND 10048) is of considerable historical interest. The king does not figure in these lists, his wine cellar presumably lying elsewhere, possibly that identified in the North-West Palace. It has been suggested that the different categories and classes of officials and workmen must have been fed in large messes, and one remembers the well-known inscription of Sargon of Agade, over 1500 years before, that '5400 men daily ate in his presence'.[63]

It is perhaps strange that the ration lists up to now discovered in Fort Shalmaneser should deal with the issue of wine to the almost complete exclusion of other, more staple commodities such as grain, but it is possible that the wine-cellars lay within the complex which we have excavated, whereas the government granaries, presumably requiring greater space and perhaps less security, lay outside and were served by a different record office. The contours of the land around the *ekal mašarti* suggest the presence of a vast parade ground, over some 200 m to the north and 450 m to the west, itself enclosed by a high ridge obviously covering a considerable range of buildings which may represent the government stores, or perhaps even further barracks, situated here perhaps for reasons of convenience or because they did not require the greater security of the inner fortress.[64]

The horse lists[65]

As elsewhere at Nimrud, the tablets recovered from Fort Shalmaneser, represent but a very small proportion of the actual archives they represent. This is perhaps most striking in the case of the so-called horse lists which were found scattered not only in room NE 50, from which the majority derived, but also in several other chambers opening onto the NE courtyard including NW 3, a room in the official residence in the north-west corner of the court. Although these tablets are little more than remnants from a much larger group of records, they provide, nonetheless, an extraordinary insight into the military administration of the *ekal mašarti*. In particular they record the official government musters of men and animals and incoming items such as chariots and horses. All refer to personnel from the cavalry and chariotry. The numbers of animals involved can be very large, for example ND 10001, the record of a BE-qu muster, in which 3,477 horses and mules are recorded.[66] Indeed a major function of the *ekal mašarti* was this annual muster which, as we know from

Esarhaddon's Nineveh inscription, was 'for the ordinance of the camp, the maintenance of the stallions, mules, chariots, weapons, equipment for war, and the spoil of the foe of every kind'.[67] A particular value of the horse lists lies in the information they provide not only about the annual muster but also concerning the organisation of the army in the late 8th century.[68] Among the more interesting texts in this respect are those that record deficiencies in the establishment of both men and animals in the provincial garrisons and the imperial posting stations, with the measures taken to bring the units up to strength. These undoubtedly reflect a later passage in the Esarhaddon inscription:

> May I – every year without interruption – take stock there during the month of the New Year's Festival, the first month, of all steeds, mules, donkeys and camels, of the harness and battle gear of all my troops, and of the booty taken from the enemy.

Among our most exciting discoveries from Fort Shalmaneser was the surviving booty.

Esarhaddon Cylinders[69]

A number of inscribed cylinders dated to the time of Esarhaddon describe his building activities at the site. Although fragments were found in the *rab ekalli*'s house, it would seem that all of these may originally have been deposited in the walls of Fort Shalmaneser. The first complete cylinder recovered (Fig. 129) was reported to have been found 'by a ploughman' in a field south of the tell, but the discovery of a second complete example in 1962 in debris below the outer wall south-east of T 27 indicates that the first example may have originated in the same location. Here the foun-

Fig. 129. Inscribed cylinder of Esarhaddon (ND 1126). This is the first example found, which was brought in from Nimrud village but had probably been found near the southern ramparts of Fort Shalmaneser. Fragments of the same cylinder text, which describes the rebuilding of the ekal mašarti, *were also found in the* rab ekalli's *house (width of cylinder 18 cm).*

dations of the outer wall had been extensively robbed, and local enquiry in 1962 elicited the information that in the early part of this century stone had been obtained from this stretch of wall for the construction of buildings in and near Nimrud village. It is thus more than likely that the previously known cylinder was unearthed during these operations and taken to the village, whence it was recovered in 1956 by the good offices of Shaikh Abdullah Nejefi.[70] Moreover, the building work described in these cylinders refers solely to the *ekal mašarti* (Fort Shalmaneser), not the South-West Palace which Esarhaddon never finished; at Nineveh also his 'new palace' lay in the same complex as the *ekal-mašarti*.[71] At Nimrud there is archaeological evidence for extensive alterations by Esarhaddon, for example to the outer wall and the throne room suite (T 1 and associated rooms).

ARAMAIC SCRIBES

A number of 7th century economic documents are found with annotations, endorsements or summaries written in Aramaic, a form of West Semitic spoken by people who occupied much of Syria and are first heard of in texts of the late second millennium BC.[72] Aramaic is written in an alphabetic script, related to the Phoenician alphabet; it was later to be the language of Imperial Achaemenid administration and of the New Testament. Early in the first millennium BC numerous clashes between Assyrian and Aramaean troops are recorded in the Assyrian royal annals. Both Assurnasirpal II's father and grandfather claimed successes against them, while his grandfather (Adad-nerari II) is the first to mention the kingdom of Bit Bahiani in the Khabur region of northeastern Syria, from which his grandson received tribute and from which comes the oldest lengthy Aramaic text. This is a bilingual Assyrian-Aramaic inscription on a basalt statue found, as is so often the case, by a farmer enlarging his field with a bulldozer at the edge of the site of Tell Fakhariyah, near modern Ras al 'Ain.[73] The date of the inscription is uncertain but is probably some time in the mid-ninth century BC.[74] Bit Bahiani was incorporated into the Assyrian provincial system during the 9th century, and if the proposed date of the inscription is correct, possibly at the time of Shalmaneser III.

The earliest uncontroversial use of an alphabetic script at Nimrud is provided by the evidence of alphabetic notations found on the bricks from T 20 in Fort Shalmaneser, which can be dated unequivocally to the reign of Shalmaneser III (p. 186). The importance of this evidence lies in the fact that it constitutes the earliest indication of the presence in Assyria of craftsmen using a western alphabet, in this case probably Aramaic,[75] and that this represents the period during which Assyria began to incorporate Aramaic-speaking kingdoms in the west. Although the use of alphabetic letters shows the widespread presence of alphabetic writing at this time, it has of course a purely practical function in that cuneiform is normally incised, and the alphabetic letters can be more simply painted on. The painted signs closely resemble those found on the ivories, but here often only single signs are cut and it is not always possible to determine whether the alphabetic script is Aramaic or Phoenician. As in the case of the marks on the glazed bricks, the single letters are almost certainly fitters' marks.

Fig. 130. Part of the reverse side of an ivory plaque depicting a sphinx. On the back is a two-line inscription in either Aramaic or Phoenician, together with a certain amount of 'doodling' (12.4 x 5.1 cm; from SW 11/12, Fort Shalmaneser; ND 12049, British Museum.)

Among the Aramaic inscriptions from Nimrud, however, are ivories bearing longer inscriptions, including the names of rulers and cities, for example Fig. 130 and the ivory fragment from SW 37 inscribed 'Hamath', modern Hama (Fig. 131), a city ruled early in the first millennium BC by a Neo-Hittite dynasty but taken over by Aramaean rulers in the late 9th/early 8th century. The set of bronze weights found by Layard in the North-West Palace bear their denominations inscribed in Akkadian and/or Aramaic, while an ivory knob found by Loftus is inscribed 'property of Milki-ram', possibly the same Milki-ramu who was eponym in 656 BC and the wealthy husband of the ZT 16 text (see p. 201).[76] A few inscriptions are in Hebrew, the most interesting of which is the fragmentary ivory also from SW 37 which has been described as 'perhaps the finest example of ancient

Fig. 131. Ivory label inscribed with three letters in Aramaic, which read 'Hamath' (9.2 x 6.5 cm; from SW 37, Fort Shalmaneser; ND 10151).

Hebrew calligraphy'. The last two lines appear to be part of a curse formula:

> (may God curse any) of my successors, from great king to private citizen who may come and destroy this inscription.[77]

Also unusual is an ostracon from Fort Shalmaneser (room SW 1) bearing two separate lists of names, one on each side. These are written in Aramaic script but the names themselves appear to be either Phoenician or Israelite.[78] Two other potsherds with alphabetic writing from the North-West Palace (room I) are illustrated by Layard.[79]

Aramaic was usually written in ink on perishable materials such as leather or papyrus. Aside from the fitters' marks, the most common written evidence for Aramaic in Assyria lies in the annotations on dockets and clay tablets, which are thought to have been added by bilingual scribes. We know also that there were specifically Aramaean scribes, who are identified in the wine texts as among those entitled to the issue of wine; one text, dated 786 BC, lists Assyrian, Egyptian and Aramaean scribes.[80] By the 8th century there must have been a considerable Aramaean component among the population, and at Nimrud their names are found among the officials, and especially the royal wives. Perhaps the best-known was Sennacherib's wife Naqi'a-Zakutu, who kept her original West Semitic name alongside its Akkadian equivalent. It was she, as the powerful Queen Mother, who was instrumental in orchestrating the succession enforced by the treaty tablets found in the Ezida throne room.

Cuneiform tablets with Aramaic annotations have been found at Nineveh but not at Nimrud.[81] However, four clay dockets written in Aramaic were found in the ZT scribal offices. Two from room 13 were simple labels in Aramaic only, 'for the palace' and 'for the house'; two others were ovoid bullae inscribed both in Aramaic and cuneiform.[82] All bore stamp seal impressions. By the late 7th century Aramaic must have been commonly spoken in Assyria. At the same time the late texts from Fort Shalmaneser clearly attest the continuing use of the Assyrian dialect of Akkadian, both as a spoken and a written language,[83] that is, Aramaic had not replaced Assyrian at this time. It was soon to do so, however, as a widely understood language with an easily used script. The latest surviving witness to the Assyrian language are the documents of Nebuchadnezzar date from Dur-Katlimmu (Shaikh Hamad) on the Khabur (p. 25).

WRITING BOARDS

Both wood and ivory writing boards were found in the well excavated by Mallowan in courtyard AB in the North-West Palace. These are discussed in more detail on p. 97.[84] The Nimrud boards were fastened together with hinges in order to form a polyptych, an early form of 'book'. These large examples are, however, exceptional, two leaves, occasionally as many as five, being the more normal size. Writing boards (*^{is}le'u*) are attested in the cuneiform texts far earlier than they have been found, and it is possible that they were introduced into Assyria from the west, along with the use of the beeswax which provided the actual writing surface. In Assyria a sulphur compound (orpiment) was mixed with the beeswax to render it more plastic, producing a yellow surface on which the writing was inscribed. In Roman times verdigris or carbon was often added to obtain a green or black writing surface. Surviving fragments of inscribed wax from the Nimrud polyptych (Fig. 62) show not only that the text was written in cuneiform but also that it was inscribed in two columns down the long axis of the boards. The script is small and neat, averaging ten to twelve lines of cuneiform to the inch in each column.[85] It is likely that Aramaic was also written on these boards, and indeed the notations on the individual hinges that provide the guide to assembling the individual boards into the Nimrud 'book' are written in alphabetic script.

Fragments of writing boards were found in ZT and in Ezida, while a tablet from the ZT archive room mentions the more ordinary writing boards with from two to five leaves.[86] Also from Ezida was a unique black stone writing board (ND 6307), the raised edge of which was decorated with sunken rosettes, presumably designed to receive some form of inlay. It was found in the north courtyard.

STAMPED BRICKS AND SYMBOLS

Some of our most important dating information comes from the use, especially in the courtyards of monumental buildings, of baked bricks stamped with the name of the royal builder. In the late 8th and 7th centuries bricks were also stamped with symbols associated with particular rulers. In Ezida, for example, there were bricks bearing a stamp depicting a Babylonian *mušhuššu* dragon, some of which also bore an inscription of Assur-etel-ilani.[87] Other stamps included a lion, found on bricks used almost certainly by Esarhaddon in the conversion of SW 5 into a residential suite. The use of such 'symbols' seems to have been a particular fashion of Sargon and his descendants.

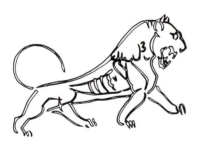

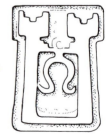

Fig. 132. Examples of stamped or incised 'symbols' found on royal objects from Nimrud. a) incised lion from duck weight of Tiglath-pileser III, North-West Palace Tomb III (after Fadhil 1990a, pl. 43d); b) one of several shells engraved with a scorpion design from the 'trinket collection', room HH, North-West Palace (length c. 7 cm, ND 1714); stamp found on sherd of large storage jar in room ZZ, NWP (3.5 x 2.4 cm, ND 1412).

They appear not only on bricks but on portable palace property, for example the lion on a duck weight of Tiglath-pileser III from Tomb III (Fig. 132a) and on the so-called Sargon vase. At the same time personal items belonging to the women of the family were often marked with scorpions, a symbol of fertility. Among a number of examples are the engraved scorpions found on the handle of a mirror which formed the cover of an electrum cosmetics box and on a gold bowl from Tomb II in the North-West Palace, both inscribed with the name of Atalia, Sargon's queen.[88] The same symbol appears on a number of shell cosmetics containers from the 'trinket collection' found in the Room HH cupboard, also in the North-West Palace (Fig. 132b),[89] which almost certainly belonged to one of the palace women, and on a sealing from that room. Pottery storage vessels also occasionally bore identifying stamps (Fig. 132c).

SEALS AND SEALING PRACTICES

The practice of sealing storerooms and containers for purposes of security began at least as early as the 7th millennium BC. At this time the seals themselves were simply stone or perhaps wood stamps with a distinctive design carved on the surface for identification. Cylindrical seals, which could be rolled on a clay surface both to provide more complex designs and to cover a larger surface area for greater security, first appear in the middle of the 4th millennium BC (Middle Uruk). These remained the most common Mesopotamian seal form until the 7th century when alphabetic scripts such as Aramaic and Phoenician came into wider usage. Unlike the more cumbersome cuneiform the alphabetic scripts were in general written not on clay but with ink on papyrus or leather. Such documents could be rolled up, the rolls often tied with string and sealed with a lump of clay on which the stamp seal provided a more practical means of authorisation or identification. In ninth century Assyria the cylinder seal was used almost exclusively, but by the late 8th century the stamp seal had returned into general use by court officials, coinciding with the extension of direct Assyrian control to Syria and the west where alphabetic writing was the more customary form.

There was in Assyria a variety of stamp seal known as the royal seal type, on which was portrayed the king himself stabbing a lion.[90] This was an official seal applied largely to bullae and dockets, and could be used only by the king or his designated representative (as in the example from the *rab ekalli*'s residence, cited above, Fig. 127). It was also used on tablets recording gifts and royal charters. Over 100 different versions have been recorded, covering some two centuries. It was long believed that the earliest example was the state seal of Shalmaneser III, found in the North-West Palace (Fig. 21, p. 43), but a recent publication identifies several exam-

Fig. 133. Bulla impression of an unusual royal stamp seal of a grandson of Shalmaneser III, presumably Adad-nerari III (only the end of the inscription is preserved), from the šakintu's storeroom in Fort Shalmaneser (S 10) (6.5 x 6.2 cm; ND 7104).

Fig. 134. Translucent pale grey chalcedony cylinder seal, found in a broken patch of pavement behind the Ezida Fish Gate. An armed god stands before the symbols of Nabu and Marduk, faced by two worshippers. The star-like effect is obtained by heavy use of the drill; originally covered with copper caps (ht 4.5 cm, ND 5262, Iraq Museum).

ples from Assur apparently of the time of Assurnasirpal II.[91] The importance of this particular seal type was first recognised by Layard, who was also the first to appreciate the significance of the impressions on the backs of the sealings which of course provide information about the containers or other objects to which they were applied.[92] An unusual royal stamp seal is illustrated in Fig. 133, on which only the lion is depicted.

By the 7th century, with the increasing preference for stamp seals, not only were cuneiform tablets being sealed with such stamps but cylinder seals had themselves come to be treated as stamps, that is, they were stamped onto rather than rolled across the clay surface. Most extraordinary is the jar sealing of this time from the *rab ekalli*'s house in Fort Shalmaneser, with seven impressions of one royal or 'palace' stamp seal, in this case possibly the decorated end of one of the seal's gold caps, and four impressions of a second smaller palace seal, encircling two 'stamped' impressions of a cylinder seal of the palace of Esarhaddon (Fig. 127).[93] Another (?jar) sealing from an adjacent room (SE 1) also bore part of the impression of a very large rectangular royal seal (almost certainly also of Esarhaddon), together with three impressions of a small round example.[94]

Seals also served as marks of status. Indeed, some designs appear to have been restricted to certain classes of people or officials, while the higher the status of the owner, the more beautiful the carving and the more expensive the materials. Some prestigious seals were fitted with gold caps, some with copper. The impressions of 16 different scorpion seals are known, constituting perhaps the equivalent of the royal seal but used for marking property of the palace women. The only example found at Nimrud came, significantly, from room HH in the North-West Palace, where other evidence attests the presence of female occupants (see p. 79).[95]

The king presumably also had his own personal cylinder seal, but that of Esarhaddon, referred to above (Fig. 127), which was inscribed with his name and genealogy, seems to have served as an official 'palace seal'; few such royal cylinder

Fig. 135. Pale mauve, translucent chalcedony seal from the Governor's Palace, room B. One of the finest cylinder seals found at Nimrud, and one notable for the presence of the cock, a bird rarely represented in Assyria at this time. It is also unusual in that the ends have been ground down (perhaps damaged in removing an original set of gold caps?). Even the head of Aššur in his winged disc has disappeared. The bottom of the seal is also unusual in that the figures do not stand on the same ground line, suggesting that the seal had been recut (ht 2.7 cm, ND 305, British Museum).

Fig. 136. Dark red stone cylinder seal from the Burnt Palace, room 45; style characterised by the linear engraving and the possible astrological motif (ht 2.2 cm, ND 2151, Metropolitan Museum of Art).

seals have survived. Other seals, for the most part to be dated to the first half of the 8th century, were also inscribed with the name and title of the owner, providing a useful source of information about the organisation of the Assyrian government. Many of these are the seals of *limmu* officials which, like the royal seals, also provide invaluable dating information. Among these are the impressions of a seal, found on documents from the Governor's Palace, of the (eunuch) governor of Kalhu who dedicated the statues in the Nabu Temple and was eponym in 797 BC.[96] More unusual is the seal of a eunuch servant not of the king but of this same governor, which probably also came from Nimrud.[97] It is rarely possible to associate uninscribed seal impressions with their owners, but one stamp seal design on a tablet of the time of

Sin-šar-iškun can be associated with its scribe.[98]

Seals can also be dated by style, but this is a far less precise method owing to the widespread survival of such objects as heirlooms or votive pieces.[99] An example of this is the use of an early second millennium BC seal 'belonging to the god Aššur' on the treaty tablets found in Ezida (Fig. 124). Two collections of ancient seals have been found at Nimrud, one consisting of ten seals recovered from a Hellenistic grave, of which one is of third millennium date (PG 21, p. 263), the other apparently a deliberate burial of temple property at the back of the Ninurta Temple sanctuary.[100]

Several different styles of seal cutting existed in the Late Assyrian period.[101] The hardest seal stones, for example carnelian and chalcedony, required the use of a cutting-wheel and drill in order to execute the design (Fig. 134). Sometimes there is no attempt to mask the very distinctive marks of these tools, and the figures are left simply as a series of drill holes, without further finishing. At other times these marks are carefully masked by skilled overcarving, a technique perfected in Babylonia and apparently introduced into Assyria at the time of the capture of Babylon by Tiglath-Pileser III (Fig. 135). Seals were also made of softer stones such as serpentine. In the 9th and 8th centuries such softer stones were often carved in what is known as the linear style (Fig. 136). As mentioned above, a number of seals were also made of faience, especially in the 7th century, though seals of this material were much more common in the late second millennium. Perhaps it was the bright colours of the glazes that made this type especially popular among the women of the North-West Palace and Fort Shalmaneser. Recently, an extraordinary number of faience seals was recovered by Iraqi excavators in the area of courtyard 80 in the North-West Palace, in the associated well and, in particular, from the underground vaulted rooms which were perhaps the 'treasury' of the palace women.[102] Especially popular in the 7th and 6th centuries was a particular type of stamp seal, carved on small conoids, often of a very beautiful blue chalcedony.[103] Several such seals have been found at Nimrud, for example in the Neo-Babylonian graves above the Adad-nerari III palace in the outer town.[104] In general the impressions of seals, whether on containers or on dockets or tablets, are found more often than the seals themselves. Indeed the rare stones that were especially in demand for the better quality seals, carnelian, for example, and lapis lazuli (especially rare in the first millennium BC), had to be imported over long distances. Their rarity of course increased their value, and many must have been looted in 612 BC. Such stones were often 're-cycled', removing them from the chronological contexts in which one might expect to find them.

Sealings are especially common on dockets, bullae and cuneiform documents

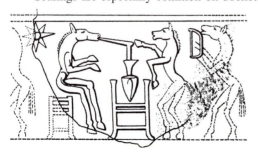

Fig. 137. Seal impression from the private throne room in Fort Shalmaneser (S 5). The partying horses are unique among Late Assyrian seals (4.2 x 3 cm, ND 7107).

that record contracts or some other form of obligation (for example, Figs. 126, 128).[105] In practice it was largely legal documents requiring witnesses that were sealed; letters were also often sealed. The range of sealed documents recovered at Nimrud has added considerably to our understanding of the use of seals in the Late Assyrian period. It would appear, for example, that as late as the time of Sargon II even people of relative wealth and importance did not necessarily use seals. The tablets of this date clearly show instead the use of fingernail impressions, the ancient equivalent of the thumb print. There is evidence to suggest that at least some of the Assyrian nail impressions may have been made with a clay tool: 'Associated with the tablets there were little cushion-shaped pieces of terracotta with incurving sides....when stamped on wet clay they reproduce exactly the curved nailmark of the *supru*'[106] (and see Fig. 126a).

Many of the sealed objects are small dockets, some of which had been attached to specific commodities, usually with string or rope the impressions of which remain visible. Among the more unusual examples are three dockets from the *rab ekalli*'s house in Fort Shalmaneser which record the review of troops and which, it is suggested, may have been applied to a wood surface, conceivably even wooden tablets which would have been inscribed with lists of the soldiers.[107] A number of bullae and sealed labels were recovered from the Governor's Palace, including a door sealing, a widely known type that was not especially common at Nimrud where doors were clearly secured by more effective methods.[108]

Fig. 138. Drawing of the impression of a veined carnelian seal from the vaults beneath North-West Palace room 75. The god Ninurta is often shown riding the scorpion-tailed drag-on, as here, but shooting arrows at the bird-tailed version. The identity of the goddess is less clear; although she resembles the warrior Ishtar. But Ishtar always stands on a lion, never a dragon, while Ninurta's consort Gula is usually associated with her dog. An extraordinary seal from an extraordinary new collection (ht 5.3 cm; IM 127812, after Hussein & Abdul-Razak 1997/98, no. 38).

CHAPTER 7

TYPES OF OBJECT AND MATERIALS FROM NIMRUD

THE 'NIMRUD IVORIES'

If one were forced to select a single category of object for which Nimrud stands out above all contemporary ancient sites, it would have to be the carved ivories. Thousands of carved ivories were registered in the excavation catalogues for the 1949–1963 seasons, and there remain many hundreds in the Iraq Museum still to be recorded. In addition there are the carved ivories found by Layard and Loftus in the 19th century and the remarkable pieces recovered by Iraqi excavators, especially in 1975 in well AJ. A number of ivories were found more recently in the well in courtyard 80. The following brief summary cannot begin to do justice to the great interest and variety of this material, and the reader is recommended to consult the final publications, some of which are still in preparation, if only for the impact of the illustrations. The well AJ ivories are illustrated in chapter 3 (and in the colour section).

Many types of object were made either entirely of ivory or covered with ivory veneer. Most commonly, the surviving ivories came from furniture, for example couches or thrones, often tables, of which the original form was not always possible to determine. There were also small, approximately circular ivory boxes (pyxides, see inter alia, Fig. 54)[1] and elaborately carved small ivory bowls, thought to have been either cosmetics containers or possibly salt cellars (Figs. 59, 116). Such objects were found in all the monumental buildings, and in the AB Palace the walls had been covered with ivory panelling (p. 132). Some ivories were coloured, some inlaid with glass or other materials (Pl. 12a); many if not most were overlaid with gold, and chryselephantine statuary was not uncommon. Indeed many of the ivories that we recovered had been tossed aside as the 612 BC plunderers of the city tore from them their gold leaf overlays. Although the inscriptions on the palace reliefs tell of the royal hunting of elephants in Syria, a large proportion of the ivories found at Nimrud, and especially those from Fort Shalmaneser, came largely through plunder, tribute and royal gifts, particularly from areas west of Assyria. Thus the Nimrud ivories represent many different schools of ivory carving. However, we lack the criteria to determine which pieces were actually made at the site, and which were not, since the craftsmen themselves were often brought to Kalhu literally as booty or 'by royal appointment'. A specifically 'Assyrian style' has been identified (for example, Figs. 31, 74), but it remains possible that other styles were copied by craftsmen at Nimrud itself. Even those with alphabetic lettering on the backs could have been made in Kalhu, since this type of writing was in use at the site already in the ninth century. But it remains more likely that much of this material arrived as tribute or gift.

The huge quantity of ivory in use or available at the site is clear from the royal annals. Ivory was brought not only from the west, both Syria and Phoenicia, but also as tribute from Chaldaean tribes to the south (p. 175). On one campaign Assurnasirpal II lists tribute from Carchemish:

I crossed the Euphrates, which was in flood, in rafts made of inflated goatskins and approached the land of Carchemish. I received tribute from Sangara, king of the land of Hatti, 20 talents of silver, a gold ring, a gold bracelet, gold daggers, 100 talents of bronze, 250 talents of iron, bronze cauldrons…beds of box-wood, thrones of box-wood, dishes of box-wood decorated with ivory, 200 adolescent girls, linen garments, purple wool, elephants' tusks (literally 'teeth'), a chariot of polished gold, a gold couch with inlay – objects befitting my royalty. I took with me the chariots, cavalry and infantry of the city of Carchemish. All the kings of the lands came down to me and seized my feet (i.e. paid homage).[2]

Such tribute lists, boasting of the acquisition of the raw material as well as large quantities of carved ivory are frequent also in the campaign inscriptions of his successors.

Some of the most exciting groups of ivories found at Nimrud came from the North-West Palace wells, of which that in court AJ yielded the most spectacular pieces. Indeed this group must undoubtedly be the most remarkable single collection of ivories recovered anywhere in the ancient world. A second well in the corner of courtyard NN, excavated by Mallowan in 1952, also produced ivories of a quality seldom seen in the excavations of the surviving buildings. Again the ivories had been thrown into the well in the sack of the palace, their gold surfaces having been ripped off. Perhaps the most famous pieces from this deposit were the two large female heads, known to us as the 'Mona Lisa' and the 'Ugly Sister' (Figs. 50, 51, pp. 90, 91), and the chryselephantine plaques depicting a lioness killing a Nubian and on which there survived heavily incrusted inlay of lapis lazuli and carnelian (Pl. 12a). The gold leaf was applied before the inlay so that the effect was of precious stones set in gold cloisons; the thin pieces of lapis inlay were actually set in an adhesive which included powdered blue frit.[3] A fourth well, in courtyard 80, excavated in 1992 by Iraqi archaeologists under the direction of Sd. Muzahim Mahmud Hussein, yielded a number of ivory objects, including small cylinders with incised Assyrian designs, two with narrative scenes, the others floral or geometric.

Although the ivories found in the wells excavated by Mallowan and, more recently, by Iraqi archaeologists constitute the most spectacular pieces found on the citadel, many other ivories, admittedly less well preserved, were found throughout the buildings investigated here. Of these, it is perhaps the Burnt Palace collection that is best known. As noted above, it was here that Loftus, in 1854–55, found the immense collection of ivories, now in the British Museum, that bears his name. Many more were found by Mallowan, especially in the throne room and literally on the throne dais. Outstanding among these were a variety of elaborately costumed ladies' heads, most of which had been burnt in the fire, resulting in an extraordinarily beautiful, if probably unintentional, shiny black surface (Fig. 79). Some of the ivory heads are of such an even and consistent, shiny black, however, that it must remain a possibility that they had been deliberately 'ebonised' by careful heating,[4] for example, Fig. 116, p. 189. Among the Burnt Palace ivories were also caryatid ladies forming the handles of objects such as mirrors and a number of beautifully carved bulls and calves, the latter originally the ornament on the lids of small ivory boxes

Fig. 139. Ivory plaque with sharply concave shape, probably one side of a cornice-shaped box. Two figures of the Egyptian god Bes, a protective deity who was the god of play and recreation, flank a palm tree beside which are two monkeys; flying ducks decorate the upper corners. This graphic scene is without parallel at Nimrud; from Fort Shalmaneser, room 37 (width 13.5 cm; ND 9434A, Iraq Museum).

(as in Fig. 54). One of the most unusual pieces from the early seasons at Nimrud was a composite object, unfortunately found cased in a half-baked mass of black earth on a Burnt Palace floor. Although incomplete and impossible to reconstruct, it serves to indicate yet again how depleted is the surviving repertoire of material objects. This remarkable fragment,[5] for that is all it is, consisted of bronze wire 'branches', to which ivory birds were attached. Lapis lazuli fruit was also present, unfortunately detached from its stems. This must have been an extraordinary 'set piece', designed for some royal table. The surviving portion of the object is only some 6.5 cm in height, and we have no way of establishing its original size or purpose.

It was Fort Shalmaneser that produced the greatest quantity of ivory objects, again including many of extraordinary beauty. Especially striking is the collection of small ivory statues of men leading or carrying animals, from a room beneath the *rab ekalli*'s house (Figs. 100, 140). In an earlier chapter we have already noted that one of the purposes of the *ekal mašarti* was for the 'mustering' and storage of 'all kinds of booty taken from the enemy'. And indeed here, during the course of the 1957–63 excavations, was recovered an extraordinary number and variety of ivories, both in terms of style and design, most of which had been relegated in antiquity to the building's large number of storage magazines. The quantity was so great that many, now in the Iraq Museum, remain to be recorded, an ongoing process under the direction of Georgina Herrmann who has published many of these ivories, including the furniture fragments, chair backs, etc. from storeroom SW 7 (discussed below), 1573 pieces from the storage magazine SW 37 and the small collections from other rooms in the arsenal, themselves totalling some 509 pieces.[6] The large number of ivories from the storage magazine SW 12, the adjacent room 11 and from the royal storeroom T 10 remain to be published. These are further described in the discussion of the rooms in which they have been found. Further ivories were found in 1987 by the Italian expedition under the direction of Paolo Fiorina in the previously undug southeastern doorway of SW 37, which led into the courtyard to the east.

The Nimrud ivories can be classified into a variety of styles, though there is not complete agreement as to the appropriate terminology.[7] Easily differentiated is a local

Fig. 140. Ivory figure in the round from the rab ekalli*'s house (see also Fig. 100, pp. 160-61), man carrying a lion on his shoulders, grasping the lead and holding a goat or ibex by the horn (ht. 12.8 cm, ND 9304, Iraq Museum).*

Assyrian style, with engraved and sometimes relief decoration reflecting the symbols of the monarchy itself. Not surprisingly, these often parallel the themes of the stone reliefs, in particular scenes of tribute and homage, and the winged genii known from the reliefs. Often found also are friezes or single inlays of animals. One of the most interesting features of the Assyrian style is the contexts in which such ivories were found. Indeed they seem to have been the predominant group in all of the major reception rooms, for example, in the North-West Palace throne room, in Ezida – seen in the chair arms and other fragments presumably from the throne itself, and in the royal suite in the queen's household in Fort Shalmaneser (rooms S 3–5). This is not to say that all the ivories in these rooms were of the Assyrian style, only that the Assyrian style seems to have been associated with these rooms in particular, and especially on the furniture. Another ivory carved in this style, depicting Assurnasirpal II himself (Fig. 19, p. 40), was found behind the famous banquet stele, just outside the North-West Palace throne room. Further ivories of this type came from the palace of Adadnerari III in the outer town and a single panel from the 1989 British Museum excavations in T 20.[8] Other types are also attributed to a local Assyrian style, including openwork panels, small composite statues, as in Fig. 56 (p. 95), and 'silhouette' figures used as inlay. A number of statue components were found in Fort Shalmaneser, in the *rab ekalli*'s house and in one of the large workrooms (NW 5). Not all the incised ivories can be attributed to the Assyrian style, since this technique is also used elsewhere (for example, Fig. 139, discussed below).

Many of the ivories are in a 'Syrian style', others are clearly Phoenician. Not surprisingly, among the Phoenician ivories Egyptian iconography is often employed. There are no true Egyptian ivories at Nimrud, with the single exception of an ivory scarab bearing the cartouche of Pharaoh Taharqa (c. 690–664 BC), who was defeated by Esarhaddon.[9] A number of Phoenician ivories that appear, at least superficially, to be Egyptian are referred to as having been carved in an 'Egyptianising'

Fig. 141. 'Egyptianising ivories' from Fort Shalmaneser, a) a crowned sun disc flanked by ba *birds rides in a boat with papyrus prows,* cloisonné *inlay, from SW 37 (7.0 x 13.3 cm, ND 10702, Iraq Museum); b) two kneeling males hold bowls on which there seems to be a mis-representation of Maat; the cartouche is surmounted by a triple* atef *crown and stands on the hieroglyph for gold, from SW 12 (5.7 x 14 cm, ND 12034, Iraq Museum).*

style (e.g. Figs. 139, 141). Other types of object also appear to be Egyptian, for example the alabaster vase illustrated on p. 41, but our Egyptological colleagues assure us that the motifs are mis-used or misunderstood and, like the ivories, would appear to have been made somewhere in the southern Levant. The Phoenician and 'Egyptianising' ivories are noted not only for their beauty but also for their strong use of colour and a cloisonné-like technique using inlaid coloured glass, as in Figs. 105, 118, 141. There are also ivories carved in a style that is partly Syrian and partly Phoenician, sometimes referred to as 'intermediate' or 'South Syrian'. Other ivories came from Urartu in north-eastern Anatolia. Ivory craftsmen seem to have shared a common pool of motifs, and among the most well-known that recur at Nimrud are sphinxes, the so-called 'St George and the dragon' (Fig. 142), the Biblical 'lady at the window', the cow and calf (Fig. 143), and also bulls and stags. The great majority of the ivories recovered came from furniture, and one assumes that the smaller items, such as mirror or fly-whisk handles, may have been carried away during the

Fig. 142. Open-work plaque, a youthful pharaoh grasps the comb of a winged griffin as he plunges a spear into the griffin's mouth, an example of the 'St George and the dragon' group, from Fort Shalmaneser SW 12 (ht 13 cm, ND 11036, Iraq Museum).

Fig. 143. Cow and calf plaque, from Fort Shalmaneser SW 12 (9.0 x 6.2 cm, ND 11097).

sack. One can hardly imagine the quantity that was actually kept in this building. The gold from the tombs is overwhelming is its splendour, and more immediately striking, but the ivories are memorable not only for their great beauty and the evidence of extraordinary craftsmanship, but for their sheer numbers.

FURNITURE

The simple fact that furniture is generally made from wood has always meant that it is seriously under-represented among recovered archaeological materials. Nonetheless, a surprising amount of evidence survives for Assyrian furniture, not only in depictions on the reliefs, wall paintings, ivories and even glazed vessels (Fig. 144) but also among the bronze, ivory and charred wood fittings and ornament recovered. At Nimrud most of these objects are of course in contexts that are either royal or associated with the king's senior officials. That is, we have virtually no record of the types of furniture, if any, used by the ordinary Assyrian family. Even the representations of furniture in military camps reflect only the royal entourage. The decoration on the furniture is in general both heavy and elaborately ornate, suggesting clearly Victorian tastes among the Assyrian upper class, even to the lion-footed table legs.

Evidence for furniture at Nimrud consists almost entirely of fittings, that is, parts of but not the whole of the original. Animal protomes were common, both in bronze and in ivory, with bitumen commonly used both as a filler and adhesive. The most 'complete' piece of furniture comes, as does the largest number of ivories, from Fort Shalmaneser. This is a possible couch or bed, or perhaps parts of more than one piece of furniture, found at the north end of NE 26 (Fig. 145).[10] As excavated, it seemed to be a complete piece, in situ, with a curved arm-rest at one end, but this reconstruction has been questioned on the grounds that its shape does not match those illustrated on the reliefs,[11] not of course proof that such a shape did not exist.

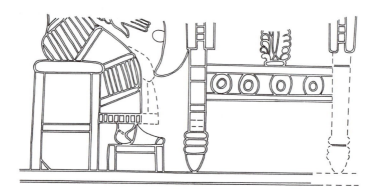

Fig. 144. Drawing of a fragment of a glazed vessel from courtyard AJ in the North-West Palace, illustrating a (? royal) figure seated on a stool, with feet on a footstool, before an elaborately decorated table; the colours used are red, black, yellow and white (surviving ht of decoration 10 cm, ND 1357).

Fig. 145. a) The NE 26 (Fort Shalmaneser) couch in situ (north end of room), showing the bronze elements of the leg and arm rest, and the shell ornament; b) detail of arm rest.

The pieces stored here were decorated with shell inlay rather than the more usual ivory, reminiscent of a craft still to be found in Damascus today. The legs were sheathed in bronze as was the upper curved surface of the arm-rest, clearly visible in the photograph as is the bronze palm capital for one of the legs. Also in the room were *ajouré* metal plaques (Fig. 146), together with shell sphinxes and other ornament of types illustrated on the reliefs as decoration for both thrones and tables.

In his relief sculpture Assurnasirpal II sits on a backless throne, literally a stool (Fig. 28, p. 54), but later kings, for example Tiglath-pileser III, seem to have used a straight-backed, chair-like throne.[12] The use of a royal footstool seems to have been *de rigueur*, as in Figs. 28, 144; indeed the emplacements for the footstool can still be seen on the Fort Shalmaneser throne base. Parts of such furniture have also been found at Nimrud, one of the most complete having been among the many bronze objects recovered by Layard in room AB in the North-West Palace:

233

Fig. 146. Copper open-work plaques, furniture ornament from NE 26, identical with those found by Layard on the room AB throne in the North-West Palace (ND 9250, 8.3 x 7.5 cm; ND 9251, 9.5 x 7.5 cm).

In the further corner of the chamber stood the royal throne. Although it was utterly impossible, from the complete state of decay of the materials, to preserve any part of it entire, I was able, by carefully removing the earth, to ascertain that it resembled in shape the chair of state of the king, and particularly that represented in the bas-relief of Sennacherib receiving the captives and spoil after the conquest of the city of Lachish. With the exception of the legs, which appear to have been partly of ivory, it was of wood, cased or overlaid with bronze, as the throne of Solomon was of ivory, overlaid with gold. The metal was most elaborately engraved and embossed with symbolical figures and ornaments, like those embroidered on the robes of the early Nimroud king, such as winged deities struggling with griffins, mythic animals, men before the sacred tree, and the winged lion and bull. As the woodwork, over which the bronze was fastened by means of small nails of the same material, had rotted away, the throne fell to pieces, but the metal casing was partly preserved. Numerous fragments are now in the British Museum, including the joints of the arms and legs, the rams' or bulls' heads which adorned the ends of the arms (some still retaining the clay and bitumen with the impression of the carving), and the ornamental scroll-work of the cross-bars in the form of the Ionic volute. The legs were adorned with lions' paws resting on a pine-shaped ornament, like the thrones of the later Assyrian sculptures, and stood on a bronze base. A rod with loose rings, to which was once hung embroidered drapery, or some rich stuff, appears to have belonged to the back of the chair, or to a frame-work raised above or behind it. In front of the throne was the foot-stool, also of wood overlaid with embossed metal, and adorned with the heads of ram or bulls. The feet ended in lion's paws and pine cones, like those of the throne.[13]

The openwork bronze plaques which are said by Layard to have been ornaments of the room AB throne are identical with those found in 1960 in FS room NE 26 (Fig. 146).[14]

Also from room AB, and found in the enormous bronze cauldrons discovered there, were four bronze palm capitals of the type seen commonly on throne and table legs (for a description of the contents of this room, see p. 96); this decorative element is also found in stone and there are fine ivory examples from well AJ.[15] Three bronze lions' paws, found in Trench P near the centre of the citadel mound, may have formed the feet of a three-legged table of the type often found in temples, for example in front of the the Ninurta Temple at Nimrud (p. 7).[16] The latter, almost certainly some form of offering table, was, however, carved in stone, as were similar tables in the Temple of the Sibitti at Khorsabad. Oddly, and despite Layard's claims (see quote above), such lion feet appear not to have been used on thrones, only on tables and footstools where they were often supported by further cone-like feet. Figures and furniture are always shown in profile on the reliefs, so that it is impossible to determine whether there were both three- and four-legged tables, although this seems likely. An ivory table leg was found in Fort Shalmaneser, and such tables were depicted among the many other motifs on ivory boxes from the AJ well (Figs. 102, 147). One of the most extraordinary features of Figure 147 is that it almost exactly duplicates a scene on the stone sarcophagus of King Ahiram, from Byblos.[17] Cross-legged stools and tables are also illustrated, particularly in the context of military camps, where it is tempting to see them as the original, easily portable, folding furniture (Fig. 148). This is suggested by the recovery at Nimrud of heavy bronze hinges that almost certainly belonged to furniture.[18] The reliefs also illustrate furniture being carried away as booty or brought as tribute, as do the stelae from Nimrud.[19]

By far the most frequent evidence for various furniture types is, however, to be found among the ivories. In Fort Shalmaneser room SW 7, for example, were found 19 curved ivory chair backs, stacked in rows at the south end of the room.[20] All that

Fig. 147. Detail of ivory pyxis from the AJ well, illustrating a Levantine sphinx-throne and an ornate Phoenician table with legs resembling the example from the Fort Shalmaneser wine store (cf. Figs. 54, 102).

235

survived, of course, was the ivory, consisting of vertical sideposts supporting a curving central section, normally 65–80 cm in width. The wooden structure itself had completely decayed, often leaving no support for the ivory, although in the ground this remained still in its original position (Fig. 149). Removing these large structures from the soil was a major challenge, and was accomplished by digging away the soil from the back of each chair and consolidating them with heavy bandaging. The whole chairback was then literally cut from the soil as a single piece, leaving a layer of earth attached to the carved surfaces, and carried the kilometre or so to the house for more careful cleaning (Fig. 150). One can perhaps imagine that these were heavy and awkward packages to deal with. Indeed, one of us spent much of the 1958 season on this task alone.

Whether these objects were all chair backs as opposed to parts of beds or couches cannot be determined with absolute certainty; in particular, they are not all of the same size. For example, a long panel associated in the soil with the scroll pattern chairback (Fig. 103) measures some 107 cm in width, considerably wider than the apparent width of the other chairs.[21] This was one of the reasons for the original identification of some of the SW 7 ivories as possibly parts of beds or couches. Certainly the furniture at the south end of the room, which had been least disturbed by the looting and subsequent collapse of the roof, appeared to have been chairs, carefully stacked with the upper one, upside down, on top of the lower chair on which the ivory panels were in their correct, upright position. It is not impossible, of course, that several types of furniture were stored in the room; certainly other types of ivory object were found there (e.g. Fig. 105).

Fig. 148. Alabaster relief from the North-West Palace throne room illustrating a military camp, including the royal pavillion, and illustrating examples of the king's domestic furniture (after Layard 1849a, pl. 30).

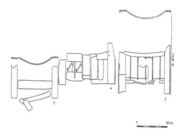

Fig. 149. Part of the plan of the positions of some of the ivory chair backs in room SW 7, showing the second and third rows with ND 7904 and ND 7906 in situ. ND 7906 is illustrated, after excavation, in Fig. 150. The full plan can be found in Mallowan 1966, figs. 337–41.

GLASS

By the time of Late Assyrian Nimrud glass had been known in the Near East for at least 1200 years. Originally viewed as a substitute for semi-precious stone, by the second half of the second millennium large numbers of elaborately ornamented glass vessels were being manufactured by what is known as the core-moulded method, where the vessel was literally built up around a clay and dung core which was later removed. Large numbers of these fifteenth/fourteenth century BC core-moulded types, largely bottles and beakers with complicated polychrome patterns swagged into the surface of the vessel, have been found at the sites of Nuzi, Tell al Rimah and Tell Brak. They are among the earliest known glass vessels.[22] It was long thought that there had been little innovation in the manufacture and use of glass in the first millennium BC, at least until Roman times, but the excavation of Nimrud substantially altered that view, in particular in the evidence for the manufacture of some of the earliest known transparent glass (earlier glasses were opaque) and in the moulding or casting of vessels, perhaps by the lost-wax process. Such 'cast' vessels were then finished by means of a wheel or some other method of grinding and polishing, a technique borrowed from the working of stone. There are, in fact, a number of very beau-

237

tiful rock crystal vessels of this date, which perhaps the transparent 'cast' glass types were designed to imitate (Pl. 8a).

One of the earliest known glass vessels made in this manner, and one of the very few that can be precisely dated, is the so-called Sargon vase, found by Layard in the North-West Palace. The inscription is accompanied by an engraving of a lion, probably a symbol of virility or fierceness used to mark royal and palace property and comparable with the scorpion signs of fertility found on property of the North-

Fig. 150. Photographs of the large ivory chair-back or bed-head ND 7906 as removed from the soil and as restored in the Iraq Museum (overall width 84 cm).

Fig. 151. Rock crystal bowl with engraved design, from the Burnt Palace 'throne room' (original d 7.8 cm, ND 1663, Ashmolean Museum).

West Palace ladies (p. 79). Layard also found three hemispherical clear glass bowls, while fragments of perhaps as many as 150 bowls of clear or greenish glass were recovered during the more recent excavations, many from Fort Shalmaneser. Not only is clear glass remarkable at this date, but some of the walls of these bowls are astonishingly thin (2–3 mm). A glass specialist, provided with no information as to provenance or date, would almost certainly identify such pieces as Roman and assume even that they had been blown, but the technique of glass-blowing is generally believed to be a Syrian innovation of the first century BC. How these extraordinary eighth/seventh century vessels were made remains to be established, although it has been suggested that the blowpipe could have been known to the Nimrud glassmakers. Some 30 vessel fragments of transparent purple glass were also found, many examples again being paper-thin. Also unique for this period are 14 fragments of glass bowls and cups embellished with deeply-cut grooves and geometric patterns, another manufacturing technique that reflects the close association of these glass bowls with their counterparts in rock crystal (Fig. 151). One puzzling aspect of the Nimrud glass is the lack of evidence for the core-moulded type of vessel, so popular in the late second millennium and which continues in use elsewhere at this time, for example in Babylonia. At Nimrud only a very few fragments were recovered (from the Burnt Palace[23]).

Pieces of inlay constituted the most common type of glass found at Nimrud. A variety of shapes has been found, used as ornament on glass vessels themselves, on furniture and on the ivories.[24] The most frequently found individual inlays were small

Fig. 152. Drawing of miniature glass plaque with painted sphinx ornament, from SW 7, Fort Shalmaneser, one of a group that represent the earliest painted glass yet found; the figure is delineated in black paint and there are traces of gold leaf (the stippled areas) and blue paint (3.2 x 4.4 x 0.2 cm, ND 7639, Iraq Museum, after Orchard 1978, fig. 1).

239

rectangular pieces; these occurred in large numbers in Fort Shalmaneser (for example, room SW 37). Most were of a cobalt blue, but there were also some deep green (? originally red) examples. Many of the square inlays had been cut to hold the petals of white rosettes, that is, the pieces of inlay were themselves inlaid. On some pieces the 'inlay' was visible on both surfaces, perhaps made by the 'cane method' by which the individual segments of second millennium mosaic glass were also formed.[25] The most extraordinary feature of the Nimrud inlays is the way the glass has survived. Most ancient glass weathers on the surface which then becomes soft, flaky and iridescent. The blue and green inlays, however, still look as though they had been manufactured yesterday. By far the most unusual inlays were two groups of painted, clear glass plaques found in Fort Shalmaneser (Fig. 152), the earliest painted glass to have been found in Western Asia.[26]

One of the most exciting glass finds from more recent excavations is a vase recovered in Tomb III in the North-West Palace (beneath room 57, p. 86). This is a globular glass bottle with a stopper terminating in a robed figure modelled around an iron peg. The pale green glass is decorated with small square inlays of dark (cobalt) blue glass inset with designs including white rosettes and seated figures with raised hands, set in horizontal bands in white or green glass frames.[27] Another unusual piece is a limestone head of a woman originally inlaid with glass.[28] It was one of at least three examples found by Layard in the temple of Ištar Šarrat-niphi. These had been mounted on wooden shafts and were perhaps originally furniture components.

A still unanswered question is whether true enamel was in use at Nimrud at this time, that is, powdered glass fused in situ. The cloisonné work on the extraordinarily beautiful armlets from Tomb II (Pl. 6a) undoubtedly involves the use of inlays of semi-precious stones, but the colour photographs suggest the possibility that some parts might be true enamel.[29] If this proves to be so, it would be the earliest use of enamel found up to now in Mesopotamia. That enamelling was uncommon or even unknown at this time, despite the 600 or more years of complex glass making that preceded it, may reflect no more than the difficulty of temperature control. The melting temperatures of these coloured glasses range between 800° and 950° C. A temperature of 900–1000° C would be necessary for fusing a good enamel.[30] The gold alloys then in use would begin to melt at somewhere between 900° to 1050° C, suggesting an entirely practical reason for the rarity of enamel-working at this time. With the ivories, on which heating would produce a colour change, the already manufactured glass had to be cut or moulded to fit.

Whether raw glass or the 'cast' glass vessels were actually made at Nimrud remains unknown. Certainly glass was widely used at the site – as inlay on the ivories, on gold jewellery, on furniture – but how much, if any, of this work was carried out at Nimrud cannot be determined on the basis of present evidence. Unfortunately the style of the object does not tell us where it was made, since we know from the inscriptions that not only were enormous quantities of such objects brought back to Nimrud as gifts or tribute from foreign campaigns but also that many craftsmen were acquired in the same way. The presence of cullet and discs of raw glass formed in rough moulds does, however, prove that there were glass-making facilities at Nimrud. Although much of this evidence post-dates the Assyrian period, the presence of a cake of raw blue glass in room HH in the North-West Palace establishes at least the manufacture of objects of glass at the site, if not the raw glass itself.[31] Mallowan found kilns at the north end of the Burnt Palace, together with glass discs and cullet, but these kilns cut the walls of the 'squatter level' which itself post-dates the 612 BC destruction. Whether the kilns were Achaemenid or Hellenistic is less certain, but some if not all of the red cullet was undoubtedly Hellenistic and we believe the kilns to be as well. Moreover, the Nimrud 'sealing-wax red' cullet is unique in having a high percentage of lead, a feature of red glasses not normally found before Roman times.[32]

FRIT AND FAIENCE

A further piece of evidence that indicates the working of glass-related materials at Assyrian Nimrud is the widespread presence of big lumps of blue frit, inter alia in a wine store in Fort Shalmaneser (room SW 6, p. 167). Here it would appear that the frit had been stored in the room above, since large pieces were actually found on top of the wine jars. Such large cakes of frit could be ground into a fine powder for use as a pigment or to make objects of moulded frit, faience (glazed frit) or glass. Our use of the term frit should be explained, since its common use in archaeology is potentially misleading. Correctly, it is applied to a specific stage in glass-making, when the materials have been ground, mixed and sintered (heated or 'fritted') but not as yet melted. Glass, frit and faience all have the same composition, the glass differing from the others by virtue simply of its vitreous nature. In archaeological usage frit has come to mean a sintered quartz body that differs from glass only in its crystalline structure but which exists as a manufacturing material in itself. The term 'faience' is used for glazed frit. It has nothing to do with the tin-glazed pottery, from which its name derives, which was made from mediaeval times onwards in Faenza and is now known as majolica. Both frit and faience occur in a variety of colours, but with frit the colour is consistent throughout while the body of a faience object is often white and always has a coloured glaze on the surface. When the glaze becomes very worn, the two materials can be difficult to distinguish. Blue frits tend to dominate, made from a natural mineral known as Egyptian Blue. The advantage these materials have over coloured stones, for which glass is often a substitute, is that they can easily be moulded.

Frit itself is a common material on Near Eastern sites from an early date and was widely used for beads and small moulded objects, both of which are found at Nimrud. Frit beads, including attractive fluted examples, seem to have been especially popular in the North-West Palace. An unusual use of frit was identified in Tomb III in the same building, where two white frit vessels were found set on gold bases.[33] Among the faience objects from the site were beads and a number of amulets in which Egyptian iconography was prevalent, objects possibly of Phoenician origin. Faience cylinder seals were also common, including one out-of-context heirloom of north Syrian, Mitanni style, that is, late second millennium.[34] Both the core-moulding technique for the manufacture of glass vessels and the elaboration of the use of moulded faience appear to originate in northern Syria in the second millennium.

Although these materials were commonly used at Nimrud, the peak of their popularity lay in the late second millennium, a period represented at Nimrud in the group of 30 faience rosettes, mace heads and an elaborate triangular faience 'buckle' found beneath the 1950 building.[35]

Another related technology is the use of glazes on pottery and other earthenware materials such as baked bricks. The glazing of earthenware is a relatively late development, the earliest glazed pottery coming again from areas under Mitanni control but post-dating the technology of core-moulded glass. It is a technically more difficult process than the glazing of glassy materials, the difficulty lying in making the glaze adhere. Technologically this is largely due to the differing coefficients of expansion involved. Hence the lack of glazed pottery, at least in any quantity, before c. 1400 BC, and at this time the range of colours was relatively limited (largely blue, some white and yellow).[36] By the time of first millennium Nimrud very attractive glazed pottery is found, generally with polychrome designs (Fig. 153). These are often rather simple jars, but a number are large and tub-shaped, that is, relatively straight-sided and flat-bottomed. Indeed it is very tempting to see them as large containers for potted plants, though we must admit this is pure speculation. On the large tubs crenellated patterns are common, and some are very elaborately decorated, see for example the ostriches and the court scene of Figs 40, 144. Horse-drawn chariots decorated another example from the Town Wall houses (room 44).[37] Unfortunately these large vessels do not survive well.

Glazed baked bricks are also found from Middle Assyrian times onwards. Such bricks were often used to frame architectural features, the most elaborate Late Assyrian example at Nimrud coming from the southern entrance of the Fort Shalmaneser throne room suite, above the door (Fig. 112). With reference to the

Fig. 153. Polychrome glazed pottery from Nimrud: large bowl from the North-West Palace and small jar from one of the wall niches in Tomb IV. Both have an all-over blue glaze, the bowl with black and white chevrons between yellow bands; the jar is a brilliant blue, with white, yellow and blue petals. The bowl was found behind the banquet stele (d 24 cm, ND 1354, Metropolitan Museum of Art).

242

North-West Palace Layard remarks that associated with the lion- and bull-colossi doorways were 'invariably large collections of baked bricks, elaborately painted with figures of animals and flowers and with cuneiform characters… on the backs of these bricks were rude designs in black of men and animals and marks having the appearance of numbers,'[38] a common feature to facilitate the assembly of complex designs. Glazed terracotta plaques with ornate patterns and central knobs were a further form of architectural decoration, either round or in the form of rectangles with concave sides (Pl. 12b); similar wall ornament is also found in metal. Individual pegs with round heads known as *siqqatu* are also found, and may have been used for fastening decorative cloth hangings to the walls. The so-called hands of Ishtar constitute another unusual architectural feature, apparently inserted as miniature corbels high in the walls of major rooms. These consisted of a flat terracotta 'arm' ending in a closed fist, which would have been visible from below, often inscribed and sometimes glazed.[39]

Pigments should perhaps be mentioned here, since their use and procurement are closely related to the procurement of the colourants used in the manufacture of frit and glass. Those used in the wall paintings in the reception room S 5 in Fort Shalmaneser were analysed by Joyce Plesters of the National Gallery,[40] whose report indicates that the red-brown plaster of the wall consisted of a mixture of clay and chalk, with a small proportion of fine grey sand. A preliminary priming coat consisted of lighter brown, finer-textured plaster. The red-brown colour is accounted for by a high ferric iron content. Borders and motifs were outlined in a coarsely ground carbon black. The blue pigment, not surprisingly, is Egyptian blue, the red a deeply coloured iron ochre, the white a mixture of calcium carbonate and sulphate, possibly a natural compound. No medium could be detected though this could have been washed out over time; the total absence of medium is also a feature of Roman wall paintings.

Fig. 154. Part of a set of 18 decorated shell objects, which had been fixed to some wooden object by means of a bronze nail driven through a perforation in the shell. From the well in room NN, North-West Palace (dimensions 5 to 11 cm across; ND 2240).

SHELL

Shell like ivory was widely used for inlay. This is perhaps most clearly seen in the fragments of furniture recovered from room NE 26 in Fort Shalmaneser, where a variety of shell plaques was found, including representations of sphinxes, a winged genie and trees similar to the patterns on the bronze plaques recovered from the same room, and also ornament for furniture (Figs. 145, 146). Some of the most attractive shell ornaments are illustrated in Fig. 154. These are carved from an Indian Ocean *Lambis* shell and are generally assumed to have been ornaments for horse harness. Other suggestions for the function of the decorated shells include shield bosses and, perhaps less likely, 'clappers' or castanets. A number of the examples found in T 10 in Fort Shalmaneser bore Hittite hieroglyphs thought to represent the name Irhuleni, a king of Hama who was a contemporary of Shalmaneser III (Fig. 6, p. 17).[41]

Another Indian Ocean shell popular in Late Assyrian times was the giant clam *Tridacna*. These large bivalves were carved with a variety of patterns reminiscent of the ivories. Often the bulbous umbo or hinge was carved in the form of a human head with outstretched wings depicted on the back of the shell. The function of these shallow 'dishes' is uncertain, but they may have served as containers for cosmetics.

METAL

Of the various types of metal found at Nimrud it is of course gold that appeals most not only to the viewing public but also to the archaeologist (especially because it does not corrode and therefore needs no cleaning!). But with the exception of thou-

Fig. 155. Silver beaker decorated with thin bands of gold overlay, found with gadrooned silver bowl in a deposit just under the floor of room C6, in the area of the queen's household, Fort Shalmaneser (ht 12 cm, ND 7845, British Museum).

sands of tiny fragments of gold leaf and the occasional crescentic earring or gold bead, very little gold was found by either the Mallowan expedition or the nineteenth century excavators of the site.[42] Indeed neither 'gold' nor 'jewellery' appears in the index of Mallowan's final volume. This picture was completely altered in 1988, with the discovery of the first of the Iraqi-excavated tombs beneath the North-West Palace, two of which alone contained superbly crafted gold objects weighing over 35 kg. However, the tombs provide us with little more than a glimpse of the wealth that must have been displayed, or simply stored, in the temples and palaces of Kalhu. To the archaeologist working there in the 1950s and 1960s the wealth of Nimrud seemed overwhelming, but it is clear from the tombs that we were seeing barely the prover- bial tip of the iceberg. On the Banquet Stele, we read, for example, that in building the Ninurta temple and renovating eight earlier temples at the site, Assur-nasir-pal II

stationed holy bronze images in their doorways. I made images of their great divinity resplendent with red gold and sparkling stones. I gave to them gold jewellery, many pos- sessions which I had captured. I adorned the shrine of the god Ninurta, my lord, with gold and lapis lazuli....installed wild ferocious dragons of gold at his throne... I created my royal monument with a likeness of my countenance of red gold and sparkling stones, and stationed it before the god Ninurta, my lord.[43]

Such statues would long ago have been the first objects to be stolen or melted down, and it is not surprising that not one has survived. Indeed the absence of gold with the exception of a few small items of jewellery and tiny fragments of gold leaf in surprisingly large quantities testifies to the efficiency and selectivity of the looting in 612 BC.

Metal vessels
The inscriptions also mention enormous quantities of metal objects brought to Nimrud as tribute or booty. Silver, gold, tin and bronze occur repeatedly. One important func- tion of metal was in providing vessels of high status – gold dishes for the king's table, and vessels that were waterproof, both for cooking and for drinking (Pl. 36). The gold bowls from the royal tombs are discussed in Chapter 3; some were inscribed with the names of their royal owners, providing important historical information as well as objects of great beauty. Owing to their poor survival silver vessels are rarely found and are therefore seriously under-represented in the archaeological record. However, a silver beaker with gold overlay (Fig. 155) and a gadrooned bowl of the same metals were the first objects found at the beginning of the 1958 season, having been hidden in antiquity just below the floor of room C6 in Fort Shalmaneser, a room which had been excavated the previous season and of which we were simply re-cleaning the floor.[44] A silver bowl with an inscription in hieroglyphic Hittite was found in tomb III.[45] Electrum, an alloy of gold and silver which survives well owing to its gold con- tent, is also found, though rarely. The most striking electrum object is the cosmetics container from tomb II in the North-West Palace, for which an electrum mirror served as the lid. These objects were inscribed with the names of two different late 7th cen- tury queens (p. 84). An electrum horse bit was recovered from the NN well.[46]

Fig. 156. Shallow bronze bowl decorated with falcon-headed sphinxes, papyrus columns and winged sun discs, probably of Phoenician manufacture. Found by Layard in the North-West Palace, room AB, the 'room of the bronzes' (d 21.7 cm, now in the British Museum).

Not surprisingly bronze vessels are the most common, and one reads of enormous quantities in the tribute lists. Note the 100 talents of bronze, bronze tubs, bronze pails and bronze bath-tubs of the Assurnasirpal II text quoted on p. 227, while Shalmaneser III's plunder from the same king included 300 talents of bronze and 1000 bronze casseroles.[47] At Nimrud the largest single collection of bronze objects, including more than 150 bowls, twelve large cauldrons, bronze furniture parts and other objects were found by Layard in room AB in the North-West Palace, known not surprisingly as the 'Room of the Bronzes' (p. 96). The most attractive of these objects were the bronze bowls (Fig. 156). Most were found in a pile behind the cauldrons; a few were recovered from within the cauldrons themselves. Although copper itself easily decays, it also acts as a preservative for adjacent objects. Thus the bowls at the bottom of the pile were the best preserved. Many are elaborately decorated with a variety of designs, of which the most common involve animals and hunting scenes.[48] As on the gold bowl illustrated in Pl. 7b, many of the designs are 'Egyptianising', presumably, as in the case of the ivories, the work of Phoenician craftsmen. Nine of the Nimrud bowls are inscribed with the names of their owners, a custom which has persisted until modern times on the copper vessels and trays of Ottoman Baghdad. The Nimrud inscriptions are alphabetic but, as often on the ivories, it is impossible to determine whether they are Phoenician or Aramaic.

Jewellery

As already remarked, prior to the discovery of the North-West Palace tombs the amount of gold jewellery known from the site was very small, the 'Nimrud jewel' with its gold chain and setting being the most striking piece. Now, from tomb II alone there are more than 80 gold earrings, some of very complex elaboration (see Pl. 5), perhaps 90 necklaces, many with gold beads, and literally hundreds of small gold stars and rosettes which had been sewn onto the clothes of the deceased. Massive gold anklets and armlets, along with various crowns and diadems were also found, one anklet weighing over 1100 g (see Pls. 4–7).

Silver jewellery is less common, at least in part because it survives less well. This is true not only of the Mallowan excavations but of the tombs as well, with only the very occasional discovery of silver lunate earrings and buttons. An unusual silver ring bearing an oval disc with granulated decoration came from Fort Shalmaneser, room T2 (ND 11450).

Fibulae

Among the other bronze objects are a large number of fibulae, the ancient 'safety pin', used to hold together folds of clothing, usually at the shoulder. Some, known as 'elbow' fibulae, are triangular in shape; other fibulae are bow-shaped. Both types were often decorated, usually with elaborate ribbing. At Nimrud the clasp sometimes appears in the shape of a hand.[49] The more ornamental gold fibulae from the tombs are described in Chapter 3.[50] The latter clearly date to the 8th century, at which time this type of pin, apparently an introduction from the west, was becoming increasingly popular in Assyria. The absence of any depiction of such objects on the stone reliefs might suggest that in Assyria they were used largely by women, and indeed many of the bronze fibulae recovered at Nimrud came from domestic quarters both in the North-West Palace and in Fort Shalmaneser. But a number were also found in the administrative area ZT and, more recently, some 25 well-preserved bronze fibulae, of both elbow and bow type, were recovered from the more formal rooms to the west of courtyard Y (North-West Palace).[51]

Other objects in bronze

Most weapons were made of iron,[52] but in Fort Shalmaneser T 20, for example, large quantities of bronze (and also iron) armour were stored, together with bronze horse harness and a large number of bronze hold fasts.[53] Bronze weights were also found, the best known group from Nimrud including 16 lion-weights found by Layard beneath one of the gate figures in the southern doorway of the North-West Palace throne room.[54] Other objects in copper/bronze include small figures of dogs, a type of apotropaic figure not recovered in situ at Nimrud; most came from the well in room NN.[55] Copper/bronze saucer lamps are found in the tombs (Fig. 48, p. 88), and there is at least one bronze pipe lamp.[56] Pins, needles and nails (also of course made of iron) are found in quantity; the heads of some bronze nails were overlaid with gold. Among the copper jewellery are bangles, earrings and buttons, but these have not been found in any quantity. The use on furniture of bronze plaques and overlay is discussed above.

Iron

The first millennium BC is commonly referred to as the 'Iron Age', and one notes a

Fig. 157. Reconstruction of iron helmet with inlaid bronze decoration, found by Layard in the North-West palace, room I, now in the British Museum (ht. 30.6 cm, after Dezsö & Curtis 1991, figs. 19-20).

large quantity of iron in the inscription quoted on p. 227. Iron is most useful for providing a cutting edge which can be resharpened, and is therefore particularly important for the manufacture of tools and weapons, the most common iron objects found at Nimrud, especially in the workshops of Fort Shalmaneser (e.g. NW 15) and in the magazines where very large numbers of weapons and armour were stored. In SW 7, for example, the whole of the north end of the room was filled with a mass of corroded scale armour to a depth of almost one and a half metres. Nearly 500 iron arrowheads were found in Fort Shalmaneser.[57]

Bronze continued to be used in considerable quantity, and some objects were even made of a combination of bronze and iron. In this category, undoubtedly the most unusual is the iron brazier with bronze turrets and iron and bronze wheels (preserved on one side, Pl. 12c); this was found by the Italian expedition in Fort Shalmaneser, in storage magazine A2, east of SW 37.[58] Here is a rare example of the type of brazier used to heat the various reception rooms and which rested, presumably, on the famous 'tram lines'.

A group of maceheads found by Layard, again from room AB, was also made of a combination of bronze and iron; five bore West Semitic alphabetic inscriptions, possibly the names of the original owners.[59] The one complete helmet from Nimrud is also of iron with inlaid bronze decoration.[60] This was found in Room I of the North-West Palace, together with sixteen fragments of iron, also with bronze inlay, belonging to at least four different crested helmets (Fig. 157). In Room AB Layard found 16 enormous bronze and iron tripods, which must have been supports for the bronze cauldrons. They apparently had bronze 'feet' (bulls' hooves or lions' paws), while the iron rods of the tripod were held together with bronze jointing pieces which had apparently been cast over the iron, testifying to a high degree of technical competence.[61] Similar rod tripods are found from Urartu to North Syria and Cyprus, and were copied even further to the west. In Assyria, as elsewhere, bronze and iron were of course also used in the manufacture of chariots and their wheels. Pieces of iron bits were also recovered, and at least one complete example.[62] Iron fetters were recovered in NW 15.

Iron daggers and swords have been found in the *ekal mašarti*,[63] including, inter alia, a cache of iron weapons in SE 16. Sword and dagger hilts, sheaths and scabbards, and even iron knife handles, could be elaborately decorated with ivory. Indeed 59 pieces of such ornament, often showing iron staining, were found in SW 37.[64] Iron projectile points were common, both socketed spearheads and various types of arrowhead.[65] Many of the iron arrowheads, especially those found along the east wall of the *ekal mašarti*, were bent or broken at the tip, suggesting that they almost certainly date from the actual sack of the city. Groups of iron weapons were also found elsewhere on the site, for example in the North-West Palace in storeroom I, where large quantities of scale armour were recovered, and in the 'room of the princess' (HH: 8 iron spears stacked in the corner). In the Adad-nerari palace in the outer town, 6 iron lances were found in a grave in room 11.

Workmen's tools were frequently found, including iron knives, saws, axes, chisels and hoes. Indeed Assurnasirpal's inscriptions often tell us of his use of axes and picks to 'smash' his way through difficult mountain terrain:

> For six days within Mount Kashiyari, a mighty mountain and rugged terrain which was unsuitable for my chariotry and troops, I cut through the mountain with iron axes and smashed a way with copper picks.[66]

Metal tools were especially common in Fort Shalmaneser where a large number of workshops were excavated. One of the most extraordinary of these was a double-handled iron saw, found in NE 50, the room to which the statue of Shalmaneser III had been taken for repair (p. 158). This stone-cutters's tool measured 1.73 m in length, width 13 cm, with a cutting edge of teeth 0.6 cm long. At one end a short tang for a wooden handle, secured by four heavy iron rivets, was preserved.[67] Iron tends to rust, and such objects were often poorly preserved, especially the knives. Iron sickles, chisels and other tools were found in the Town Wall houses, while a surprising amount of iron came from the soundings in the outer town, to the north of the ziggurat. The latter included hoes, daggers and scale armour.

The surviving texts make it clear that much military equipment, especially of metal, came to Fort Shalmaneser as booty or tribute. However, a large proportion of these metal objects must have been made at Nimrud, or at least locally in Assyria, since very large quantities of the metals themselves appear in the tribute lists. But nowhere in the excavated areas of Nimrud have we found any evidence of actual smelting or metal-working. It is likely, of course, that such workshops would be found only in the outer town, away from residential areas.

Other metals
Very little lead was found, and no surviving tin, although considerable tin must have been available for alloying copper.

HORSE HARNESS
The riding and harnessing of horses in ancient Mesopotamia dates back to the end of the third millennium BC, but it was not until the time of the Assyrian Empire that cavalry was widely employed, together with the horse-drawn military chariots which were an early second millennium development.[68] The Assyrian reliefs illustrate both the vehicles and the decoration with which the harness was embellished; examples of the latter have been found at Nimrud in some quantity. Among these were decorated ivory 'cheek-pieces' or 'blinkers', of which a large number were found in the Iraqi excavation of well AJ (Fig. 55). Room T 20 in Fort Shalmaneser seems to have been used specifically for the storage of horse harness, including a bronze 'blinker' decorated with the lotus buds that formed one of the most common forms of ornament on the ivory examples. Also found in this room were more than 150 bronze bosses used to decorate leather bridles.[69] Another important collection of horse trappings was recovered by Layard in room AB in the North-West Palace (the 'Room of the Bronzes'). The very large quantity of horse harness found in the *ekal mašarti* reflects the military functions of this building, and we know from the 'horse texts' (pp. 123, 215) that a major government office organised the acquisition of the horses needed for the Assyrian army. Among the less common pieces were an iron snaffle-bit from NW 15, and an electrum bit from the NN well in the North-West Palace.

The reliefs show the decoration of headstall straps with small ornaments, often circular discs or rosettes like those found in Fort Shalmaneser. Similar decoration is also made of shell, often with concentric circle ornament and a bronze stud in a centrally-pierced hole (Fig. 154). Such objects were found in particular in well NN and in Layard's 'Room of the Bronzes', along with other elements of horse harness. Whether these were actually used as harness decoration is uncertain, but in T 20 they were again found with both horse harness and armour. Frontlets or noseguards also survive in the archaeological record, for the most part of ivory but also in limestone.[70] From the 8th century onwards bronze bells and tassels were often suspended from a strap which passed around the neck. A large collection of such bells was found by Layard in two of the bronze cauldrons in room AB, of which nearly 80 examples survive in the British Museum. Prophylactic rituals sometimes required the use of bells to drive out evil demons.

POTTERY
As on all archaeological sites in Western Asia, after c. 7000 BC pottery is the most commonly found type of object. It is also the type of object most often used for purposes of dating. However, at Nimrud this situation was reversed, since it was our original intention to attempt to date Late Assyrian pottery more precisely by the associated cuneiform texts. This proved to be misguided optimism, and the reader should be warned of the unreliability of attributions 'to the time of Sargon' in the early

reports. Even in rooms where tablets can be securely dated to the 8th century BC, it cannot simply be assumed that other objects are necessarily of the same date.[71] In general the monumental buildings continued in use until 612 BC (even the Governor's Palace). The only place on the tell where stratified levels with in situ material were investigated 'extensively' was the area of the Town Wall houses, but even here relatively little pre-612 BC material was actually excavated.

In the excavation of Fort Shalmaneser we were more aware of these dating difficulties, and here a large quantity of pottery which was in use in 612 BC and in the immediately following 'squatter levels' has been published; pottery of earlier date remains ill-attested at the site.[72]

Palace Ware
By far the finest pottery at Nimrud is the so-called Palace Ware, consisting of thin-walled bowls and beakers made from a very fine greenish-buff to cream fabric. In some cases the fragile beaker walls are literally of eggshell thinness. The production of the beakers in particular is of an extraordinary competence, in that even the finest examples were actually thrown, that is, they were neither moulded nor cut-down in the green-hard state, methods used by later Achaemenid potters to produce their so-called 'eggshell ware'. The indentations on the beaker bodies are the unavoidable fingertip marks made by the potter in removing the vessel from the wheel. Further indentations were deliberately added for symmetry.[73] In general the late 7th century beakers have small ring bases (Fig. 158A). Very well-made, thin-walled bowls are also found in this fabric.[74] Two large deposits of Palace Ware were recovered, one in a ZT cupboard (Fig. 23, p. 47), the other on a 'table' in the Governor's Palace (Fig. 84). One of the most interesting objects made in this fine fabric is a rhyton in the shape of a ram's head recovered from the vaulted room 34 in the Town Wall houses (Fig. 158b).[75] The type of stamped ornament used on the rhyton is found on other types of vessel at Late Assyrian Kalhu, often in combination with a lotus pattern. The design illustrated in Figure 159, with impressed 4-winged genii, is up to now unique, but a number of examples have been found with the lotus and rosette patterns. These are most common on large, open jars with ledge-like rims.

Glazed pottery (see also p. 242)
A number of polychrome glazed jars of a variety of sizes was found (Fig. 153). These survive well, but the glazed tub-like, straight-sided vessels were clearly more fragile and were often found only as sherds (e.g. Fig. 144, p. 232). This is unfortunate since the decoration on these vessels was often quite elaborate, even amusing (see also the ostriches, Fig. 40, p. 72). Favourite patterns included scenes involving the king very like those on the stone reliefs. It is tempting to see these highly decorated, tub-like vessels as containers for garden plants but, as noted above, this is pure speculation.

Painted pottery
A very small number of cosmetics bottles are decorated with horizontal painted bands. All the examples found in Fort Shalmaneser, together with a number of other

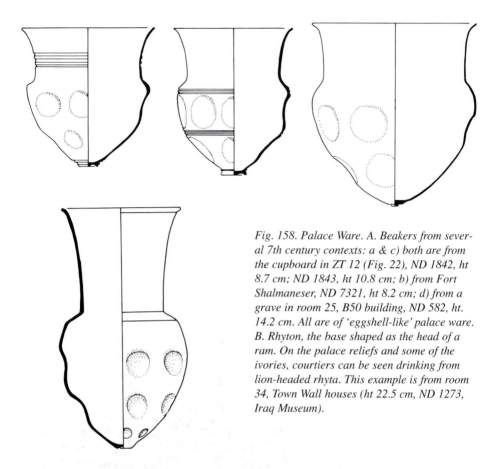

Fig. 158. Palace Ware. A. Beakers from several 7th century contexts: a & c) both are from the cupboard in ZT 12 (Fig. 22), ND 1842, ht 8.7 cm; ND 1843, ht 10.8 cm; b) from Fort Shalmaneser, ND 7321, ht 8.2 cm; d) from a grave in room 25, B50 building, ND 582, ht. 14.2 cm. All are of 'eggshell-like' palace ware. B. Rhyton, the base shaped as the head of a ram. On the palace reliefs and some of the ivories, courtiers can be seen drinking from lion-headed rhyta. This example is from room 34, Town Wall houses (ht 22.5 cm, ND 1273, Iraq Museum).

miniature jars and bottles, came from corridor E in Area S, that is, clearly among the loot from the area of the queen's household and, as one would expect, confirming their presence among the possessions of the women of the royal family and their female servants.[76] An attractive Cypriote painted bottle, perhaps a gift, was found in the North-West Palace, room 74, again in the domestic quarter of the building.[77]

There are a small number of attractive, burnished red and grey tripod vessels, which must also have served some special function (Fig. 160).[78]

Undecorated pottery
Most Late Assyrian pottery is undecorated. Among the more interesting types is a group of small, straight-sided drinking vessels, some of which are identical with the tea-glasses found today in every Iraqi house (see Fig. 164, p. 257). For this reason these are referred to in the reports by the Arabic term *istikan*.[79] Both 'pipe-lamps' and 'saucer-lamps' are found, the latter a simpler version of the metal lamp illustrated in Fig. 48, p. 88.[80]

Storage jars are found both in the houses and the large magazines. Very large jars are often marked with their capacity, especially those designed to hold grain or wine (see p. 166–67). Such very large containers are often set into the floor or into purpose-built benches. Some even have bung holes in the base.

APOTROPAIC FIGURINES

In the world of ancient Assyria a variety of rituals and 'magical' practices was employed to protect individuals from harmful spirits and disease. One part of these rituals involved the manufacture of various types of small sun-dried clay figurines which were then buried beneath the floors of houses or other types of residence, most commonly palaces, for the protection of their inhabitants. They were often placed in boxes of clay or stone, usually in the corners of rooms, sometimes in doorways (Fig. 161). At Nimrud a large number of these figurines were recovered in situ, especially in the Burnt Palace, Ezida and Fort Shalmaneser. Cuneiform texts are known which describe both the figurines themselves and the appropriate ritual of their manufacture and deposition. As prescribed in the texts, some Nimrud types bore a lime plaster coating, with details added in red or black paint.

Among the most common examples at Nimrud were the so-called *apkallu* which always occur in groups of seven. These represent the seven 'wise men' or 'sages' who were thought to have lived before the epic flood. According to the texts the *apkallu* appeared in different forms, some human, some cloaked in fish skins and others as winged bird-headed figures, resembling the eagle-headed 'griffin-demon' of the reliefs (Fig. 162). The latter are particularly associated with the Burnt Palace where their use appears to date to the time of Adad-nerari III. The excavation of the Burnt Palace examples provided both excitement and entertainment for the dig staff, and there was great competition among us to be allowed to open the boxes and

253

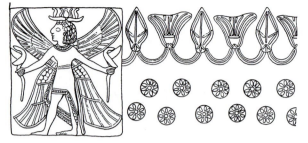

Fig. 159. Reconstruction of stamped decoration on a large open jar from Nimrud, found by Rassam in the 19th century, possibly in the Kidmuru Temple (after Herrmann & Curtis 1998, fig. 5).

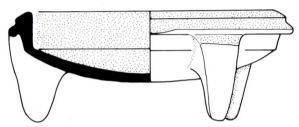

Fig. 160. Red-burnished tripod vessel, from the west wall of Fort Shalmaneser (d 15 cm).

Fig. 161. Brick box in the SE corner of Room S 64, Fort Shalmaneser, containing a spearman or lahmu figurine, inscribed vertically behind one arm, 'Enter, spirit of peace', and behind the other, 'Depart, spirit of evil' (ht 11.5 cm, ND 9445).

254

Fig. 162. Sun-dried clay figurine of eagle-headed apkallu *type; known in magical texts as the 'wise ones', they were found in boxes of seven, in particular under the floors of the Burnt Palace; the clay was covered with a white gypsum plaster and the wings were often painted on the back in black stripes (ht 14 cm, ND 3522).*

Fig. 163. Prophylactic clay figurine of a lion-man, holding a mace across his right shoulder, inscribed 'the one who admits the...', from south box outside west door of corridor E, Fort Shalmaneser (ht 11.5 cm, ND 8190, Musée Cinquantenaire, Bruxelles).

remove the row of neat little figures contained within, as in Fig. 77 (p. 126), with its seven warrior figures or *lahmu* (see also Fig. 161). This was another common type at Nimrud, the so-called 'hairy' figure, a protective and beneficient deity who appeared in human form, usually with long curly hair and a beard. The ritual texts prescribe that such figures should hold before them a spade (symbol of the god Marduk) and that they should be covered with gypsum plaster over which water should be painted in a black wash. They were also to be inscribed on the right arm, 'Enter, spirit of peace', and on the left, 'Depart, spirit of evil'. Proper *lahmu* had six 'spiral tresses' at the end of their long hair,[81] but at Nimrud many similar figures with the same inscription lacked this particular detail. This type was the most common in sector S of Fort Shalmaneser, was predominant also in the Burnt Palace foundation boxes, as in Fig. 77, and was found in the AB Palace. The *lahmu* is usually referred to as the 'spear man type' in the excavation reports.

Layard found a set of fish-*apkalle* in the South-West Palace,[82] and the symbolism of the man with fish cloak is common on the reliefs, on the cylinder seals and even on the gate figures. This type was also found in the Burnt Palace, where the gate figures themselves were 'fishmen'; the figurines sometimes display a dorsal fin on the back. Oddly, none of the dog figurines known elsewhere, especially from Nineveh, were found at Nimrud. These were often inscribed with such suitable instructions as, 'Don't think, bite' or 'Loud is his bark'.[83] Bronze dog figurines were found, however, which presumably served the same purpose; a set of these was recovered from the well in room NN in the North-West Palace.[84] Other 'animal' types found at Nimrud include the mythical dragon-like *mušhuššu* (in the dig register originally catalogued as a dog) found together with a *lahmu* figure and a miniature copper spear in a box deposited at the jamb of a doorway in Fort Shalmaneser, Corridor E.[85] Another Corridor E box contained a lion-headed human, clasping an object in the right hand in a position which led to the identification of this type among the dig staff as the 'telephoning' lions (Fig. 163). Bird figurines were found under the floor of a room in a building to the west of the so-called Town Wall Palace, one of which bore an inscription of Assurbanipal.[86] Found with them was an extraordinary bifrons figurine, with a human body and the faces of a lion and a man; it was covered with lime plaster and had once been painted with what resembled cross braces and a girdle.[87] The largest collection of apotropaic figurines came from one of the long barrack-rooms in Fort Shalmaneser (SE 5), some 30 fragments including five different types, together with two examples of the miniature copper symbols that they sometimes held. These were not a primary deposit but seem to have been discarded here. Perhaps the most likely explanation is that they had been placed here simply as a repository while repairs were being undertaken to the building after the damage suffered during the attack of 614 BC. Green explains the unusual number of figurines by the suggestion that this was some kind of 'sick-bay'.[88] This seems very unlikely, though it is just conceivable that renewal of the magical protection of the room had been rendered necessary by the 614 attack (see p. 163).

CHAPTER 8

POST-ASSYRIAN NIMRUD

Throughout the text we have had occasion to refer to Hellenistic burials above the Assyrian buildings and to 'squatter occupation' within them. The archaeological evidence indicates that not long after the sack in 612 BC the surviving local population returned to Kalhu and created shelter for itself within the remains of the monumental buildings. Their material remains, and especially the pottery, proved to be indistinguishable from those of the immediately pre-612 occupation, and one of our difficulties in interpreting these materials was to ascertain whether they represented objects simply reused by the squatter occupation or whether the pottery and even objects of metal were continuing to be produced by surviving craftsmen.[1] It became clear that the post-612 levels had been created by levelling off the collapsed debris to create new floors some 60–90 cm above the original ones, and that the pottery and other objects were actually in use in the squatter dwellings (Fig. 164). At the same time, joins were occasionally found between the floor debris and the material on the squatter floors, clearly indicating that some of the later floor material had originated in the earlier destruction debris. The fact that the squatter material was indistinguishable from that of the inhabitants of the imperial city is of course is not surprising, since we are dealing with essentially the same population, and this would mean the same potters, craftsmen and masons.

How long this 'village life' survived we cannot determine, though the fact that their material possessions remained indistinguishable from those of the residents of imperial Kalhu suggests that the reoccupation did not last for long. The character of this temporary resettlement is, however, significant. It was confined to the fortified areas, that is, the citadel and the arsenal. In the case of the arsenal a deliberate attempt was made to put the building in a posture of defence by rebuilding the north gate,

Fig. 164. Squatter level above room NE 49, Fort Shalmaneser, showing the remains of a jar which had been sunk into the floor, surrounded by a number of small 'tea glasses' or istikanat.

which had been dismantled for repair in 614 BC and had not as yet been re-erected at the time of the final onslaught in 612 BC.[2] We have no means of knowing what authority was responsible for this reconstruction, but it was not the Assyrian government, which lingered on in Harran until 608 BC but never again exercised control over the homeland. But this evidence clearly reflects insecurity in the countryside, which is indeed demonstrated by the fate of these refugees. Within the walls of the *ekal mašarti*, for example, three apparently brief levels of post-Assyrian occupation were identified. None could be precisely dated. All in turn came to a violent end. The possibility that those responsible were peoples from the hills to the north-east, who had suffered much at Assyrian hands, is perhaps supported by historical evidence that the Babylonians, who had fallen heir to Assyrian military responsibilities in this area, found it necessary in 608 and 607 BC to campaign in the hills north-east of Assyria.[3]

After the disappearance of these final remnants of the city population of Kalhu, there is very little surviving evidence until the Hellenistic period. Neo-Babylonian graves were found dug into the walls of the Adad-nerari III palace in the outer town, and there is some suggestion of later rebuilding, probably in the 5th century, especially in the area of Ezida and the Burnt Palace (Phase H, p. 125), and also above the AB Palace where vestiges of mud-brick partition walls were found, dividing the Assyrian chambers into smaller, often carefully paved rooms. Unfortunately very little material was discovered in direct association with this phase, and there are none of the cuneiform records that provided our earlier historical framework.[4] Moreover, the pottery here shows little similarity to that known from the Late Assyrian levels. Our best guess attributes this material to the Achaemenid period, but we are hampered in our understanding by the lack in northern Mesopotamia of well-dated Neo-Babylonian and Achaemenid parallels. This ignorance has certainly led to an under-identification of sites of this date, but the relative lack of archaeological evidence at Nimrud at this time may reflect no more than the degree of stability and security re-established under Achaemenid rule. For the huge mounds of ruins, once the great citadels of Assyrian cities, had become less attractive to these later settlers, except in times of danger when their inaccessibility became an advantage. And it was precisely these citadels which, until the recent period of rescue excavation, had attracted the almost exclusive attention of modern excavators. History tells us that Xenophon passed by Nimrud in 401 BC, at which time the tell was deserted, its name forgotten, but the local villagers took refuge on the ziggurrat:

> The Greeks marched on safely for the rest of the day and reached the river Tigris. There was a large deserted city there called Larisa, which in the old days used to be inhabited by the Medes. It had walls twenty-five feet broad and a hundred feet high, with a perimeter of six miles. It was built of bricks made of clay, with a stone base of twenty feet underneath. At the time when the Persians seized the empire from the Medes, the King of the Persians laid siege to this city but was quite unable to take it. A cloud, however, covered up the sun and hid it from sight until the inhabitants deserted the place, and so the city was taken. Near the city there was a pyramid of stone, a hundred feet broad, and two hundred feet high. Many of the natives from the neighbouring villages had run away and taken refuge on it.[5]

Nonetheless, our excavations have demonstrated that at some time in the Achaemenid period and later, in Hellenistic times, there were small settlements, perhaps a few houses at most, on the southern part of the citadel mound. We know that, after Xenophon, Alexander passed through this area, and the battle in which he finally defeated the last Achaemenid, Darius III, was fought not far to the northeast of Nimrud (331 BC).[6] Nineveh would appear to have been a city of some importance under the succeeding Seleucid kings, and it is clear from the reports of the 19th century excavators of Nimrud that there were many Hellenistic tombs on the site, especially in the southeastern and central parts of the tell. Layard recounts the discovery in the area of the Central Palace of terracotta sarcophagi in some number, with grave goods consisting of glass, agate, carnelian and amethyst beads, cylinder seals, mirrors, copper and silver ornaments and jewellery. Other tombs in this area were built of baked bricks. These lay just under two metres above the Assyrian buildings. Of the south-eastern area he remarks that he dug 'to a considerable depth' without meeting any traces of building, although much pottery and fragments of inscribed (baked and therefore easily recognised) bricks. Here he also discovered terracotta sarcophagi of which the lids were stone slabs re-used from the monumental buildings. One such sarcophagus was long and narrow, a second 'resembling a dish cover in shape'. George Smith also investigated this area, observing that,

> all the eastern and southern portions of the mound of Nimroud have been destroyed by being made a burial-place. The ruins had been excavated after the fall of the Assyrian empire, walls had been dug through, and chambers broken into, and the openings filled up with coffins. These coffins were various in shape, no two being alike. Most of them were so short that the bodies had to be doubled up to get them in. The coffins were of terracotta, some of them ornamented and painted; but the commoner graves of the same period only contained large jars or urns in which the remains were packed, the poorest being buried without any covering at all. Generally the coffins were covered with one or two stone slabs from the neighbouring palaces, and then closed up with large sun-dried bricks. These burials are of all ages; some I opened belonged to the period of the successor of Alexander the Great, in the third century BC. From the tombs I obtained beads and ornaments, rings, bracelets, etc.[7]

Hellenistic burials were found by the Mallowan expedition above the North-West Palace, the Governor's Palace, the Town Wall houses, indeed over the whole of the site, although no great number of graves was identified before the 1957 excavations, discussed below. Analysis and identification of these finds was impeded not only by the lack of comparative material from Northern Mesopotamia, but in the particular case of Nimrud our inability, up until 1957, to find an area of the mound that had not already been ransacked by the earlier excavators. It was not until we started to work in the area of Ezida and the Burnt Palace that we began to find isolated groups of in situ material of this date – not simply graves but, for example, a Hellenistic house overlying the north-west corner of Ezida.[8] A reliable sequence was still lacking, however, and in 1957, in an attempt to fill this gap, we made a sounding on a small plateau east of the AB Palace, which showed little superficial sign of previous disturbance. It was also our objective to re-examine here the Assyrian build-

ing beneath (the AB Palace, p. 130), the existence of which had been briefly reported by Layard and Loftus.

The sounding revealed that more than seven metres of ancient debris overlay
the AB Assyrian building. The time, to say nothing of the expense, of removing such
an overburden of soil forced us to restrict our subsequent excavations to three
trenches, the longest of which was some 50 x 6 m. The plans of these trenches can
be seen in Figs. 82, 165. At the same time we reopened a large pit dug by Layard a
short distance to the west, in which the throne room of the AB Palace was re-
exposed, but here the overlying deposits had been extensively disturbed. These excavations established the presence on the south-eastern part of the tell not only of the
small village already referred to but of undisturbed parts of the Hellenistic cemetery.

On the basis of these excavations a series of six building levels was identified
and approximately dated by the coins found within them:[9]

Level 1   after 140 BC (no legible coins).
Level 2   begins c. 145 BC (coin of Demetrius II Nicator, 146–140 BC)
Level 3   a late phase of Level 4, post-150 BC
Level 4   begins c. 180 BC (coins of Aradus, 170–169 BC, and Alexander Bala,
           150–145 BC)

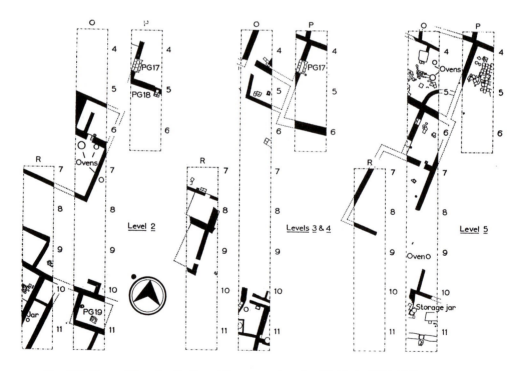

*Fig. 165. Plans of Trenches R, O, and P, excavated south of Ezida in 1957: Hellenistic
levels 2-5.*

Level 5   begins c. 220–210 BC; Rhodian jar handle (dated 190–180 BC)
Level 6   begins approximately 250–240 BC; one house destroyed by fire, hoard
           of tetradrachms; coin of Seleucus III (226–223 BC)

This 3rd/2nd century village settlement seemed to differ little in character or in size from any one of the smaller villages that dotted the plain around Nimrud at the time we were excavating there. The houses were irregular agglomerations of two, three or four rooms, ranged about small courtyards in which were bread ovens of the type still in use today for the baking of flaps of unleavened bread. Brick-covered drainage pits may have served as a secondary source of rainwater, since the river had by now changed its course to the western side of the valley. At this time, moreover, the deep Assyrian wells of the citadel seem largely to have gone out of use, although at least one well in the North-West Palace, that in room AJ, originally built by Shalmaneser III and from which the very splendid ivories came, had continued in use not only after the sack but later still. Indeed, at some time, probably in the Hellenistic period, the level of the well-head had been raised by nearly two metres, the steps leading up to it lying in what was now open ground (Fig. 53, p. 93). By then, however, most of the other wells seem to have been covered over by the decaying and collapsing Late Assyrian walls.

The material equipment of the Hellenistic inhabitants reflected in almost equal measure the survival of traditional Mesopotamian types and the introduction of new fashions as a result of the conquest by Alexander and the domination of his Seleucid successors. The external connections of the area at this time can be seen both in the coinage, with a great predominance of coins from the mints of Syria and Asiatic Greece, and the pottery, among which were pieces imported from the

Fig. 166. Hellenistic coins from Level 6: a) Silver tetradrachm of Lysimachus; obverse, head of deified Alexander, reverse, seated Athena holding victory in right hand, mint uncertain (Asia Minor 297-281 BC; ND 6191). b) Silver tetradrachm of Seleucus III, head on obverse, seated Apollo on reverse, mint Antioch 226-222 BC (ND 6196). c) Silver tetradrachm of Attalus I (?), obverse, head of Philetaerus, reverse, seated Athena (? 241-197 BC; ND 6197).

Fig. 167. West end of throne room AB 3, showing intrusive Hellenistic graves dug into the Assyrian mud-brick dais and the floor of the room. PG 21 is in the middle foreground.

Levant or from the more important provincial towns, closer to home. Within these post-Assyrian levels the only major change in the character of the pottery occurs after the destruction of Hellenistic Level 2, glazed wares being noticeably more common in the otherwise relatively impoverished settlement of Level 1. At this time the pottery also takes on a more Parthian aspect.

In the trenches was found a continuous sequence of six building levels, summarised above, extending from a depth of 40 cm below the surface to somewhat over three metres. Below the sixth level lay a depth of barren, fallen mud-brick, interrupted only by occasional graves dug from the upper levels. In the trenches themselves we reached only the tops of the Assyrian buildings. However, two graves, sunk into the collapsed mud-brick of these buildings, can be attributed to Level 6. These were constructed of baked- and mud-brick, respectively, and were covered with re-used stone slabs, just like those reported by Layard. The capstones of PG 13, for example, bore part of the standard inscription of Shalmaneser III. Both burials were devoid of grave goods and both were exceptions to the general rule of burial outside the houses. In PG 13 the skull was found reversed, suggesting that the body had been decapitated. The overlying house had been destroyed by fire, and among the debris was our only notable find from this level, a hoard of six silver tetradrachms, buried under the floor. At least four of these bore the superscription of Lysimachus, king of Thrace (297–281 BC) (Fig. 166a); another is dated to the reign of Seleucus III

Fig. 168. Fragment of stamped Rhodian amphora handle, bearing a name which occurs between 200 and 180 BC in the Pergamum series, found in Level 5 debris, south side of AB room 3 (ND 6072, Iraq Museum).

Fig. 169. Stamped wine-jar handle, from a Thasian amphora, the stamp including a name and the depiction of a bunch of grapes, from a Hellenistic rubbish pit dug down into the north court of the Burnt Palace (ND 4485).

(226–223 BC) (Fig. 166b), while the sixth bore the head of Philetaerus of Pergamum and was probably minted under Attalus I (241–197 BC) (Fig. 166c). Also found in this level were a fragment of a glass rod, iron tools, two chert arrowheads of possible third millennium date, and a number of bone 'spatulae', a common type of object of which the purpose remains uncertain, although it could have been a type of writing tool, used either to inscribe the waxed boards then used for writing, or perhaps for ink on leather or papyrus, although no traces of ink were found on them. The flat, rounded end was presumably used to rub out and smooth the wax surface, or conceivably as a burnisher for some entirely different purpose.

Although the Level 6 village did not extend as far east as the AB Palace, a number of graves found here almost certainly belong to this time (PG 20–23, Fig. 167). PG 20 contained two skeletons in a terracotta coffin, the only example of a double interment. A copper anklet and an alabaster bottle were found here. In PG 23 were two iron knives, a miniature hedgehog pendant and 36 beads of carnelian, lapis lazuli, serpentine and frit. It was PG 21, however, that yielded the richest collection of objects found in any Hellenistic grave dug by the Mallowan expedition. This abutted directly (and accidentally) onto the mud-brick dais of the Palace AB throne room. It contained 10 cylinder and stamp seals, amulets, a silver bangle and pendants, and a large number of beads, as in PG 23. One coin was also found, a silver drachm of Alexander the Great.[10] This does not, of course, provide any close indication of the date of the grave, since silver coins remained in used for upwards of a century and old specimens seem to have been considered particularly acceptable currency for the passage of the Styx. Indeed the striking parallel in equipment, and the wealth that it implies, between PG 21 and PG 5 (Level 5, see below) tends to reinforce the conclusion that they both date from the same prosperous phase of the settlement, about the end of the third or beginning of the second century BC.

Level 5 lay some 60–70 cm above Level 6, the plan showing basically a rebuilding with only minor variations on its predecessor, and in good quality mud-brick. Again, the finds were relatively few in number, but included further bone spatulae, an iron arrowhead and a bronze signet ring bearing the device of a winged victory.[11] Two of the Level 5 graves were comparatively rich in grave goods. PG 10, a jar burial of an infant, contained four copper bangles and about 75 beads of carnelian and frit. PG 5, a brick chamber roofed with stone slabs, yielded a more elaborate collection of personal ornaments, including beads of carnelian, rock crystal, agate and lapis lazuli, four silver pendants, one representing a dog, four bronze bangles and two much worn cylinder seals. Seven small bronze coins of Seleucus III and a small bronze recumbent cow or calf were also buried with the dead woman.[12] The area above the AB Palace was occupied at this time by an enormous rubbish pit used by the inhabitants of the nearby village. One of the most interesting finds from this pit was a Rhodian jar handle (Fig. 168) bearing the name of the eponym Pratophanes, to be dated between 190 and 180 BC.[13] The stamped handle of a wine jar (Fig. 169) had previously been found in a late rubbish pit near the well in the north court of the Burnt Palace, in this instance testimony to the export of Greek wine from the island of Thasos, at the northern end of the Aegean. The wines of Thasos were famous both for their bouquet and for their strength, and from the fifth century onwards were traded not only within Greece, but all over the Mediterranean and even through the Black Sea. Stamped Thasian jar handles have been found at many sites in Western Asia, including Antioch, Troy and Babylon. This is the only known example from Assyria, but we can be reasonably certain that the export of this famous wine to the east had been much stimulated by the conquests of Alexander and his Seleucid successors.

Levels 4 and 3 represent only minor modifications of the same plan. Parts of two houses were uncovered. These were smaller and of less careful construction than those of the preceding levels, perhaps to be explained by the extension of the village eastwards at this time to the hitherto unoccupied site above the AB Palace. Bone spatulae were again found here, and iron tools and weapons. Of interest also was the head of a veiled terracotta figurine. Above the east end of the AB throne room was a small house, built on the accumulated rubbish of Level 5. This had been destroyed by fire, preserving for us a number of common domestic objects such as pottery, spindle whorls and spatulae. A coin of Seleucus IV (187–175 BC) was also recovered, confirming the approximate date of the house. Many of the burials in this phase were almost entirely devoid of grave goods. PG 15, however, yielded a single silver drachm of Aradus (dated to the year 170–169 BC), and PG 8 an attractive, thin-walled bowl with notched triangles below the shoulder, of the same general type as one found in a grave overlying the south end of the Nabu Temple, excavated in 1956.[14]

That the Level 4 houses continued in use until after 150 BC is shown by the discovery of a small bronze coin of Alexander Bala and a drachm of the same reign, both dated between 150 and 146 BC. A relative revival in prosperity is demonstrated in Level 2, the houses being extensive and regular in plan, with well-built walls, again of good quality mud-brick. Small finds were few in number but the destruction

Fig. 170. Hollow terracotta figurine, Hellenistic type depicting mother and child, from a pit cut into the south wall of Ezida sanctuary NTS 2, probably early second century BC (ht 17.2 cm, ND 5202, Iraq Museum).

of the settlement by fire served to preserve a useful range of well-dated pottery. Also found here were a number of fragments of moulded mother-and-child figurines, of which the best-preserved example comes from a rubbish pit cut into the south wall of the NTS 2 shrine in Ezida (Fig. 170). The Level 2 destruction represents the effective end of the Hellenistic sequence. Although a higher ground surface was identified, the surviving traces of buildings were too meagre to form any coherent plan. However, there appeared here a number of distinctive changes in pottery types, and we believe this level to belong to a period after the imposition of Parthian control in this area.[15]

The excavation of the 1957 trenches enabled us to reassess the evidence previously recovered in the area of Ezida and the Burnt Palace. In particular Phase I can now be attributed to the Hellenistic occupation identified in the trenches, and this allows us to place the important evidence for glass-making somewhere in the century between 250 and 150 BC. This includes not only the kilns but the extraordinary red cullet that was recovered here (p. 241). There is also a quantity of sherds from the robber trench which are closely comparable with the red and stamped wares of the Hellenistic levels 2–4, while an unstratified silver drachm of Alexander the Great was found near the fish gate. In fact the sequence overlying the Nabu Temple corresponds very closely with that observed above the AB Palace: an extension of the village, represented by isolated houses and burials. But no trace was found here of Parthian Level 1.

Pottery

The well-dated Hellenistic pottery that was recovered from the 1957 trenches proved in itself to constitute a major contribution to our understanding of this period. Indeed it remains the only well-stratified material of this date to have been published from

Fig. 171. Large, triple-handled storage jar with impressed decoration, from Hellenistic level 2 above AB 3 (ht 56.5 cm, ND 6622, British Museum).

northern Mesopotamia.[16] The Nimrud pottery is unlike that known from the Greek cities of the eastern Mediterranean and at sites such as Samaria and Dura. At Nimrud only a few pieces of the usual black- or red-varnished wares were found and there was no true 'Hellenistic Pergamene'. The absence of the latter is perhaps not surprising since it does not appear in western Asia until the second half of the second century and the Nimrud village probably came to an end sometime in the third quarter of the same century. The few examples at Nimrud of the earlier red-varnished ware typical of sites like Tarsus and Antioch are all bowls of a single type, with isolated palmette stamps in the base.[17] Several black-varnished ring-based bowls were found with rouletting and, again, palmette stamps in the base. Perhaps the most distinctive local pottery type, widely distributed across northern Mesopotamia and north-eastern Syria includes a carinated bowl type and the shallow 'fish plate', usually ring-based, with an orange-red paint at the rim; sometimes it seemed that the vessel had actually been dipped in the paint. This red-painted ware is an imitation of western pottery types, themselves inspired by Attic models. Only from the very latest level are there vertically grooved local imitations of 'Hellenistic Pergamene'. Of particular interest is a unique baby's feeding bottle, which was moulded in two halves; this was recovered from Level 4/3. An example of this type, now in the Fitzwilliam Museum in Cambridge, is decorated with the representation of a small child crawling, while those from the Agora in Athens actually have teeth marks on the protruding 'nipple'.[18] Another distinctive feature of the Hellenistic pottery at Nimrud is the use of impressed stamp decoration on the plain wares (Fig. 171). From

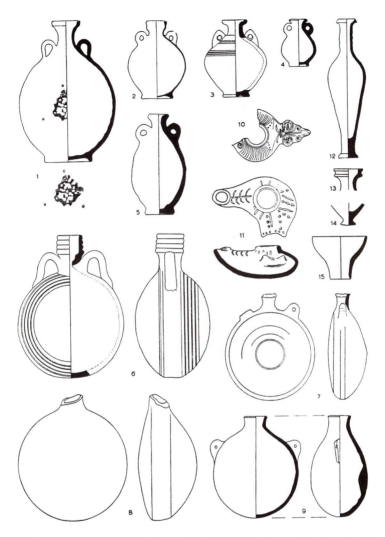

Fig. 172. Selection of pottery from the Hellenistic trenches, including glazed bottles (1–5), lamps (10–11), an unguentarium (12, ht 22 cm) and a number of water flasks (6–9).

Level 4 onwards a number of glazed jars and bottles were found, the glaze itself originally a deep blue-green, which weathers to a light, sometimes silvery blue. A yellow glaze is sometimes used, but there are no dark green glazes. Several Hellenistic lamps and a single *unguentarium* (oil bottle) have been found (Fig. 172)

    The excavations described in the preceding pages have provided a picture, however incomplete, of the foundation and development of a small village on the south-east corner of the mound. Kalhu had been an artificial creation of the great kings of late Assyria, and had no natural advantages, such as an important highway or river crossing, to ensure its survival. In this it differed markedly from Assur and Nineveh which survived the destruction of their political power. It is thus not surprising that the Hellenistic villages differ little in character from those of the 1950s. Although the external connections of the area under Seleucid rule can be seen in the coinage, with a great predominance of coins from the mints of Syria and Asiatic Greece, since the same pattern is found all over Mesopotamia at this time, it may also reflect simply the numerical distribution of coinage in circulation and may not, therefore, imply any especially close links across the northern plain.

The pottery provides our largest body of evidence and is probably a valid example of the type of western influence that existed in Assyria at this time. Although the actual quantity of imported pieces is small, there are a number of new wares and decorative motifs that clearly derive from the Hellenistic pottery of Syria and Cilicia. At the same time the Mesopotamian ceramic tradition remained strong. The graves also reflect the varying fortunes of the village, Level 5 producing two collections of jewellery that imply considerable wealth. It is interesting, but certainly not surprising, to see among the grave goods a number of small antiquities, especially in the form of cylinder seals, stamp seals and amulets recovered from the earlier levels at the site, for which the villagers, or at least their wives, had a considerable affection almost certainly joined with a regard for their magical properties. The only standard feature of the graves is the practice of flexed inhumation; with a few possible exceptions the graves were sited outside the houses yet within the limits of the village, this lack of a defined cemetery perhaps continuing the Assyrian tradition. They consisted in many cases of simple cists of baked or mud-brick, sometimes covered with capstones, but occasionally either filled directly with earth or provided with a wooden lid. 'Bath-tub' coffins are also found, usually with both ends rounded, in contrast with the bronze examples with one flat end found in the Assyrian tombs of the 8th century. One post-Assyrian example, found above Ezida, also had a flat end;[19] although it seems likely to have been Hellenistic, we cannot establish its date with certainty.

We have already remarked that at the time of Xenophon (401 BC) the tell at Nimrud was uninhabited, suggesting a period of reasonable security. Indeed the abundance and excellence of food in the countryside is remarked on by Xenophon.[20] It is possible that the founding of the Hellenistic village sometime in the middle of the third century may have reflected the rise of the Arsacid dynasty of Parthia, who had begun to make serious inroads on the Seleucid provinces of Mesopotamia not long after that time. It is tempting to see the prosperity of Level 5 as a reflection of the long reign of Antiochus III the Great (222–187 BC), who made great efforts to re-establish Seleucid authority in the east. This was, however, no more than a temporary recovery, and by 130 BC the Parthians were in control of all Mesopotamia to the banks of the Euphrates. At what stage they conquered the northern plain we do not know, but it seems safe to assume that their advent is reflected at Nimrud in the destruction of the Level 2 village some time after 146 BC, and the appearance of their distinctive pottery in the short-lived upper level. The final establishment of their authority, which was to last more than three centuries, presumably brought with it the conditions of peace and order in which villages could once more exist in safety on the plain.

EPILOGUE

Nimrud is one of a small number of ancient Mesopotamian sites that were excavated by the pioneers of the nineteenth, and have been further excavated in the twentieth, century. As an Assyrian capital it is unusual in that the imperial city is immediately accessible and relatively undisturbed, despite the damage inflicted in the 612 BC sack and by the subsequent squatter and Hellenistic populations. Both Nineveh and Assur were important Parthian cities, with monumental structures overlying the Assyrian city, whereas in the later first millennium BC Nimrud was little more than an occasional small village and a burial ground. Khorsabad was of course equally accessible but it lacks the longer history and the variety of Nimrud. Unfortunately, except in the (apparently rare) areas of private housing, most of the excavations at Nimrud also proved to be investigations of what was essentially a single level, that of the destruction of the city. Thus further exploration of the Town Wall houses would be rewarding, as well perhaps of areas in the outer town where ancient reconstruction and refurbishment may not have been quite so efficient in removing stratified materials. We continue to lack, inter alia, a well-stratified pottery sequence, for dating purposes the most useful single type of object since pottery, unlike tablets, ivories or cylinder seals, is rarely stored for long periods of time. Further excavation of the monumental buildings would continue to be productive in the sense of adding to our knowledge of the plan of the city and of the material possessions of the upper classes but, beyond the possible discovery of more cuneiform tablets, it would do little for our wider understanding of the social and economic situation of the ordinary Assyrian citizen.

Mallowan's objectives were both simple and straightforward.

> We kept before us two primary objectives. First, to discover more ivories, for I was convinced that many more remained to be found. Second and much more important, to discover cuneiform records, for apart from the royal standard inscriptions which accompanied the Assyrian bas-reliefs, no clay tablets in the cuneiform script had ever been recorded by Layard and it seemed incredible to me that so large a city could have been devoid of economic, business, historical and literary texts. I would have staked my life that in the end we would find all these things, and find them we did.[21]

But such 'unscientific' goals would hardly satisfy the awarding committees of modern funding bodies. Mallowan was of course an archaeologist of his time. In fact, his work at Nimrud has been described as the last of the great nineteenth century expeditions, and although he shared an Institute with Gordon Childe, he was little concerned with social or economic questions, except to the extent that these could be understood from the written documents. There was an understandable emphasis on the spectacular, as there was in Layard's time, since impressing the British public was an important part of fund-raising. His London lectures were always highly successful, to say nothing of social, occasions. Moreover, the emphasis on 'finds' in the material sense was understandable, since in the generous days of the archaeological 'division', that is, the division of the more common antiquities between the expedition and the local Department of Antiquities, the expedition's share of the finds provided an important source of funding, museums contributing to the excavations in the hope of receiving in return objects for their collections. The major finds of course went directly to the Iraq Museum. In this attitude Mallowan was in accord with the distinguished 1950s Director-General of the Iraqi Antiquities Department, who commented in *Sumer* in 1956 on 'one of the most interesting and fruitful seasons in the long history of Iraq':

> With four to five expeditions, both Iraqi and Foreign, working in the field, year after year, one certainly expects remarkable additions to the unique collections of the Iraq Museum. Archaeological activity in the field is never an easy undertaking. It is, indeed, one of the most exacting scientific tasks imaginable. It carries a high sense of responsibility to Science, History, the Antiquities discovered and also to the highest cultural interests of the country in whose soil it undertakes excavations.
>
> Happily, gone are the days when foreign expeditions working in Iraq had to think only in terms of unearthing antiquities and in shipping them to their respective countries, often at the expense of the ancient sites themselves. The price of ignorance and indifference was colossal for the country in the loss of its great antique treasures. The only excuse and perhaps consolation is that Iraq did not then exist as an independent state.[22]

These comments lead us to consider whether the nineteenth century excavation of important sites like Nineveh and Nimrud is to be regretted, even condemned. The parsimony of potential sponsors in England, including both the Government and the British Museum, led Layard to 'obtain the largest possible number of well-preserved objects of art at the least possible outlay of time and money.' It is difficult to judge what would otherwise have been the progress of our knowledge of the culture and history of what was, from the vantage point of the western world, one of the most important areas of the ancient world, and one that provided, via the classical world, the foundations of many of our own traditions and institutions.

Certainly one can regret both Layard's lack of funds and his lack of experience. It is clear that large numbers of delicate antiquities were lost – 'entire when first exposed to view, it crumbled into dust as soon as touched.' 'They fell to pieces as soon as exposed.'[23] Thus Layard writes of ivories and metal in particular. We doubt, however, that even among modern 'scientific' field archaeologists one could easily find any single individual who has not had at least one such disaster, and one could argue, taking a broader view, that Layard's mistakes are of less account than his careful recording and drawing, which undoubtedly helped to lay the basis for a more technical and scientific approach to work in the field. Nonetheless, one is aware, especially when working at a vast site like Nimrud, of the enormous amount that was destroyed, not only the objects themselves but, far more seriously, the contexts in which they were found, by far the most important component of archaeological evidence.

At the same time, it must be admitted that there was little interest among the Ottoman officials, and stone and other materials were being removed from the ancient sites for re-use, with no appreciation of their historical value. Perhaps it was in this context that the work of those like Layard made its greatest contribution, in demonstrating both to the general public and the academic community, not only in the West but in the Near East as well, the depth and importance of the archaeological information that was there to be found. In recent years, rescue operations on smaller sites have helped to increase the chronological span of Late Assyrian evidence, and the work of the State Board of Antiquities and Heritage in Iraq has itself not only added spectacularly to the archaeological information from the site but has been instrumental in preserving the site for future generations.

In 1852 Rawlinson wrote off Nimrud as having little further left to offer. His contribution to the decipherment of cuneiform was fundamental, but we hope that this volume has demonstrated how wrong he was about the potential of the archaeology of Nimrud. Indeed, as this volume goes to press, the latest news from Baghdad reports exciting new finds by our Iraqi colleagues in the Ishtar Temple, including cuneiform tablets and many beautiful cylinder seals as well as the two lion colossi. More remarkable discoveries certainly lie ahead.

NOTES AND REFERENCES

INTRODUCTION

[1] Genesis x.11,12.

[2] The earliest recorded European traveller in the Near East was a 12th century rabbi, Benjamin of Tudela in the kingdom of Navarre, who visited Mosul, recognising the ancient site across the river as Nineveh, but providing a seriously exaggerated estimate of the extent of its walls, perhaps in a pious desire to demonstrate the veracity of the book of Jonah (iii.3). His account, written in AD 1178, was printed in Hebrew in 1543 and in Latin in 1575. It is not possible here to provide a history of exploration in ancient Assyria, but we recommend Seton Lloyd's *Foundations in the Dust* (1947) as the most readable general book on the subject.

[3] N & R I, xxv.

[4] N & R I 4; see also p. 258, this text.

[5] Genesis x.11,12; N & R I, 7–9.

[6] Saggs 1984, 302–3.

[7] N & R I, 29–30.

[8] N & R I, 20.

[9] N & R I, p. 66.

[10] Cooper's drawing of the rock sculptures of Bavian is reproduced in Curtis and Reade 1995, fig. 2.

[11] Published in Barnett 1956.

[12] See Gadd 1936, appendix 4, 9; his plan of Nimrud is reproduced in Barnett and Falkner 1962, colour plate at end of volume.

[13] Canto V, 61; the reference is to his two Memoirs on the Ruins of Babylon (1813, 1818).

[14] Lloyd 1947, 137; Curtis & Reade, 1995 fig. 5.

[15] Some of these cartoons are reproduced in Waterfield 1963, e.g. 318, 400, the latter accusing him of 'playing the Nineveh Bull in the Stambul China-shop'.

[16] Lloyd 1947, 161.

[17] Mallowan 1977, 242–43.

[18] The terrace in 1962 is illustrated in Curtis & Reade 1995, Fig. 6, long minus its fruit trees.

[19] A list of references to the Iraqi work can be found in Postgate & Reade 1980, 306; from 1972 onwards, occasional summaries of excavations at Nimrud are published in the journal *Iraq*.

[20] Postgate 1973, p. xvi and text 14.

[21] Mallowan 1966, 53 (ND 3415, Wiseman 1953).

CHAPTER ONE: THE LAND OF ASSYRIA – SETTING THE SCENE

[1] N & R I, 38 ff. and II, 67.

[2] The issues raised here are more fully discussed in Oates 1968, chapter 1. See also Postgate 1992.

[3] We are indebted to Nicholas Postgate for this information.

[4] This time on an ivory fragment, illustrated in Mallowan 1966, fig. 482. Hazael is a common name, and it must be admitted that it cannot be proved that the name on the ivory is that of this particular king. However, both the inscribed shells and this fragment were found in the same storeroom (T 10), suggesting at least their possible contemporaneity.

[5] Parpola & Watanabe 1988, text 1.

[6] The text of the stele is published in Grayson 1996, 180.

[7] The translation of LÚ.SAG/*ša reši* as 'eunuch' is not agreed by all scholars, but it should be noted that the king's officials are specifically described as *ša reši* and *ša ziqni* ('bearded'). For a further note on the power of the governors at this time, see Zawadzki 1997.

[8] Grayson 1996, 203.

[9] Grayson 1996, 231–33.

[10] Grayson 1996, 209–12; the stele itself is most recently published in C. Postgate, Oates and Oates 1997, pl. 13.

[11] Grayson 1996, 204–05.

[12] The Tell Abta stele of Bel-Harran-bel-uṣur, Grayson 1996, 241.

[13] Tadmor 1994, 9.

[14] His texts make no statements as to his ancestors, but on a brick inscription from Assur he is described

as a son of Adad-nerari, while the latest version of the Assyrian King-List makes him a son of Assur-nerari V (Grayson, CAH 73).

[15] The official inscriptions of Tiglath-Pileser III are published in Tadmor 1994.

[16] Grayson CAH, 87.

[17] Details of the history of the period from Sargon until the fall of Assyria can be found in the Cambridge Ancient History III, 2, 1991.

[18] Millard 1994, 60; the campaign is thought to have been against Tabal (Cappadocia), Grayson 1975, 238.

[19] Tadmor, Landsberger and Parpola 1989.

[20] J. Oates 1986, 94–96, 114.

[21] Grayson 1975, 81 (Chronicle I iii, 34–35).

[22] Illustrated in Mallowan 1966, fig. 583.

[23] Porter 1997, 258.

[24] According to Parpola (1983, 230ff.) he suffered from *Lupus erythematosus*.

[25] Grayson, CAH 138–39.

[26] Illustrated in Parpola & Watanabe 1988, fig. 20.

[27] Parpola & Watanabe 1988, treaty 8.

[28] See Brinkman CAH; Oates CAH; and references. A fundamental argument revolves around the 'king' of Babylon after 648, whose name, Kandalanu, appears only in date formulae or in chronological documents. That is, there is no independent evidence that he existed other than as a possible 'throne name' for Assurbanipal. Both 'died' in 627 BC. But the evidence is far more complicated than is indicated by this relatively straightforward question.

[29] J. Oates 1965, 136.

[30] Kühne 1993.

[31] Larsen 1976, 192 ff.; for a detailed discussion of the Late Empire, Millard 1994.

[32] Illustrated in Millard 1994, frontispiece, and see p. 8.

[33] Grayson 1996.

[34] Anabasis III, 4.

[35] N & R I, 8.

[36] N & B 656–57.

[37] Mallowan 1966, figs. 29–34.

[38] As suggested by Reade (Postgate & Reade 1980, fig. 1). A gate has also been identified in this area by recent Iraqi excavators.

[39] Rassam 1897, 226.

[40] Mallowan 1966, fig. 29.

[41] Mallowan 1966, figs. 33–34.

[42] Tadmor 1994, 173.

[43] Grayson 1992, 290; the translation 'squirrel' is suggested by Nicholas Postgate.

[44] Oates 1968, 46 ff, and pls. 2–3.

[45] N & R I, 80–81; Luckenbill II, 1927, 278–79.

[46] See further discussion in Oates 1968, 47–49.

[47] Grayson 1992, 226.

CHAPTER TWO: MAJOR PALACES ON THE CITADEL

[1] Inter alia, Meuszynski 1981; Winter 1979; for the Tell al Rimah orthostat, see C. Postgate, D. Oates and J. Oates 1997, pl. 8b.

[2] Heidel 1956, 31.

[3] Wiseman 1952; Grayson 1991, 288. It should perhaps be noted that the text is inscribed on a stele and not a 'large stone slab'.

[4] Mallowan 1966, figs. 103, 104.

[5] The missing piece was identified in 1953 by J.O; unfortunately it was not separately catalogued but I am certain that it came from the 612 BC destruction debris (either Town Wall houses Level 3 or Level 2), a location also implied by Mallowan (1954, 69). See also p. 138.

[6] The translation of the cuneiform word for the oil seed common at this time remains a matter of debate. Most cuneiform scholars are persuaded that it is sesame, yet archaeological evidence of sesame remains rare or non-existent while large quantities of linseed are found (see Helbaek in Mallowan 1966).

[7] ND 3414, 3483, possibly to be dated to the time of Esarhaddon on the arguments of Grayson, CAH 137. See also Parpola 1983, xxii–xxiii.

[8] The administrative tablets, including those from rooms 14/16, were published in Parker 1961.

[9] See Fig. 158, also Mallowan 1966, 178–79.

[10] ND 2307, Parker 1954, 37; see also discussion in chapter 6, p. 46.

[11] For a detailed reconstruction of the throne room bas-reliefs and those of the façade, see Meuszynski 1981.

[12] See inter alia Meuszynski 1981; Winter 1981; Reade 1979, 1980; Paley and Sobolewski 1987, 1992.

[13] Barbara Parker Mallowan 1983.

[14] Moortgat 1969, 134.

[15] It is likely that there was some form of clerestory lighting (see also p. 172).

[16] Abu Al-Soof 1963.

[17] N & R II, 203; in fact two of the surviving throne room reliefs had fallen backwards, suggesting that part of the mud-brick wall itself had been removed.

[18] Abu Al-Soof 1963; Reade 1968, 69, n. 2; Paley and Sobolewski 1992, 12, 17.

[19] See discussion by David Oates in Oates, Oates and McDonald, *Brak* 2, 388.

[20] Black and Green 1992, 115.

[21] Parpola 1987, letters 110 (ND 2765, from ZT 4) and 119.

[22] For Sargon's Khorsabad plans, see Loud and Altman 1938, and esp. pl. 86.

[23] Meuszynski 1981.

[24] N & R I, 128; see also N & B 601, where the actual weights are listed; the Sennacherib weight is no. 12. Three of the Shalmaneser V set are illustrated in Curtis & Reade 1996, 193. See also Kwasman and Parpola 1991, xxiv–xxv.

[25] Turner's Type F reception suite (1970, pl. 39)

[26] Reade 1985, pl. 40 a & b. See also Paley and Sobolewski 1987, 65 ff.

[27] Winter 1981, 34.

[28] Also illustrated in Meuszynski, *Et.Trav.* 5, 1974.

[29] N & R II, 8 ff.

[30] The 'wind door' is presumably an air shaft of the type still in use in traditional houses in Iraq and the Gulf (Persian *badgir*). These were found in other buildings at Nimrud, and are visible in the photograph of the bathroom in the outer town palace of Adad-nerari III (Fig. 88).

[31] Luckenbill 1927, 72–73.

[32] N & R II, 11.

[33] K.F. Müller, *Mitteilungen der Vorderasiatische-aegyptischen Gesellschaft* 41, 3, 59 ff.

[34] Polish work in this area is reported in Paley and Sobolewski 1992, where the gate is mistakenly identified as consisting of 'lion-*lamassu*' (p. 35).

[35] Meuszynski 1981, plan 2.

[36] Illustrated in Mallowan 1966, fig. 62.

[37] ND 485, '1 homer, 2 *sutu*, 5 *sila*', Wiseman & Kinnier-Wilson 1951, 115.

[38] Wiseman & Kinnier-Wilson 1951, ND 805, 486; see also Postgate 1973, nos. 250–63. Postgate suggests an alternative reading, 'copper', for the original translation 'wool'. We are grateful to Christopher Walker for the information that the tablet is no longer sufficiently legible for the problem to be resolved.

[39] Mallowan 1951, pl. 10, 1.

[40] Mallowan 1966, 116.

[41] See footnote 39.

[42] We are extremely grateful to Muzahim Mahmud Hussein for his very helpful information about the recent excavations in the southern part of the North-West Palace.

[43] See Postgate 1973, pl. 97: i and j from Level I, and k from Level III.

[44] ND 485, attributed in the catalogue to 'Room HH, upper fill'; see also Wiseman & Kinnier Wilson 1951, 115.

[45] Postgate 1973, 261; Mallowan 1950, 178.

[46] Mallowan 1966, 118.

[47] Mallowan 1950, 180.

[48] Hussein and Abdul-Razaq 1997/1998.

[49] Hussein & Abdul-Razaq 1997/1998, no. 41.

[50] Hussein and Abdul-Razaq 1997/1998.

[51] Courtyard 65 is illustrated in Hussein, in press.

[52] N & R II, 15–16; Reade 1968, 70; see also Turner 1970, 198.

[53] N & R II, 14–17; Grayson 1996, 201.

[54] Illustrated in Gadd 1936, pl. 8, right.

[55] A plan and photographs appear in Meuszynski 1976, and Mierzejewski & Sobolewski 1980; other useful references include Reade 1968, 1980.

[56] Barnett & Falkner 1962; Meuszynski 1976; Mierzejewski & Sobolewski 1980.

[57] Barnett and Falkner 1962, 4; Reade 1980; Mallowan 1953, 5.

[58] As far as we can determine, the inscriptions remain unpublished; they are referred to as the 'Standard Inscription' of Assurnasirpal II, found also on his palace walls. This does not resolve the identification of the Centre Building, since the Standard Inscription appears both in palace and temple dedications (for example in the Ninurta Temple). Indeed, according to Grayson (1991, 268) 'a parallel text is included as part of most long inscriptions of Assurnasirpal'. Unfortunately it is the upper parts, that is, the more informative beginning, of the Centre Building inscriptions that are lost. The plan as known up to now is also unhelpful in determining the purpose of the building, though it does not suggest the usual lay-out of a palace.

[59] Mierzejewski & Sobolewski 1980, fig. 14.

[60] Tadmor 1994, 173.

[61] N & R II, 19.

[62] Mierzejewski & Sobolewski 1980, 'West Area II'; see also fig. 12.

[63] N & R II, 30. The best source for this building is the discussion by Falkner in Barnett & Falkner 1962, 20 ff.

[64] Mallowan 1952, 5.

[65] Some of the original walls were observed by Robert Hamilton when he carried out the survey of the mound in 1949 (comment published in Mallowan 1950).

[66] N & R II, 27.

[67] Falkner and Barnett 1962, 23.

[68] The most useful plan together with a discussion of the building can be found in Barnett and Falkner 1962. The plan of the southern suite constitutes Turner's Reception Suite Type C (1970, pl. 45).

[69] Illustrated in Barnett & Falkner 1962, pl. 109.

[70] A better-preserved though wrongly restored model from Nineveh is illustrated in Curtis and Reade 1996, 100, no. 44. This was found by George Smith, who uses its illustration on the cover of our American edition of *Assyrian Discoveries*.

[71] N & R I, 350, 376; II 26.

[72] A number of references from the annals of Tiglath-pileser III and several 7th century kings are listed in *CAD* (H), 184–84; see also Winter 1982, 357 ff.

[73] See the plan published in Loud and Altman 1938, pl. 75 and the plain, stone column bases, pl. 41.

[74] For the most recent plan of Sennacherib's palace at Nineveh, see Reade 2000, fig. 11, on which similar column bases have been restored.

CHAPTER THREE: TOMBS, WELLS AND RICHES

[1] This is clear in the Middle Assyrian laws, see for example Driver and Miles 1935, 407, section 40. It is interesting that there is no such requirement in the surviving Babylonian laws.

[2] Mallowan 1966, fig. 59.

[3] Illustrated in Mallowan 1966, 114.

[4] ND 1713, 1714; see Mallowan 1966, figs. 56, 57.

[5] Mallowan 1966, 114.

[6] The definitive publication on the tombs, *Nimrud, A City of Golden Treasures,* is now in press in Baghdad, by the excavator Muzahim Mahmud Hussein and the epigraphist, Amr Suleiman.

[7] Details of the skeletons themselves can be found in Schultz and Kunter 1998, summarised in Damerji 1999, 12. Note that Damerji 1999 appeared as an article in the same journal as Schultz and Kunter (1998), but was also published as a separate volume (1999).

[8] For a general discussion of fibulae with figural ornament, see Curtis 1994.

[9] Hussein, in press; the skeleton would appear to be Schultz & Kunter 1998, no. 2.

[10] Illustrated in Hussein, in press, fig. 10.

[11] Damerji 1999, fig. 19. See also Hussein and Suleiman, in press. A number of fascinating colour

photographs showing the objects in situ and in the interior of the sarcophagus itself are published in these volumes; see also Damerji 1991.

[12] We are very indebted to Jeremy Black for advice on the transliteration of this name, of which the literal meaning is 'Open up, chief porter'; the actual Neo-Assyrian dialect form written in the text is Biṭ.ukidigulu; for Pituh-idugallu, see Deller 1991.

[13] Fadhil 1990; Damerji 1999, 52 and fig. 19.

[14] Damerji 1991, fig. 3.

[15] Damerji 1999, figs. 20, 21.

[16] Crowfoot 1995, 113.

[17] Kathy Tubb in Crowfoot 1995.

[18] Illustrated in Damerji 1991, figs. 5,6. The mirror can be seen in situ in Damerji 1999, figs. 21.2 & 22.1.

[19] Information on the palaeopathology of the skeletons comes from the very detailed report of Schultz and Kunter 1998.

[20] Illustrated in Damerji 1991, Fig. 3.

[21] Visible in Damerji 1999, fig. 36.

[22] Fadhil 1990.

[23] Damerji 1999, fig. 39.

[24] We are indebted to Dominique Collon for the detailed description of this piece.

[25] Note that Grayson (1996, 201) remarks that this must be a eunuch of an earlier Adad-nerari, but he was unaware that these were secondary burials.

[26] Curtis 1983.

[27] Schultz and Kunter 1998, 124.

[28] Information from Schultz and Kunter 1998.

[29] Previously read *abarakku*.

[30] Published in *Sumer* 39, 1983 (Arabic section). We are grateful to Lamia al-Gailani Werr for information about Humaidat. A vaulted brick tomb at Til Barsip contained a terracotta coffin similar to that in Tomb IV at Nimrud (Bunnens 1997, fig. 5).

[31] These objects are illustrated in Mallowan 1966, chapter 9.

[32] Mallowan 1966, fig. 70.

[33] Published in Safar & al-Iraqi 1987.

[34] See Safar and al-Iraqi 1987.

[35] *Iraq* 38, 71.

[36] ND 2243 (Orchard 1967 ref) from well NN, and ND 7 IM 79575, see Safar and al-Iraqi 1987, pp. 126–27.

[37] The finds in Room AB are described in N & B 176–200; see also Curtis and Reade 1995, esp 134–47; the lens-like object is illustrated on p. 127.

[38] Wiseman 1955; Howard 1955; see also Fales & Postgate 1992, section 7.

[39] Illustrated in Curtis and Reade 1955, fig. 198.

[40] Payton 1991; see also Symington 1991.

[41] Wiseman 1955, n. 70.

[42] We are grateful to Georgina Herrmann for this information; the objects themselves remind us of the second millennium BC faience cosmetic containers from Tell al Rimah (D. Oates 1965, pls. 18b, 19a).

[43] The gold caps on this seal closely resemble one illustrated in Collon 1987, no. 391. Both seals have a design on the lower cap, in the case of the new example from Nimrud, a very fine figure of a horse (Hussein & Abdul-Razaq no. 36). See also p. 222 & n. 93, ch. 6.

[44] Adapted from Luckenbill 1926, and Grayson 1991, 252–53 (Monolith inscription).

CHAPTER FOUR: TEMPLES, MINOR PALACES AND PRIVATE HOUSES

[1] N & B 125–29, esp. plan 2 and p. 127.

[2] Smith 1875, 75.

[3] The name was originally read as *Ištar belit-mati*. See Grayson 1991, 283.

[4] Julian Reade reminds us that the Ninurta Temple inscription was referred to by Layard as the 'monolith inscription' whereas that on the stele was Rawlinson's 'Great Monolith inscription', a cause for some confusion in the references to these texts; see N & B 353, and Grayson 1991, text 1, p. 191, and text 17, p. 237. Rawlinson's Great Monolith was inscribed with over 568 lines of text.

[5] Grayson 1991, 291.

[6] Cole & Machinist 1998, letter 128.

[7] J. Oates 1974, pl. 28:5, found outside the entrance of the approximately contemporary shrine at Tell al Rimah; the entrance of the Nimrud temple is illustrated in N & B, opposite p. 361.

[8] The unidentified temples listed in the inscriptions are the temple of Enlil (referred to with that of Ninurta, and possibly the same building), Ea-šarru and his wife Damkina, the storm god Adad and his wife Šala, Gula (goddess of healing), Sin (the moon god), and the Sibitti (the Pleiades).

[9] Grayson 1991, 352.

[10] Grayson 1991, 304.

[11] Wiseman 1953, 149, ND 3491 and 3492.

[12] Mallowan 1966, 87.

[13] Compare, for example, the plans of the shrines of Nabu and Tašmetum, Fig. 67.

[14] We are grateful to Nicholas Postgate for the translation (following Borger *BiOr* 28, 1971, 66a):

1 NIR.GAL.ZU	takil-ka	He who trusts on you,
2 NU TEŠ	ul ibaš	shall not be put to shame,
3 ᵈAG		Nabu.

[15] Illustration in Mallowan 1966, fig. 198.

[16] Dalley & Postgate 1984, tablet 95 from room NE 50.

[17] Rassam 1897, 9–10; Smith 1875, 74; see also Gadd 1936, 150–51.

[18] Rassam 1897, 11, 14; text Grayson 1996, 180.

[19] ND 5400, Mallowan 1966, 266.

[20] Oates 1957, 29; Rassam 1897, 9–10; a drawing by Boutcher of one of the servant-figures can be found in Gadd 1936, pl. 8,1.

[21] Grayson 1996, 226, text 2002.

[22] Established during restoration work, Mahmud (Hussein) and Black 1985–86 (added to the Mallowan plan, Fig. 67).

[23] The new plan (Muzahim Mahmud Hussein 1995, 33) shows a wall blocking the west end of NTS 5; no trace of this was found in the 1950s, and there would appear to be no comment on this reconstruction in the 1995 text. However, the presence of a monumental (? *bit hilani*) entrance on the north side of NTS 15, discussed here, suggests that there must have been such external access.

[24] See note 23.

[25] Mahmud (Hussein) & Black 1985–86.

[26] These façades have now been restored, see Hussein 1995, 31.

[27] Mallowan & Glynne Davies 1970, pls. 8–9, 20–21, 44–45; also no. 85.

[28] For a more detailed description of the archaeological and textual evidence, see Oates 1957; the relevant texts are reconsidered in Postgate 1974, together with an important text from the Nabu Temple throne room (ND 4318, now in the Iraq Museum), which lists various rooms in the Ezida complex. The Esarhaddon letters are republished in Cole & Machinist 1998.

[29] Most recently published in Cole & Machinist 1998, no 78; see also Oppenheim 1967, 168.

[30] It is of interest that ND 4318 (see note 28) specifically lists a bedroom within the Ezida complex.

[31] Cole & Machinist 1998, no 56.

[32] Generally translated 'mayor' or 'inspector' of the Nabu Temple and, following Nicholas Postgate, the 'mayor of Kalhu'.

[33] Cole & Machinist 1998, no. 70, and see accompanying footnote; 'stretch' or 'release' his legs may be connected with the ritual 'footrace' (*lismu*) of Nabu, tempting though another interpretation may be.

[34] Parpola 1987, letters 110–13.

[35] Cole & Machinist 1998, letter 130.

[36] See Black and Green 1992, 136–37.

[37] We are grateful to Nicholas Postgate for the translation 'first fruits' (a form of offering), and for the translation 'polishing' in the final line.

[38] Cole & Machinist 1998, letter 134.

[39] Postgate 1974 (and see footnote 28).

[40] Cole & Machinist 1998, letters 82–123; see also Postgate 1974b, 7–18.

[41] See Chapter 6, p. 213.

[42] Curtis 1983a, fig. 2.

[43] The stratigraphic investigation of the Burnt Palace was carried out largely by John Reid, joined by David Oates in 1955.

[44] Oates & Reid 1956, 24.

[45] Oates & Reid 1956, pl. 4.

[46] For the location of these boxes see Oates & Reid 1956, fig. 2.

[47] The changes in plan are best seen in Oates & Reid 1956, figs. 1–3.

[48] ND 5005, ND 5004, illustrated in Oates & Oates 1958, pl. 24:8, pl. 28:15.

[49] Oates & Reid 1956, pl. 8.

[50] It is possible that some of these ivories were deliberately blackened (see discussion on p. 227).

[51] A number of these ivories are illustrated in Mallowan 1966, 212 ff.

[52] D. Oates 1958; N & R II, 38 ff.

[53] Oates 1958, 109–10. George Smith (1875, 79) describes a number of rooms on the south edge of the mound, presumably a part of this palace, served by a drain incorporating bricks of Shalmaneser III.

[54] Smith 1975, 78.

[55] Parker 1962, pl. 17:1.

[56] Illustrated in Mallowan 1950, pl. 30.

[57] Illustrated in Mallowan 1966, fig. 7.

[58] ND. 252, 240; Postgate 1973, nos. 170, 171 and pl. 95. Note that the wording of ND 240 closely parallels that on the stone inscription, Fig. 75.

[59] Note especially that palace ware beakers with ring bases, Mallowan 1966, 51; Mallowan 1950, pl. 32, can be compared with J. Oates 1959, nos. 16, 59, while an unpublished beaker is identical with no. 66. See also Fig 158, p. 252.

[60] The trench is illustrated on the plan, pl. 26, in Mallowan 1950; in this report the faience rosettes seem to be attributed to the lower level in the 1950 building itself, but see the report in the *ILN* of July 29th that year. There is no question but that this material is of Middle Assyrian date. See also Tucker 1992.

[61] ND. 3463, Wiseman 1953, 146. The tablet specifies only that the house is in Kalhu.

[62] The earliest dated tablet of Šamaš-šarru-uṣur is 666 BC, while 20 tablets are dated by post-canonical *limmu*. Of the latter, ND 3429 is dated by the *limmu* Bel-iqbi (sometime around 620 BC), while ND 3438 is possibly even later. The tablets are published in Wiseman 1953. See also p. 210 in this volume.

[63] Published in Lines (J. Oates) 1954.

[64] N & R II, 41; see also Mallowan 1952, 4; 1954, 139.

[65] Mallowan 1954, 69. The level is unfortunately not recorded, but was certainly either Level 3 or Level 2. My own memory and Mallowan's comment suggest Level 2, perhaps with the ivories in room 42, but I cannot be absolutely certain of this so many years later. I am certain, however, that it was part of the 612 BC destruction debris (J.O.).

[66] ND. 3467, room 33; see Wiseman 1954, 146.

[67] Illustrated in Mallowan 1954, pls. 33–34.

[68] Mallowan 1954, pls. 31, 32.

[69] Sections through some of the rooms, drawn by John Reid, are illustrated in Mallowan 1954, pl. 29.

[70] The plan of the Adad-nerari III palace is published in *Iraq* 16, 1954, pl. 35.

[71] ND 3419, Wiseman 1953, 140; ND 3301, 3302; see Parker 1955. Pl. 17:3; Neo-Babylonian stamp seals: Parker 1955, pl. 19:1,2,8.

[72] Mallowan 1954, 162.

[73] ND. 5498, 5302–03. The birds are illustrated in Mallowan 1957, pl. 11.

[74] The 'date before Sargon' favoured in Postgate & Reade, 1980, would seem unlikely, since the building post-dates, indeed actually cuts into, that to the west.

CHAPTER FIVE: FORT SHALMANESER – THE EKAL MAŠARTI

[1] ND 7054 and ND 7067, see Læssøe 1959, 39; in addition, a text from the *šakintu*'s archive (ND 7072) and one from SE 8 (ND 7010), all from the 1958 season (Dalley & Postgate 1984).

[2] The Nebi Yunus inscription is published by Alexander Heidel and Leo Oppenheim in Heidel 1956.

[3] The excavations here were directed by David Oates from 1958 to 1962, and in 1963 by Jeffery Orchard. Preliminary reports can be found in *Iraq* 21–25, 1959–63.

[4] We are indebted to John Curtis for this information.

[5] N & B 164–67.

[6] For the Esarhaddon cylinder inscriptions, see p. 216 and Læssøe 1959, n. 1

[7] Grayson 1975, Chronicle 3, pp. 92–94.

[8] Illustrated in Mallowan 1966, fig. 305.

[9] For further details, see Oates 1962, 4 ff.

[10] Grayson 1975, 93.

[11] See illustration in Mallowan 1966, fig. 380; a photograph of the inscription appears in Reade 1982, fig. 78.

[12] E.g. ND 10014, 10015 (Dalley and Postgate nos. 96, 97), which are chariot inventories but also refer to the replacement of both chariots and their component parts.

[13] ND 10082; Dalley & Postgate no. 117.

[14] Oates 1959, 109 and pl. 26; Oates 1961, 12.

[15] ND 6232–37. The inscriptions are identical with Grayson 1991, ANP text 26; the Shalmaneser text is Grayson 1996, text 1.

[16] The 41-line inscription is published by Kinnier-Wilson (1962) and in Grayson 1996, 58 ff. An alternative possibility is that there was a shrine of 'Adad of Kurbail' at Kalhu (Oates 1962, 16), but there is no mention of such a shrine in any surviving inscription.

[17] There is evidence for a handle at only one end of the Nimrud saw; we have, perhaps wrongly, assumed that it must have been a frame saw because of the difficulty of controlling a tool of this length. A similar iron saw is illustrated in N & B 159. Those on the Nineveh reliefs appear to have been true frame saws, see Layard *Monuments of Nineveh* II, pl. 12 (we are indebted to John Curtis for this reference.)

[18] For the analyses of the raw materials in the room, see Oates 1962, 17–18.

[19] Published in Dalley & Postgate 1983, texts 119–49.

[20] ND 10001, Dalley & Postgate 1983, text 103.

[21] Formerly read *abarakku;* for discussion of tablets, see Kinnier-Wilson 1972, 105 ff.

[22] Illustrated in Oates 1962, pl. 6b.

[23] ND 9222, a thin rectangular copper object with three longitudinal slots and a protruding knob, found by the jamb of the west door of NE 7.

[24] Illustrated in Oates 1961, pl. 5b.

[25] The other pieces in this group are illustrated in Mallowan 1966, figs. 443–448 and colour VII.

[26] Illustrated in Oates 1959, pl. 26a. There is a general description of the SE sector in this report.

[27] Inscription published in Læssøe 1958, 40; see also Oates 1959, 113 and pl. 27.

[28] ILN Jan 17, 1959, p. 100, fig. 7.

[29] ND 7520, 7527–29.

[30] Oates 1959, 112.

[31] ND 8159.

[32] Dalley & Postgate 1983, no. 27.

[33] Millard 1961.

[34] Laessøe 1959, 19, and see p. 145.

[35] This ivory is illustrated in Herrmann 1992, pl. 48:250.

[36] Indeed we know already, from the results of the Italian excavations in the late 1980s, that there exists another door on the east side of SW 37, approximately opposite the doorway to SW 10, and two doors to the west, and that the southern east-west magazine between SW 37 and SW 8 does not exist. Moreover, further rooms seem to have been constructed in the small south-east courtyard at the time of Esarhaddon. We are grateful to Paolo Fiorina for this information.

[37] ND 6231, cf Segal 1957, and p. 219.

[38] Illustrated in the *ILN,* Nov. 23, 1957, 874, fig. 13.

[39] For the most part these were removed from the ground by the Sharqatis and J.O., in 1958 with the assistance of Carroll Wales, who was responsible for the initial cleaning and preservation. A plan of the room was drawn by David Stronach (Oates 1959, fig. 1); see also Herrmann 1974, pp. 4–5.

[40] Orchard 1978; see also Brill 1978.

[41] ND 10150, 10151; Herrmann 1986, pl. 331; and see comments by Alan Millard in the catalogue to this volume, pp. 236–37.

[42] Herrmann 1986; Orchard 1967.

[43] Fiorina 1998, and in press.

[44] As depicted on a relief from Nineveh, N & B 647.

[45] A 9th century floor was identified in room T 4 (p. 179).
[46] Pl. 12c, and Fiorino 1998. The distance between the grooves in the FS throne room was 1.60 m.
[47] Grayson 1996, 139–40 (text 62).
[48] For further details of this Babylonian incident, see J. Oates 1986, 109–10. The epigraph 'labelling' this scene is published as Grayson 1996, text 59, p. 138.
[49] Munn-Rankin 1954, 86.
[50] Grayson 1996, 138.
[51] Parpola and Watanabe 1988, 4–5.
[52] The throne base reliefs are published in full in Oates 1963, and in Mallowan 1966, 448–49.
[53] Grayson 1996, 139.
[54] Further detail can be found in Oates 1963.
[55] Wiseman 1952, with correction from Læssøe 1958, n. 1; see also Millard 1962.
[56] For further discussion of this and other constructional problems in the throne room area, see Oates 1963.
[57] Oates 1962, 25–26.
[58] Mallowan 1966, fig. 582.
[59] For fuller description, see Oates 1962, 27.
[60] Report published in *Iraq* 55, see Curtis et al. 1993.
[61] His inscriptions were found on doorsills between T 21 and T 27 (2 slabs), in the north-east entrance to T 27, the central doorway on the west side of T 25, the north doorway between T 25 and T 26, and on the small slab which housed the bolt of the south door of T 23.
[62] A possibly similar suite of rooms can be found in the North-West Palace, west of court Y, opening onto a terrace further to the west.
[63] In room T 22 glazed crenellation bricks had been used to create a waterproof dado along an area of wall adjacent to the stone paving slabs, along the west and on part of the south wall, but this was not their primary context; indeed no attention had been paid to the original pattern.
[64] Heidel 1956, 33; CAD, vol. M, 406, for *matgiqu*.
[65] N & B 164–67. Some of these glazed bricks, which probably date from the time of Esarhaddon, are now in the British Museum.
[66] Detailed descriptions of the panel itself and the process of reconstruction can be found in Reade 1963.
[67] Curtis et al. 1993, 26–27 and figs. 21–26.
[68] Dalley & Postgate 1984, 11.
[69] Læssøe 1959, 40.
[70] The wall paintings are further discussed in Oates 1959; note that the position of the hands has been corrected in the later drawing, reproduced here, following Oates 1959.
[71] For a list of the foundation boxes found in the S sector, see Oates 1959, n. 29.
[72] Herrmann 1992, pls. 1–12.
[73] J. Oates 1959, pl. 38: 87, 90, 91.
[74] 85 pieces are published in Herrmann 1992, from the 1958 and 1960 seasons, and it should perhaps be noted that at the same time hundreds of ivories from SW 37 were catalogued in the 1958 season alone.
[75] See Herrmann 1992, pl. 39.
[76] Illustrated in Mallowan 1966, fig. 367.
[77] Cole & Machinist 1999, letters 81–133, and see p. 123, this volume.
[78] Perhaps illustrated most strikingly in Oates 1963, pl. 3b.

CHAPTER SIX: THE WRITTEN EVIDENCE
[1] BM 12334, found by Rawlinson in 1852 (Gadd 1936, 82); see also Tadmor 1994, 193.
[2] Instrumental in this conservation in the 1950s and 60s was Mr C.A. Bateman of the Department of Western Asiatic Antiquities (now 'Ancient Near East').
[3] II Kings xv:19, an identification first made by Schrader in 1878, see Tadmor 1994, 280, n. 5.
[4] Grayson 1991, 282.
[5] Most recently Grayson 1991, 1996; Tadmor 1994. The later inscriptions, not as yet covered in the Toronto series, can be found most conveniently in English in Luckenbill 1927. There are also several more recent German editions of the Assyrian royal texts, see Borger 1956, 1996; Fuchs 1994; Frahm 1997.

[6] Saggs 1955, 24. A more detailed discussion of this period in Babylonia can be found in J. Oates 1986, chs. 4–5. See also letter 66, Saggs 1963, 73, and Saggs 2001.

[7] Saggs 1963, 72.

[8] II Kings xx.12; Is. xxxix.1.

[9] Gadd 1953, 130; Frame 1995, 149. The 'substitute' document is now at Yale. See also Tadmor 1997, 333–34.

[10] Gadd 1953; Mallowan 1966, fig. 107. For (Nabu)-mukin-zeri and Marduk-apla-iddina, and for the Sargon cylinder from Warka, see Frame 1995, pp. 132, 135, 146.

[11] Gadd 1954.

[12] ND 3411, see Gadd 1954, 198 ff.

[13] Saggs 1955; see also Parpola 1987, letters 171–176.

[14] Originally translated 'jump around', i.e. 'beat them up', but we are indebted to Nicholas Postgate for the information that this should be read as 'grovel'.

[15] Saggs 1956; see also the offer by the Assyrian *rab šaqe* to the people of Jerusalem to transport them to a fruitful "land like their own land", II Kings xviii. See also Gallagher 1994, 57.

[16] Saggs 1958, ND 2759; see now Postgate 1973, 21 f. and Parpola 1987, letter 1.

[17] Postgate 1973, 29.

[18] Preliminary publication in Wiseman 1953; Parker 1954.

[19] Parker 1961, 18–21.

[20] ND 2307. Parker 1954, 37. The *šakintu* official seems to have been responsible for the supervision of the domestic wing of the palace; see also the archive of a *šakintu* in Fort Shalmaneser, p. 213.

[21] Postgate 1979, 99–103. This is, of course, the North-West Palace *šakintu*.

[22] Deller and Fadhil 1993.

[23] Millard 1994, 120; see also p. 19.

[24] ND 815, Wiseman and Kinnier Wilson 1951; Postgate 1973, no. 247. The 1951 tablets from the NWP are published in Postgate 1973, 230 ff.

[25] ND 814, see Wiseman 1951. With reference to the large quantities of wool, see ch. 2, n. 38.

[26] The conservation and restoration work was carried out by Mr. C.A. Bateman.

[27] For further details see Wiseman 1958, 5.

[28] Watanabe 1985; George 1986; Collon 1987, 131.

[29] An institution which at Assur seems to have been closely associated with the *bit alim*.

[30] George 1986, 140–41.

[31] Wiseman 1958, 21.

[32] The translation follows Wiseman 1958, with slight emendation following Parpola & Watanabe 1988.

[33] See Grayson CAH, 140, and discussion above, chapter 1, p. 24.

[34] Wiseman & Black 1996.

[35] Mahmud & Black 1985–86.

[36] ND 5417, Wiseman & Black 1996, 4. Grayson (1996, 172) suggests a possible attribution to Shalmaneser III.

[37] Wiseman & Black 1996, n. 41.

[38] See Curtis & Reade 1995, no. 219 (K8520); the obverse of Fig. 125 can be found in Mallowan 1962, Fig. 256.

[39] Parker 1957.

[40] Wiseman & Black 1996, 5.

[41] Discussed in Postgate 1973, 17–18.

[42] Postgate 1973, no. 170, and comment on 171.

[43] See preliminary publication of the tablets by Wiseman 1953: the *limmu* Bel-iqbi, ND. 3429, is found in a text which is unequivocally dated to the time of Sin-šar-iškun (Fig. 70).

[44] Wiseman 1953, 136.

[45] The tablets from Fort Shalmaneser are published in Kinnier-Wilson 1972 and Dalley & Postgate 1984. We owe the information contained in this section to the authors of these two volumes, and to the information provided by Professors D.J. Wiseman and J. Læssøe at the time of the excavations.

[46] Dalley & Postgate 1984, text 12, and see note 50.

[47] Cole & Machinist 1998.

[48] Cole & Machinist 1998, letter 107.

[49] On the basis of the name of the officer in charge, Dalley & Postgate suggest a date of the time of

Sargon (p. 74), but the same name appears in the *rab ekalli*'s archive as a witness in text 17, dated by a post-canonical *limmu*.

[50] Inter alia ND 7001, dated by the *limmu* Aššur-matu-taqqin, from the *rab ekalli*'s bathroom; = Dalley and Postgate 1984, no. 6. ND 7010, which refers specifically to the military use of the palace, is dated by the same *limmu* (Dalley & Postgate no. 12).

[51] Dalley & Postgate 1984, texts 1–5, 28, 84.

[52] Dalley & Postgate 1984, texts 1–27.

[53] Dalley & Postgate 1984, texts 20–22; Parker 1962, 38.

[54] ND 7032, ND 7033, Dalley & Postgate 1984, nos 21, 22.

[55] Dalley & Postgate 1984, no. 75.

[56] Dalley & Postgate 1984, texts 28–45.

[57] Text 39, Dalley & Postgate 1984. For the post-canonical *limmu*, see Whiting in Millard 1994, 75.

[58] Discussed in extensive detail in Kinnier-Wilson 1972; see also Dalley & Postgate 1984, 22–25 and texts 119–49.

[59] The calculation of equivalent weights and measures is far from straightforward. This figure, based on our own measurements at Nimrud, carried out by filling two different jars with grain, established a *qa* of 1.83 or 1.84 litres (Parker 1957, 127–28; Oates 1959, 103). See also p. 167, this volume. Nicholas Postgate argues for a *qa* of .84 litres, but this is based on an Old Babylonian jar from Tell al Rimah (Postgate 1978). Our experience of Iraq at the time of the Nimrud excavations showed that even in recent times measures varied from one city to another. A *qa* of similar size to that measured by us at Nimrud is reported also from Nippur (Postgate 1978, 74–75).

[60] D. Oates 1959, n. 10; and see n. 59.

[61] In Kinnier-Wilson 1972, xiv.

[62] Kinnier-Wilson 1972, 135.

[63] Kinnier-Wilson 1972; Mallowan questions this suggestion, noting that feeding in messes would not always have been a practical proposition (ibid. p. x). Dalley and Postgate 1984, 24, note the fact that the wine lists and the horse lists are sometimes found together, suggesting the possibility that the same event in the military calendar gave rise to the muster of equids and the feasting of the army with members of the royal family and foreign emissaries. For the Sargon of Agade quotation, see Frayne 1993, 29.

[64] See also p. 148.

[65] Dalley & Postgate 1984, texts 85, 98–118.

[66] Dalley & Postgate, tablet 103. The horse lists are published on pp. 7–22, 167–235.

[67] Oates 1962, 24; Heidel 1956.

[68] Dalley & Postgate 1984, 27 ff.

[69] Wiseman 1952; Millard 1961; Hulin 1962.

[70] Oates 1963, 33.

[71] Wiseman 1952, line 42, originally read *ekal mahirti*; see Læssøe 1959, Millard 1961, n. 13.

[72] Time of Tiglath-Pileser I (1114–1076 BC), see Grayson 1991, 34.

[73] Millard & Bordreuil 1982; text also published in Grayson 1991, 389.

[74] This date is partly based on the assumption that the father of the ruler celebrated in the inscription is the same Šamaš-nuri as the eponym for 866 BC (Millard and Bordreuil 1982, 139).

[75] Note by Alan Millard in Curtis et al. 1993, 35–37.

[76] The alphabetic inscriptions are discussed in Millard 1962.

[77] Millard 1962, 45–49; see also Herrmann 1986, 236.

[78] Segal 1957.

[79] Layard 1849a, pl. 85.

[80] Kinnier-Wilson 1972, 138, text 9.

[81] Millard 1972. There are also Aramaic epigraphs on 5 dockets from Tell Halaf and 6 from Assur.

[82] Millard 1972; 1983.

[83] Dalley & Postgate 1984, 2.

[84] See also the inventories of tablets and writing boards published in Fales & Postgate 1992, section 7.

[85] Wiseman 1955.

[86] ND 2653.

[87] A *mušhuššu* brick is illustrated in Curtis & Reade 1995, 107.

[88] For the glass vase inscribed with the name of Sargon, see p. 238; the electrum example is published in Damerji 1991, Fig. 3. The image of a scorpion was also engraved on an alabaster vase found at Assur,

belonging to the wife of Sennacherib (Andrae 1904, 12).

[89] See p. 79; also Parker 1955, fig. 2.

[90] Sachs 1953; Herbordt 1992, 123–45.

[91] Herbordt 1996.

[92] N & B title page and 154, 161.

[93] We are indebted to Dominique Collon for information about this sealing; the caps, which were horizontally ridged, may well have resembled Collon 1987, 391, 359. See now also the new seal, with a similarly ornamented cap, from the well in courtyard 80 (NWP) (Hussein & Abdul-Razaq 1997/1998, no. 36).

[94] ND 7050.

[95] Parker 1955, 111.

[96] Seal of Bel-tarṣi-iluma; Parker 1955, pl. 21, 1; see also Postgate 1973, pl. 95.

[97] Illustrated in Collon 1987, seal 342; see also Grayson 1996, 229.

[98] Parker 1962, pl. 22, 2 and fig. 10 (ND 7001).

[99] Seal styles are not discussed in detail in this volume, since there is a large literature on this subject. The general reader is referred to the section by D. Collon in Curtis & Reade 1995. The Nimrud seals and sealings have been published by B. Parker (1955, 1962).

[100] Parker 1962, pls. 13–15, 16, 17.

[101] These different styles are clearly illustrated in the section on seals and sealings by D. Collon in Curtis & Reade 1995.

[102] Hussein & Abdul-Razaq 1997/1998.

[103] An example is illustrated in colour in Curtis & Reade 1995, fig. 193.

[104] Parker 1955, pl. 19:1,7,8.

[105] A number of examples are illustrated in Parker 1955, pls. 20–29, some of which bear impressions of both cylinder and stamp seals.

[106] Mallowan 1950, 173.

[107] Dalley & Postgate 1984, 74, dockets 21–23; see also the section on writing-boards, p. 219.

[108] Postgate 1973, pl. 96:173.

CHAPTER SEVEN: TYPES OF OBJECT AND MATERIALS FROM NIMRUD

[1] These are described as circular in all the excavation catalogues, but in the early seasons we never found a complete example. According to Georgina Herrmann and Dominique Collon the Nimrud boxes are not truly circular but are flat on one side, owing to the sub-circular tusk cavity.

[2] Grayson 1991, 217, from the lengthy inscription on the stone slabs in the Ninurta Temple..

[3] For manufacturing details see the notes by H.J. Plenderleith, in Mallowan 1966, 139–41.

[4] For a study on the effect of burning on ivory, see Robins et al. 1983; see also discussion in Herrmann 1986, 60. A number of the Burnt Palace ivories are illustrated in Mallowan 1966, 212 ff.

[5] ND. 1677.

[6] The recent ivory publications are listed in the bibliography and include Orchard 1967, Mallowan and Glynne Davies 1970, Mallowan & Herrmann 1974, Herrmann 1986, Herrmann 1992; see also Safar & al-Iraqi 1987.

[7] See Herrmann 1992, 3, n. 5.

[8] Curtis et al. 1993, fig. 20.

[9] Illustrated in Herrmann 1992, no. 178.

[10] Oates 1961, 14 and pl. 8; Mallowan 1966, figs. 321–30.

[11] Inter alia, Curtis 1996, 175.

[12] Illustrated in Barnett & Falkner 1961, pls. 8, 18.

[13] N & B 198–200; some of the British Museum pieces are illustrated in Curtis & Reade 1995, 124–25.

[14] Compare N & B 198 and 200, reconstructed in Curtis & Reade 1995, 126.

[15] Safar & al-Iraqi 1987, figs. 93–96.

[16] These objects are illustrated in Curtis 1996, and N & B 179; see also B. Mallowan 1993, pl. 67. For 3 bronze lions' paws from a possible 3-legged table, see Curtis & Reade 1995, 126.

[17] Porada 1973, pl. 1a & fig. 5.

[18] Curtis 1996, 179.

[19] See for example the Rassam Obelisk of Assurnasirpal II, Reade 1980, pl. 3.

[20] For plan, see Oates 1959, fig. 1; also Mallowan & Herrmann 1974, 4–5.

[21] Illustrated in Mallowan & Herrmann 1974, pls. 106, 107. The possibility of a join between the two pieces has been questioned, largely owing to the apparently excessive width, but it was very clear at the time of excavation (and indeed this still shows on the photographs) that they constitute a single long strip.

[22] The major study of Near Eastern glass is Oppenheim et al. 1970. The Nimrud and Nuzi glass is published in this volume; for the Brak glass see Oates et al. 1997. A report on the Nimrud glass by Von Saldern is appended to Mallowan 1966.

[23] See Barag in Oppenheim et al 1970, figs. 45, 46.

[24] See discussion in Curtis 1999; also von Saldern in Mallowan 1966, figs. 593–94.

[25] Curtis 1999.

[26] Orchard 1978; Brill 1978.

[27] We are indebted to Dominique Collon for information about this important object. A rim fragment of clear glass with similar rosette inlay was found in Fort Shalmaneser, room SE 13 (von Saldern in Mallowan 1966, fig. 590).

[28] Curtis & Reade 1995, fig. 89.

[29] See also Damerji 1999, fig. 30; Moorey 1994, 214–15.

[30] Ogden 2000, 166.

[31] Turner 1955, 58.

[32] See chapter 8. Von Saldern assumes that these kilns are Assyrian (Mallowan 1966, 633), but their post-Assyrian position is made clear on the section published in Oates and Reid 1956, where the 'heavy ash deposit' is associated with these kilns. For the analysis of the red glass, see Plenderleith in Turner 1955, 67. See also p. 265.

[33] Damerji 1999, fig. 41, in the background of the photograph; the frit part of the vessel appears to have moulded figures on the outside, but this part of the photograph is not very clear.

[34] Parker 1962, pl. 11:4 (correctly described as ND 4164 on p. 30, but mistakenly illustrated as no. 4 on pl. 11). Seals are further discussed in chapter 6.

[35] Mallowan 1950, 174; see also *ILN* July 29, 1950. The excavation catalogue attributes them to the 1950 Building, Room VII, Level III, but these are undoubtedly from a Middle Assyrian deposit beneath the building. The faience pieces could date from anytime in the 13th–12th century BC, perhaps even slightly later.

[36] At sites like Nuzi, Alalakh, Tell al Rimah and Tell Brak; for discussion see Moorey 1994, Oates et al. 1997. Polychrome glazed vessels were virtually unknown before the Late Assyrian period.

[37] ND. 3125, cf Mallowan 1954, 151.

[38] N & R II, 13. See also p. 59 and Curtis et al. 1993.

[39] Curtis & Reade 1995, 104.

[40] Oates 1959, 127–29.

[41] For 'castanets', see Barnett 1963; Curtis & Reade 1995, 169.

[42] The gold jewellery is published by Curtis & Maxwell-Hyslop (1971).

[43] Grayson 1991, 291.

[44] The beaker is illustrated in colour in Curtis & Reade 1995, 143; see also J. Oates 1954, pl. 34b. The gadrooned bowl is illustrated, together with the beaker, in Mallowan 1966, 428–29.

[45] The name reads 'Sandasarmas', a 7th century (?) king of Cilicia. See Hawkins 2000, 570, no. XII. 15; pl. 327.

[46] Illustrated in Mallowan 1966, fig. 70 (ND 2180), there described as 'bronze'.

[47] Grayson 1991, 18, from Shalmaneser III's 'Kurkh monument'.

[48] Six of these are illustrated in colour in Curtis & Reade 1995, figs. 100–105.

[49] Stronach 1959, pl. 51:10–12; this paper provides a general discussion of bronze fibulae, as well as publishing some examples from Nimrud.

[50] See also Curtis 1994.

[51] Hussein, in press. More elaborate bronze fibulae do exist, decorated for example with images of the demon Pazuzu and birds of prey, as are the gold fibulae, but we know of none from Nimrud (see Curtis and Reade 1995, 174).

[52] The metal objects from the 1957 season are published by Stronach (1958); a number of projectile types are illustrated here.

[53] Curtis, Collon & Green 1993.

[54] See p. 53, and Curtis & Reade 1995, 193.

[55] Illustrated in Mallowan 1966, 146–47.

[56] ND 2177, from ZT.

[57] We owe this information to John Curtis.

[58] See Fiorina 1998.

[59] Illustrated in Curtis & Reade 1995, 176.

[60] Curtis & Reade 1995, 172–73.

[61] Curtis & Reade 1995, 144–45.

[62] Illustrated in Stronach 1958, pl. 35:1.

[63] For example, a dagger from T 20 (Curtis et al. 1993, Fig. 17; and an iron (?steel) sword from S 67.

[64] ND 9021–9079.

[65] Stronach 1958.

[66] Quoted from the 'Kurkh Monolith', found in 1861 near modern Diyarbakr in southeastern Turkey (Grayson 1992, 259). Kashiyari (Kašiiari) is the Assyrian term for the modern Tur Abdin.

[67] Oates 1962, 17 (ND 10987). A similar saw was found by Layard (N & B, 195) (see also note 17, ch. 5).

[68] There is much literature on this subject; see, inter alia, Moorey 1986; Curtis & Reade 1995, 161 ff; J. Oates, in press.

[69] Those from T 20 in the *ekal mašarti* are illustrated in Curtis et al, 1993, fig. 15. See also discussion in Curtis and Reade 1995, 161 ff.

[70] Large numbers of these and the cheekpieces are published in Orchard 1967.

[71] This comment refers not only to assertions made in the preliminary excavation reports but also to the comments in J. Oates 1954, referring to 'Sargonid material in the ziggurrat area', and 'Sargonid levels' generally, especially in the Burnt Palace.

[72] J. Oates 1959. Some Middle Assyrian sherds were recovered in the deep soundings, and surface sherds of painted Ninevite 5 attribution have been found, especially on the south-east area of the mound.

[73] The production of these vessels is discussed in Rawson 1954.

[74] Oates 1959, nos. 20, 27–29, 59.

[75] Animal-headed drinking cups are discussed in Curtis 2000.

[76] Oates 1959, 134.

[77] Hussein, in press, fig. 27.

[78] See Oates 1959, no. 16; red tripod vessels were also common in the Town Wall houses. Small cosmetics bottles from Fort Shalmaneser can be found on pl. 38.

[79] Oates 1959, pl. 36 and esp. 43–48.

[80] For colour photographs of these lamp types see Curtis & Reade 1995, 160; other Nimrud pottery types are illustrated in this catalogue, including several *istikanat* (p. 155).

[81] Mallowan 1954, pl. 19; Green 1983, pl. 13.

[82] N & R II, 37.

[83] Recently illustrated in Curtis and Reade 1995, 116.

[84] Mallowan 1966, 146–47.

[85] Illustrated in Mallowan 1966, fig. 359. The companion piece was not a lion-headed figure, pace Green 1983, 95; the *lahmu* and 'dog' pair are catalogued as ND 8183.

[86] See p. 143 and Mallowan 1957, 24 and pl. 11,2.

[87] ND 5296.

[88] 1983, 89.

CHAPTER EIGHT: POST-ASSYRIAN NIMRUD

[1] The Fort Shalmaneser pottery is published in J. Oates 1959.

[2] Oates 1961, 10–11; 1962, 1–13.

[3] Grayson 1975, 97 (chronicle 4). For a discussion of the possible post-612 BC role of the Babylonians and the Medes in this area, see Curtis 1997, 14, and Dandamayev 1997, 41.

[4] In Babylonia cuneiform writing remained in use as the learned language of mathematics and astronomy until the first century AD (see, inter alia, J. Oates 1986, 143), but no post-seventh century tablets have been found in Assyria with one possible (unreadable) exception, from Tell Fisna on the upper Tigris, possibly of Hellenistic date (Black 1997). Among the very small number of objects from Nimrud that we believe to be of this date, are pottery vessels found in the area of the Burnt Palace and above the AB Palace; these include Oates & Oates 1958, pl. 28:13, 14, and esp. 18, and pl. 24:4, 28; see also p.

119. For a further comment on Assyria at this time, see Oates 1968, 58 ff.

[5] Xenophon, *Anabasis,* III, 4; translation from Warner 1949, 118.

[6] Oates 1986, 139.

[7] N & R I, 352–53; II, 17–25; Smith 1875, 80.

[8] Illustrated in Mallowan 1957, pl. 6, 1.

[9] The coins are published in Jenkins 1958.

[10] Jenkins 1958, pl. 31:1; the seals are illustrated in Parker 1962, pls. 16–17.

[11] Illustrated in Oates & Oates 1958, pl. 19:c; the metal objects are published in Stronach 1958.

[12] Illustrated in Oates & Oates 1958, pl. 19:b.

[13] Oates & Oates 1958, 120 and footnote.

[14] Oates & Oates 1958, 123, and cf. Pl. 24:8.

[15] The Level 1 pottery types include Oates & Oates 1958, pl. 21:13, 15; pl. 23:32–4; pl. 24: pl. 14–17.

[16] This pottery is published in full in Oates & Oates 1958, and the illustrations are repeated in Oates 1968.

[17] For example, Oates & Oates 1958, pls. 21:3, 23:9.

[18] Oates & Oates Pl. 23:18.

[19] Mallowan 1957, pl. 6,2.

[20] *Anabasis* III, 4.

[21] Mallowan 1977, 251.

[22] H.E. Dr. Naji al-Asil, *Sumer* 1956, 3.

[23] N & R I, 353.

CHRONOLOGY

Assur-uballit I	1363–1328 BC	Sennacherib	704–681
Shalmaneser I	1273–1244	Esarhaddon	680–669
Tukulti-Ninurta I	1243–1207	Assurbanipal	668–627 (?)
Tiglath-pileser I	1114–1076	Assur-etel-ilani	626–623 (?)
Adad-nerari II	911–891	Sin-šumu-lišir	623 (?)
Tukulti-Ninurta II	890–884	Sin-šar-iškun	–612
Assurnasirpal II	883–359	Assur-uballit	611–609
Shalmaneser III	858–824		
Šamši-Adad V	823–811	*Babylonian rulers mentioned in text:*	
Adad-nerari III	810–783	Marduk-zakir-šumi I c. 854–819	
Shalmaneser IV	782–773	Marduk-balassu-iqbi c. 818–813	
Assur-dan III	772–755	Nabu-mukin-zeri	731–729
Assur-nerari V	754–745	Merodach-Baladan II	721–710
Tiglath-pileser III	744–727	Šamaš-šum-ukin	667–648
Shalmaneser V	726–722	Kandalanu	647–627
Sargon II	721–705		

RECOMMENDED GENERAL READING

Curtis, J.E. and J.E. Reade (eds) 1995. *Art and Empire, Treasures from Assyria in the British Museum*. London: British Museum Press.

Damerji, Muayyad Said Basim 1998. *Gräber Assyrischer Königinnen aus Nimrud, Jahrbuch des Römisch-Germanischen Zentralmuseums* 45, 1998; and 1999, Department of Antiquities and Heritage, Baghdad and Römisch-Germanischen Zentralmuseum, Mainz.

Layard, Austen Henry 1849. *Nineveh and its Remains* (2 vols). London: John Murray.

Layard, Austen Henry 1853. *Discoveries in the Ruins of Nineveh and Babylon*. London: John Murray.

Mallowan, M.E.L. 1966. *Nimrud and its Remains* (2 vols). London: Collins.

Oates, David 1968. *Studies in the Ancient History of Northern Iraq*. The British Academy: Oxford University Press.

Saggs, H.W.F. 1984. *The Might that was Assyria*. London: Sidgwick & Jackson.

Abbreviations:

CAD	Chicago *Assyrian Dictionary*.
CAH	*Cambridge Ancient History*, III, 2, 1991.
N & R I, II	Layard 1849.
N & B	Layard 1853.
NWP	North-West Palace.

BIBLIOGRAPHY

Abu es-Soof, Behnam 1963. Further Investigations in Assurnasirpal's Palace, *Sumer* 19, 66–73.

Agha, Abdallah Amin 1985–86. Notes on the plan of the Nabu Temple, Nimrud, *Sumer* 44, 42–47 (Arabic section).

Agha, A.A. and M.S. al-Iraqi 1976. *Nimrud.* Baghdad.

Ainachi, Mahmud 1956. Reconstruction and Preservation of Monuments in Northern Iraq, *Sumer* 12, 124–32 (Arabic section).

Albenda, P. 1991. Decorated Assyrian Knob-Plates in the British Museum, *Iraq* 53, 43–53.

Andrae, W. 1904. Aus zwölf Briefen von W. Andrae, *Mitteilungen der Deutsche Orientgeschellschaft* 21, 10–38.

Barnett, R.D. 1956. *Catalogue of the Nimrud Ivories in the British Museum.* London.

Barnett, R.D. 1963. Hamath and Nimrud, *Iraq* 25, 81–85.

Barnett, R.D. and M. Falkner 1962. *The Sculptures of Aššur-nasir-apli II, Tiglath-Pileser III, Esarhaddon, from the Central and South-West Palaces at Nimrud.* London: British Museum.

Black, Jeremy 1997. Hellenistic Cuneiform Writing from Assyria: The Tablet from Tell Fisna, *Al-Rafidan* 18, 229–38.

Black, Jeremy and Anthony Green 1992. *Gods, Demons and Symbols of Ancient Mesopotamia.* London: British Museum Press.

Borger, R. 1956. *Die Inschriften Asarhaddons, Königs von Assyrien.* Graz.

Borger, R. 1996. *Beiträge zum Inschriftenwerk Assurbanipals.* Wiesbaden.

Brill, R.J. 1978. Some Miniature Glass Plaques from Fort Shalmaneser, Nimrud, *Iraq* 40, 23–39.

Brinkman, J.A. 1991. Babylonia in the shadow of Assyria (747–626 BC), *CAH*, 1–70.

Brinkman, J.A. 1993. Babylonian Influence in the Šeh Hamad Texts Dated Under Nebuchadnezzar II, *State Archives of Assyria Bulletin* 7, 133–38.

Budge, E.A. Wallis 1920. *By Nile and Tigris* II. London: John Murray.

Bunnens, G. 1997. Til Barsip under Assyrian Domination, in Parpola & Whiting (eds), 17–28.

Cole, Steven W. & Peter Machinist 1998. *Letters from Priests to the Kings Esarhaddon and Assurbanipal.* State Archives of Assyria 13. Helsinki University Press.

Collon, Dominique 1987. *First Impressions. Cylinder Seals in the Ancient Near East.* London: British Museum Press.

Collon, Dominique 1995. "Filling Motifs", in U. Finkbeiner, R. Dittmann and H. Hauptmann (eds), *Beiträge zur Kulturgeschichte Vorderasiens*, 69–76. Mainz: Verlag Philipp von Zabern.

Crowfoot, Elisabeth 1995. Textiles from Recent Excavations at Nimrud, with contributions by M.C. Whiting and Kathryn Tubb, *Iraq* 57, 113–18.

Curtis, John 1983. Late Assyrian Bronze Coffins, *Anatolian Studies* 33, 85–93.

Curtis, J.E. 1983a. Some Axe-heads from Chagar Bazar and Nimrud, *Iraq* 45, 73–81.

Curtis, John 1992. Recent British Museum Excavations in Assyria, *Journal of the Royal Asiatic Society*, 3rd series 2, 147–65.

Curtis, J.E. 1994. Assyrian fibulae with figural decoration, in M. Dietrich & O. Loretz (eds), *Beschreiben und Deuten in der Archäologie des Alten Orients*, Altertumskunde des Vorderen Orients 4, 49–62.

Curtis, John 1995. "Stützfiguren" in Mesopotamia, in U. Finkbeiner, R. Dittmann and H. Hauptmann (eds), *Beiträge zur Kulturgeschichte Vorderasiens*, 77–86. Mainz: Verlag Philipp von Zabern.

Curtis, John 1996. Assyrian Furniture: the Archaeological Evidence, in Herrmann (ed), 167–80.

Curtis, John (ed) 1997. *Mesopotamia and Iran in the Persian Period: conquest and Imperialism 539–331 BC*. British Museum Press.

Curtis, John 1999. Glass inlays and Nimrud ivories, *Iraq* 61, 59–69.

Curtis, John 2000. Animal-headed Drinking Cups in the Late Assyrian Period, in R. Dittmann, B. Hrouda, U. Löw, P. Matthiae, R. Mayer-Opificius & S. Thürwächter (eds), *Vario Delectat, Iran und der Westen, Gedenkschrift für Peter Calmeyer*. Alter Orient und Altes Testament 272, 193–213. Münster: Ugarit-Verlag.

Curtis, John, D. Collon and A. Green 1993. British Museum Excavations at Nimrud and Balawat in 1989, *Iraq* 55, 1–37.

Curtis, J.E. and K.R. Maxwell-Hyslop 1971. The Gold Jewellery from Nimrud, *Iraq* 33, 101–12.

Curtis, J.E. and J.E. Reade (eds) 1995. *Art and Empire, Treasures from Assyria in the British Museum*. London: British Museum Press.

Dalley, S. & J.N. Postgate 1984. *The Tablets from Fort Shalmaneser*. Cuneiform Texts from Nimrud III. BSAI.

Damerji, Muayyad Said 1991. The Second Treasure of Nimrud, in M. Mori, H. Ogawa and M. Yoshikawa (eds), *Near Eastern Studies, Dedicated to H.I.H. Prince Takahito Mikasa on the Occasion of His Seventy-Fifth Birthday*, 9–16.

Damerji, Muayyad Said Basim 1998. Gräber Assyrischer Königinnen aus Nimrud. *Jahrbuch des Römisch-Germanischen Zentralmuseums* 45, 1–84.

Damerji, Muayyad Said Basim 1999. *Gräber Assyrischer Königinnen aus Nimrud*. Baghdad: Department of Antiquities and Heritage, and Mainz: Römisch-Germanischen Zentralmuseum.

Dandamayev, M. 1997. Assyrian Traditions during Achaemenid Times, in Parpola & Whiting (eds), 41–48.

Deller, Karlheinz 1966. Neo-Assyrian Epigraphic Remains of Nimrud, *Orientalia* 35, 179–94.

Deller, Karlheinz 1991. On some Names of some Divine Doorkeepers, *NABU* 14–16.

Deller, Karlheinz and Abdulillah Fadhil 1993. Neue Nimrud-Urkunden des 8. Jahrhunderts v. chr., *Baghdader Mitteilungen* 24, 243–70.

Deller, Karlheinz and Alan R. Millard 1993. Die Bestallungsurkunde des Nergal-apil-kumuja von Kalhu, *Baghdader Mitteilungen* 24, 217–42.

Dezsö, Tamas and John Curtis 1991. Assyrian Iron Helmets from Nimrud now in the British Museum, *Iraq* 53, 105–26.

Bibliography

Driver, G.R. & J.C. Miles 1935. *The Assyrian Laws*. Oxford: Clarendon Press.

Fadhil, Abdulillah 1990. Die in Nimrud/Kalhu aufgefundene Grabinschrift der Jaba, *Baghdader Mitteilungen* 21, 461–70.

Fadhil, Abdulillah 1990a. Die Grabinschrift der Mullissu-mukannišat-Ninua aus Nimrud/Kalhu und andere in ihrem Grab gefundene Schriftträger, *Baghdader Mitteilungen* 21, 471–82.

Fales, F.M. & J.N. Postgate 1992. *Imperial Administrative Records* I. *Palace and Temple Administration*. State Archives of Assyria VII. Helsinki.

Fiorina, Paolo 1998. Un Braciere da Forte Salmanassar, Nimrud, *Mesopotamia* 33, 167–81.

Fiorina, Paolo, in press. Store and Store Rooms at Fort Shalmaneser, *Actes du colloque*, Det Danske Institut i Athen.

Frahm, E. 1997. *Einleitung in den Sanherib-Inschriften,* Archiv für Orientforschungen, Beiheft 26. Vienna.

Frame, Grant 1995. *Rulers of Babylonia from the Second Dynasty of Isin to the End of Assyrian Domination (1157–612 BC)*. RIM Babylonian Periods 2. University of Toronto Press.

Frayne, Douglas 1993. *Sargonic and Gutian Periods (2334–2113 BC)*. Royal Inscriptions of Mesopotamia 2. University of Toronto Press.

Freestone, I.C. 1991. Technical Examination of Neo-Assyrian Glazed Wall Plaques, *Iraq* 53, 55–58.

Fuchs, A. 1994. *Die Inschriften Sargons II Aus Khorsabad*. Göttingen.

Gadd, C.J. 1936. *The Stones of Assyria*. London: Chatto and Windus.

Gadd, C.J. 1953. Inscribed Barrel Cylinder of Marduk-apla-iddina II, *Iraq* 15, 123–34.

Gadd, C.J. 1954. Inscribed Prisms of Sargon II from Nimrud, *Iraq* 16, 173–201.

Gallagher, W.R. 1994. Assyrian Deportation Propaganda, *State Archives of Assyria Bulletin* 8, 57–65.

Garelli, Paul 1991. The Achievement of Tiglath-pileser III: Novelty or Continuity? in M. Cogan & I. Eph'al (eds), *Ah, Assyria … Studies in Assyrian History and Ancient Near Eastern Historiography Presented to H. Tadmor*. Scripta Hierosolymitana 33, 46–51. Jerusalem.

George, A.R. 1986. Sennacherib and the Tablet of Destinies, *Iraq* 48, 133–46.

Grayson, A.K. 1975. *Assyrian and Babylonian Chronicles*. Texts from Cuneiform Sources V. Augustin: Locust Valley, NY.

Grayson, A.K. 1991. *Assyrian Rulers of the Early First Millennium BC* I *(1114–859 BC),* RIM Assyrian Periods 3. University of Toronto Press.

Grayson, A.K. 1991b. Assyria: Tiglath-pileser III to Sargon II (744–705 BC), *CAH,* 71–102; Assyria: Sennacherib and Esarhaddon (704–669 BC), *CAH,* 103–141.

Grayson, A.K. 1993. Assyrian Officials and Power in the Ninth and Eighth Centuries, *State Archives of Assyria Bulletin* 8, 19–52.

Grayson, A.K. 1996. *Assyrian Rulers of the Early First Millennium BC II (858–745 BC),* RIM Assyrian Periods 3. University of Toronto Press.

Green, Anthony 1983. Neo-Assyrian Apotropaic Figures, *Iraq* 45, 87–96.

Harper, P. O. and H. Pittman 1983. *Essays on Near Eastern Art and Archaeology in Honor of Charles Kyle Wilkinson*. New York: Metropolitan Museum.

Hawkins, J.D. 2000. *Corpus of Hieroglyptic Luwian Inscriptions* I. Inscriptions of the Iron Age. Untersuchungen zur indogermanische Sprach-und Kulturwissenschaft NF 8. Berlin: de Gruyter.

Heidel, Alexander 1956. A New Hexagonal Prism of Esarhaddon, *Sumer* 12, 9–37.

Herbordt, S. 1992. *Neuassyrische Glyptik des 8.–7. Jh. v. Chr.*, State Archives of Assyria Studies I. Helsinki..

Herbordt, S. 1996. Ein Königssiegel Assurnasirpals II (?), *Baghdader Mitteilungen* 27, 1996, 411–17.

Herrmann, Georgina 1986. *Ivories from Room 37 Fort Shalmaneser*. Ivories from Nimrud IV. BSAI.

Herrmann, Georgina 1989. The Nimrud Ivories, 1, The Flame and Frond School, *Iraq* 51, 85–109.

Herrmann, Georgina 1992. *The Small Collections from Fort Shalmaneser*. Ivories from Nimrud V. BSAI.

Herrmann, Georgina (ed) 1996. *The Furniture of Western Asia Ancient and Traditional*. Mainz: Verlag Philipp von Zabern.

Herrmann, Georgina 1996. Ivory Furniture Pieces from Nimrud: North Syrian evidence for regional traditions of furniture manufacture, in Herrmann (ed), 153–64.

Herrmann, Georgina 2000. Ivory carving of first millennium workshops, traditions and diffusion, in C. Uehlinger (ed), *Images as media. Sources for the cultural history of the Near East and the Eastern Mediterranean*. Fribourg: University Press.

Herrmann, G. & J.E. Curtis 1998. Reflections on the four-winged Genie: a pottery jar and an ivory panel from Nimrud, *Iranica Antiqua* 33, 107–34.

Howard, Margaret 1955. Technical Description of the Ivory Writing-Boards from Nimrud, *Iraq* 17, 14–20.

Hulin, P. 1963. The Inscriptions on the Carved Throne-Base of Shalmaneser III, *Iraq* 25, 48–69.

Hulin, P. 1969. Another Esarhaddon Cylinder from Nimrud, *Iraq* 24, 116–18.

Hussein, Muzahim Mahmoud 1985–86. Excavation and conservation in the southern and south-east parts of the Nabu Temple, Nimrud, *Sumer* 44, 48–54 (Arabic section).

Hussein, Muzahim Mahmoud 1995. Excavations and Restoration Work in the Temple of Nabu, Nimrud, *Sumer* 47, 28–34 (Arabic section).

Hussein, Muzahim Mahmoud 1996. Excavations in the west wing of the southern part of the Palace of Ashurnasirpal II in Nimrud, the Sixteenth Season, *Sumer* 48, 5–24 (Arabic section).

Hussein, Muzahim Mahmoud, in press. Excavations of the Department of Antiquities & Heritage in Nimrud, 1988–1993.

Hussein, Muzahim Mahmoud and R. Abdul-Razaq 1997/98. Seals from Nimrud, *Sumer* 49, 177–191 (Arabic section).

(Hussein), Muzahim Mahmud and Jeremy Black 1985–86. Recent Work in the Nabu Temple, Nimrud, *Sumer* 44, 135–55.

Hussein, Muzahim Mahmud and Amr Suleiman, in press. *Nimrud, A City of Golden Treasures*. Baghdad (in English and Arabic).

Ibrahim, Jabir Khalil and Abdulla Amin Agha 1983. The Humaidat Tombs, *Sumer* 39, 157–71 (Arabic section).

al-Iraqi, Myesser S.A. 1982. Bas-reliefs from the North-West Palace at Nimrud, *Sumer* 38, 93–102 (Arabic section).

Jenkins, G.K. 1958. Hellenistic Coins from Nimrud, *Iraq* 20, 158–68.

Kinnier-Wilson, J.V. 1962. The Kurba'il Statue of Shalmaneser III, *Iraq* 24, 90–115.

Kinnier-Wilson, J.V. 1972. *The Nimrud Wine Lists*. London: BSAI.

Kühne, Hartmut 1993. Vier Spätbabylonische Tontafeln aus Tall šeh Hamad, Ost-Syrien, *State Archives of Assyria Bulletin* 7, 75–107.

Kwasman, T. and Simo Parpola 1991. *Legal Transactions of the Royal Court of Nineveh* I. Helsinki: University Press.

Læssøe, Jørgen 1959. Building Inscriptions from Fort Shalmaneser, *Iraq* 21, 38–41.

Læssøe, Jørgen 1959a. A Statue of Shalmaneser III, from Nimrud, *Iraq* 21, 147–57.

Larsen, M.T. 1976. The Old Assyrian City-State and its Colonies. *Mesopotamia* 4, Copenhagen.

Layard, Austen Henry 1849. *Nineveh and its Remains* (2 vols). London: John Murray.

Layard, Austen Henry 1849a. *The Monuments of Nineveh*. London: John Murray.

Layard, Austen Henry 1853. *Discoveries in the Ruins of Nineveh and Babylon*. London: John Murray.

Liverani, Mario 1979. The Ideology of Assyrian Empire, in M.T. Larsen (ed), *Power and Propaganda. Mesopotamia* 7, 297–318.

Lloyd, Seton 1947. *Foundations in the Dust*. Oxford University Press.

Loud, Gordon and Charles B. Altman 1938. *Khorsabad II. The Citadel and the Town*. Oriental Institute Publications 40.

Luckenbill, D.D. 1927. *Ancient Records of Assyria* II. University of Chicago Press.

Madhloom, Tariq 1970. *The Chronology of Neo-Assyrian Art*. London: Athlone.

Mallowan, Barbara 1983. Magic and Ritual in the Northwest Palace Reliefs, in Harper and Pittman, 33–39.

Mallowan, Barbara 1986. The Assyrian Tree, *Sumer* 42 (special issue), 141–45.

Mallowan, Barbara (Parker) 1993. Assyrian Temple Furniture, in M.J. Mellink, E. Porada & T. Özgüç (eds), *Studies in Honor of Nimet Özgüç, Aspects of Art and Iconography: Anatolia and its Neighbours,* 383–87. Ankara.

Mallowan, M.E.L. 1950. The Excavations at Nimrud (Kalhu), 1949–1950, *Iraq* 12, 147–83.

Mallowan, M.E.L. 1951. The Excavations at Nimrud (Kalhu), 1949–50. Ivories from the N.W. Palace, *Iraq* 13, 1–20.

Mallowan, M.E.L. 1952. The Excavations at Nimrud (Kalhu), 1951, *Iraq* 14, 1–23.

Mallowan, M.E.L. 1952. The Excavations at Nimrud (Kalhu), 1949–50. Ivories from the N.W. Palace, *Iraq* 14, 45–53.

Mallowan, M.E.L. 1953. The Excavations at Nimrud (Kalhu), 1952, *Iraq* 15, 1–42.

Mallowan, M.E.L. 1954. The Excavations at Nimrud (Kalhu), 1953, *Iraq* 16, 59–114.

Mallowan, M.E.L. 1954. The Excavations at Nimrud (Kalhu), 1953 (continued), *Iraq* 16, 115–63.

Mallowan, M.E.L. 1956. The Excavations at Nimrud (Kalhu), 1955, *Iraq* 18, 1–21.

Mallowan, M.E.L. 1957. The Excavations at Nimrud (Kalhu), 1956, *Iraq* 19, 1–25.

Mallowan, M.E.L. 1958. The Excavations at Nimrud (Kalhu), 1957, *Iraq* 20, 101–108.

Mallowan, M.E.L. 1966. *Nimrud and its Remains* (2 vols). London: Collins.

Mallowan, Max 1977. *Mallowan's Memoirs*. London: Collins.

Mallowan, M.E.L. & Leri Glynne Davies 1970. *Ivories in Assyrian Style*. Ivories from Nimrud II. London: BSAI.

Mallowan, Max and Georgina Herrmann 1974. *Furniture from SW.7 Fort Shalmaneser.* Ivories from Nimrud III. London: BSAI.

Meuszynski, Janusz 1971–1978, a series of reports on the Polish work at Nimrud, published in *Études et Travaux. Travaux du Centre d'Archéologie Méditerranéenne de l'Académie Polonaise des Science.* Warsaw (*EtTrav*).

Meuszynski, Janusz 1975. The Throne-Room of Aššur-nasir-apli II, *Zeitschrift für Assyriologie* 64, 51 ff.

Meuszynski, Janusz 1976. Neo-Assyrian Reliefs from the central area of Nimrud Citadel, *Iraq* 38, 37–43.

Meuszynski, Janusz 1981. *Die Rekonstruktion der Reliefdarstellungen und ihrer Anordnung im Nordwestpalast von Kalhu (Nimrud),* Baghdader Forschungen 2.

Meuszynski, Janusz and Hazim Abdul Hameed 1974. Ekal Assur-nasir-apli, First Report on Reliefs: Rooms "B" and "L", *Sumer* 30, 111–19.

Mierzejewski, A. and R. Sobolewski 1980. Polish Excavations at Nimrud/Kalhu, *Sumer* 36, 151–62.

Millard, Alan 1961. Esarhaddon Cylinder Fragments from Fort Shalmaneser, Nimrud, *Iraq* 23, 176–78.

Millard, Alan 1962. Alphabetic Inscriptions on Ivories from Nimrud, *Iraq* 24, 41–51.

Millard, Alan 1965. The Assyrian Royal Seal Type Again, *Iraq* 27, 12–16.

Millard, A.R. 1972. Some Aramaic Epigraphs, *Iraq* 34. 131–37.

Millard, A.R. 1983. Assyrians and Arameans, *Iraq* 45, 101–08.

Millard, Alan 1994. *The Eponyms of the Assyrian Empire 910–612 BC,* Assyria Studies II. University of Helsinki.

Millard, Alan 1997. Observations from the Eponym Lists, in Parpola & Whiting (eds), 207–16.

Millard, A.R. and P. Bordreuil 1982. A Statue from Syria with Assyrian and Aramaic Inscriptions, *Biblical Archaeologist*, summer, 135–41.

Moorey, P.R.S. 1986. The Emergence of the light, horse-drawn chariot in the Near East, c. 2000–1500 BC, *World Archaeology* 18, 196–215.

Moorey, P.R.S. 1994. *Ancient Mesopotamian Materials and Industries.* Oxford: Clarendon Press.

Moortgat, A. 1969. *The Art of Ancient Mesopotamia.* London: Phaidon.

Munn-Rankin, J.M. 1956. Diplomacy in Western Asia in the Early Second

Millennium BC, *Iraq* 18, 68–110.

Oates, David 1957. Ezida: the Temple of Nabu, *Iraq* 19, 26–39.

Oates, David 1958. The Assyrian Building South of the Nabu Temple, *Iraq* 20, 109–13.

Oates, David 1959. Fort Shalmaneser – an interim report, *Iraq* 21, 98–129.

Oates, David 1961. The Excavations at Nimrud (Kalhu), 1960, *Iraq* 23, 1–14.

Oates, David 1962. The Excavations at Nimrud (Kalhu), 1961, *Iraq* 24, 1–25.

Oates, David 1963. The Excavations at Nimrud (Kalhu), 1962, *Iraq* 25, 6–37.

Oates, David 1965. The Excavations at Tell al Rimah, 1964, *Iraq* 27, 62–80.

Oates, David 1968. *Studies in the Ancient History of Northern Iraq*. The British Academy: Oxford University Press.

Oates, David and Joan Oates 1958. Nimrud 1957: The Hellenistic Settlement, *Iraq* 20, 114–57.

Oates, David, Joan Oates and Helen McDonald 1997. *The Excavations at Tell Brak I: the Mitanni and Old Babylonian Periods*. Cambridge: McDonald Institute Monographs.

Oates, David and J.H. Reid 1956. The Burnt Palace and the Nabu Temple; Nimrud Excavations, 1955, *Iraq* 18, 22–38.

Oates (Lines), Joan 1954. Late Assyrian Pottery from Nimrud, *Iraq* 16, 164–67.

Oates, Joan 1959. Late Assyrian Pottery from Fort Shalmaneser, *Iraq* 21, 130–46.

Oates, Joan 1965. Assyian Chronology, 631–612 BC, *Iraq* 27, 135–59.

Oates, Joan 1974. Late Assyrian Temple Furniture from Tell al Rimah, *Iraq* 36, 179–84.

Oates, Joan 1986. *Babylon*. London: Thames and Hudson.

Oates, Joan 1991. The fall of Assyria (635–609 BC), *CAH,* 162–93.

Oates, Joan, in press. A note on the early evidence for horse in Western Asia, in M. Levine, C. Renfrew and K. Boyle (eds) *Prehistoric Steppe Adaptation and the Horse*. McDonald Institute Monograph.

Ogden, Jack 2000. Metals, in Paul T. Nicholson and Ian Shaw (eds), *Ancient Egyptian Materials and Technology*, 148–76. Cambridge: CUP.

Oppenheim, A. Leo 1967. *Letters from Mesopotamia*. Chicago.

Oppenheim, A.L., R.H. Brill, D. Barag, A. von Saldern 1970. *Glass and Glassmaking in Ancient Mesopotamia*. Corning, NY: Corning Museum of Glass.

Orchard, J.J. 1967. *Equestrian Bridle-Harness Ornaments. Ivories from Nimrud* I, 2. London: BSAI.

Orchard, J.J. 1978. Some Miniature Painted Glass Plaques from Fort Shalmaneser, Nimrud, *Iraq* 40, 1–21.

Paley, S.M. and R.P. Sobolewski 1987. *The Reconstruction of the Relief Representations and their Positions in the Northwest-Palace at Kalhu (Nimrud)* II, Baghdader Forschungen 10. Mainz: Philipp von Zabern.

Paley, S.M. and R.P. Sobolewski 1992. *The Reconstructions of the Relief Representations and their Positions in the Northwest-palace at Kalhu (Nimrud)* III, Baghdader Forschungen 14. Mainz: Philipp von Zabern.

Parker (Mallowan), Barbara 1954. The Nimrud Tablets 1952 – Business Documents,

Iraq 16, 29–58.

Parker (Mallowan), Barbara 1955. Excavations at Nimrud, 1949–53; Seals and Seal Impressions, *Iraq* 17, 93–125.

Parker (Mallowan), Barbara 1957. The Nimrud Tablets, 1956 – economic and legal texts from the Nabu Temple at Nimrud, *Iraq* 19, 125–38.

Parker (Mallowan), Barbara 1961. Administrative Tablets from the North-West Palace, Nimrud, *Iraq* 23, 15–67.

Parker (Mallowan), Barbara 1962. Seals and Seal Impressions from the Nimrud Excavations, 1955–58. *Iraq* 24, 26–40.

Parpola, Simo 1983. *Letters from Assyrian Scholars to the Kings Esarhaddon and Assurbanipal*, Part II, commentary and appendices. Alte Orient und altes Testament 5/2.

Parpola, Simo (ed) 1987. *The Correspondence of Sargon II* I: *Letters from Assyria and the West*. Helsinki University Press.

Parpola, Simo & Kazuko Watanabe 1988. *Neo-Assyrian Treaties and Loyalty Oaths*. State Archives of Assyria II. Helsinki.

Parpola, S. & R.M. Whiting (eds) 1997. *Assyria 1995*. Helsinki: The Neo-Assyrian Corpus Project.

Payton, Robert 1991. The Ulu Burun Writing-Board Set, *Anatolian Studies* 41, 99–106.

Porada, Edith 1973. Notes on the Sarcophagus of Ahiram, in *The Gaster Festschrift, Journal of the ancient Near Eastern Society of Columbia University* 5, 355–72.

Porter, Barbara N. 1997. What the Assyrians Thought the Babylonians Thought about the Relative Status of Nabu and Marduk in the Late Assyrian Period, in Parpola & Whiting (eds), 253–60.

Postgate, Carolyn, David Oates & Joan Oates 1997. *Excavations at Tell al Rimah: The Pottery*. London: Aris and Phillips.

Postgate, J.N. 1973. *The Governor's Palace Archive*. Cuneiform Texts from Nimrud II. BSAI.

Postgate, J.N. 1973a. Assyrian Texts and Fragments, *Iraq* 35, 13–36.

Postgate, J.N. 1973b. *Taxation and Conscription in the Assyrian Empire*. Studia Pohl: Series Maior 3. Rome: Biblical Institute Press.

Postgate, J.N. 1974. The bit akiti in Assyrian Nabu Temples, *Sumer* 30, 51–74.

Postgate, J.N. 1976. *Fifty Neo-Assyrian Legal Documents*. Warminster: Aris & Phillips.

Postgate, J.N. 1978. An Inscribed Jar from Tell al Rimah, *Iraq* 40, 71–75.

Postgate, J.N. 1979. On Some Assyrian Ladies, *Iraq* 41, 89–103.

Postgate, J.N. 1979b. The Economic Structure of the Assyrian Empire, in Larsen (ed) *Power and Propaganda*. Mesopotamia 7, 193–221.

Postgate, J.N. and J.E. Reade 1980. Kalhu, in *Reallexikon der Assyriologie und vorderasiatischen Archäologie* V, 303–23. Berlin: Walter de Gruyter.

Postgate, J.N. 1992. The Land of Assur and the yoke of Assur, *World Archaeology* 23, 247–63.

Rassam, H. 1897. *Asshur and the Land of Nimrod*. New York.

Rawson, P.S. 1954. Palace Wares from Nimrud – Technical observations on selected examples, *Iraq* 16, 168–72.

Reade, J.E. 1963. A Glazed-Brick Panel from Nimrud, *Iraq* 25, 38–47.

Reade, J.E. 1965. Twelve Ashur-nasir-pal Reliefs, *Iraq* 27, 119–35.

Reade, J.E. 1968. The Palace of Tiglath-Pileser III, *Iraq* 30, 69–73.

Reade, J.E. 1979. Assyrian Architectural Decoration: techniques and subject-matter, *Baghdader Mitteilungen* 10, 17–49.

Reade, J.E. 1979a. Narrative Composition in Assyrian Sculpture, *Baghdader Mitteilungen* 10, 52–110.

Reade, J.E. 1980. The Rassam Obelisk, *Iraq* 42, 1–22.

Reade, J.E. 1980a. Space, Scale and Significance in Assyrian Art, *Baghdader Mitteilungen* 11, 71–74.

Reade, J.E. 1980b. The Architectural Context of Assyrian Sculpture, *Baghdader Mitteilungen* 11, 75–87.

Reade, J.E. 1982. Nimrud, in John Curtis (ed), *Fifty Years of Mesopotamian Discovery*, 99–112. London: BSAI.

Reade, J.E. 1985. Texts and Sculptures from the North-West Palace, Nimrud, *Iraq* 47, 203–14.

Reade, J.E. 2000. Ninive (Nineveh), in *Reallexikon der Assyriologie und Vorderasiatischen Archäologie* 9, 387–433.

Robins, G.V., C. del Re, N.J. Seeley, A.G. Davis and J.A-A. Hawari 1983. A Spectroscopic Study of the Nimrud Ivories, *Journal of Archaeological Science* 10, 385–95.

Sachs, A.J. 1953. The Late Assyrian Royal-Seal Type, *Iraq* 15, 167–70.

Safar, Fuad and al-Iraqi, M. S. 1987. *Ivories from Nimrud* (in Arabic). Baghdad: Ministry of Culture and Information.

Saggs, H.W.F. 1955. The Nimrud Letters, 1952 – I, The Ukin-Zer Rebellion and Related Texts, *Iraq* 17, 21–56.

Saggs, H.W.F. 1955. The Nimrud Letters, 1952 – Part II, Relations with the West, *Iraq* 17, 126–160.

Saggs, H.W.F. 1956. The Nimrud Letters, 1952 – Part III, Miscellaneous Letters, *Iraq* 18, 40–56.

Saggs, H.W.F. 1958. The Nimrud Letters, 1952 – Part IV; the Urartian Frontier, *Iraq* 20, 182–212.

Saggs, H.W.F. 1959. The Nimrud Letters, 1952 – Part V, Administration, *Iraq* 21, 158–79.

Saggs, H.W.F. 1963. The Nimrud Letters, 1952 – Part VI, The Death of Ukin-zer and other letters, *Iraq* 25, 70–80.

Saggs, H.W.F. 1984. *The Might that was Assyria*. London: Sidgwick & Jackson.

Saggs, H.W.F. 2001. *The Nimrud Letters, 1952*. Cuneiform Texts from Nimrud V. BSAI.

Sax, M., N.D. Meeks and D. Collon 2000. The early development of the lapidary engraving wheel in Mesopotamia, *Iraq* 62, 157–76.

Schultz, M. and M. Kunter 1998. Erste Ergebnisse der anthropologischen und paläopathologischen Untersuchungen an den menschlichen Skeletfunden aus den neuassyrischen Königinnengräbern von Nimrud, *Jahrb. Römisch-Germanisches Zentralmuseum* Mainz 45, 85–128.

Schwartz, Glenn M. 1989. The Origins of the Aramaeans in Syria and Northern Mesopotamia: Research problems and potential strategies, in O.M.C. Haex, H.H. Curvers and P.M.M.G. Akkerman (eds), *To the Euphrates and Beyond. Archaeological Studies in Honour of Maurits van Loon*, 275–91.

Segal, J.B. 1957. An Aramaic Ostracon from Nimrud, *Iraq* 19, 139–45.

Shukri, Akram 1956. Conservation and Restoration of Assyrian Sculpture at Nimrud, *Sumer* 12, 133–34.

Smith, George 1875. *Assyrian Discoveries*. London: John Murray.

Stronach, David 1958. Metal Objects from the 1957 Excavations at Nimrud, *Iraq* 20, 169–81.

Stronach, David 1959. The Development of the Fibula in the Near East, *Iraq* 21, 181–206.

Symington, Dorit 1991. Late Bronze Age Writing-Boards and their Uses: textual evidence from Anatolia and Syria, *Anatolian Studies* 41, 111–23.

Tadmor, Hayim 1982. The Aramaization of Assyria: Aspects of Western Impact, in H-J. Nissen & J. Renger (eds), *Mesopotamien und seine Nachbarn*, 449–70. Berlin: Dietrich Reimer.

Tadmor, Hayim 1994. *The Inscriptions of Tiglath-pileser III King of Assyria*. Jerusalem: Israel Academy of Sciences and Humanities.

Tadmor, H. 1997. Propaganda, Literature, Historiography: Cracking the Code of the Assyrian Royal Inscriptions, in Parpola & Whiting (eds), 325–38.

Tadmor, Hayim, Benno Landsberger and Simo Parpola 1989. The Sin of Sargon and Sennacherib's Last Will, *State Archives of Assyria Bulletin*, III.1, 3–51.

Tucker, David 1992. A Middle Assyrian Hoard from Khirbet Karhasan, Iraq, *Iraq* 54, 157–82.

Turner, Geoffrey 1970. The State Apartments of Late Assyrian Palaces, *Iraq* 32, 177–213.

Turner, W.E.S. 1955. Glass Fragments from Nimrud of the Eighth to the Sixth Century BC, *Iraq* 17, 57–68.

Watanabe, K. 1985. Die Siegelung der "Vasallenverträge Asarhaddons" durch den Gott Aššur, *Baghdader Mitteilungen* 16, 377–92.

Waterfield, Gordon 1963. *Layard of Nineveh*. London: John Murray.

Waterman, Leroy 1930. *Royal Correspondence of the Assyrian Empire*. Ann Arbor.

Winter, Irene 1981. Royal Rhetoric and the Development of Historical Narrative in Neo-Assyrian Reliefs, *Studies in Visual Communication* 7.2, 2–36.

Winter, Irene 1979. Art as Evidence for Interaction: relations between the Assyrian Empire and North Syria, in H. Nissen and J. Renger (eds), *Mesopotamien und seine Nachbarn,* 355–82. Berlin: Dietrich Reimer Verlag.

Winter, Irene 1981. Is there a South Syrian Style of Ivory Carving in the Early First Millennium BC?, *Iraq* 43, 101–30.

Winter, Irene 1983. The Program of the Throneroom of Assurnasirpal II, in Harper and Pittman, 15–31.

Wiseman, D.J. 1951. Two Historical Inscriptions from Nimrud, *Iraq* 13, 21–26.

Wiseman, D.J. 1952. An Esarhaddon Cylinder from Nimrud, *Iraq* 14, 54–60.

Wiseman, D.J. 1952. A new stela of Aššur-nasir-pal II, *Iraq* 14, 24–44.

Wiseman, D.J. 1952. The Nimrud Tablets, 1951, *Iraq* 14, 61–69.

Wiseman, D.J. 1953. The Nimrud Tablets, 1953, *Iraq* 15, 135–160.

Wiseman, D.J. 1955. Assyrian Writing-Boards, *Iraq* 17, 3–13.

Wiseman, D.J. 1958. The Vassal-Treaties of Esarhaddon, *Iraq* 20, Part 1.

Wiseman, D.J. 1968. The Nabu Temple Texts from Nimrud, *Journal of Near Eastern Studies* 27, 248–50. BSAI.

Wiseman, D.J. and J.A. Black 1996. *Literary Texts from the Temple of Nabu, Cuneiform Texts from Nimrud IV.* BSAI.

Wiseman, D.J. and J.V. Kinnier Wilson 1951. The Nimrud Tablets, 1950, *Iraq* 13, 102–22.

Xenophon, *Anabasis* (trans. by Rex Warner 1951, 2nd ed, *The Persian Expedition*, Penguin Classics).

Zawadski, Stefan 1994. The Revolt of 746 BC and the Coming of Tiglath-pileser III to the Throne, *State Archives of Assyria* 8, 53–54.

Zawadski, S. 1997. The Question of the King's Eponymate in the Latter Half of the 8th Century and the 7th Century BC, in Parpola & Whiting (eds), 383–89.

SOURCES OF THE ILLUSTRATIONS

All photographs of the objects from the Iraqi excavations in the North-West Palace are published by kind permission of the State Organisation of Antiquities and Heritage, Baghdad. The photographs of Nimrud tombs I–III and all the gold objects were taken by Dr Donny George Youkhana. Photographs and drawings of Tomb IV, and Figs. 37, 39, 48, 49, are published with the generous permission of Sd Muzahim Mahmud Hussein. The three colour photographs for Plates 3b, 5a and 7a, taken by Dr Donny George, were kindly supplied by Dr Michael Müller-Karpe, from the publication by Dr Muayad Said Damerji in the *Jahrbuch des Römisch-Germanisches Zentralmuseum Mainz* 45, 1998. The frontispiece is reproduced by courtesy of the *Illustrated London News* Picture Library. Pl. 12b and Figs. 1a, 2, 5, 7–9, 16, 25, 26, 28, 42, 44, 156, are reproduced by courtesy of the Trustees of the British Museum, and Figs. 29, 50, 79, 86, 87, 103, 126b and 136, by kind permission of the Metropolitan Museum of Art, New York City. Pl. 12c is reproduced by courtesy of Dr Paolo Fiorina. The photographs from the British expedition are the property of the British School of Archaeology in Iraq; these were taken in the field largely by Barbara Parker, but also by other expedition members, including Nicholas Kindersley and David Oates. Figs. 36 and 64 were taken by Dr Georgina Herrmann; we are extremely grateful to her and to Dr Lamia Al-Gailani Werr for copies of many of the Iraq Museum photographs. The copyright of Pls. 1, 2a, 11a, and Figs 1b, 14, 17, 32, 72, 108, 109, 111, 145, 150a and the photographs on the back cover is held by the authors.

INDEX